GNVQ Advanced
Information Technology

Dave Evans
Geof Foot
Peter Hodson
Tim Hutchings
Keith Norris
Mike Watkins

Edited by
Peter Hodson and Mike Watkins

Letts Educational
Aldine Place
LONDON W12 8AW
1997

Acknowledgements

The editors would thank all their colleagues who have generated ideas throughout the development of the text. The authors of individual units deserve recognition for their ability to react to the changing requirements as the specification for the units evolved throughout the year. Keith Norris and Tim Hutchings in particular have been a strength at all stages.

Catherine Tilley at DPP has constantly encouraged us when the going got tough and the editors thank her for the support. Liz Hodson has proof read much of the text and has simplified it on many occasions, for which we are grateful. Mike Ready is thanked for his contribution on the communications access. Liz Elwin has been splendid in typesetting this book with great patience and making helpful improvements. The editors thank her for that support. Finally, Pat Bayley is thanked for a last minute typing input that rescued us from further delays.

The various examples used throughout the text have been prepared using Microsoft Office products, all of which provide an ideal platform for the GNVQ IT programme. We thank Colin Walker and BTEC for their kind permission to use questions from the BTEC question bank, and Feedback Instruments for the use of their Instructors' manual for the Traffic Control module MIC 937.

Any remaining errors remain the editors' responsibility and they would welcome any feedback, recommendation on changes or re-emphasis that would be helpful in enabling students to successfully complete this GNVQ.

A CIP catalogue record for this book is available from the British Library

ISBN 1 85805 111 8
Copyright P.J. Hodson & M. Watkins © 1995

First edition 1995; reprinted December 1995
Reprinted 1997

Typeset by Elizabeth Elwin

Printed in Great Britain by
W M Print, Walsall, West Midlands

About the authors

The authors are all staff at The University of Glamorgan and are active in the delivery of BTEC or GNVQ programmes.

Peter Hodson is Head of the Department of Computer Studies, University of Glamorgan. He has been involved in the developments of Advanced Level GNVQ in IT during the original writing of the unit specifications and has worked with NCVQ on monitoring the pilot year in test centres.

Mike Watkins has worked in computing for twenty-seven years. He is currently a Principal Lecturer at the University of Glamorgan and is course leader on the HND Computing Scheme. The major areas of interest include data modelling, database implementation and information engineering. His research interests are in computer based learning.

Dave Evans is a Principal Lecturer in Dept. of Computer Studies

Geof Foot is a Senior Lecturer in Dept. of Electronics and IT

Tim Hutchings is a Senior Lecturer in Dept. of Computer Studies

Keith Norris is a Senior Lecturer in Dept. of Computer Studies

Lecturers' Preface

This book provides comprehensive coverage of the eight mandatory units in GNVQ Advanced Information Technology

The text is structured to follow the GNVQ unit definitions as closely as possible, with each unit dealt with in a separate chapter, and each element given a separate section in that chapter. As individual colleges or schools will tackle the units in a different sequence, the units in the text have been written to allow this, and each is as independent of the others as the topic allows. Where appropriate, cross-referencing of material has been undertaken. Where material has been fully covered in another unit, it is not rigorously treated on a subsequent occasion.

To produce a book against the new specification in such a short time has required a team approach. The text has been authored by a number of staff at the University of Glamorgan, with the editors introducing a house-style which closely follows the unit specification, to ensure a comprehensive coverage of the material.

How to use this book with your students

The text is designed to support units taught through a combination of lectures and practical sessions. The text follows the GNVQ specification closely and can therefore form an underpinning framework for the course, enabling students to see clearly how the topics they are being taught meet the requirements of the course.

Assessment material

Throughout the text are embedded short questions (with answers at the unit ends) that can be used in class or by students themselves to check they have understood the basic points being made. These are intended to confirm the learning process only.

Each unit also contains a series of in-text tasks that provide a scheme of activities necessary to generate the evidence required for each student's portfolio. Some tasks are practical in nature and will require the student to spend time on a computer system. Others require students to undertake on-site visits or to review a case study. Each task is referenced to the particular performance criteria it addresses, and, if appropriate, to a core skills criteria too. The Lecturers' Supplement (see below for full details) gives answers and guidance to the tasks.

At the end of each unit is a specimen external test paper in the style of the multi-choice questions of the actual papers. Answers are also in the Lecturers' Supplement.

Lecturers' Supplement

A supplement to the book is available to lecturers, which contains answers to tasks and tests papers, guidance on delivering the unit and on meeting some of the requirements of the specification. There is also a pack available of approximately 75 OHP masters (on paper) of diagrams from the book. The supplement is free to lecturers adopting the text as a course text (please apply on college headed paper giving details of the course and likely bookshop supplier) and can be supplied for a charge of £3 to lecturers who are using it as a reference text. The OHP masters pack costs £15 and is photocopiable.

Students' Introduction

Studying a GNVQ

GNVQs have been introduced to give a work-related qualification that is broadly based. It also provides a route into Higher Education. The programme consists of eight mandatory units plus four optional units, with the opportunity of adding further units from a range of additional units provided by your Examining Body (e.g. BTEC, City and Guilds, RSA etc.). Careful choice of optional or additional units will help you get a job in your preferred area or enhance your opportunity of gaining the place you may want in Higher Education.

You will also be assessed in Core Skills, which are specified as Communication, Application of Number and Information Technology. It is assumed that the core skill in Information Technology will be automatically covered in this programme, so only Communication and Application of Number skills are addressed (see under *How to get the most out of this book*).

The key terms used in a GNVQ programme need a little explanation:

❑ A **unit** is a separately identified and assessed area of study. To achieve a GNVQ you will be tested on 12 units.

❑ An **element** is a topic of study within a unit covering a major piece of work in the subject. There are typically 3 or 4 elements in each unit.

❑ **Performance criteria** (PCs) represent the skills and knowledge you need to gain within each element. Each element consists of a number of performance criteria and you have to demonstrate your competence in each of these.

❑ **Range statements** exist within each element, defining the extent of knowledge required to cover the performance criteria.

❑ **Evidence indicators** represent the work you have undertaken in demonstrating that you have acquired the necessary skills to meet the performance criteria. They are the proof you need to be assessed as competent in the element/unit.

❑ **Assessment** is the measure of how well you have met the performance criteria. For the mandatory units assessment will be a combination of reviewing your portfolio of evidence containing your work plus an externally set test. All the work you have undertaken in a unit, such as coursework and project assignments are aimed at providing the evidence indicators needed. Each performance criterion needs to be completed, with all the range covered, before a pass is recorded. You should carefully keep all your work in your Portfolio of Evidence, since it may be reviewed by staff who are involved in the quality assurance issues relating to verification of evidence.

How to get the most out of this book

The book is organised in exactly the same way as the eight mandatory units of the GNVQ Advanced Information Technology. It is designed to support a combination of lectures and practical sessions. Each *unit* is separately identified, with each *element* presented as a separate section of a chapter. Embedded, short self-assessed questions are introduced which allow you to check whether you have understood the basic points being made. These questions are not part of the formal assessment and are there to give you an early feedback on how well you have understood the material. Suggested answers to these questions are provided at the end of each unit.

Within each unit is a series of tasks which cover all the performance criteria of that unit. These are intended to provide a framework of activities necessary for you to assemble the evidence required for your portfolio. Each task is clearly labelled with the performance criteria (PC) that it addresses. Completion of each of the tasks will put you well on your way to completing this aspect of assessment. Remember to file your work from these tasks carefully in your portfolio.

The top right-hand corner of certain tasks indicates which core skills may be assessed during completion of that task. We have used a nomenclature of C to represent communication skills and N a numeracy skill. They are all level 3 core skills with 4 elements in the communication skills and 3 elements in the application of numbers. Hence C3.2 means a communication skill at level 3 with element 2 evidence.

At the end of each unit is a specimen test paper based on multi-choice questions. The style of each paper is similar to that which you will take with your Examining Body, although they may structure the paper into topics rather than randomly fire questions at you.

Completing the tasks

The work you undertake in collecting the evidence of your skills and competence is supported by the task structure. The approach you need to take should be varied to suit the particular requirements. Some tasks are practical in nature and need time on computer systems. Others require you to undertake on-site visits or to review a case study. This style of investigation should be carefully documented and contribute to an active-learning approach.

Peter Hodson
Mike Watkins

December 1995

Contents

by **Keith Norris** and **Geof Foot**

Unit 1

Information Technology Systems

Introduction

The unit aims to introduce you to the components of an information technology system. In particular the operation of a microprocessor is covered in some detail. Examples of industrial and commercial applications for IT are considered to give a context in which systems may be found.

Finally the practical issues of installing and configuring a PC system are covered, enabling you to understand all the major system files required in a stand alone environment.

Element 1.1

Investigate Industrial and Commercial Information Technology Systems

Introduction

This first element introduces the way in which Information Technology may be used in both the Commercial and Industrial contexts. Several systems will be reviewed in this element and the framework to analyse and evaluate these systems will be introduced.

To cover the range of this element it is envisaged that investigations will be carried out by visits to local commercial and industrial organisations which have extensive computing systems. Where this is difficult to fully implement, case studies should be used to reflect real systems. This element also integrates well with Element 2.4, where the whole Information Technology system is investigated. Hence these two elements can be taught and covered together or Element 1.1 can act as a leader for Element 2.4.

1.1.1 Commercial Systems

Booking Systems

A typical example of a commercial system is a booking system used by the local travel agent. If you want to travel anywhere, the local agent (by means of an IT link to the tour operator or airline) can gather relevant information for you. Such information includes details on the availability of flights, the time of departure and arrival or relevant information about your proposed travel or holiday. The time it takes to access this information is a few seconds. You can make your booking through the system and pay your deposit. All this is achievable by means of a PC (with the appropriate software), a modem to give you access to the telephone system and a remote system as shown in figure 4.3. In effect you have one computer in the travel agency 'talking' to another computer at the travel provider e.g. tour operator, airline, rail or ferry service. In the future this system may develop to the extent that if you have the appropriate equipment you will be able to make such bookings from your home. In conjunction with your television you may also be able to make purchases in a similar way with a television channel dedicated to advertising products just like a shopping catalogue. Satellite television already has something similar to this already but you have to use your telephone rather than your PC.

Electronic Funds Transfer

Handling cash and physically transferring large sums of money is a high security risk. It is preferable to establish an electronic means of transferring money between locations, reducing some aspects of security concerns (and maybe raising others!).

The technical term used by banks for this facility is BACS, the Banks Automated Clearing System. One example of the use of BACS enables the payment of an employees salary directly into their bank account with the minimum of paper work, time and personnel involvement. The employer informs their bank of the details of the payment to be made. This information is then put into the bank's computer and the system takes over. The BACS system debits the employer's account and communicates with the employee's bank account so that a credit transfer takes place. The transaction involves no paperwork in the form of cheques and occurs almost instantaneously.

> ### *Task 1.1*   PC 1   *C3.2*
>
> *Obtain information either directly from a major bank about their BACS system or investigate how the system works by using the information in the library. It is important that you keep a good record of the books and information that you use as this will be useful in providing evidence on information gathering. Using this information explain how the BACS system works with the aid of a block diagram. In addition, find out how the direct debit system interacts with the BACS system.*

Electronic point of sales system

It is common place for goods to be purchased using credit or debit card facilities rather than cash. Details of the account to be debited are taken from the magnetic strip on the card. This approach to payment is known as Electronic Point of Sale (EPOS). It reduces all the paperwork which requires manual data entry at a later stage.

A system which is now very common is the use of credit cards when we make a purchase in a shop. Figure 1.1 shows the block diagram for such a system from a consumer's viewpoint.

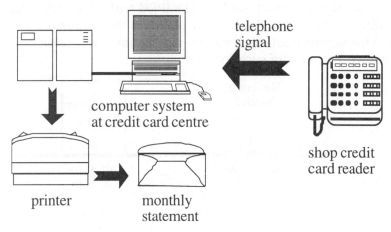

Figure 1.1 Consumer's view of EPOS

The amount to be debited is entered into the credit card reader, a telephone call is made to the credit card centre by pressing the appropriate preset button and the credit card swiped through the machine. During this action, the magnetic strip on the back of the card is read to determine the buyer's personal details i.e. card number and this is transmitted to the centre. The credit card number is compared to the data in the computer to see if it is valid. Checks are made to see if the card has been reported stolen or if the owner has exceeded their credit limit. If everything is alright, then the transaction can go ahead and the computer communicates to the shop that this is the case. The purchaser signs the credit card slip, the shop assistant presses a button to indicate that the transaction has been completed. This is electronically sent to the computer at the credit card centre. The computer adds the purchase price to the credit card holder's statement which is totalled at the end of the month, printed and sent through the post to the customer.

Because the transaction has been completed with the involvement of the central computer (in real time), the possibility of fraudulent use of the card is reduced, i.e. it prevents the use of cards which have been reported stolen.

Stock control

The volume of stock (e.g. goods for sale or raw material for manufacturing) held by any organisation needs careful monitoring. Putting stock on the shelf is the equivalent in business terms of putting money on the shelf. If you hold more stock than is necessary for your immediate business needs, you could be tying up money and preventing other business opportunities from occuring.

Hence the need to accurately record stock movement such as goods received and goods sold is a key issue in managing this process. As you may suspect, information technology plays an important role in this process. Recording everything that is sold can be automated. The use of a bar code system is important to this system. Manufacturing organisations frequently use this approach to monitor the progress and movement of components in the workshops or stores.

An application familiar to everybody is the supermarket where information on the goods sold is captured at the till. Not only does this calculate the bill, but it automates the stock control process by recording the goods sold. A similar approach is implemented on the goods inward side, when stock is replenished. Hence stock control, order processing and EPOS can be closely linked systems.

The vast majority of products sold are identified with a bar code which consists of a series of lines of different thickness. The bar code identifies the product so that when it is read by a laser beam at the supermarket check-out it is automatically recognised and the price registered. Figure 1.2 shows the layout of such a system.

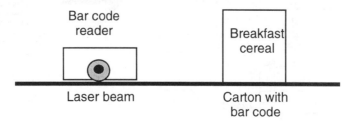

Figure 1.2 A Bar Code reader in a retail store

When the bar code is read, the item and price are identified and added to the shopper's bill where the total is calculated for payment to be made. In addition the bar code reader at the till can be considered as part of a master computer which is being used to monitor stock control. The master computer has an up to date record of the stock on the shelves and when the till registers that a box of cereal has been bought, the stock of cereal is deleted by one.

Question 1.1

Should each bar code label attached to the same product be identical?

Task 1.2   PC 1

Draw a typical bar code from a product and investigate how the bar code is read. In your investigation you should explain the purpose of the following aspects of the bar code:

Corner mark, right- and left-hand bar guards, the light margin, the centre pattern, the flag digits, the modulo check digit, OCR-B Human readable characters

Question 1.2

Should each product have a separate bar code identifier?

Order processing

Orders may be raised or received by an organisation. If we are able to automate the process, then many of the delays and mistakes can be avoided. Placing of orders can be actioned by setting threshold levels i.e. when the stock reduces to a pre-set level, we automatically place an order to replenish. Many organisations are moving to an electronic means of exchanging orders based on Electronic Document Interchange (EDI). Indeed some large organisations insist that all transactions with them are actioned using EDI. The computer systems to monitor the placing or receipt of orders and the stock movement control need to be integrated or at least able to exchange data.

Payroll Processing

One of the most sensitive issues in a commercial operation is ensuring your employees are paid correctly and on time. Any inaccuracies or non-payment creates tension and potential conflict.

The payroll suite of programs is often based on one of several standard packages which may be altered for the particular needs of individual organisations. The correct calculation of pay and expenses with the appropriate deductions of statutory or authorised payments (e.g. tax, national insurance contributions or trades union fees) is a standard function. The output of the payroll suite would be data prepared for EFT.

1.1.2 Industrial Systems

Design

Today, with the use of Information Technology, the role of design has almost taken on a new meaning as the manual element has almost disappeared. There is no need for a pencil and paper to make the traditional sketch or to draw the design – all can be done using computer graphics. Computer Aided Design (CAD) is the term used to describe such activities where computers particularly with high resolution graphics backed up with sophisticated software packages, are used to design complex objects such as cars or the layout of integrated circuits etc. Such complex drawings can be done in a fraction of the time and modifications are extremely easy. The layout of such a system is shown in figure 1.3. However the design doesn't end with the drawing. Once the outline has been finished it can be tested using software to model the practical use to which the design is to be put. For example in the case of the car, with the appropriate software the design of the car can be tested aerodynamically to ensure that when the car is travelling at high speeds, the vehicle meets minimum air resistance. In the case of the integrated circuit and printed circuit board (PCB) design, the software can model operating conditions to ensure the circuit works correctly and components do not over-heat.

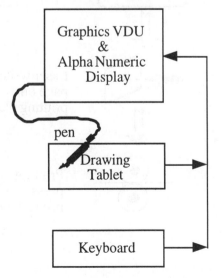

Figure 1.3 Block diagram of a typical CAD workstation

In many cases the CAD system can be directly connected to the manufacturing process. For example, the CAD system can design a metal component which has to be machined on a lathe. The lathe can be a numerically controlled machine operated by a computer which holds the design in software. Such a system shows the link between CAD and CAE (Computer Aided Engineering) and full automation as found in Flexible Manufacturing Systems (FMS). Another example is the design of PCB's. Once designed using CAD software, it is a relatively simple step to automatically make the board, drill holes and place the components ready for soldering.

Task 1.3   PC 1   C3.3

Investigate, either by visiting a local manufacturer or using the resources in the library, an application of Computer Aided Design being used to manufacture a product. Illustrate your investigation with diagrams so as to show the layout of the system.

The newspaper industry is an example where automation using Information Technology has occurred in recent years. With Desk Top Publishing (DTP) software, it is possible to design a newspaper page by page, including photographs and text. The composed page is then 'burned' into a printing plate by means of a laser and the plate used to print the page. A block diagram of this arrangement is shown in figure 1.4.

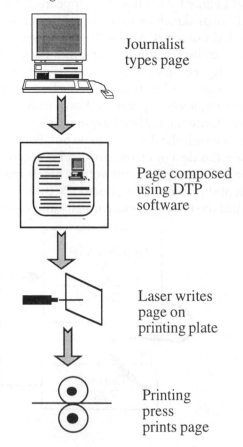

Journalist types page

Page composed using DTP software

Laser writes page on printing plate

Printing press prints page

Figure 1.4 DTP for Newspaper production

Process Control

A process control system attempts to influence the outcome or conditions of a system. It frequently measures the outcome and takes action to bring the value it measures closer to the value that we wanted. An example is probably the best way of explaining this. If you wanted to keep a pot on a domestic cooker at simmering, you might frequently inspect the pot to see if that is still happening. If it wasn't, you could adjust the heat to the hob. This is a process control activity, the simmering pot is the process and you are the monitoring function.

Let us consider an industrial application. Electrical energy is a major part of our everyday lives. Can you imagine what life would be like without it? Dinorwic Power Station was built to meet our everyday needs for electrical energy. The problem that Dinorwic solved was meeting the need when a sudden surge for electricity occurred. Such a surge occurs when there is a sudden drop in temperature and everyone switches on an electric fire. But by far the worst type of demand for electricity, which to some extent is totally unpredictable, is when a commercial break at the end of a very popular tv serial occurs and everyone gets up to put the kettle on for a cup of tea. Conventional power stations cannot cope which such a sudden increase in demand as it takes up to 12 hours to get a power station to generate electricity for the National Grid. But Dinorwic is totally different, in a matter of 10 seconds 1,320 Megawatts of electrical power can be generated, which is sufficient to keep those electric kettles going! Hence Dinorwic power station is ideal for generating electrical power when the demand is great.

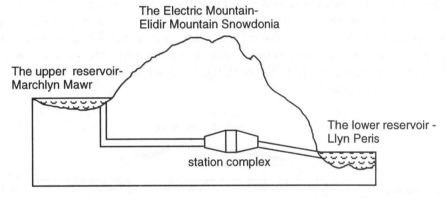

Figure 1.5 Dinorwic Power Station

The control principle used to provide this massive amount of electrical energy in so short a time is very simple. Figure 1.5 shows the basic layout. When electrical energy is required a valve is opened, allowing water from the upper reservoir to flow through a pipe down to the lower reservoir via the station complex. This sounds very simple, but the amount of water involved is considerable. In just 90 minutes the amount of water used is the same as that used by London in a whole day. In the station complex there are 6 giant pump turbines to generate a maximum of 1,800 Megawatts of power. Electricity can only be produced in this way for up to 5 hours but this is usually sufficient to cope with the heavy demand periods. When the electrical power consumption is low, during the night, the function of the station complex reverses its role. Instead of the turbines generating electricity, they pump water from the lower reservoir up to the upper reservoir to replenish the water level ready for the next demand for electricity. Information Technology has a very important role to play to make Dinorwic come on line in the way in which it does, both in terms of monitoring and control.

Question 1.3

Why can Dinorwic only generate electricity for a period of 5 hours?

Robotics

Robotics is an exciting use of IT with many applications, particularly in the industrial sector. In particular, the use of robots to perform jobs in hazardous areas where it would not be possible for human activity to take place is paramount to some activities. The use of robots by bomb disposal teams, or in nuclear processing plants are examples of pretty hazardous activities. Robots are covered in Element 2.4 where other examples and details may be found.

Environmental Control

Control is a very important part of our everyday lives. If there was no control we would have chaos. In terms of nature, the weather is a natural form of environmental control. For plants to grow they need sunshine and water. These two ingredients need to be applied in the correct amount. Too much rain would mean little sunshine and the plant would be drowned in water. Whereas too much sunshine would mean that the plant would shrivel and die.

In the UK the weather is sometimes too cold and hence the requirements for plant growth are not ideal. In order to have the correct amount of sunshine (light and warmth) and rain (water and humidity) a greenhouse is used to compensate for the poor weather. Figure 1.6 shows such a greenhouse where the heat, light and water inputs to the plants is carefully controlled to promote growth.

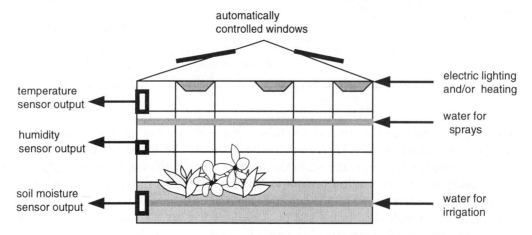

Figure 1.6 A computer controlled Greenhouse

The greenhouse shown in figure 1.6 has a number of inputs to get the required environmental effects. For example:

- ❏ water for irrigation which would consist of a pipe with holes in it buried under the soil;
- ❏ water for the overhead sprays which in effect is a sprinkler system used to water the plants and keep the atmosphere humid;
- ❏ electric lighting and heating, lighting to prolong the 'day' and heat for warmth;
- ❏ automatically controlled windows are used to cool down the greenhouse if it gets too hot by opening the windows.

To achieve this control of the environment in the greenhouse, it would be necessary to measure the variables that effect plant growth. These measurements would then act as outputs from the greenhouse such as:

❑ a temperature sensor used to ensure that the temperature does not drop too low (frost will kill plants) or too high (will burn the plant leaves);

❑ moisture content of the soil, if the soil gets too dry for too long the plants will die with lack of water;

❑ a humidity sensor used to ensure that the atmosphere in the greenhouse is not too dry.

Task 1.4 PC 1 *C3.1*

Investigate, by visiting a local garden centre or nursery, the techniques involved in controlling the temperature, humidity and irrigation of the greenhouses. Explain, with the aid of diagrams how this is achieved.

Traffic Control

The control of traffic at a road junction is a good example of the use of Information Technology and is something with which we are all familiar. Figure 1.7 shows a typical junction. The sequence of the change of lights as a car approaches a junction and the Red traffic light is showing is ideally controlled by means of a microprocessor. Red, Red and Amber then Green for the traffic to proceed through the junction. To stop the flow the sequence is from Green to Amber and then finally Red to stop. The sequence of lights has a certain time interval dependant upon a number of factors e.g. is traffic approaching from the adjacent roads meeting the junction? More complex control can involve the use of a pedestrian crossing or filter for traffic to turn right across on-coming traffic. Element 2.4 considers some of these problems.

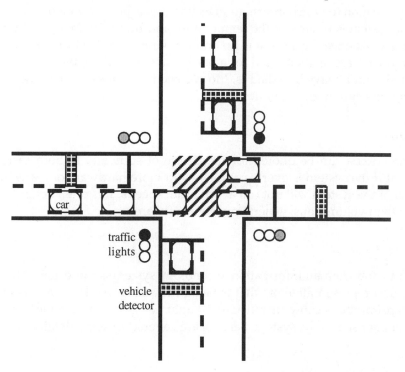

Figure 1.7 Traffic control system at a road junction

1.1.3 Criteria for Analysis

Purpose

Information Technology may be used to solve a problem. That problem can come in a number of different forms:

☐ The application may be very labour intensive or the tasks that have to be performed may be unpleasant or dangerous to human health. The task may be very monotonous and boring and unsuitable for humans to do. All these are reasons why information technology should be applied to an application. Typical examples are the use of Robots for paint spraying because of the unhealthy working environment that this creates (see Element 2.4).

☐ The application may be repetitive and continuous. The example of the control of traffic lights falls into this category and due to its logical sequence is an ideal application to be solved by information technology.

☐ The application may be complex with a number of different inputs and outputs and too much for a human being to cope with. Hence a microprocessor would be ideal as it can cope with a number of inputs and outputs, controlling to a good degree of accuracy.

☐ The application of Information Technology is a more efficient solution as it saves time and requires less human input. An example of this would be CAD and its related applications.

So there are multiple opportunities for the use of Information Technology. Wherever it does the role more efficiently and economically, it is an ideal solution.

Hardware

The choice of hardware is important and should be kept to a minimum, but fit for the purpose for the application to which information technology is being applied. For example, if the microprocessor system is to control the temperature and humidity in a greenhouse, there is no real need for a VDU once the system is up and working. The size of memory should be sufficient and no more or less. Is there need for a hard disk or will a floppy disc be sufficient? The question that should always be asked is, 'do we need this piece of hardware' and if there is any doubt 'can the system do without it'?

Software

The same criteria can be quoted for the choice of software. In both cases it is important to realise that if the system is overly complex with more hardware or software than is necessary, the speed of the system will not run at optimum speeds. It is often better to have purpose built software than voluminous, general purpose software.

Data

The data to and from an Information Technology system is important. The input data must be accurate and representative of what is being measured. All too often a computer control system fails primarily because insufficient thought has gone into the measurement data from the sensors being used in the system. Sensors are covered in some detail in Element 2.4.

People

One of the purposes of Information Technology is to make the quality of life better for people. This may be aiding the task that they are doing or to use their talents elsewhere to better effect. Hence an important criteria for analysis must be the effect of the technology on people and the quality of life that it brings. The social implications of technology can have a significant impact on the success or otherwise of information technology introduction to a situation.

Processing activities

When we analyse a problem with a view to introducing information technology solutions, we must analyse the existing processes. The way in which existing systems handle a problem may perfect for the current approach taken. However a redesign of the methodologies may reveal that a different approach, using IT solutions, will improve the system. Hence it is not always computerisation of the current processes that give the best outcome. It could be a radically different approach that yields a better solution.

Input and output

The inputs and outputs of an information technology system very much depend upon the complexity of the processing tasks that it has to perform. The greenhouse example has a number of different types of input i.e. temperature, humidity and dryness of the soil. The types of measurements needed for the input will partly dictate the device used. The range of input values will also strongly influence the analysis. Hence, the devices used will depend on the application being considered. Systems are rarely identical except in the mass production areas such as embedded systems used in washing machine control. Generally the more inputs and outputs there are, the more complex the information technology system.

Advantages

There are many advantages of using an Information Technology system and they very much depend upon the application. Generally the processing happens that much faster. Usually the tasks are carried out more accurately and efficiently than if they were being performed by humans. This is because people get tired, easily loose concentration and make errors. If robots are employed, or other automation equipment used, such equipment is able to work in areas unsuitable for humans.

Thus, in making an analysis of the advantages for implementing an I.T. solution, we need to list all the positive issues that are identified. It is often useful to list these in a ranked order, since Element 1.1.4 on evaluation can take account of such information.

Limitations

There may also be some disadvantages. For example, people may have to be re-deployed or re-trained to work elsewhere (if there is work available). This could of course be a benefit if the type of work created is more interesting and has a higher skill content. The problem is that there is usually less of such work than prior to the introduction of IT systems. Initial costs can be expensive and the pay back time for these costs to be recovered can be quite long. In order to maintain this type of equipment technically skilled personnel have to be employed to look after it.

It may be that special or purpose built accommodation is required for the new set up. This may need the re-organisation of other parts of the operation. The investment needed here will reduce the organisation's ability to seek other business opportunities.

Impact on environment

This also depends upon the applications. Usually it is the application which is the major concern in terms of the impact on the environment rather than the supporting information technology. However there are examples where the use of information technology associated with measurement and control can have a very positive effect on the environment. Consider the generation of electricity by means of a coal fired power station. The coal is burnt to produce super heated steam with a high kinetic energy, sufficient to drive the turbine blades connected to a generator. This is similar to the Dinorwic example where we had high pressure water driving the turbine blades. The problem is that in burning the coal, sulphur dioxide is given off and this is the major cause of acid rain. Hence it is very important to try to keep to a minimum the amount of sulphur dioxide given off by the coal. By using analytical sensors the sulphur dioxide can be monitored and the signal used to reduce the emission of these toxic gases.

Question 1.4

Figure 1.8 shows part of a coal fired power station and in particular the cooling tower and the boiler house chimney. Which of the two is guilty of giving off sulphur dioxide to the atmosphere?

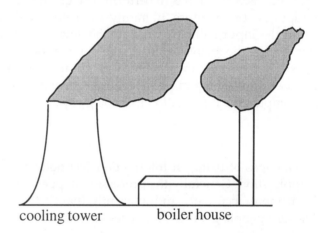

cooling tower   boiler house

Figure 1.8 A coal fired power station

1.1.4 Criteria for Evaluation

Comparison with other systems

One criteria for evaluation is simply to ask the question, 'is the application better with the use of Information Technology and in what way is it better?'. This type of comparison is essential and requires a knowledge of the faults and limitations of the application prior to the use of information technology.

A frequently used approach in comparative techniques is to list the major points that you want to see in a system. Some of these may be essential features, others may just be nice to have. You may well rank the nice to have features in order of importance to you. This ranking may have evolved from the analysis previously undertaken. For each of the proposed approaches, a comparison of performance against each of the features will establish whether all the essentials are present and how well the 'nice to have' features are met.

Selection can be based on this style of comparison, but may also include a number of other criteria, such as:

❐ is the proposed hardware and software already available or is development needed?

❐ is the software a shrink-wrapped solution?

❐ are there multiple vendors in the market?

❐ will there be adequate support for the implementation, including on-going maintenance?

Costs

Another factor which has to be considered is the cost. Is the cost justified in terms of the improvements gained and will the improvements be such that the overall system will save sufficient money to pay back the original investment. How long will this pay back take? In the UK the pay-back period is often set on a shorter basis than our competitors. Frequently in the UK we are looking at a 3 year period, whereas in Japan this may well be a 7 year period. It is also difficult to quantify some benefits in the equation. We will examine benefits in the next section.

There are a few additional factors here. It may be that we have to implement the proposal to stay in business. For example, if you went into the travel agent and they weren't able to connect to the tour operator's central system and give you an immediate choice of options, you may may well go elsewhere. Equally in choosing car insurance, the broker should be able to give you a choice of quotes from an interrogation of a central database. You may be less impressed if they had thumbed through a few ragged books.

Hence they need to implement simply to stay in business.

Benefits

Other factors which have to be considered are the benefits that the application now has with the addition of information technology. This may be measured in terms of increased speed of operation, increased efficiency, or improvements in accuracy and quality. Once this evaluation is complete it is always necessary to rethink the situation and reconsider what other changes or additions to the system could be included to make further improvements. It is in effect a cycle of perfection and you only stop when either the improvements are impractical or too expensive to justify the additional improvement made.

Identification of potential improvements

It is not unusual to identify additional improvements that can be delivered at the same time as implementing the original specification. The original system to be changed will have been identified through some formal process. The additional benefit may result from the analysis and investigation undertaken. For example, it may be that a dentist has implemented a database to record the treatment given to patients so they can charge the correct fee to the patient and health service. A simple additional benefit would be a periodic scan of the database to check when patients last received treatment and send out a reminder for a check up.

Task 1.5   PC 2 & 3

Using the information gathered for task 1.2 with respect to the bar code reader, investigate either by means of a visit to a large supermarket or by research in the library and contacting outside agencies, how the check-out system interfaces with stock control. Write a detailed report on your analysis and evaluate the system employed ensuring that each topic in Elements 1.1.3 and 4 is covered in both cases.

Task 1.6   PC 2 & 3

Write a detailed report for another commercial IT system. Your choice can cover any of the following: airlines, holiday or hotel booking systems, mail order companies. Gather as much information as possible either by visits to local commercial establishments or by research in the library and contacting outside agencies. Use the criteria for analysis and evaluation as the basis of your report.

Task 1.7   PC 4 & 5

Using the information gathered for task 1.4 on controlling a greenhouse environment, extend the notes to produce a report. Use the criteria for analysis and evaluation (covered in Elements 1.1.3 and 4) as the basis for the report.

Task 1.8   PC 4 & 5

Repeat the exercise described in task 1.7 for another industrial IT system. Your choice can cover any of the following: domestic systems e.g.. washing machines and central heating systems, car speeding cameras systems and photographic processing facilities, the manufacture of bottles, automobiles and plastic pipes, the use of robotics in any of these plus CAD and CAM.

Investigate Components of an Information Technology System

Introduction

An investigation into the elements representing a computer system will provide an ability to:

❏ describe types of available hardware and their purposes;

❏ explain the effect of system specification, and variations, on performance;

❏ describe the differing types of software and the purpose of each.

1.2.1 Types of hardware

The general operation or facility provided by any computer system is that of processing some form of input into some form of output through the use of a processor. To aid the processor achieve the desired outcome additional devices may be used as a form of intermediate information store.

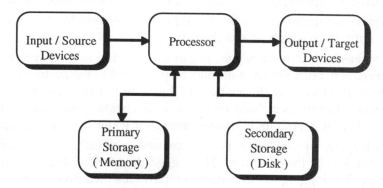

Figure 1.9 Overall view of a computer system

The overall view of a computer system as shown in figure 1.9 consists of four classes of hardware component:

❏ Input devices – Provide the means to present information for processing and include keyboard, mouse, tracker-ball, scanner, video source, joystick, light-pen, touch-screen and bar-code reader;

❏ Processor – A processor is a hardware component which obeys instructions to process input information in some pre-defined manner into output information. Traditionally, a processor used in a personal computer system is known by the term micro-processor. The term processor and micro-processor are often used to mean the same thing and are freely interchanged. The term processor is also associated with control devices. Such devices provide for the localised controlling of equipment in an intelligent manner. Examples include the control unit in central heating systems, domestic washing machines and alarm systems;

❑ Storage devices – These devices provide for the storage of information. The information may represent instructions associated with a processor or data to be processed by a processor. Storage devices exist in two forms, primary storage and secondary storage. Primary storage devices are memory components whilst secondary storage devices are cheaper, mass storage devices such as hard disks;

❑ Output devices – The results produced by a processor are reported (output) through the use of an output device. Output devices include printer, plotter, display-screen or monitor, speaker and robotic-arm.

1.2.2 Purposes of hardware

Hardware components (devices) are used in various ways providing for:

❑ Data capture;

❑ Processing;

❑ Storage;

❑ Output.

Data capture

Hardware used to capture, obtain or input data may do so in different ways:

❑ Manual – information may be entered into the system by the user through the use of a data entry device such as a keyboard;

❑ Automated – information may be obtained by the system automatically without user intervention. Such information may be presented to the system via a link with a remote system. The receiving device detects the receipt of the information and processes it as necessary. Examples include a thermostat in a heating system signalling to a control unit and a domestic washing machine sensing for water level and temperature;

❑ Data logging – a data logger is a device used to record and store information at a source independent of the computer. The logged data is later input to the computer for processing. The logging device usually employs it's own processor to control it's operation and some form of storage in which to store the supplied inputs. The input may be entered in the form of user keyed values or through the use of a device such as a bar-code reader. Data loggers may represent simple hand-held units such as electronic meter readers whilst larger devices maybe Point Of Sale (POS) devices;

❑ Sensed – information entered into a system does not necessarily have to be in a human readable textual form. The input may be obtained (sensed) through the use of devices such as temperature, pressure, positional and sound (microphone) sensors. The system samples (inputs) the available information and processes it as necessary. Sound sensing can be used in voice recognition packages, the user entering commands by speaking into a microphone rather than typing the commands in via a keyboard.

Question 1.5

Explain how manual and sensed data capture techniques differ.

Processing

Hardware devices such as processors are used to process or interpret input information and produce output information. They achieve this by following a sequence of instructions which carefully detail the exact actions required by the process, such as, add and subtract.

Storage

To process information a processor needs to be supported by additional devices which provide the means to store both the instructions to be performed and the data upon which to perform the instructions. Such data stores take the form of:

- ❐ Permanent – this form of storage is provided by primary storage (main memory) in the form of ROM (Read Only Memory) as detailed in Element 1.2.3. The contents of such memory elements cannot be changed and represents predefined instructions and data;

- ❐ Temporary – this form of storage is provided by primary storage in the form of RAM (Random Access Memory) as detailed in Element 1.2.3. The contents of such memory elements can be amended as necessary and would normally contain some or all of the program and data currently being run;

- ❐ Auxiliary – also known as secondary storage this form of storage is provided by devices such as disk drives and tape streamers. Disks and their associated drives are detailed in Element 1.2.3. Disk drives take the form of Floppy, Hard and CD-ROM.

Question 1.6

Identify the storage forms a processor may use.

Output

The hardware available to present results derived through processing include:

- ❐ Screen display – Information may be presented to the user in a temporary visual form through the use of a suitable screen display or monitor. The information may represent readable text or some form of image;

- ❐ Sound – Output in the form of sound is produced by converting some internal numeric form through the use of suitable sound generating hardware. The generated sound may represent synthesised spoken word or music. At the simplest level this may be an alert 'bleep';

- ❐ Print – Similar to screen display output, information may be presented to the user in a permanent visual form through the use of suitable printing hardware. The information presented to the printer may ultimately represent readable text or some form of image and be presented on a variety of mediums including paper and transparency sheets;

❏ Movement or Physical Control – Just as input information does not always have to represent a readable form, so to can the output information. It may represent a command to a movable device such as a robotic-arm. Consider an automated drilling machine capable of drilling at different drilling speeds and differing rates of drill-bit advance and withdrawal. The output of the process can be the sequence of commands to achieve this accurate drilling operation.

Task 1.9   PC 1

Using computer systems in your place of work, home or where you study:
❏ *undertake an investigation into the differing types of hardware and how this hardware is used;*
❏ *produce a report detailing the findings of your investigation.*

1.2.3   System specification

Defining the specification of a required system is a complex task faced by both commercial and domestic users. It should be noted that due to the ever continuing advances being made in system technology, the system purchaser should accept that any acquired state of the art machine, irrespective of price and all embracing specification, will almost immediately be superseded by a cheaper and better system in a very short time.

The user's software requirements will dictate the hardware specification. Should there be a need to run a range of software packages for various purposes, then the hardware must be more generalised, accommodating each package's needs. However, should there be a well defined single software requirement, then the hardware specification can reflect the true needs of the software. The software may place considerable demands on the system as follows:

❏ disk space to store the software on the system;
❏ disk space to store desired run-time information;
❏ processor time, software may be heavily computation based;
❏ memory (RAM), a minimum requirement;
❏ high resolution displays which require both additional processor time and memory to update the display in an acceptable time-scale.

A lack of adequate resources in any of these areas may cause considerable execution delays or not being able to run the desired software at all.

Question 1.7

A flawed system specification may result in execution delays. Identify the reasons why such instances may arise.

The following issues may also need to be taken into account:
❏ Window based software employing graphical user interface techniques demand greater all-round processing power. Generally, such packages comprise a large quantity of soft-

ware, utilise large amounts of memory, demand greater processor throughput and need to use and update high-resolution graphical screen displays rapidly;

❑ Command-line (non-window) based software places lesser demands on the overall interfacing capabilities of the system. Generally, the advantages associated with this software are the disadvantages of window based software and visa-versa;

❑ Database users need to store and query large amounts of structured information and thus require greater disk storage capacities, faster disk access times and processor speed to facilitate searching the stored information.

A system is specified in relation to the following components:

❑ Processor type;

❑ Number of processors;

❑ Processor speed;

❑ Cache;

❑ Primary storage (main memory – RAM or ROM);

❑ Secondary storage (disk devices);

❑ Input/output devices (such as keyboard, monitor and printer).

Processor type

Processor manufacturers continually strive to provide processors capable of moving information faster and in larger quantities. Newer versions (models) of processors are continually emerging. Presently, the majority of personal computers and many intelligent peripheral devices such as laser printers use INTEL 80xxx or MOTOROLA 68xxx processors.

Number of processors

There exist processors whose architecture is specifically geared to working in unison or parallel with other similar processors. The concept is that of sharing the workload and where possible performing tasks in parallel thus increasing the overall throughput of the system. Each supporting processor will typically perform a specialist role, which it can do faster than the main processor, for example, a maths co-processor will execute a range of arithmetic operations.

Processor speed

Generally, processors do something each time an internal clock or time source 'ticks'. Each clock tick is the signal to start an action, for example, the execution of a program instruction may be completed in one or more clock ticks depending on how complex the instruction is. The more ticks per second, the more actions can be undertaken by the processor per second. The internal structure of the processor must be capable of operating at the frequency of the time source. Thus, one measure of a processor's capability is that of it's clock frequency. A single model of processor may be available in one of many differing clock frequency ratings. A higher clock frequency does indicate a processor's ability to operate faster but should not be considered in isolation of the rest of the system. A clock rate of 33 MHz means a clock tick occurs every 1/33,000,000 of a second.

Cache

It is possible to identify support devices such as main memory and disk drives which operate much slower than the processor. Cache mechanisms represent components which lie between the processor and devices as shown in figure 1.10.

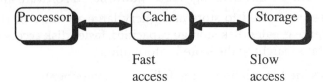

Figure 1.10 Cache usage

Their purpose is to hold the set of stored information most recently accessed by the processor. When referenced again, a copy may be more readily available in the faster cache area rather than waiting for the slower device to respond. If too little cache is available then the contents are frequently being replaced by only the most recently accessed information. If too much cache is provided then excessive time may be spent searching the cache storage, in which case, it would be more efficient to obtain the information from the attached device.

Primary storage – main memory (RAM and ROM)

A processor uses main memory as a fast access area denoting the program instructions to be executed and the information upon which to perform such instructions. Memory exists in various forms providing the processor with differing facilities. The most basic forms are:

- ❑ ROM – Read-Only-Memory – The contents of such memory devices can only be read and never changed. Such memory is used to provide pre-defined executable instructions and information. The information stored in ROM is not lost when power is removed from the system. Individual ROM memory elements may be randomly accessed;
- ❑ RAM – Random-Access-Memory – Unlike ROM, the contents of RAM can be amended. However, it's name does not truly reflect it's usage as RAM represents memory which can be both read from and written to. RAM is available in various forms, such as SRAM and DRAM. Basically, SRAM is faster than DRAM but is considerably more expensive. SRAM is usually used in small quantities in cache mechanisms whilst the cheaper DRAM is used to represent the usual form of main memory.

It is the amount of available RAM by which a system's memory is specified. Generally, the more RAM a system has the better, provided the processor has the capacity to reference such quantities.

The last factor concerning memory is that of response times. When a processor generated request is received by memory, memory must either store information provided by the processor into some memory location or provide the contents of some memory location for use by the processor. As memory technology has developed, the speed with which memory responds to such requests has improved. Typically, present DRAM memory response times can be as short as 60 nano-seconds or 60 ns whilst SRAM response times are faster at 15-20 ns. A nano-second is 1/1,000,000,000 of a second.

Secondary storage

Secondary storage differs from primary storage in that the information is stored on an external device such as a disk. Such storage is slower than main memory and is not lost when power is switched off. Disks are measured in terms of their:

❏ storage capacity – the quantity of information that may be stored;

❏ access (response) times – the speed of response to requests;

❏ data transfer rates – the quantity of information transferable in one read or write operation.

Many disk technologies presently exist in attempts to store greater quantities of information and improve transfer rates:

❏ Floppy disks – Such disks can be both written to and read from. They are so-named because their structure is that of a flexible disk coated with a recording surface. These disks are cheap to manufacture and do not require specialised environments in which to run. The recording surfaces are very susceptible to contamination or damage and subsequently provide low density storage capacities when compared to the other forms of disks. They require simple drives to operate them and also provide slower response times and data transfer rates than hard disks and CD-ROMs;

❏ Hard disks – Like floppy-disks, hard disks are disks which are coated with a recording surface. The disk is rigid and therefore a greater storage density is achievable. Hard disks are usually housed in a sealed drive unit in order to prevent air-borne contamination of the surfaces permitting greater storage capabilities. These devices provide both faster access times, data transfer rates and storage capacities than those provided by floppy-disks. Unlike floppy-disks which consist of a single disk, a hard disk drive may comprise several disks attached to the same common axle. Present-day software development trends appear to have little regard to a system's disk limitations. Newer software packages require greater disk storage simply to store the software;

❏ CD-ROM (Compact Disk Read Only Memory) – CD-ROM provides the ability to store large quantities of disk based information in a read only manner. CD-ROM is well suited in the distribution of large unchangeable software packages and data. A CD-ROM drive reads the information stored on a CD-ROM through the use of a laser beam. The surface of the CD-ROM reflects (scatters) the beam in a manner unique to each value stored. The CD-ROM drive converts the reflected light into meaningful data. A CD-ROM typically holds 680 Mbytes of storage.

Devices

A system will employ a keyboard and VDU (Visual Display Unit) or monitor to permit the user to interact with the running system. If the system represents a multi-user system then many such pairs of keyboards and display units will be available permitting the system's capabilities to be shared amongst the connected users. The display unit may be specified in various ways denoting it's ability to display text and high-resolution graphics. A system specification may include the following devices:

❏ Mouse – A pointer device permitting a more flexible means of communicating input to the system via point and click techniques. A mouse may be connected by dedicated control hardware or via a serial port dependent upon it's design;

❏ Printer – It is generally necessary to be able to provide a hard-copy representation of the results derived from processing. Printers do not usually form part of the central system but a specification may indicate the form a required printer must take. Printers may be specified as serial or parallel dependent upon the manner in which information is transferred between them and the system as outlined in figure 1.11.

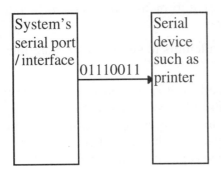
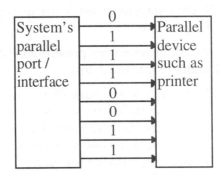

Figure 1.11 Serial and parallel transfer

In general, a parallel method is faster as the information is transferred as a pattern of parallel bits. The serial method is regarded as slower because each element constituting the information is transferred one after another. Both parallel and serial devices have other specifications associated with them, for example, serial devices may be further specified dependent upon their transfer rates;

❐ Video – Much research and development is being undertaken to provide computer-based full-motion video capabilities, the motion being measured in terms of frames per second. Present-day hardware does not yet readily provide facilities to reproduce full-screen displays and the hardware that does exist is expensive. However, available hardware generally permits displays within a smaller area of the monitor. More readily available using affordable hardware is the ability to capture a single frame from some attached video source;

❐ MODEM – A modem is a device to send data using a telephone connection. Such devices are used in pairs, one at each end of the telephone line. The telephone connection permits the attached devices to be used as if connected by a short cable where in reality they may even be in different countries;

❐ Network – Networking individual systems through the use of network interfacing hardware and associated software provides many benefits including information and resource sharing. The techniques associated with networking systems are detailed in Unit 4;

❐ Sound – Sound processing hardware provides an alternative way to output information and, through speech recognition techniques, to input information.

Consider the following typical system specification of an IBM compatible PC:

❐ Intel 80486DX2-66 MHz – indicates the processor model and frequency

❐ 8 Mbyte RAM Upgradable – main memory capacity which can be increased by additional memory modules

❐ 256 Kbyte secondary cache – cache memory between the processor and main memory

❑ 540 Mbyte with 256 Kbyte cache – one hard disk comprising 540 Mbyte of storage. The drive employing a 256 Kbyte cache facility

❑ 3.5" 1.44 Mbyte FDD – one 3.5" floppy-disk drive

❑ SVGA Colour Monitor – monitor capable of displaying high-resolution graphics

❑ 1 Mbyte Local bus Graphics Accelerator Card – hardware driver or controller to control the operation of the high resolution display monitor

❑ 102 key Keyboard – particular style of keyboard

❑ Serial Mouse – pointer device possibly connected via serial port defined below

❑ 2 × Serial ports – two serial adaptor ports permitting connection of peripherals such as printers and modems which employ serial connectors

❑ 1 × Parallel port – one parallel adaptor port permitting connection of peripherals such as printers which employ parallel connectors

❑ Tower or Desktop case – the style of case to house the main system components

This specification defines a complete system, even down to the housing used to hold the processor and it's supporting components. It does not provide the reader with details of the quality or original manufacturer of the individual components.

Much emphasis is presently placed upon the ability to upgrade a system with future technology as and when required. It should be noted that a supplied system reflects one in which the components are usually well matched or balanced. It may be possible to replace one component of the overall system in the future but if the remaining components cannot interact fast enough to accommodate the change, then an information bottle-neck may occur prohibiting any real increase in system performance.

1.2.4 System performance

It should be noticeable from reading the above points concerning system specification that the overall performance of a system is dependent upon many factors:

❑ Speed and model of processor(s);

❑ Number of processor(s);

❑ Speed and capacity of primary storage (main memory);

❑ Speed and capacity of secondary storage (disks);

❑ Other factors such as cache mechanisms and hardware connecting the components.

Speed

The overall speed associated with the system depends upon the access times associated with the supporting hardware and clock frequency of the processor(s). The overall performance will degrade if for some reason an information bottle-neck exists within the system. Such bottle-necks may exist for many reasons including the inability of a component supporting the processor to respond to processor requests quickly enough. This leaves the processor waiting for the device to complete such requests.

Consider a system in which memory modules are employed with slow access or response times. The processor would be continually waiting upon memory to complete it's task. Indeed the system would probably run in a similar manner even if an alternative lesser capability (cheaper) processor was employed. Further consider upgrading the memory modules with modules incorporating faster response times. The processor may be incapable of servicing the memory adequately, and so here, the memory modules would always be waiting upon the processor.

Upgrading the specification of a system after it's original supply must be thought through correctly to avoid introducing information or processing bottle-necks.

Parallel processing

Where applicable, a system may be designed to process information in a parallel manner whenever possible. Here, many processors may be employed to process individual pieces of information in parallel. The more the workload or processing requirements can be shared-out and undertaken simultaneously, the greater the overall through-put of the system and the faster it operates. However, it should also be noted that additional processing is also necessary to manage the communication between the processors, deducing when it is more efficient to operate in a parallel manner and when parallel processing cannot occur.

Question 1.8

Identify one way a system may employ more than one processor.

Quality

The specification of a system does not only specify the speed with which information can be moved around the system but also the quality of the individual components. Personal Computer systems are usually advertised based upon a particular specification. However, separate independent system builders may provide apparently similar equipment but the fundamental components constituting the system may vary considerably in quality.

Efficiency

As previously mentioned, a supplied system reflects one in which the components are usually well matched or balanced. However, it is possible to construct a system in which the devices although both logically and physically compatible do not communicate efficiently, for example, slow memory modules which cause the processor to continually wait for completion of a required task thus wasting processor power.

1.2.5 Types of software

Software may be categorised as belonging to one of the following software types:

- ❐ Operating Systems;
- ❐ User Interface Systems;
- ❐ Network Operating Systems;
- ❐ Communications;
- ❐ Programming languages;
- ❐ Applications.

Operating Systems, User Interface Systems, Programming Languages and Applications are detailed in Unit 6.

Network operating systems

Networked operating systems are covered in Unit 4.

Communications

The software associated with communications between computer systems is detailed in Unit 4.

1.2.6 Purposes of software

The following represents an introduction to the purposes of software. Information pertaining to software and the purposes associated with particular software forms are detailed in various units.

System initiation

When a computer system is powered-up, a boot-strapping procedure is always actioned. Initially, the computer system is a collection of hardware components in which the RAM component of main memory is empty and the associated ROM component contains some pre-defined instructions and data. The boot-strapping process initiates the loading of the software representing the operating system into the system and sets up the system configuration in order to manage the information flow around the system and execute further user specified software. The boot-strapping process generally represents:

❐ Power-On SelfTest (POST) – a test procedure verifies the correct operation of the system's hardware components;

❐ System Load – if the POST is successful, a small subset of instructions held in ROM is executed, triggering the loading of further instructions into memory. Execution of this newly loaded code then loads the remainder of the basic system into main memory;

❐ System Configuration – if the System Load was successful, the now resident software is configured completing the initialisation of the Operating System.

Question 1.9

What are the three steps involved in the System Initiation Process?

Simplify user interaction

It is essential to simplify the user interface to any software package in order that the user, even a non-technical user, may employ a package in a productive and flexible manner. Present window-based applications all employ a similar form of user interaction irrespective of originator. Such standardisation permits a user to easily become familiar with the facilities provided by new packages. The user may select a required option through the use of point-and-click techniques. Figure 1.12 shows a window-based Graphical User Interface (GUI) in which numerous icons (graphical objects) are visible. The user may select the option associated with the displayed icon by pointing at the icon with the attached pointer device, possibly a mouse, and confirming their selection in some manner, possibly clicking a button on the pointer device.

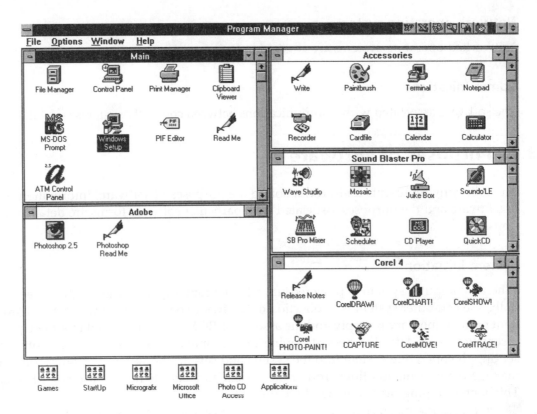

Figure 1.12 A Graphical User Interface (GUI)

Work group sharing

The term **Work Group Sharing** can be viewed as being a group of users sharing the same computer resources for a common purpose. The users usually represent a subset of individual personal computers connected together in some form of network. Although any computer connected to the network has access to common resources, only the declared users of the work group have access to their own subset of shared resources. It is important to note that each user of the work group is bound to the group by a purpose. This purpose may be departmental within a corporate organisation, such as Sales Department or project oriented in which a collection of users possibly employed in different departments are temporarily brought together for a common purpose. It is possible to have many separate work groups on a single networked system, each separate work group sharing their own set of resources.

Question 1.10

How does work group sharing differ to the usual form of networking capability.

Communicating

The purpose of this software form is to provide the user with the means to communicate with a remote or distant system via some physical connection. The connection may be via a public telephone line, private telephone line or more specialised link as further detailed in Unit 4. Generally, the communication software provides the user with the ability to transfer information from one end to another in a

manner as error-free as possible. The transferred information may represent user entered commands to a remote computer and the associated responses, executable code or data representing information of some relevant form. A range of software from file transfer to electronic mail exists.

Production of software

Some form of software must be used to easily develop or produce further software. New software designs are usually entered in some readable form and must be translated into a form more readily understood by a computer. Any software which aids the production of further software is regarded as a Software Development Tool. The development process and associated development tools are detailed in Unit 6. At the simplest level, an editor is used to create readable code, a compiler or assembler translates this representation into a specific machine code. Such software are examples of software production tools.

File management

Information is stored on secondary storage devices such a disks in the .form of files. A single file may contain information representing executable code or data (including textual information). Any operating system must provide the user with sufficient software facilities to provide for the routine management of the files, that is, to save them and retrieve them. To aid the system identify precisely which file(s) are being referenced, additional details identify the unique name by which the file may be referenced, the size of the file and even the time and date the file was created or amended. The procedures associated with file management include:

- ❑ Creation;
- ❑ Amendment;
- ❑ Deletion;
- ❑ Copying;
- ❑ Renaming.

Processing

A computer and any programs run upon it provide the user with the ability to process information in some manner. The information may represent:

- ❑ Textual documents;
- ❑ Numerical data;
- ❑ Graphical information;
- ❑ Structured data.

Many software packages exist to process each of the above information forms. These categories embody a vast pool of application packages but traditionally, the office administrative processing of such information was undertaken by individual packages:

- ❑ Textual documents being processed by text editors, word processors and desk top publishing packages;
- ❑ Numerical or statistical information being processed by spreadsheet packages;
- ❑ Graphical information being processed by a drawing package or presentation manager package;

❑ Structured data being processed by a database manager package.

Question 1.11

Generally, in terms of office administration, what may processed information represent?

Modelling

Application software can be used to:

❑ model or simulate a real situation or system;

❑ provide a simplified version of a process.

Modelling software covers many diverse applications including mathematical, medical, solid object modelling and Virtual Reality. Virtual Reality techniques permit the user to explore modelled scenes which may actually exist, represent imaginary locations or even in-accessible locations. We often want to run a model with a range of inputs to see which set of data gives the outcome closest to the ideal answer sought.

Controlling

Software can be used to control the management of various devices such as domestic washing machines, micro-wave ovens and even photocopiers. Inputs to such software represent sensed information from sensors whilst the output represents triggers initiating some action to take place. In a domestic washing machine, one stage of a wash programme may not begin until the water has reached a desired temperature.

Expert Systems

An Expert System is a software package providing the end-user with access to a computerised form of human expert to obtain a solution to a specific problem. It can act out the decision making process of the human expert and draw conclusions based upon the responses to a question and answer session. Areas in which Expert Systems applications have been developed include Medical diagnosis, Finance and Law.

Question 1.12

What facilities are provided by software packages concerned with the following areas?

❑ *Modelling;*

❑ *Controlling;*

❑ *Expert Systems.*

Task 1.10 PC 3

Using the computer system(s) used in task 1.9:

☐ *undertake an investigation into the different types of software. Describe the purpose of each piece of software identified;*

☐ *produce a report detailing the findings of your investigation.*

Task 1.11 PC 2

Using typical personal computer systems in your place of work, home or where you study:

☐ *undertake an investigation into the system specification of two different machines;*

☐ *produce a report detailing the findings of your investigation clearly identifying the effect each specification has on the performance of the relevant computer system.*

Investigate the Operation of a Micro-processor System

Introduction

Microprocessors are used extensively in commerce and industry for purposes such as word processors, numerical control of machine tools etc. They also form the heart of all microcomputer systems. Modern microcomputers focus on the system microprocessor to build a system with specific characteristics. Although microprocessors are increasingly complex devices, this element considers the basic features of microprocessors and how they operate.

1.3.1 Components

The basic functional units of a microcomputer are the microprocessor (or CPU), the memory which is primarily used to store programs and data, and the input and output ports which interface to the connected peripherals.

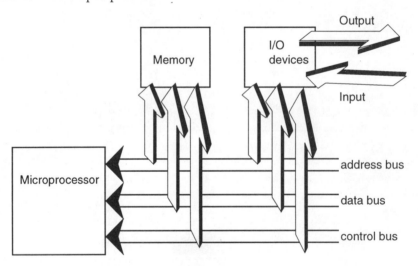

Figure 1.13 Basic Microcomputer

Central Processor Unit (CPU)

The processing unit is responsible for the execution of basic machine instructions. These instructions are read from memory and executed by the CPU. The peripheral devices connect to the computer via the input and output ports. Hence the processor has some instructions reserved to drive these interfaces correctly.

The CPU needs to send the right signals to the various components to action things at the right time i.e. it issues orders to do things by sending appropriate commands or signals. In this way the various components pass information or data between one another along the highways. The control of this data, so it arrives at the right time at the right place is the major aspect of data flow.

The basic features of the microprocessor are shown in figure 1.14.

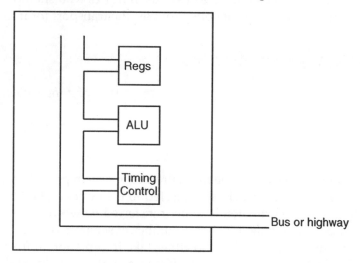

Figure 1.14 Basic microprocessor

The Central Processing Unit (CPU) usually comes in the form of an integrated circuit. It consists of a timing and control unit, an arithmetic logic unit (ALU) and a number of registers. The timing and control unit manages the internal operation of the ALU and registers so that each instruction is correctly obeyed. The arithmetic unit performs addition, subtraction and logical operations on the data. The CPU therefore controls the interpretation and execution of instructions within the microprocessor system.

Memory

The memory in the microprocessor system stores the program instructions and data. The memory comes in a variety of forms depending on its purpose, i.e. short term storage or long term storage. The latter type is called ROM, Read Only Memory. The content of the memory isn't changed after it is permanently placed in the memory during manufacture of the chip. The short term memory tends to use volatile memory and is known as RAM, Random Access Memory. The content of this type of memory is lost when the power supply is switched off. Hence it is necessary to store it on disk before switching off the power supply.

Bus

The bus is the means by which the memory, the central processing unit and the input and output ports all communicate with one another. For this purpose the bus consists of a group of connecting wires between the devices. They are normally a type of multi-strand or copper track carrying multiple signals in parallel. The number of parallel wires or tracks is part of the design specification for each system. There are three main types of bus in the microprocessor system, the data bus, the address bus and the control bus. These three buses are collectively known as the computer highway:

- ❑ The data bus is used to carry data between the memory or the input/output ports and the other components;
- ❑ The address bus identifies which memory location or input/output port is involved in the transfer;

❐ The control bus consists of a number of control lines which are used by the microprocessor to synchronise the data flows along the highway.

If we look at all three together, the address bus indicates who should be involved, the control bus says when to do it and the data bus provides the transport for it to happen.

Question 1.13

Why is the address bus uni-directional, whilst the data bus is bi-directional?

Input and output

The input/output (I/O) ports of the microprocessor system provide communication interfaces with the external peripheral devices connected to the system. The I/O is used for interfacing and controlling when information is to be transferred between these devices and the CPU or the main memory. Usually the I/O has a number of separate outlets or ports. The port associated with each unit can be arranged to either take information in from a peripheral device or transfer the information out to a device. Hence a port is usually bi-directional, allowing the flow of data in two directions, in and out. The number of lines it has depends whether it is a serial port (e.g. VDU's) or a parallel port where the number of output lines would depend upon the word length. A parallel port is a lot faster than a serial port. Element 4.1.5 in Unit 4 has further detail on this topic.

Task 1.12 PC 1   C3.3

Using a library or other resource, draw a detailed block diagram showing the components of a microprocessor system communicate with one another. Your diagram should include the following components:
CPU, Memory (i.e. ROM and RAM), the data highway (comprising of the address bus, the data bus and the control bus) and the I/O ports.

1.3.2 Functions

Instructions

To operate correctly, a microprocessor needs to be told what to do This is done by means of instructions given to the system. A whole series of instructions have been established for each family of microprocessors. The proper name for such a series is an instruction set. Instruction sets are 'key words' which are used by the programmer to tell the system what to do. For example, a simple instruction would be ' MOV C,B' which means move or transfer the contents of register B to register C. In some ways learning the instruction set is like learning a foreign language, but instead of a dictionary you use an instruction set manual.

Each type of microprocessor system will have its own unique set of instructions and commands in binary code although there is a lot of commonality between one system and another. When an instruction is executed by the microprocessor system, a bit pattern is read from the program part of the memory and held in the microprocessor unit where it is interpreted as a unique code. This code will start a sequence of control actions designed to implement the required instruction. In the case of the example quoted, MOV C,B we have a three words or bytes. The first is known as the operation code (as it tells the system what to do). The other two bytes locate the data, in this case a register address indicating where the data is located. This part of the instruction is known as the operand. Microprocessor systems have three main types of instruction corresponding to one of the following types of function:

❏ data transfer;

❏ arithmetic and logic;

❏ test and branch.

We have already recognised that data transfer is moving data from one location to another. An example of the arithmetic and logic instruction would be ADD A,C add the content of register C to the content in register A. It is also important that we can carry out tests on specific conditions (e.g. is the data content equal to zero?). The result of such a test may determine which part of the program is to be implemented next. Instructions which follow this type of facility are within the test and branch group of instructions.

Microprocessor manufacturers publish the instruction set for their system so that the processor can be programmed to perform the task required by the designer or programmer.

Calculations

We have already covered the simple operation of ADD as an instruction for a microprocessor, but there are many other instructions. The calculations are performed by the Arithmetic Logic Unit within the CPU of the microprocessor system. We should remember that the microprocessor only works with binary information, i.e. '1's and '0's. All calculations are performed under the control of the ALU. Data may be read from the memory or an I/O port, manipulated by executing a sequence of instructions and the result held in memory or output through one of the ports.

The way in which addition and subtraction is undertaken within the microprocessor may seem quite long, especially if you performed the same steps manually, but the microprocessor does it in a fraction of a second. Multiplication and division are far more complex than addition and subtraction and in the majority of microprocessor systems they are not included. In order to perform multiplication and division it is necessary to use a subroutine.

Data Flow

Data flow involves is the movement of data along the data bus between the various microprocessor registers or between a processor register and a memory location. For example when the instruction MOV A,B is executed, the content of register B is transferred to the register A. Other instruction formats locate the data needed by the instruction using an address mechanism. An address points to the location of data or a program segment held in storage. The address can refer to storage in either a register or in a memory or both. It is necessary to both read from and write to the memory, depending on the action required. The flow of data around the system at the right time is controlled by the timing and control functions. It is closely coupled with the way in which instructions are read and actioned. We will see how these functions are actioned in Element 1.1.4.

Figure 1.15 shows how the memory locations can be identified with an 8-bit address. Longer bit formats are also used on some systems.

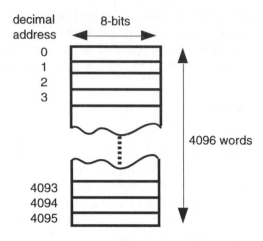

decimal
address   8-bits

0
1
2
3

4096 words

4093
4094
4095

Figure 1.15 Address structure of the main memory

Storage

In order to read information stored in a memory or write information to a memory location it is essential to know the address. If the address is not known the information cannot be located. Figure 1.15 shows only 4096 memory locations, but a hard disk inside a computer might typically have 40 million address locations in which to hold information. For large scale storage other than the hard disk, we have the floppy disks which have the advantage that they can be transferred from one microprocessor system to another. Other forms of storage used are magnetic tapes, where retrieval can be slower than the disks, but is ideal for storing a lot of data which might need to be referred to in the future.

Task 1.13 PC 2   *C 3.3*

Investigate and explain, with the aid of diagrams, the function of the components that make up the Central Processing Unit.

1.3.3 Elements

Program Counter

To remember which is the next program instruction to be executed, we need to have a pointer to the next location in memory which holds that instruction. The program counter is such a pointer and indicates the next instruction that is to be fetched and executed. Whilst this instruction is being performed the contents of the program counter is incremented to point to the next instruction. And so the process repeats itself.

Question 1.14

At the start of an instruction, will the program counter always point to the next instruction in a sequence of instructions?

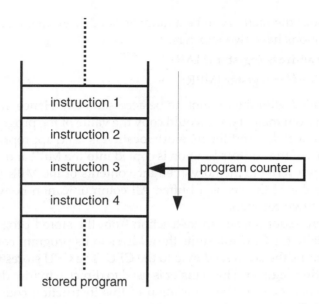

Figure 1.16 The program counter

Memory Registers

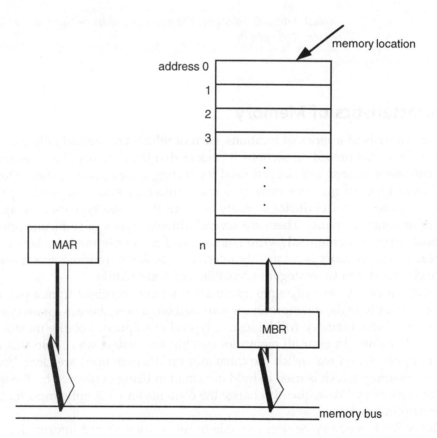

Figure 1.17 Use of memory registers

We could consider the memory to be a number of adjacent memory locations. Each collection of memory locations have two registers:

❑ **memory address register** (MAR);

❑ **memory buffer register** (MBR).

The MAR is loaded with the location to be accessed next. Hence, if we are going to fetch the next instruction from memory, we would copy the value of the program counter into MAR. The MAR address is decoded and the memory location is used appropriately. If the cycle is a read then the contents of the address location is copied into the MBR and other parts of the CPU use this value. If it is a write to memory, then the contents of the MBR is copied into the memory location. Hence the MBR acts as a buffer. All communication between the memory and the CPU is via these two registers.

When the processor fetches an instruction from the stored program it does so in two distinct parts. Initially the CPU transmits the address in its program counter to the memory, then the memory returns the addressed byte to the CPU. The CPU stores this instruction byte in the **current instruction register**. This register is used to direct activities during the remainder of the instruction execution cycle. The translation of this instruction code into processing action is performed by the instruction decoder and by the relevant control circuitry within the CPU.

Task 1.14 PC 3   *C3.2*

Investigate and report on the main elements of the Intel CPU and the memory associated with it.

1.3.4 Characteristics of Memory

Memory consists of a series of locations, each of which are individually identified by its own address. From the preceding sections it is clear that the memory is an essential feature of the microprocessor system and not just used for storing information or data. There are a number of different types of memory used by a microprocessor system depending upon the type of storage required. Semiconductor memory is the most popular type used today, especially in the form of integrated circuits. There are several different types of semiconductor memory used, the most common being read/write memory and read only memory better known as ROM. The read/write memory is frequently referred to as RAM (random access memory). Memory can be classified into two categories, volatile and non-volatile.

Volatile memory can only store information whilst energised from a power supply. When the mains supply to the microprocessor is turned off, unless there is a battery backup the information in volatile memory will be lost. A typical example of volatile memory is that used in pocket calculators. To clear all memories quickly, the easiest way to do this is to turn off the power supply. When we switch the calculator on the memories are clear. Volatile memory is working memory which is used to hold information being generated by the user. Hence RAM is volatile memory. We frequently change the contents and it is only important for the duration of the current activity.

Non-volatile memory devices are able to retain their stored information when the mains supply has been turned off. Hence this type of memory is used to store programs which are continuously used and parts of the operating system such as DOS. Typical memory devices which are non-volatile are read only memories (ROM's). ROM's are also used to load the remaining part of a program or operating system from the specified loading device.

Question 1.15

Why do we need both ROM and RAM styles of memory?

Task 1.15   PC 2

Investigate and explain, with the aid of diagrams, how ROM and RAM memory devices actually store data within the device.

1.3.5 Stages in the machine instruction cycle

The machine instruction cycle is the complete process of fetching one instruction from a memory store, decoding and executing it by the central processing unit. During a **fetch** cycle the selected instruction which could be one, two or even three bytes long is read from memory and placed in the instruction register. The instruction register is examined to **decode** the instruction i.e. to determine what the instruction is and what sequence of operations needs to be performed by the microprocessor to obey the instruction. During the **execute** phase, the instruction is obeyed by undertaking the actions determined during the decode phase. Each instruction consists of a number of machine cycles, ranging from one to five cycles. A machine cycle is required each time the microprocessor accesses the memory or an I/O port. The fetch part of the instruction cycle being one machine cycle for each byte of information to be fetched. The number of machine cycles during the execute phase depends upon the particular instruction. Each machine cycle would contribute to the actions needed to obey the instruction.

All control operations described are kept in sequence and governed by a master timing device or clock. This is usually done by a quartz crystal oscillator producing very accurate timing. The waveforms are to trigger components within the microprocessor system so that they respond to information at the right time.

Task 1.16   PC 4

With reference to appropriate text books explain graphically the stages of the fetch/execute cycle indicating the components and elements that are used at each stage of the cycle.

Install and Configure a Stand Alone Computer System

Introduction

The following text identifies the steps necessary to provide an operational stand alone computer system. In this element we will use the components described in the earlier elements to build a system. The various stages to achieve this are:

❑ Connect hardware components together to meet the specification;

❑ Configure the operating system software to meet the specification;

❑ Install relevant applications software;

❑ Test the computer system;

❑ Review the system and make recommendations for improvement of the specification.

The tasks presented in the text are practical by nature assuming the relevant hardware and software is available to produce a basic stand alone system as detailed below.

1.4.1 Hardware components

Assuming the stand alone system comprises the following components:

❑ Main processor unit;

❑ Keyboard;

❑ Mouse;

❑ VDU (Visual Display Unit/screen-display/monitor);

❑ Printer;

❑ Ports (Serial and Parallel);

❑ Cables.

These components will constitute a system as depicted in figure 1.18.

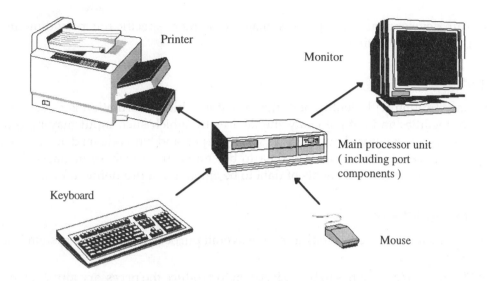

Figure 1.18 A stand-alone computer system

Such systems are supplied separately packaged, with each of the main identified components packed in it's own box. The monitor, main processor unit and printer will have their own power cables. The monitor, keyboard and mouse will also be supplied with cables by which they connect to the main processor unit. These cables carry both data and signals between the devices. The data cable connecting the printer to the main processor unit may be provided with the printer or as a separate component. The documentation supplied with the system will identify the power points and connecting ports to which all cables attach.

Question 1.16

The monitor, keyboard and mouse will be connected via data and signal cables to which unit?

1.4.2 Specification

The specification associated with the system will identify the following aspects concerning the overall usage of the system:

❐ Purpose;

❐ Input;

❐ Processing activity;

❐ Output;

❐ Hardware (components and system performance);

❐ Software (Operating System and applications).

Purpose

The specification will identify the overall purpose to which the system and it's resident software are to be put. The purpose may be to support the day-to-day activities of an office through the use of office administration software, develop software through the use of software development tools, process images or another specific role providing the user with a computer based solution.

Input

The specification will identify both the format in which information is to be presented to the system facilities and subsequently the devices by which such input may be provided. Such devices include keyboard, mouse, joystick, light-pen and bar-code reader. Consider a database manager package. The structured data to be stored in a database managed by the package requires the individual elements of data to be entered in a pre-defined format.

Processing activity

The specification as well as indicating the overall purpose to which the system is to be put will also identify the:

❐ processing activities to be undertaken to produce the necessary inputs to the system and collate the results derived. The user or operator must gather the information as necessary for subsequent input but should not be expected to needlessly process the information from one form into another repeatedly. The processing should aid the user and not incur additional administrative burdens;

❐ processing/computations to be undertaken upon the input information. Consider a spreadsheet manager package. The inputs presented to an individual spreadsheet through the use of the package will process the inputs in a pre-defined manner to achieve the desired results.

Output

The specification will identify both the format with which the results are to be presented and subsequently the devices through which such output is to be provided. Again consider the database manager package. Structured data stored in a database may be queried in some manner to derive output. The output may represent some form of report detailing the outcome of the query. Such a report will reflect a pre-defined format as identified in the specification. The output device may represent a temporary form such as a screen-display or a more permanent paper-based form via a printer.

Hardware

The specification will identify the precise component type of each of the hardware components constituting the stand-alone system. The components must individually and when built into a complete unit meet the overall system performance as detailed below.

Question 1.17

Why do we need a hardware specification?

❐ Main processor unit – this being the main component of the stand-alone system, it's specification will indicate: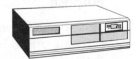

- the type of micro-processor used including it's associated clock frequency;
- the amount of available main memory;
- the amount of cache supporting main memory;
- the number of disk drives together with the type, capacity and possibly the response time associated with each;
- the standard used to internally connect the individual components;
- the unit's ability to be upgraded. This is measured in various ways including the number of expansion slots available for inclusion of add on cards providing additional facilities and the number of free memory slots permitting the insertion of additional memory modules;
- ports (Serial and Parallel) indicating the number and types of devices which may be externally connected to the main processor unit.

❏ Keyboard – the specification will indicate: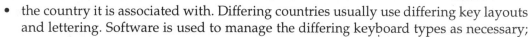
- it's suitability for connection to the main processor unit;
- the country it is associated with. Differing countries usually use differing key layouts and lettering. Software is used to manage the differing keyboard types as necessary;
- the number of keys indicating the style and function key availability.

❏ Mouse – the specification will indicate the mouse type. Such devices are usually available in various forms:
- serial – connected via a serial adaptor externally accessible on the main processor unit;
- dedicated – connected via a specific mouse adaptor externally accessible on the main processor unit;
- add on card – located in an available expansion slot inside the main processor unit, the connection being externally accessible.

Question 1.18

Identify three different types of mouse.

❏ VDU (screen-display or monitor) – the specification associated with a VDU will indicate it's:
- screen size;
- display capabilities, that is, it's resolution, such as, Super Video Graphics Adaptor (Super VGA) as available for IBM PCs and compatibles;
- associated display adaptor, the controlling hardware card inside the main processor unit which also governs the manner by which the VDU ultimately connects to the main processor unit.

❏ Printer – the specification will indicate:
- the form of the printer such as laser or ink jet;
- the manner by which the printer connects to and communicates with the main processor unit. Printers may use serial or parallel connecting and communication methods. Both serial and parallel methods may be further specified depending upon the printer used, for example, where a serial inter-

face is used, the printer's specification will also indicate the maximum rate at which information may be transferred to the printer.

Question 1.19

By what two methods may a printer connect to the main processor unit?

❑ Cables – these must be of the right specification (compatible plug and socket types) to make the correct connecting between the main processor unit and the individual external devices.

Software

The specification will identify each software package to be used in the stand-alone system. Such packages represent both the relevant operating system software and application software. Particular note should be paid to such packages to ensure they are compatible for the particular stand-alone system. The software will normally state the operating system or the hardware environment on which it will run, for example, IBM PC(and compatibles) and MS-DOS (including relevant version). Many present-day software developers produce variations of a specific package in order that it may be run on each available system. Such systems differ to the extent that the version available for one specific system cannot be used on another.

It should be noted here that the hardware requirements each software package identifies may also indicate other basic hardware requirements to run the package such as disk storage space, disk space to run and the type of display. It is essential to ensure that all such requirements are met by the stand-alone system.

Task 1.17   PC 1

Assume the stand alone system is to provide a specific software capability such as word processing. Using the definitions associated with such a system as detailed here:

❑ *familiarise yourself with the specification of the complete system and familiarise yourself with the individual different hardware components of the system. Check that all the components are there. If you are satisfied that all the components are available, carefully read the assembly instructions noting any precautionary points. Identify the tools necessary to connect the components.*

❑ *assemble the stand-alone system by connecting the separate hardware components together in the manner and order specified in the relevant assembly documentation. Be careful not to attempt to force any connections and follow any precautions previously identified. There may be a particular reason why a connection may not be made such as a tight fit or even in-compatible connectors. Particular care over making connections with "pins and sockets" is needed to avoid damaging the connectors.*

DO NOT attempt to power-up the system at this point.

1.4.3 Configure

Once a system as specified has been connected together, it may be necessary to adjust some components in order to make them compatible with the other components constituting the system. It may be necessary to adjust switch settings in the main processor unit to identify:

❏ the type of display adaptor used and the monitor attached;

❏ the quantity and type of additional memory modules if the specification required a higher than standard requirement;

❏ the settings associated with adaptor connections which ultimately connect to external devices.

Question 1.20

Why do we need to adjust switch settings in the main processor unit?

It may also be necessary to adjust further settings in both the main processor unit and the external devices in order to make them compatible and reflect the hardware specification of the stand-alone system. Such changes are particular to the specific hardware devices used and so the reader should refer to the documentation supplied with the hardware to ascertain the precise changes necessary.

Task 1.18 PC 1

Check the assembled stand-alone system to ascertain if any setting adjustments are necessary. Such adjustments may have been completed during the assembly stages as and when identified in the assembly documentation.

Task 1.19 PC 2

Install the operating system onto the stand-alone system.
❏ Familiarise yourself with the procedure associated with the installation, noting any important points identified.
❏ Install the operating system software as directed.

Date and time

As well as configuring the hardware, once the operating system has been successfully installed, it is usually necessary to set the correct system date and time. The system needs the time and date to successfully manage files and record when the files were created or amended. The system time may be recorded using 12-hour clock or a 24-hour clock. The system date format varies dependent upon the country associated with the operating system. The USA standard uses m/d/y (month/day/year) whilst the UK standard is d/m/y.

Task 1.20 PC 2

For your system, check out the relevant command(s) to check and, if necessary amend the system's time and date settings.

It is now easier to configure a system than previously. Usually devices are more able to intelligently establish the configuration of the resident hardware and subsequently adjust the settings accordingly. Thus the main processor unit may be able to automatically determine the amount of main memory available or even the type of display adaptor and therefore monitor connected to it.

1.4.4 Install

As with hardware assembly and configuring, the installation procedures associated with present-day software packages, both operating system and application software, normally use some form of automated installation and self-configuration.

The steps necessary to achieve a software installation, whether done manually or automatically under software control are:

❒ Create directory;

❒ Install the software in directory;

❒ Set defaults;

❒ Install device drivers.

Create directory

Software is best installed in separate areas on a disk to simplify the administration of the overall system. Therefore, to install a piece of software, the first step is to create a suitably named disk area or sub-directory in which the software to be installed may reside. As an example assume:

❒ an IBM PC or compatible system is available using the MS-DOS operating system;

❒ the present disk hierarchy is as shown in figure 1.19;

❒ a new piece of software is to be installed into a sub-directory called DRAWPACK;

❒ the new software requires a sub-directory in DRAWPACK called TEMP to be available.

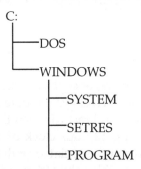

Figure 1.19 Example MS-DOS sub-directory hierarchy

The sub-directories may be created by the commands:

MD C:\DRAWPACK
MD C:\DRAWPACK\TEMP

where MD represents Make Directory. Notice that the TEMP sub-directory depended upon the DRAWPACK sub-directory being available and so DRAWPACK had to be created first. The resulting disk hierarchy is shown in figure 1.20.

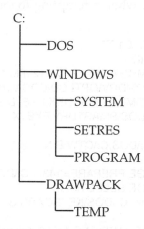

Figure 1.20 Resulting MS-DOS sub-directory hierarchy

Install the software in the directory

The software associated with a particular package should reside in a suitable disk area or sub-directory permitting easy location by both the system in it's processing and the system user. On running the software it may expect the existence of specific named disk areas or sub-directories. If such a directory structure is not respected, then run-time errors can be expected. Most current software is supplied with install procedures which automatically create the necessary disk areas or sub-directories in which the new piece of software is to reside together with any necessary additional disk areas or sub-directories. Such procedures may typically be initiated by entering the relevant command in a non-window based environment or by manipulating an icon in a window-based environment.

Question 1.21

Identify two reasons for installing a software package in a separate specific disk area or sub-directory.

Set defaults

When an operating system is loaded or the system is switched on it configures itself to reflect both the attached hardware and any declared software needs associated with available individual software packages. This is usually achieved through the processing of some start-up instructions. The user or system may at some point amend this list of instructions to reflect changes required in the run-time environment. Thus, it is possible to set default information for use by the software when it is run. The information may indicate the disk areas or sub-directories to be searched in order to locate certain files.

Consider figure 1.21 which shows an example of an AUTOEXEC.BAT file used on IBM PCs and compatibles. The configuration process, prior to passing control to the user, actions the instructions contained in this file as if they were entered directly from the keyboard. The file includes commands which set up default information for use whilst the operating system is active, namely, the *SET* and *PATH* commands:

❐ The SET command associates some information with a named item for later reference;

❐ The PATH command indicates the order in which the specified disk areas or sub-directories are to be searched when attempting to locate specific files.

```
@ECHO OFF
SET BLASTER=A220 I5 D1 T2
SET SOUND=C:\SBPRO
C:\SBPRO\SBP-SET /M:12 /VOC:12 /CD:12 /FM:12 /LINE:12
LH /L:1,19664 C:\CDROMDRV\OPTI-CD\CDCACHE /H:LASERWAV /K /DC /X:512
LH /L:1,32096 C:\CDROMDRV\MSCDEX.EXE /D:$cdcache /M:8 /V /E
LH /L:0;1,45456 /S C:\DOS\SMARTDRV.EXE /X
PROMPT $p$g
PATH C:\WINDOWS;C:\DOS;C:\QTW\BIN;
SET TEMP=C:\DOS
MODE CON CODEPAGE PREPARE=((437) C:\DOS\EGA.CPI)
MODE CON CODEPAGE SELECT=437
LH /L:1,16656 KEYB UK,,C:\DOS\KEYBOARD.SYS
C:\MOUSE\MOUSE
LH /L:1,16944 C:\DOS\SHARE.EXE /L:500 /F:5100
DOSKEY
SET LIB=C:\QTW\LIB;
SET INCLUDE=C:\QTW\INC;
```

Figure 1.21 Example AUTOEXEC.BAT

The other commands are examples to install and/or configure device drivers for a Sound-Blaster audio card, a CD-ROM drive, a mouse and a keyboard translator amongst other necessary commands to provide a specific MS-DOS environment. As well as the **SET** and **PATH** defaults, a software package may also use it's own information files which further define other default information. The form used will be specific to the software package and the user should refer to the associated documentation for further explanation.

Install device drivers

A software package may require the run-time availability of specific devices and subsequently the code to manage such devices. Such code routines are known as device drivers. In order to make them available for use by a software package, such device drivers must firstly be installed.

Consider figure 1.22 which shows an example of a CONFIG.SYS file as used on IBM PCs and compatibles when booting-up with the MS-DOS operating system. The file is used to configure the operating system to the user's software requirements and includes a number of device installation instructions such as a memory management driver and a CD-ROM driver.

Question 1.22

What are device drivers and why do we use them?

```
DEVICE=C:\DOS\HIMEM.SYS
DEVICE=C:\DOS\EMM386.EXE NOEMS
BUFFERS=15,0
Files=40
DOS=UMB
LASTDRIVE=Z
FCBS=16,8
DEVICEHIGH /L:1,12048 =C:\DOS\SETVER.EXE
DOS=HIGH
COUNTRY=044,,C:\DOS\COUNTRY.SYS
DEVICEHIGH /L:1,15792 =C:\DOS\DISPLAY.SYS CON=(EGA,,1)
STACKS=9,256
DEVICEHIGH /L:1,13424 =C:\CDROMDRV\CDMKE410.SYS /D:LASERWAV /SBP:220 /N:1
```

Figure 1.22 An example CONFIG.SYS

Task 1.21   PC 3

Select a software package as defined by the specification in Task 1.17 and install it onto the stand-alone system.
DO NOT *attempt to run the software package at this point.*

Question 1.23

How do the MS-DOS files CONFIG.SYS and AUTOEXEC.BAT logically differ?

1.4.5 Test

Following an apparent successful installation of a software package, it is necessary to test the software to check it's correct operation. This may be achieved through the following steps:

- ❑ Power-up;
- ❑ Access software;
- ❑ Enter data;
- ❑ Save data;
- ❑ Inspect print.

However, although these steps confirm the correct initial operation of the new software, more thorough testing of numerous sub-functions of the software must be undertaken to confirm that it operates in the expected manner. Any feedback or error reports provided whilst attempting these steps should be carefully noted in order to refer to the relevant documentation and find a suitable correction. You should also note that the steps must be successfully completed in the correct order. If a problem is encountered during one step, no subsequent step should be attempted until the current problem is resolved.

Power-up

The installation of a software package may have required the modification of the set of instructions which automatically configure the operating system during the boot-strapping procedure. To test the correct operation of the new software, the operating system must be configured correctly and re-started. This step may highlight any inconsistencies between the original configuration instructions and the new instructions or even the incorrect specification of the new instructions.

Access software

Attempting to access the new software will initially ascertain that all the files needed for the application have been located correctly and are accessible. Errors reported at this point would possibly indicate:

- ❏ the improper locating of relevant files;
- ❏ missing files;
- ❏ invalid declarations specifying the locations of files.

Initially starting the software does not confirm the correct availability and locating of all the files needed for the new software package. It is possible that only when a sub-function of the software is initiated, the associated files are accessed and further error reports will possibly be triggered. Consider the window based environment shown in figure 1.12 of Element 1.2. Any application may be selected by double-clicking the icon associated with the application.

Enter data

Having apparently started the new software package successfully, it is necessary to enter some appropriate information to check the correct operation. Consider a word processing package. Testing that the software accepts the data correctly involves the user entering some suitable text and checking that it is received and displayed properly.

Save data

Software generally takes input and processes it to generate output. Thus an important aspect concerned with the testing of a new software package is the software's ability to correctly save the output in some suitable form and verify it's availability. Having successfully confirmed that the software handles text entry, the user may attempt to save the text. The user may then, through further suitable facilities provided by the software or even the operating system, subsequently confirm that the text has indeed been successfully saved.

Print

In the normal processing of input into output, a program usually provides the user with the ability to generate a hard-copy (that is, print-out) of the previously entered and saved data. It is necessary to confirm that the software communicates with an attached printer correctly. This may be achieved by selecting a suitable sub-function of the new software to generate the hard-copy. Failure to generate such a print-out may not necessarily be a problem solely associated with the new software. If problems occur, alternative software should be run to confirm whether the fault lies with the new software or the printer facility.

Task 1.22   PC 4

Devise a test plan for the software package installed in Task 1.21. Test the package to see if it operates correctly.

Task 1.23   PC 5

Having completed Tasks 1.17 through 1.22, review the specification identified in Task 1.17 and produce a document outlining recommendations for improvement of the specification.

Answers to questions in Unit 1

Answer 1.1   Yes, if the product is identical, the bar code must be identical also.

Answer 1.2   To uniquely identify a product, there must be a separate bar code for the product. A 400gm jar of coffee will have a different bar code to a 880gm jar of coffee of the same brand.

Answer 1.3   The length of time that Dinorwic can generate electricity is controlled by how much water can be held in the upper reservoir. Once that is below a certain level, generation of power ceases.

Answer 1.4   The large cloud over the cooling towers is merely water vapour from the cooling steam. However the smoke coming from the boiler house will contain sulphur dioxide, hopefully not too much!

Answer 1.5   Manual information may be entered or typed into the system by the user through the use of a data entry device such as a keyboard whilst sensed information may be obtained using devices such as temperature, pressure, positional and sound (microphone) sensors.

Answer 1.6   Storage forms may be:
- ❏ Permanent;
- ❏ Temporary;
- ❏ Auxiliary.

Answer 1.7   A lack of adequate resources in any of the following areas may cause considerable run-time information bottle-necks:
- ❏ disk space to store the software;
- ❏ run-time disk space;
- ❏ processor time;
- ❏ memory;
- ❏ high resolution displays which require both additional processor time and memory to update the display in an acceptable time-scale.

Answer 1.8   A maths co-processor to specifically handle calculations.

Answer 1.9   The steps to initiate an operational operating system are:
- ❏ Power-On SelfTest (POST);
- ❏ System Load;
- ❏ System Configuration.

Answer 1.10   Work group sharing makes it easier for users to locate and use shared (common) resources for a specific purpose. Each user belonging to the work group has access to both shared information and shared devices. It is possible to have many separate work groups on a single networked system, each separate work group sharing their own set of resources.

Answer 1.11   The processed information may represent:
- ❏ Textual documents;
- ❏ Numerical data;
- ❏ Graphical information;
- ❏ Structured data.

Answer 1.12   Modelling software can be used to:
- ❏ model or simulate a real situation or system;
- ❏ provide a simplified version of a process.

Controlling software can be used to control the management of various devices such as domestic washing machines, micro-waves and even photocopiers.

Expert Systems software provides the end-user with access to a computerised form of human expert to obtain a solution to a specific problem.

Answer 1.13   The address bus carries information from the microprocessor and indictes who should respond i.e. memory location or I/O device. Hence it needs to be a uni-directional bus. The data bus carries information to or from the memory and I/O devices and therefore needs to be bi-directional.

Answer 1.14   No. It might be that the last instruction was a brach or jump instruction. If that were the case the natural sequence of instructions is broken and a new instuction location needs to be identified. The program counter is adjusted to point to the out of sequence instruction.

Answer 1.15   ROM and RAM perform different funtions. RAM is volatile memory and holds data only as long as the system is powered up. Any information held in RAM can be overwritten by other data under the control of the operating system. ROM is permanent memory and cannot be overwritten. It is pre-loaded with information that is necessary to keep the system operational.

Answer 1.16   Main processor unit.

Answer 1.17   The specification describes the individual components and the overall performance. We need to know how well the system must perform and this can be recorded formally in the specification.

Answer 1.18   The different types of mouse are Serial, dedicated and add-on-card.

Answer 1.19   A printer may connect either using a serial or parallel method.

Answer 1.20   To configure the system to the exact configuration of the attached devices. The adjustments may be necessary to indicate the type of processor attached, amount of available memory or adaptor settings for external devices.

Answer 1.21   Firstly, it is easier to manage the files associated with a single software package if only those files pertaining to the package reside in a disk area/sub-directory.

Secondly, the software package when run may expect the existence of a specific disk area or sub-directory.

Answer 1.22   A device driver is a piece of code to manage an attached device.

Answer 1.23   CONFIG.SYS is a configuration file processed during a boot-up and configures the operating system to the user's software requirements.

AUTOEXEC.BAT is a file of commands processed each time the system is booted-up prior to the configuration process passing control to the user at the end of the boot-up. It contains commands which the user could alternatively enter at the keyboard.

Unit 1 Sample Test Paper

1   High Street banks have always been leaders in the use of business computers.
    Which of the following was introduced for customer convenience?

    A   printing customer account statements using high speed laser printers
    B   using Magnetic Link Character Recognition for reading cheques
    C   electronic fund transfer between banks
    D   installing cash dispensing machines

2   A library has been computerised.
    This has improved the service to library users by:

    A   increasing the number of books that may be borrowed
    B   reducing the charges for overdue books
    C   providing a faster book enquiry service
    D   having more books available for borrowing

3   Which of the following represent primary storage?

    A   Input devices
    B   Processor
    C   Memory
    D   Secondary storage

4   A clock source has a frequency of 66 MHz.
    How often does a clock tick occur?

    A   once every 1/66,000 of a second
    B   once every 1/66,000,000 of a second
    C   once every 1/66,000,000,000 of a second
    D   once every 1,6,600 of a second

5   What form of application software provides file transfer facilities?

    A   File Management utilities
    B   Communication software
    C   Software Development Tools
    D   Operating System software

6   How is information stored on CD-ROM detected?

    A   As reflected light
    B   As electrical signals
    C   As magnetic fields
    D   As voltage levels

7   Which of the following devices does not form part of a Central System?

    A   Hard-disk
    B   Monitor
    C   Mouse
    D   Printer

8   A processor's speed is directly dependent upon which of the following?

    A   It's clock source
    B   The amount of main memory available
    C   The number of devices attached to processor
    D   User response times

9   SRAM and DRAM are examples of what form of storage?

    A   Primary
    B   Secondary
    C   Auxiliary
    D   Permanent

10 What form of memory is used in Cache components?

    A   ROM
    B   DRAM
    C   VRAM
    D   SRAM

11 Generally, how does a parallel transfer of information compare to a serial transfer of information?

    A   Slower
    B   At same rate
    C   Faster
    D   Varies

12 What category of software is associated with file servers?

    A   User Interface Systems
    B   Networked Operating Systems
    C   Applications software
    D   Stand-alone Operating Systems

13 Virtual Reality is a term associated with what form of software?

A   Modelling
B   Expert Systems
C   Controlling
D   File management

14 What three forms is a mouse found in?

A   Serial, Parallel and Dedicated.
B   Parallel, Dedicated and Add on card.
C   Serial, Dedicated and Add on card.
D   Serial, Parallel and Add on card

15 What impact does a software specification have on the associated hardware specification?

A   It specifies the software permitted to be stored on the hardware
B   It specifies the minimum hardware needs to run the software
C   It specifies the software which may be run on the hardware
D   It determines the cost of the associated hardware

16 Why does an operating system use date and time stamps?

A   to manage a system's availability
B   to record when a file is created and deleted
C   to provide the user with an accurate clock
D   to manage files and record when they are created and amended

17 What format is adopted to represent UK dates?

A   d/m/y
B   m/d/y
C   y/m/d
D   y/d/m

18 Why is it now easier to configure the hardware than on earlier systems?

A   Components intelligently establish the configuration of the resident hardware and adjust their configuration accordingly
B   Components are always supplied pre-configured
C   No configuration is necessary
D   The relevant switches are more easily accessible

19 What is a device-driver?

A   A piece of Applications software
B   A piece of Systems software
C   A piece of hardware
D   An operating system

20 What does the cabling connecting the components and devices associated with a computer system carry?

A   Power
B   Data and control signals
C   Data signals and power
D   Power, data signals and control signals

21 What form of communication methods may printers use?

A   Serial and/or parallel
B   Asynchronous and parallel
C   Serial and bi-directional
D   Serial, parallel and SCSI

22 A new range of CAD workstations is introduced into a design office.
    Which category of work would these new workstations MOST affect?

A   manual
B   technical
C   clerical
D   administrative

Questions 23 to 25 share answer options A to D:
These are examples of developments in the application of information technology:

A   media-based training
B   provision of information services
C   changes in retailing
D   data communications

To which development do these activities BEST relate?

23 Sending a message electronically using a network.

24 Finding out travel details for a holiday.

25 New ways for students to learn.

26 Random Access Memory is an example of:

   A   volatile memory

   B   CD ROM

   C   non-volatile memory

   D   a floppy disc

27 An example of a Bi-directional bus is the:

   A   control bus

   B   data bus

   C   address bus

   D   highway bus

28 The number of different messages that is possible from a 4-bit word is:

   A   4

   B   8

   C   16

   D   32

29 The read/write line in a microprocessor forms part of:

   A   control bus

   B   address bus

   C   data bus

   D   input port

30 When the instruction, 'fetch' has been performed the next operation done by the microprocessor is to:

   A   fetch the next instruction

   B   fetch more data

   C   decode the instruction

   D   execute the instruction

by **Peter Hodson** and **Geof Foot**

Using Information Technology

Introduction

The exchange of written information between people has moved rapidly from handwritten format to digital format over a relatively short period. Take a simple example in the banking sector. In the past, every time a customer wrote out a cheque, a bank clerk would write details on the customer's file and update a copy of the customer's account statement. When typewriters became fashionable, some of this activity became typed information to improve the appearance. Indeed some bank clerks claimed that such changes would alter the public's perception of bank personnel. They were afraid that the banks wouldn't employ staff with good, clear handwriting, since all they had to do now was type!

Today, of course, computer systems replace all of this activity. Account details are kept in digital format on computer systems. Millions of transactions a day are processed by exchanging digital information between the various banks. We would need a vast army of bank clerks to handle such a volume of transactions if it were still undertaken manually. Many services wouldn't be available and bank charges would be even higher.

In this unit we will examine the impact that information technology has had on processing commercial documents and the extended facilities that we now have in presenting this information. Such facilities allow us to create graphics, technical drawings and images. Of course with this ability comes a requirement to follow some standard structures and conventions in layout and presentation style. We will examine these issues in the first two elements of this unit.

Having created a base of information we are able to quiz the model to predict the way in which changes alter the system we are representing. This allows us to predict the impact of any changes. Take an easy example of a pub. Assume we set up a spreadsheet which details the cost of buying in the beer, the cost of labour and the income from sales. This will allow us to calculate the profits of the pub. If we decide to pay the bar staff more per hour the change in profit will be shown immediately.

Computers can also be used to keep control of systems. Frequent inputs of information to a computer such as the current temperature in a heating system can be quickly processed. For repetitive processing of data read from sensors, computers are much more effective than people.

The last two elements of this unit will look at how we can model data and develop control systems.

Process commercial documents

Introduction

In this element we will look at the way in which computer systems have helped us to manage to process documents. To do this well, commercial organisations and businesses have created several different formats for specific information. Each are used by convention in particular situations. For example, documents used within a business will have a different format to those sent outside the organisation.

For most businesses, their image to the public or its trading partners is influenced by the way the business communicates. The quality and appearance of letters and documents plays a big part in creating that image. Companies will often try to create a logo which represents and easily identifies them. If you see a big yellow M, you are probably thinking burgers! If we can capture such benefits and include them in the communication, then we give an advantage to the business.

Hence we need to identify the different communication formats used in business and look at how the computer systems can help us create and maintain such quality.

2.1.1 Specification

Each organisation knows the value of creating a corporate style. If we can carefully design the style for the different areas of communication, then anyone receiving that communication should:

- ❒ immediately recognise the organisation;
- ❒ be able to get the information they require from it;
- ❒ retain their positive view of the organisation.

Type of document

The range or types of document that are frequently exchanged include:

- ❒ Agenda;
- ❒ Memoranda;
- ❒ Minutes;
- ❒ Reports.

Documents which are seen outside organisations include:

- ❒ Business letters;
- ❒ Invoices;
- ❒ Newsletters;
- ❒ Advertisements.

Each of these can be developed with a house-style. If everyone uses the house-style then the image of an organisation develops and the effectiveness of the communication is enhanced and maintained.

For internal communication an effective, but easy to use house-style is important. If the format demanded is too difficult or complex to use, people simply stop using it....or don't even start! Perhaps memos are the most common internal document exchanged, so a simple house-style is helpful. If you want everyone to use it there are several options. You could create special stationary for a memo and ask everyone to use it.

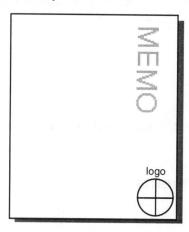

Figure 2.1 Example of Memo Stationary

Question 2.1

Can you think of other types of special stationary that might be used in an organisation?

Of course if you are preparing lots of different types of documents, it can be frustrating to keep changing the stationary in the printer. Not many printers have enough separate paper trays to hold every type of stationary that could be required without having to reload a tray.

An alternative approach is to create a standard format or template. This would look like a form on the screen with the blanks to be filled in. Once complete, it can be printed on blank paper. Many software applications provide templates which can be selected for use, e.g. presentation software templates as covered in Unit 6.

Purpose

When an organisation creates the design layout for each type of document, each format should meet the need and purpose of the communication. A range of purposes exist including:

- ❑ casual communication;
- ❑ semi- formal, internal mail;
- ❑ formal internal;
- ❑ formal external.

Also the options to be text based or to include graphics and tables, captured from databases or spreadsheets, may be required. For each purpose, the best display format should be selected. It is well known that a picture or table can frequently convey more information to a reader than a large volume of text.

Page attributes

The layout of the page is important. It is the reason that house-styles are created. Following the style means you have a designed layout. The main points to consider are:

☐ page size;

☐ orientation;

☐ quality of paper.

Once this top level has been decided, then the detailed points which contribute to the layout can be considered. These include:

☐ margins;

☐ spacing;

☐ fonts;

☐ headers and footers.

Each of these, plus a few extra points, will be covered in a little more detail later in this unit.

2.1.2 Commercial documents

Agenda

An agenda should cover several key points which tell the reader:

☐ that a meeting is taking place;

☐ the issues being discussed.

The key points covered are:

☐ the title of the meeting;

☐ the location of the meeting;

☐ the date and time of the meeting;

☐ a list of the topics being covered;

☐ any other reports or paperwork needed for the meeting.

Here is a typical example:

The second meeting of the
Newtown Scout Leaders to be
held at the Scout Hut on 6th July
1995 at 7.00 pm

Agenda

1. Minutes of last meeting
   (please bring these)
2. Matters arising
3. Planning for activity weekend
4. Planning for Autumn Barbeque
5. Any other business
6. Date of next meeting

Figure 2.2 Typical Agenda

Question 2.2

Should agenda be distributed a few weeks before the meeting takes place or at the meeting, in case people forget to bring their copy with them?

Business letter

The layout of business letters has to follow standards that are commonly used. The position of basic information is normally set up as a blank form or template, allowing the typist to quickly fill in the areas created. This ensures a standard layout and speeds up the preparation time. The following example shows the areas or zones we need to create.

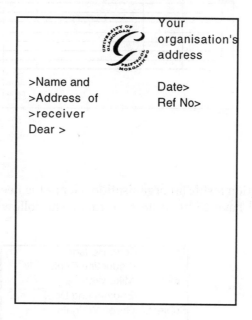

Figure 2.3 Business letter layout

The position of any logo used and the sender's address will depend on the house-style created. The pointer '>' shows the typist the position to move to and begin entering the appropriate data. In designing the position of the addressee, we must remember that its position is important if we are using envelopes with view windows i.e. the letter must fold to display the address in the correct position of a window envelope.

Invoice

An invoice is the form generated when asking the customer to pay for the goods or services supplied. The form must include the following information:

- ❑ both the supplier's and customer's addresses;
- ❑ relevant dates;
- ❑ reference numbers, e.g customer's order number, invoice number;
- ❑ description of goods or services;
- ❑ VAT as appropriate;
- ❑ total payment required and date due.

An example of an invoice is shown in figure 2.4.

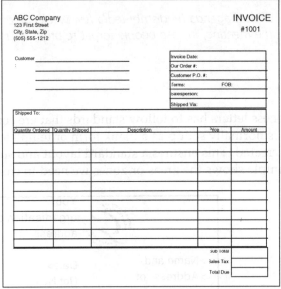

Figure 2.4 Example invoice (American style)

Memoranda

Used for communication inside an organisation. Hence the need for addressing is reduced and the structure doesn't have to be quite so formal. The following example shows the typical structure.

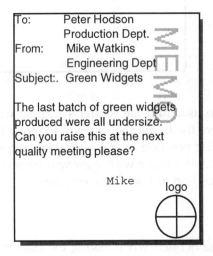

Figure 2.5 Example memo

Minutes

To remember what was discussed and what decisions were made at meetings, a record of the events in the form of minutes of the meeting are kept. It is interesting how people's memories can conveniently fade if such events are not recorded. It is good practice to record who was going to do the things decided and when they should be done by. These are frequently called the 'actions'. Minutes often have a column for actions that arise from the meeting and give a convenient way of reminding people that something needs to be done.

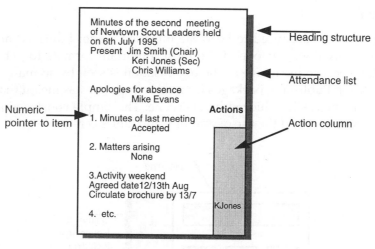

Figure 2.6 Typical Minutes Layout

Question 2.3

Why do you think an action column is a convenient way of reminding someone that they need to do something?

Question 2.4

How wide should we make the action column?

Report

This provides an opportunity to record a little more detail on a particular topic or issue. There are many thousands of reports written each day. They range from small investigations on sales performance, productivity or technical reports through to major national surveys such as a report on the national curriculum.

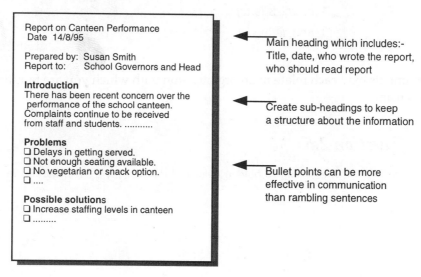

Figure 2.7 Typical Report Layout

Newsletter

These are normally produced to keep the intended reader informed about the activities of a group or organisation. It is one of the most important formats to get right in a commercial organisation because the image of the organisation is seen by so many people. The introduction of Desk Top Publishing packages for microcomputers has meant that many features of full publishing can be easily achieved by everyone. The simple construction of columns of print, just like a newspaper and the use of graphics and tables can create quite a professional appearance.

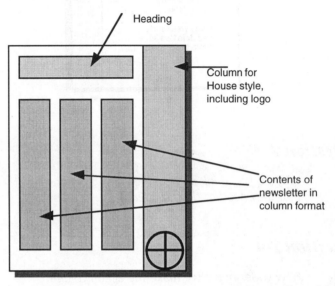

Figure 2.8 Possible Newsletter Layout

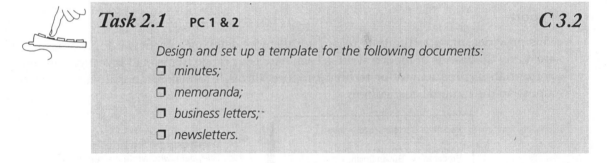

Task 2.1   **PC 1 & 2**   *C 3.2*

Design and set up a template for the following documents:
- *minutes;*
- *memoranda;*
- *business letters;*
- *newsletters.*

The documents may each relate to an organisation with which you are familiar e.g. school club or sports team

Question 2.5

Is it essential to have a column for house style as shown in figure 2.8?

2.1.3 Page Attributes

Paper size

There are standard sizes of paper available in what is known as the 'A' series. Each change in number means the page size is twice as big (or half the size) of the next in the range. Approximate sizes within the range are shown in figure 2.9.

A3	297 × 420 mm
A4	210 × 297 mm
A5	210 × 148 mm

Figure 2.9 Size of paper

In choosing the size of paper for any document we should remember:

- ❏ will it need to be filed in a normal size filing cabinet?
- ❏ will it need to be read at a distance e.g. on noticeboards?
- ❏ will it need to be put in a notebook folder or personal organiser?
- ❏ what is the purpose of the document?

Orientation

The orientation of the page may be either:

Figure 2.10 Page Orientation

The particular orientation used will be influenced by the type of document and the page contents and its layout. For example, if you were constructing a table of information with a number of columns, the presentation would be better in landscape format.

Item	Number sold	Value per item	Total	VAT rate	Gross total
Chair	2	£ 69.99	£ 139.98	17.5%	£ 164.48
Table	1	£ 160.00	£ 160.00	17.5%	£ 188.00

Figure 2.11 Landscape format for sales description table

 Question 2.6

Can you identify another situation which would be better in landscape than portrait orientation?

Widows and orphans

This is probably a layout issue rather than a page attribute but is considered here to meet the range statement specification. Where a line appears on its own at the top or the bottom of the page and has become detached from the main body of text, they are known as widows and orphans. Many of the latest wordprocessing packages allow the user to specify that widows and orphans should not be allowed.

2.1.4 Layouts

Margins

The page layout needs to know how much space you want to leave around the edges of the paper to present the information effectively. These spaces or margins will reflect a few basic issues. If the document is going to be filed in a folder or bound in some way, the left hand side of the page needs to be wide enough to do this without loosing sight of any of the content of the page. A report may well be produced and have multiple copies made with the pages backed up by printing on both sides of the page. In this case the right hand margin needs to be as wide as the left hand side.

All of the document should have the same basic margins. If we reviewed our business letter layout in figure 2.3, the name and address area would be included in the margin setting as well as the contents of the letter, i.e. nothing appears in the margins.

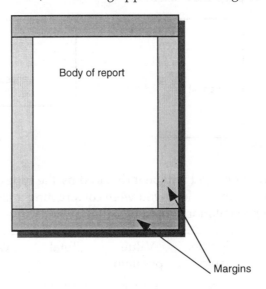

Body of report

Margins

Figure 2.12 Margin setting

All wordprocessing packages have a facility for setting the left and right hand margins. Most also allow you to set the format of how big the space at the top and the bottom of the page should be. This can either be achieved using the ruler provided on the package or the margins routine as shown in figure 2.13.

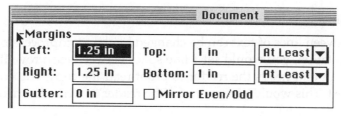

Figure 2.13 Setting margins

Justification

The layout of the page can be selected to have the contents justified in one of several ways:

❑ left alignment;

❑ right alignment;

❑ justified alignment.

The appearance of the document using justified alignment is better when the typeface is small. If it is much bigger than 10 point, then the appearance is often one of distorted spacing between words.

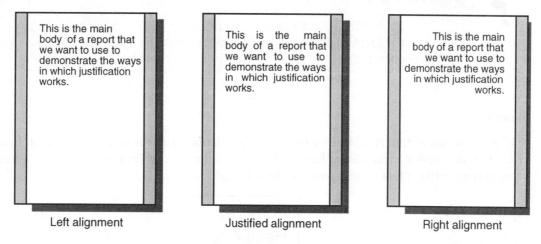

Figure 2.14 Justification

Indents and Tabulations

It is common practice to show the relationship of paragraphs in a text by indenting the whole paragraph. The result is often known as a sub-paragraph. If we only wish to move a single piece of data to the next pre-set position, then we use a tab (tabulation) function. Columns of data are usually set up by using a tab feature to get each entry aligned, rather than trying to use the space bar to get alignment. Both features can be set up on a ruler. In the example shown in figure 2.15 the tabulations have been automatically set up at each ½ inch mark (Sorry its an American package working in inches and not a metric system! Still, we are only half European because we still use miles).

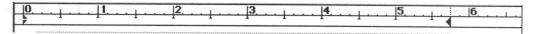

Figure 2.15 Example of a ruler

Line spacing

The space between lines of text can be changed by the wordprocessing (or DTP) package. In a normal presentation, you would set 1 line space between each row. If you know that the document is a draft and needs the reader to proof read the copy, you could double space (2 line spaces) the text. This would give room for the reader to write down any comments or changes needed.

It may be that one and a half line spacing is appropriate, especially if the reader is known to have a sight impairment, or if rows of data are presented. In this case, keeping a clear gap between the data across the page helps.

Lines of text with one line spacing	Lines of text with one and a half line spacing	Lines of text with two line spacing

Figure 2.16 Line Spacing

Question 2.7

When checking a draft document presented with two line spacing, can you think of a potential problem that could occur when the final copy is made with one line spacing?

Fonts

Different styles of font can be used to suit the particular purpose of the document. In a formal business document a traditional font such as Times, Roman or Palatino would be selected. For a club newsletter, a less formal font can be selected.

Courier
Helvetica
New York
Times
Optima
Palatino
Frutiger

Figure 2.17 Examples of fonts

Once the font style has been selected, the size of the font is chosen. For standard documents, this is normally 10 or 12 point. Large sizes are selected for particular features such as headings, front pages, display posters or a presentation document for overhead projection slides.

Times 10 point

Times 12 point

Times 14 point

Times 18 point

Figure 2.18 Typeface size

Question 2.8

Should we change fonts within in a single document to emphasise particular words or sections?

Page numbering

It is normal in any document of more than one or two pages to give each page a number. This helps a reader to locate or identify the information quickly. A book index wouldn't be much use if the pages weren't numbered. Several conventions exist which include putting the number either on one of the top or bottom corners or in the middle of the page. If material has been typeset, the position may alternate corners to either page as in the example of this book.

Headers and footers

Many wordprocessing packages provide the facilities to put a header or footer on every page. The information can be either fixed or variable. Fixed information could be the title of the document or chapter in a book. Variable information could be the date and time. For example if the date footer was implemented, then today's date would be printed in any listing taken today.

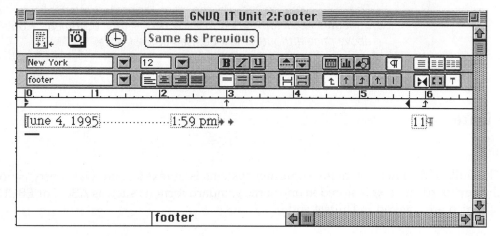

Figure 2.19 Example footer window

Column Layout

Some documents such as newsletters are frequently presented in the classic style of a newspaper with columns of text. Some internal documents may also be enhanced by having columns, especially when we are using graphics, tables and clip art.

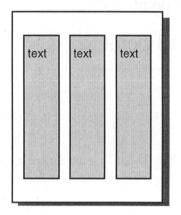 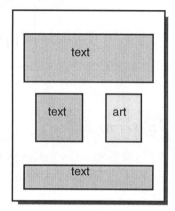

Figure 2.20 Column Layout

Document note

Reports and internal documents are often enhanced by having footnote or summary information. A footnote will have a marker in the text indicating a reference at the bottom of the page or end of the document. This marker will typically be a number and the footnote[1] shows the additional information associated with that marker[*]. The two examples here will generate a footnote at the bottom of the page.

Task 2.2   PC 2   *C 3.2*

Now that you recognise the need for page attributes such as margins, page numbering, columns and document notes, look at your work from task 2.1. Edit the layout to include the page attributes listed above. Not all the attributes need to be used in each of the four document. However all the above page attributes must be used at least once.

2.1.5 Data

Text

The bulk of data held on many computer systems is in text format. Data entry is normally via the keyboard and text is stored in one of the standard formats such as ASCII or EBCDIC, details of which are covered in Units 4 and 6.

---

[1] This is an example of a footnote. In a report it is likely to be the details of where further information on a topic may be found.

[*] It is possible to use non-numeric markers provided each marker on the page is unique.

Tables

Some wordprocessing packages allow you to create tables of data directly. Otherwise, if you want tables of information, numerical data or formula created data, it needs to be created in another package such as a spreadsheet and copied into the wordprocessed document. Copying like this is known as importing material.

Subscriptions in pence						
name	Week1	Week 2	Week 3	Week 4	Week 5	Total
Jim	20	20	20	20	20	100
Cerys		20	20	20	20	80
Helen	20	20			20	20	80
Nicholas	20	20	20	20	20	100
Hannah		20	20	20	20	80

Figure 2.21 Imported table

Graphics

This could take various formats as seen in the next element. The basic format could be a graphical representation of tabular information. The data in figure 2.21 could be represented as:

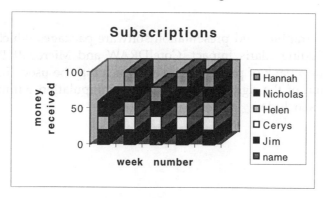

Figure 2.22 Graphical representation

Alternatively, artwork known as clip art or diagrams constructed in a drawing package can be imported into the document. Of course the size and position within the document is important in trying to get the right appearance.

Here is a example of clip art which can be used whenever we are showing something relating to detection or investigation. Perhaps this is someone trying to find the last bug in their program!

Figure 2.23 Clip art

2.1.6 Edit document

Text

The preparation of a text based document using a word processor is rarely completed without some change being required to it. This may be a small adjustment to the layout. Most word-processors provide a good range of edit facilities for text including:

- ❑ delete;
- ❑ insert;
- ❑ copy;
- ❑ move;
- ❑ enhance.

Each edit facility usually requires you to select the appropriate text and then begin the action. Some of these edit functions, such as a move, are a combination of basic edit functions like cut and paste i.e. cut out from one area and paste into another. An enhancement to text may be a simple change to a word to put the text in bold, underlined or italics to highlight its position or importance. Frequently text that has been prepared elsewhere can be re-used by copying it from the original document and inserting the text into the new document.

Graphics

There are many graphics and presentation software packages which allow us to create such documents, including Claris Impact, CorelDRAW and Microsoft PowerPoint. Many of the packages provide a bank of prepared clip art which may be used. To get the material into the right position and of the right size needs some manipulation within the package. Basic edit tools for graphics include:

- ❑ size;
- ❑ rotate;
- ❑ copy;
- ❑ move;
- ❑ manipulation;
- ❑ colour.

For example a box with a line can demonstrate some of the characteristics.

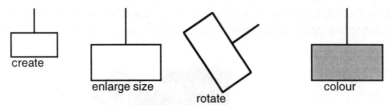

Figure 2.24 Graphics manipulation

Move and manipulation editing usually occurs when you are creating some graphics work which combines two or more features. If we take the box and line examples, it was possible to have created either of the following two outputs depending on the sequence of drawing.

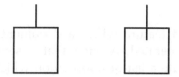

Figure 2.25 Sequence if creating graphics

One represents the line drawn first and the box second. The other is the box first and the line second. We could then of course colour or fill the box with a pattern (including white) to create the final effect in figure 2.24.

Question 2.9

If we had created the second graphic shown in figure 2.25 and then filled the box with a 'pattern' that was a white space, what would the graphic now look like?

Tables

These can be created in most wordprocessing packages or in a spreadsheet and copied across to the document by importing the table. The basic structure is rows and columns to create a grid or matrix effect. Each grid point contains an item.

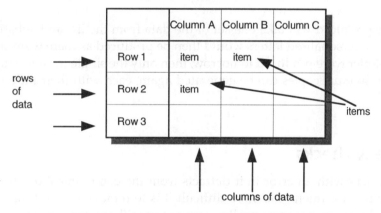

Figure 2.26 Table structure

Once a table has been established, the edit tools allow us to insert or delete another:

- ❏ row;
- ❏ column;
- ❏ item.

2.1.7 Software

Search and Replace

The search facility enables us to find the location of a word wherever it occurs in a document. That word may then be changed or replaced. For example if a company changed its name, the search and replace facility could be used to update all of its documents and reports etc. containing the old name.

Mail merge

This is a particularly good feature where a document needs to be personalised but many personalised copies are generated. A letter that is sent to a number of people is a typical application. We would create a list of information which will be used for every distribution. This list may be created by direct data entry into the list or generated from a database.

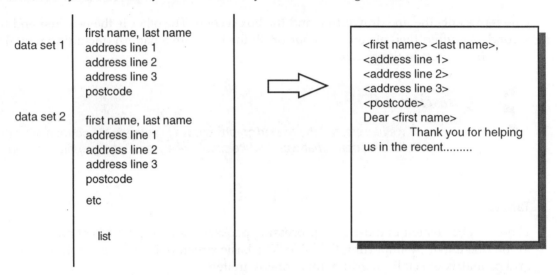

Figure 2.27 Mail merge

Each letter produced will take one set of the data from the list and substitute this into the letter. As many personalised letters would then be produced as there were sets of data on the list. If another letter were produced tomorrow, then only the single master letter needs creating and multiple individual copies can be generated again, each with their individual or personalised information.

2.1.8 Accuracy checks

Any document with an error in it detracts from the communication that is being attempted. The larger the document, the more difficult it is to remove all the little glitches. Wordprocessors can help us remove some spelling errors but will not detect misused words.

Spell-checker

A complete check on a document or part of a document against the dictionary database can be undertaken. There may be new words that are correctly spelt but were not known to the supplied dictionary. Facilities to add your personal dictionary, which will be part of a spell-check, are available in many packages. For example Microsoft Word doesn't have my town name included, but I use it regularly in correspondence. Hence I have included it in my user dictionary.

Proof read

In addition to spell-checker, we still need to proof read the material. This second check will hopefully spot all the errors. Unfortunately there is a tendency to read what you expect to see and not what is actually there.

Question 2.10

Identify in the following text what would be noted by spell-checker and what could be subsequently spotted by proof reading.

'It was good to sea you again at the recent meeting. Thr venew is two close to the rail station and the noice level is high'.

Question 2.11

Proof read the following text to determine if an error exists.

It is often difficult to proof read a document that you have created because the the text is so familiar, you read what you expect to see.

2.1.9 Security checks

Data held on computer systems are a valuable asset to any business and should be carefully protected. Some data may be confidential or personal information covered by the Data Protection Act. It is good practice to keep to regular security procedures to protect information.

Confidentiality

It should be recognised that access to some data must be restricted and the originator may be required by their organisation to take precautions to protect it. It may be that the file can be secured either by networked security software or on a local disk with special security software. To access protected data requires the use of a password which was set up when the document was first protected.

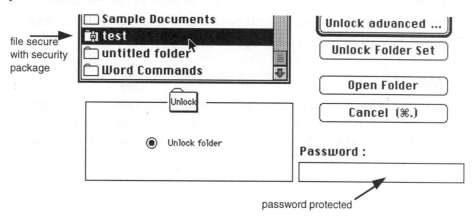

Figure 2.28 Folder protected by security software

Some organisations require their employees to sign an agreement of non-disclosure because the data is so sensitive. This means the employee must not release the data and the non-disclosure agreement can become part of the job contract. To disclose the data and let outside organisations or people see it would break the agreement and could result in dismissal.

File saving and Back-ups

A version of Murphy's Law says 'What can go wrong, will go wrong'. Computer systems and in particular new releases of software are prone to containing errors. Have you ever entered data, not saved the file and 'lost' it trying to do something to it? Although this rarely happens, it is new environments, such as implementing new versions of software, that often create such situations. The lesson is save your file regularly, probably every 30 minutes. This can be set to happen automatically in many wordprocessing packages. Of course the disk copy which contains this saved file could get damaged or corrupted. Hence back-up copies should be taken at regular intervals. This may be at the end of a session in a computer laboratory or at times of the day when you take a break. It is advisable to use at least two back-up disks and alternate the disk onto which you take the copy. Certainly daily back-ups of important files must occur. Network systems probably do this for you automatically.

Retain source documentation

If a complete disaster occurs and all the data held in digital format on the computer system is 'destroyed', all is not lost if the original documentation that was used to create the data is still available. For example this text was originally handwritten and I kept these notes until I had released the work to the publisher. If my Macintosh computer had lost all the text (perhaps a virus could have been introduced unknowingly to the system, which wasn't detected by the virus detection software, and attacked the files or corrupted the data), I could have recreated the text, albeit somewhat laboriously.

Theft

Unfortunately theft of computer systems, both hardware and software is all too common. Indeed sometimes you may not even be aware that someone has stolen a copy of your software or data. To protect systems we could:

- physically secure the hardware;
- introduce protection of the software or data areas to prevent unauthorised use;
- use procedures to control unauthorised copying or removal of software or data;
- prevent illegal software being imported into your system.

Copyright

To write a book, a piece of software or to create data requires a considerable effort. To protect that work and stop others from copying it needs a conscious effort. Copyright protection is available and makes any infringement illegal. Hence copying a piece of software or data in breach of its copyright is an illegal activity.

Task 2.3   PC 3, 4 & 5   C 3.3

Create a newsletter for a club or your school or college. The newsletter must contain some graphics and a table of information, which may be created in another package and imported into your wordprocessing package.

When you create the first draft of text, before you import any graphics and tables, save the file and back it up. Once the imported data has been positioned correctly, secure the file by saving it again.

Use a spell-checker to correct any spelling errors and proof read the layout.

Task 2.4   PC 2 & 4   C 3.4

The publishers of your newsletter have decided that they would like the name of the current contributors in a footer at the bottom of the page. Edit your newsletter to include that information.

Task 2.5   PC 4 & 6

The publisher has now recognised that distribution of your newsletter needs to be managed. They have asked if a mail-merge facility could be used. Set up a mail list of at least four people to be recipients of the newsletter. Position on your newsletter an area to indicate the name of the recipient...that could be the top corner of the page! Print the newsletter using the mail-merge facility.

Process presentational and technical graphic designs

Introduction

This element builds on the work achieved in Element 2.1. It is largely a practical element based on drawing or presentational packages. Here's your opportunity to become a computer artist! Most organisations understand that effective communication, especially in presentations at seminars or training sessions, are a key issue. The presentation software packages available such as Microsoft's PowerPoint, Claris' Impact and CorelDRAW all allow the creation of good quality graphics. They may be sequenced to automatically or manually present a slide show. Alternatively they can be copied onto acetates for overhead projection.

This element can be studied separately or combined with the work in Unit 3. Some of the evidence indicators required in Elements 3.1 and 3.4 can also provide the evidence required for this element. If you are studying Unit 3 at the same time, then combine or substitute the tasks of both units.

2.2.1 Graphic Design Software

Bit map and vector graphics

A graphic file can be represented in two basic ways. The whole drawing could be seen as a file with each minute item (or dot) in the graphic being held as a single bit of information in the file. In fact several bits of information will be held for each dot if it is a colour picture. We can change any bit in the graphic as an individual piece of information, but we can't edit elements as an entity i.e. we couldn't say that an individual line within a big image could separately be made shorter, leaving the rest of the image the same.

In a vector graphic, each element is defined in vector format. Hence we know a start point, a direction in which the vector is heading and it's length. So we define the graphic by the characteristics of the element. Each characteristic can be edited and manipulated individually within the whole image. So an individual line in a big graphic image could be changed. Figure 2.29 is an example of a bit-map image and the straight line in figure 2.30 is a vector graphic.

Question 2.12

Is figure 2.35 a bit-map or vector graphic?

Chart

Representation of data in chart form is generally recognised as being easier to interpret than wordy statements. Whether the chart is presented as tables or graphic format, such as piecharts and histograms, is influenced by the sophistication of the intended reader. Detail on charts is given in Element 2.2.3.

Slide Show presentation

The presentation software packages normally allow you to create a series of graphic pages or slides. The order of the pages or slides in the file is called the slide sequence. This sequence may of course be re-ordered at any time. Once it is created, the output of the computer system can be projected either onto the monitor or onto a large screen. Large screen presentation can be achieved either by taking the output of the computer to a display panel mounted on top of an overhead projector or directly into a projection system.

The package can then use this file to present a slide show. In automatic mode, each slide will be projected for a time period which the presenter can specify. Alternatively, a manual operation can be used, with the next slide being displayed on request.

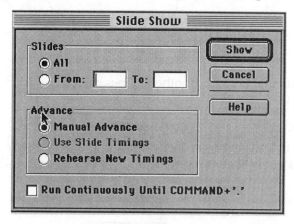

Figure 2.29 Establishing a slide show

Question 2.13

Why is a slide show a convenient way to make a presentation?

Task 2.6   PC 1   C 3.2

Survey the graphic design software packages you have available at your centre. Write notes on the main features in the package(s) which show how the following points are supported:

❑ *bit-map;*

❑ *vector;*

❑ *chart;*

❑ *slide show.*

2.2.2 Components

Most graphical images are made up of a combination of basic lines, shapes and attributes. Once these have been mastered, anything can be constructed, given enough time and patience. The major components will be considered here.

Lines

There are perhaps four basic line formats:

- ❑ straight;
- ❑ arc;
- ❑ curve;
- ❑ freehand.

straight   arc   curve   freehand

Figure 2.30 Basic types of lines

With these fundamental lines, most other shapes can be constructed.

Shapes

It would be quite tedious to revert back to building everything from basic lines. The presentation software package is likely to provide a range of shapes to use.

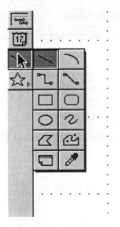

Figure 2.31 Example of shapes available in Impact

Typically most packages provide the following shapes:

- ❑ rectangles;
- ❑ circles;
- ❑ polygons.

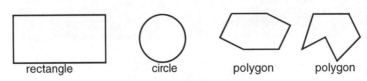

rectangle   circle   polygon   polygon

Figure 2.32 Basic shapes

Question 2.14

Why do we have rectangles rather than a square as a basic shape?

Colour and shade

Most computer systems offer colour output. The use of colour on a slide presentation or in a printout can be helpful in making a point more clearly. Colour also adds to the interest level. There are some situations where colour cannot be used cost effectively. For example where pages are printed directly onto acetates to produce overhead slides. The cost of this may be too high for some purposes e.g where a large number of slides are used in a college or school.

The cost of publishing a book using colour would make it's retail price much less attractive to many potential readers. The option for colouring or shading everything in the range of shapes leaves much to the imagination and creativity of the user of the package.

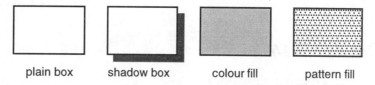

| plain box | shadow box | colour fill | pattern fill |

Figure 2.33 Examples of colour and shading

In selecting the shade or colour, it is worth noting that pale colours do not project well. Bold, strong colours may be needed which may look odd on the monitor, but better on projection.

Question 2.15

Do we need to worry about colour combinations?

Text

The style and size of text in presentations and technical graphic design needs careful consideration. Normal size print at 10 or 12 point does not make good projection. The standard templates supplied with the presentation software have pre-set text size which recognises these display requirements. Using a heading and a series of bullet points is widely recognised as a good style, rather than presenting too much detail on any single slide. Most slide templates have pre-set sizes for bullet points and allow a smaller typeface size to elaborate these main points.

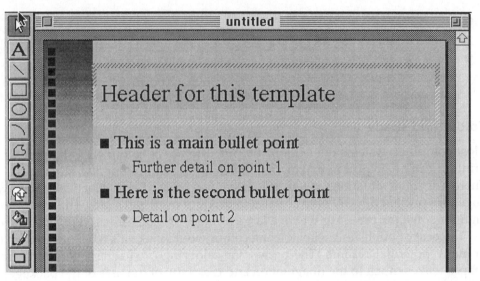

Figure 2.34 Example template with text features

 ## Question 2.16

What is a bullet point?

If you open a supplied template you will see that the fonts used are the bold, solid and traditional type rather than a fussy style. A font appropriate to the intended audience should be recognised e.g. a modern style may be more acceptable to a youth club than a business sales presentation!

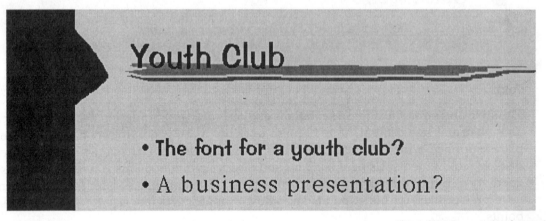

Figure 2.35 Presentation font styles

Attributes

Each diagram drawn can use a range of attributes such as a style, thickness or fill. Line thicknesses can be used to show the relative importance of component parts of a diagram. Thin lines may be fine in printed output, but will not project well. However the term 'line' in presentation software is also used to refer to the border around an object. Together with object fills and shadows, they define the attributes of an object.

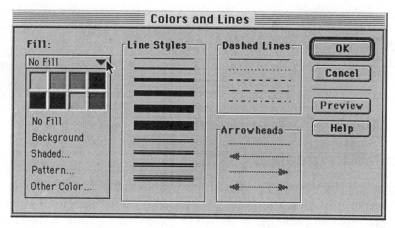

Figure 2.36 Typical range of fills

Brush and Spray

A number of presentational packages allow you to create graphics using features that emulate artists 'tools'. Hence you can select a thickness of brush and colour of paint and brush that effect onto the page using the mouse for control. An erase tool to clean up mistakes is usually available. Equally a spray tool with a variety of spray contents is often available to create an aerosol spray effect. You can elect to spray dots, stars, snow etc. in many packages.

Figure 2.37 Brush and spray effect

Question 2.17

Is the spray effect shown in figure 2.37 a bit-map image or a vector graphic?

Task 2.7   PC 2   C 3.4

Use the presentation software available at your centre to create each of the line types in figure 2.30 and each of the shapes in figure 2.32. Label each of the graphics with identifying text.

Task 2.8   PC 2 & 5   C 3.4

Use your software package to draw a diagram of the front of your school, college or house. Shade or colour the diagram to reflect the different building materials.

Task 2.9   PC 2 & 5   *C 3.4*

Use the brush and spray tools to add surrounding detail to the building drawing created in task 2.8 such as trees, shrubs and paths. You may also import clip art to help.

2.2.3 Presentation graphics

The range of graphics used in presentations includes charts and pictures. These can be created in a package or imported from one package into the presentation software. An example of moving data between packages is shown in figure 6.3. Graphic images used to represent artwork such as pictures are normally created and stored as a bit-map image.

Slide show

As we suggested in Element 2.2.1 a series of pages can be placed in a file to form a slide series. These slides can be selected in sequence or have an alternative choice of paths set up (selection) in the more sophisticated versions of software. The display could be simply via the monitor if the group receiving the presentation is small, or projected onto a large screen for bigger groups.

Charts and pictures

In any communication it is widely accepted that pictures, diagrams and charts etc. can more easily convey information to the reader than a text description. Figures 2.21 and 2.22 are examples of the two representations that are both more helpful to the reader than a wordy description of the data. These were generated in a spreadsheet, in this case Excel. The range of charts available include histograms, piecharts etc. and can be selected within the package to represent the numerical data entered. Figure 2.38 shows a range of charts available.

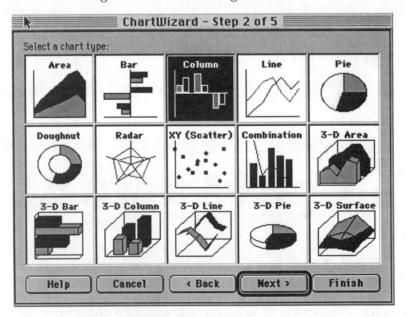

Figure 2.38 Range of charts

It is possible that you have an image or picture that you wish to include in a presentation that only exists in paper format. It is relatively easy to scan the picture to create a bit-map image of the original. Most pictures exist in bit-map format.

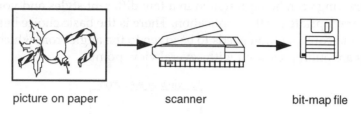

picture on paper   scanner   bit-map file

Figure 2.39 Scanning process

To enhance a presentation, it may be helpful to include relevant pictorial information from clip art or diagrams that have been scanned into digital format. A good range of clip art exists and choosing something appropriate is helpful in getting over your message. For example, if you were preparing a document to discuss printers, you could choose an image from one of the following pieces of graphics.

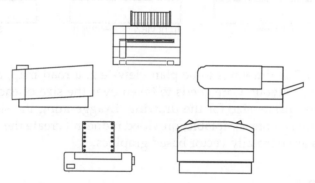

Figure 2.40 Examples of printer graphics

Question 2.18

Why do software packages provide clip art rather than let you create your own?

Task 2.10   PC 2   C 3.2

Create two or more slides describing either your school, college or house. One slide should include the diagram produced in task 2.9 and the other slide(s) should have text describing the building. For example the text could indicate the address of the building, its purpose, number of students attending, key subjects taught etc.

2.2.4 Technical drawings

Layout

Technical drawings can be represented in a few different styles and you need to decide which is the most appropriate for the application. There is the basic choice between 2-D and 3-D representation and consideration needs to be given to the angle from which the object is drawn. 2-D drawings are often presented with several view points.

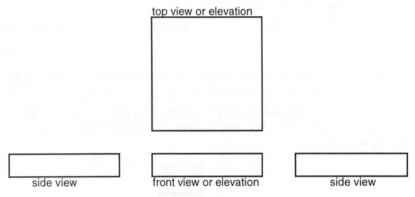

Figure 2.41 Paving slab

It is common for 2-D drawings to be plan views e.g. a road map, a kitchen design, a garden design or an office layout. Care needs to taken over the size of each object to make sure it is scaled to an appropriate size for the drawing. Exaggerating the size of an object by a small amount for clarity is quite acceptable, provided it doesn't create the wrong impression of scale. These drawings are normally vector based graphics.

Product design

In the manufacturing sector, draughtsman have historically hand drawn the product with full specification of size, tolerances, materials used etc. Component parts are represented in 2-D format, a typical example being the modification of figure 2.41 to include the necessary detail.

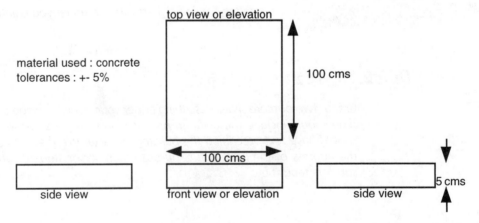

Figure 2.42 Paving slab design

Block schematic

Vector graphics are often used to draw block schematics, such as an organisational structure of chief, line management, supervisors etc., or the flow of signals in a computer system. A less obvious example is the exploded view of a number of component bits that make up an a product. This shows the block structure of a product and are often drawn in 3-D format.

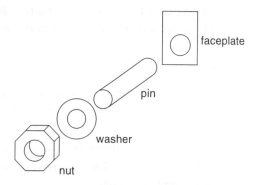

Figure 2.43 Exploded view

An example of block schematics has been used in many units in this book. Examples include figures 1.1 and 3.10.

> ## Question 2.19
>
> *Why are exploded views in 3-D a useful representation for assembly of component parts?*

2.2.5 Design specification

This section of the element is putting into practice all of the issues that have been covered so far in the unit. The major issues we need to consider are the design and layout of any document.

Graphic type

We have already seen that bit-map and vector graphics exist. Wherever we can work with vector graphics it is more helpful because the size of the file to hold the image is much smaller than a bit-map. If we have many bit-map images to hold, it is quite common to use a data compression package to reduce the file size.

The selection between bit-map and vector is often pre-determined by what it is that you are trying to represent.

Purpose and context

Preparing presentational and technical graphic design takes a lot longer than one might imagine. The effort put into the preparation should be controlled by the purpose of the work. For material that will be used many times over, that will have thousands of copies made or that is created for external or commercial work, then there is a good reason for spending time getting the quality right. Smaller, one-off jobs need less consideration. E.g. if you were drawing a map to send to a friend to reach your house, it may not be as carefully prepared and as accurate in scale as if you were preparing a map for the location of a business which was being printed on several thousand brochures.

The layout and information presented should recognise the skills of the intended reader. If you are preparing a 3-D assembly design of a product kit for home assembly the reader will have a different skill level to a reader of a 3-D assembly design of a manufacturing product in an engineering workshop. The first situation needs to be clear, with straight forward graphics and no fussy detail. The second can include detail of materials used, the tolerances for fitting, the stock numbers and other manufacturing detail. Hence the context is important.

Context and dimensions

We have just noted issues relating to context. This should be detailed enough to pass on all of the key information and not loose important information. If however the document is for a presentation, it is worth remembering:

- ❏ slides with too much information cannot be read easily at a distance;
- ❏ slides are usually created to support the presentation and act as a supporting structure, reminding the viewer of the key points;
- ❏ too many slides per minute or hour and the viewer will suffer from slide fatigue.

The design needs to consider how best to portray the information without loosing detail. That will influence how much separate documentation will need to be created. For example, if it is a map that is being created, the result may be a series of maps with different levels of information:

- ❏ A top level map showing the town in relation to other towns in the region. Major roads and motorways will be included;
- ❏ A lower level showing the town only with major features of railway, bus and main roads;
- ❏ A detail map showing the street names, landmarks such as pubs, schools and shops.

Task 2.11 PC 3

Draw two or more maps showing the position of your school, college or home. Each map should address the different levels of detail suggested above. Put each of the maps into the slide show set up for task 2.10.

If the work is a technical drawing, then normally the objects are carefully drawn to scale. The scale should be shown e.g.1 mm : 100 cm. Normally the units are specified (i.e. mm, cm, miles etc.) as plus/minus some fixed level or plus/minus a percentage measurement e.g ±1 m or ±1%.

Image and page attributes

Your design or artistic skills can be demonstrated here as you select the width, height, colours and shade. All of these have been previously mentioned. It is only practice and experience that shows you what will work well for a particular situation. We still need to remember that the graphic design needs to fit onto a specified page size which has been selected for the purpose. The output may then be portrait or landscape and may require margins setting up. All of these issues are a culmination of previous topics and need practice to get perfect.

Task 2.12 PC 3 & 4

C 3.4

Using basic shape and vector graphics, construct the following two diagrams. Use different thickness lines to enhance any major features and colour your diagram as appropriate.

Put appropriate dimensions on the drawings which relate to products with which you are familiar.

Model Data

Introduction

Businesses will frequently set up a model of their existing or proposed activities. This allows the organisation to see what the likely affect of changing one of the parameters in this model would be. At a simple level the model can be based on a spreadsheet. More sophisticated modelling, based on queueing theory for example, exists to predict more complex situations. For example, supermarkets will have modelled what would happen in 30 to 60 minutes time if 100 people arrive at the store over a 10 minute period. This model will predict the length of the checkout queues for a range of open checkout positions. This is a classical problem, but one that is important since you need to know in advance if more checkouts need to be opened in order that queue lengths stay below a particular size.

In this element we will concentrate on the use of spreadsheets to provide the level of evidence needed for your portfolio. Other models involve the use of vector based graphics, simulation and games packages.

2.3.1 Purpose of model

Compress time

We model a range of systems to know what the impact of existing or changing parameters will have on the system. The timescale needs to be relatively quick, since the model answer needs to be faster than letting the event occur naturally. For example, a model may be a weather forecasting system. If the daily prediction takes longer to model than 24 hours, having the model answer later than the time of prediction is not too much help.

What is needed is a model that makes reasonably accurate assumptions and significantly compresses the time scale.

Cost saving

It is usually cheaper to model data than have the real event happen. For example, if we wanted to know how strong a piece of equipment is we could model the effect of putting a bigger load or greater strain on it. The model could show the damage caused to the equipment without destroying anything. Where the equipment is expensive to build, a modelling approach should be cost effective. For example we would want to model how a space ship will perform in space before sending up a manned flight!

Given that a model is quicker to run, the cost of labour spent on the live project should be reduced. Since salaries represent significant proportions of many development costs, then a real reduction in salary costs can be achieved by reducing the time to determine the outcome of a change.

Safety

There are some tests that are difficult, even hazardous to undertake in real life situations. For example the nuclear industry working with hazardous material has to establish extensive safety procedures and precautions to undertake any testing. If we could model the test, then the hazardous nature could be removed.

Question 2.20

Can you think of another area where modelling would be appropriate?

Convenience

Most models can easily be set up on personal computers which are readily available and easy to use. To undertake a modelling test and keep re-running the model with a variety of conditions is normally more convenient than going to the location where an actual test can be carried out, with all the necessary set up procedures involved. Virtual reality brings us closer to providing this as an approach in many situations.

Hypothesis testing

If a model has been set up, it is helpful to know what will happen if particular changes to the parameters are made. It is common to set up a business model on a spreadsheet and look at the result of change.

For example consider a hotel spreadsheet. At the moment the hotel charges £50 per night and can sell 50 rooms out of the 75 rooms in the hotel. With current staffing levels etc. there is a fixed cost of £1380 and each occupied room costs £10 per night to service (clean sheets etc.). We believe the market is price sensitive and a 10% increase in price results in a 10% reduction of guests. The reverse is also believed to be true. A model of this would suggest:

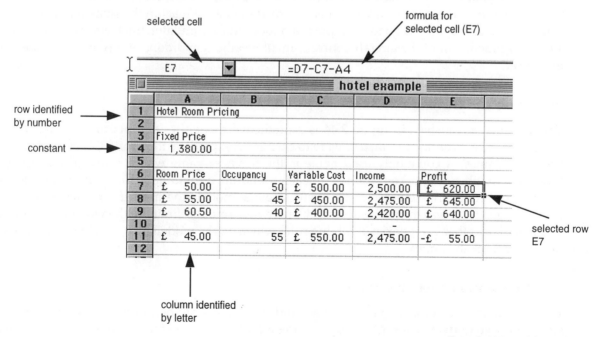

Figure 2.44 Spreadsheet of hotel

Task 2.13 PC 1, 2 & 3   N 3.1

Research has shown that guests are attracted by small additional comforts in the room (e.g. bowls of fruit and sweets, luxury toiletries etc.). An increase in the variable costs of £5 per night per room would attract another 10% more business.

Create a spreadsheet as in figure 2.44. Model the impact of the proposed change in service level on the spreadsheet.

Task 2.14 PC 1, 2, 3 & 4   N 3.1

Further evidence would suggest that if the quality of service were improved by adding more staff (at additional fixed cost of £150 per night), then a further increase of 10% in room bookings can be achieved.

Model this new set of data on the spreadsheet and produce a report of the output from the original data in figure 2.24, task 2.13 and this task. The report may be in pictorial format to show where maximum profits can be gained.

It is equally possible to set up a model on a database package such as Access and quiz the model with what-if queries in the form of SQL. Further detail of this approach is given in Element 7.3.4. The work that you do in Element 7.3.4 can be used for your portfolio in this unit.

2.3.2 Computer models

Simulation

A computer model can be built to look, as far as possible, like the real situation. The view of the model and its response to any input is designed to make it react in the same manner as the situation it is simulating. A good example is a pilot training simulator. Such a simulator allows a pilot to practice all of the aircraft controls, in all weather conditions at any major airport in the world.

Prediction and Gaming

The example spreadsheet in figure 2.44 is a predictive model. It attempts to show what the profit would be if certain parameters were to change i.e. it predicts the profit. Other models are based on games. A commonly used game is the business game where teams of players go through a number of knockout rounds. In each round the individual teams will set their marketing and production strategies. The business game models the input from each team and grades which team was the most successful. Successive rounds eliminate the worst performing team(s). Many other games exist involving rules which can be modelled, including many of the new virtual reality games.

Three dimensional representation

If a 3-D model is created, its visual impact and its features can be more readily understood. Computerised drawing packages may assist in presenting a model for viewing from any angle.

Town planners and architects gain enormous benefit from such software, since the way in which a proposal will fit into the existing environment can be seen more clearly. This can show how shade will be cast throughout the year so the location of some features such as a swimming pool will be sited to maximise its function. Alternatively the impact on existing buildings can be demonstrated.

Question 2.21

Would modelling the data communications traffic on a computer network, so we can determine the performance over a range of network loads, be a sensible activity? Would this be a simulation or a 3-D representation of the model?

Task 2.15 PC 1   N 3.3

Within the classification of computer models defined in this element (simulation, prediction, gaming, 3-D) how would you define the models created in tasks 2.13 and 2.14? Write brief notes explaining why the model(s) fit the classification(s).

2.3.3 Data parameters

Input values

Data input can be from existing information held on database, read directly from sensory devices or input from the keyboard. The data representation in the form of integer, real numbers or appropriate formats can be pre-set or adjusted later in the model.

Constraints

The model created in figure 2.44 could have resolved the problem of finding the point where maximum profits occurred without the repeated modelling that we have undertaken. The advanced features of the spreadsheet called solver could have been used. Within solver, constraints are allowable, which set the maximum values of variables used in the formula line. For instance in our hotel example the maximum occupancy figure is 75 because we don't have any more rooms than this. Hence 75 would be an occupancy constraint in the calculation.

Variables

As we have implied from the data input, the values may represent anything that is relevant to the system we are modelling. Providing each variable or data element has a relationship to another value in the model, then it is relevant to the system. Variables could represent response times, speed, cost, time, dimensions, scale, position etc.

Calculations using operators

Once the variables have been input to the model the relationship between elements can be defined in terms of operators. (Indeed this could be defined before the data input). The standard operators of arithmetic, relational and logical as covered in Element 6.2.6 can be used. An example of a spreadsheet using these operators is shown in figure 2.44. Such operators are often part of a formula which calculate the value of some cells. Constant values as well as variables can be declared to the system and again this can be seen in figure 2.44.

2.3.4 Rules of operation

Formula

The value of some cells in a spreadsheet may be calculated using operators and other variable inputs. The relationship is expressed as a formula e.g the cell is the sum of all of the cells in the column above. The formula which dictates how the value of such a cell is calculated is not usually displayed in the cell, since this normally displays the result of the calculation. The formula is normally hidden, but if a cell is selected it is displayed elsewhere in the calculation zone. Hence the formula line shows how any cell has been set up or defined.

Cell references, relationships and variable changes

Figure 2.26 shows the construction of a matrix which is the basic structure of a spreadsheet. A column and a row define any item or cell, e.g. column 1, row 2 is a single cell. In Element 2.3.1 we have seen the impact of changing the variables and setting up formulae to show the relationships between input and outputs. In a spreadsheet the columns are usually identified by letters and the rows are identified using numbers. Figure 2.44 shows how a particular cell is identified. Any input cell can have its value changed as part of the modelling.

Input and output methods

In Element 2.3.3 we noted the various sources of input which enable data capture by a range of input devices which do not restrict ourselves to the keyboard. Equally the output from our model can be extended beyond the normal display and a range of reporting methods which will be noted in Element 2.3.5. Hence this data can be exported from the spreadsheet (or other modelling software) and used as input to another system. In Excel (and other packages) you can create and save sets of input values that produce different results as scenarios representing what-if assumptions.

Task 2.16 PC 2   *N 3.2*

For the work in task 2.14, write notes on three data parameters and four rules of operation used in the model. For example, these could be notes on the arithmetic operator, variables, formulae, cells, affect of variable change or relationships.

2.3.5 Reports

The representation of the output value can be displayed as a chart or in pictorial format. Figures 2.26 and 2.38 are examples of the representation available. Any sub-section of the spreadsheet can be selected for representation to produce an abstract of the output. The whole table (or set of tables) could be produced to show the full numerical analysis that has been undertaken.

2.3.6 Effectiveness

The cost of commercial modelling software such as a spreadsheet is relatively cheap, costing between £100 and £200. Once the user becomes proficient at setting up a spreadsheet then many models can be easily established. It takes perhaps a day to learn the basic features of Excel and a day or so to become reasonably proficient at modelling and displaying the output in a format needed.

The comparative cost of modelling to setting up the real system (if that was possible) should be significantly lower. If we consider the hotel model we used earlier, our model was easy to set up and any changes to see what-if this change were made, is instantly displayed. One alternative to not modelling would be to have employed the extra staff or changed the room prices and waited to see what the result actually was. A prudent manager would want a little more confidence that such changes were going to be beneficial before implementation, hence the modelling role.

Time invested in setting up the model is well spent. It can begin as a simple overview and increasingly become more detailed as refinements are made. It can be constructed by setting up a series of related information and combining the various spreadsheets into a single overview. The benefit of this approach is that any small change is seen throughout the whole of the model and its impact recognised. There is no possibility that the calculation will not be implemented in one area, so the model has greater accuracy than any manually performed calculations.

Certainly where repetitive changes are made to the model to undertake what-if queries on the system, it is much more efficient to have established the model than repetitively undertake manual calculations with all the possibilities of an error being introduced. Data integrity checks can also be built into models that will be frequently used to make them more robust and reliable. This helps prevent any inconsistent data being entered.

2.3.7 Suggestions for improvement

Once the model has been run it is often possible to see how a more refined model could be beneficial. This could take the format of a more sophisticated formula or changes in the data parameters. Models should be fit for the purpose and the amount of time invested in setting up and running the model should be commensurate with the system that is being modelled. If it were a nation's economy, then it is unlikely that a model created in half an hour would be appropriate. Equally a spreadsheet to add up a column of numbers and calculate mean results with the standard deviation should not take long.

The tools available in the modelling software are constantly improving and enable us to construct some of the outputs in a simpler manner than earlier releases. Future improvements will almost certainly follow, hopefully not at the expense of making the products too big and overly rich in features that the user rarely (or never) uses.

Develop a control system

Introduction

We can now develop the ideas introduced in Element 1.1 where we investigated industrial and commercial information technology systems. This element is a development from the Intermediate Level GNVQ Information Technology. It contains information about sensors and actuators used in control. This knowledge is required to understand what is happening in a control system. Even so, this is only an introduction to the technical concepts.

One of the advantages of this element is that it integrates with material elsewhere in the Advanced Level GNVQ. For example, some of the tasks outlined involve the use or writing of programs. Hence in doing some of the tasks in this element the evidence gained will be of use to you elsewhere within the qualification.

2.4.1 Control systems

Environmental Control

Control is a very important part of our everyday lives. If there were no control we would have chaos. The weather is a form of environmental control which manages the water cycle. Other examples might be the control of the temperature in a freezer or the conditions in a greenhouse.

We often want to control the environment in our homes or place of work etc. The most common form of environmental control found in the home is a central heating system. The central heating system is used to control the temperature at a comfortable level in a range of about 20°C to 25°C.

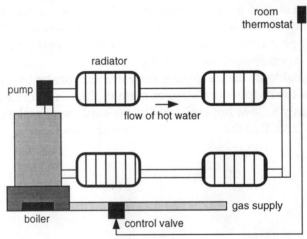

Figure 2.45 The central heating control system

The gas supply provides the boiler with fuel which is burnt to heat up the water. A pump is then used to circulate this hot water around the central heating system. As the hot water circulates, the radiators heat up and consequently warm the room in which they are located. So the room does not become too hot, a thermostat is used. When the temperature of the room reaches a pre-set value, determined by the thermostat, the gas supply is shut off from the boiler. The boiler and the circulating hot water cool down, resulting in the radiators giving off less heat to their surroundings and eventually causing the room temperature to fall. When it falls below the pre-set value, the thermostat switches on the gas supply to the boiler. This heats up the water and the radiators and the process repeats itself.

Question 2.22

The way in which the central heating system in figure 2.45 is controlled is only one such method. Can you suggest alternative ways of controlling the temperature?

Process Production Control

Let us consider the simple example of a process production control system. One such system we are all familiar with is controlling the level of water in the tank found in a domestic flush system of a toilet. This system consists of a 'ball-cock' system which opens and closes a valve and, when open, lets water into the tank. The ball is basically a float which follows the level of water in the tank. As the water level falls, the float falls and it opens the valve to replenish the water in the tank. When the water level rises, so the valve slowly shuts until at a preset value, shown as horizontal in the figure 2.46. The valve shuts the water off preventing overflow.

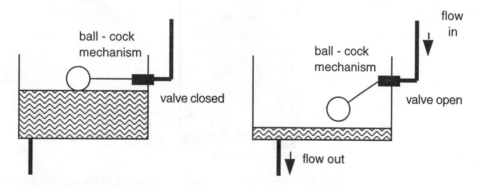

Figure 2.46 The domestic level controller

The advantage of this type of system is that a constant volume of water is available in the tank. In an industrial system, the level of liquids and solids in tanks can be achieved in a number of ways. Figure 2.47 shows a probe being used to measure the level of liquid in the tank. It can also be used for solids but is not the most accurate technique as explained later. The output from the probe uses some electronic or mechanical type circuit which opens and closes an inlet valve to stop or allow the flow of water into the tank. The probe can use a number of different techniques to give its output e.g. Capacitance, Resistance, Pneumatic Pressure (called a bubbler tube). Whatever the nature of the output from the probe, it is proportional to the level of liquid in the tank. Hence it can be used as an indicator or used for a control device to open and shut an inlet valve.

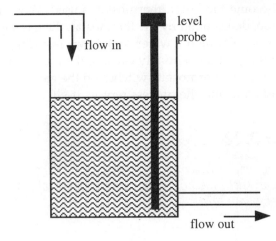

Figure 2.47 The industrial level controller for liquids

The system described cannot be used very accurately with powdered solids in the tank because they do not have a flat surface in the same way as a liquid. Powders tend to form into a pyramid as shown in figure 2.48.

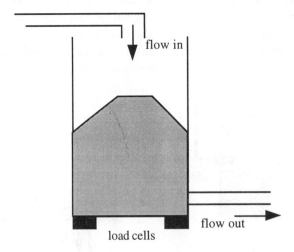

Figure 2.48 The industrial level controller for solids

To get a reasonably accurate measure of the contents in the tank, an average level would have to be obtained which may be difficult to achieve. Therefore an alternative approach is used that could also be used to measure the level of liquids. The level in the tank is calculated from the the weight of its contents.

Another example of process production control is the handling of the temperature of a furnace. Temperature is a variable that is frequently measured and used to control the heat of ovens and furnaces. A typical example is found at home in our kitchens. Frequently when cooking something in the oven, part of the instructions suggest the preferred value of the temperature. Similarly in industry, furnaces have to be held at a fixed temperature. In the example shown in figure 2.49, the furnace is being used to heat up steel blocks, known as ingots, to a certain temperature. The process is known as annealing and requires good temperature control. If the temperature falls below that required, the process of annealing does not work. Should the temperature gets too high, energy is wasted in heating the furnace more than necessary which is expensive.

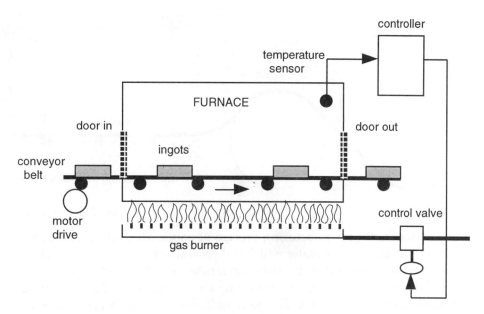

Figure 2.49 The temperature control of a furnace

Controlling the temperature in the above furnace has added complications. A door has to be opened to put an ingot into the furnace and when it has been annealed a door has to be opened to take it out. Every time the door is opened, cold air will enter the furnace lowering its temperature. In addition a cold ingot put into the furnace will draw heat to raise its temperature and in doing so also lowers the temperature of the furnace. Therefore, keeping the temperature of the furnace at a constant temperature is quite complicated and requires sophisticated control. A computer is able to provide this control. Preset values of temperature would be stored in memory and the computer would monitor the temperature of the furnace using a suitably connected sensor. The measured temperature would then be compared to that stored in memory and the difference would be used to open or shut the control valve, feeding gas to the furnace gas burners.

Task 2.17 PC 1   C 3.4

Investigate, using your library resources, how a kitchen oven works in terms of the temperature control for cooking purposes. Illustrate with a simple diagram.

SAFETY NOTE : DO NOT TAMPER WITH THE COOKER AT HOME.

Quality control

An example of quality control can be seen in the manufacture of paper. The thickness of paper during its manufacture is very important. If it is too thin there is the danger that it will break or tear because of the pulling forces associated with its manufacture. When it is being used in a photocopier a similar problem could result. On the other hand if the paper is too thick the manufacturer is wasting raw material. When using paper like this in a photocopier the machine would have difficulty in picking up the extra heavy paper. Hence the thickness of the paper is very important.

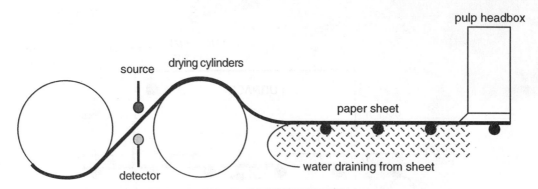

Figure 2.50 Controlling the thickness of paper

Figure 2.50 shows the manufacturing process of paper. The pulp which comes from the head-box is mainly in the form of water which is then drained on a wire mesh. The very delicate, wet sheet of paper is then dried on heated cylinders to form the sheet of paper. The thickness of the paper is determined by means of measuring the amount of radiation that passes through the paper from a radioactive source. The more radiation that the detector measures the thinner the paper.

The thickness of the paper gives an indication of its quality. For photocopiers a typical requirement would be a mass of 80 grammes per square metre and this would be given by the thickness of the paper as well as its density.

Security

A typical example of a control system used for security would be an anti-theft device similar to the type used in museums and art galleries. The sensor used for this system consists of a transmitter producing a beam of light (a laser beam) or sound and a receiver which detects the presence of the beam. If the beam is broken by someone passing through it, an alarm is sounded, doors are shut or the police are called automatically. Automated video camera systems are another example of a security control system.

Task 2.18 PC 1   C 3.4

Investigate and explain, with the aid of simple diagrams, how to prevent a book being stolen from a library using anti-theft devices.

Transport System

One of the most familiar forms of transport system known to us all is that of a car. You may be either learning to drive a car or indeed have passed your driving test. Driving a car is an extremely complex control system and those of you who are learning or have learnt will know how many operations there are and how many have to be performed at once.

Question 2.23

List the operations that you have to perform in making a right turn when driving a car.

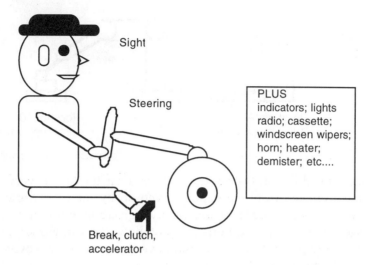

Figure 2.51 Manual control of a car

The car driver uses sight as the sensor to monitor the road and see if something is in the way. In order to avoid a crash the driver might decide to break, turn the steering wheel to swerve around the other car, or .....? The important thing to note is that the car driver is an integral part of the control operation to drive the car safely.

Figure 2.52 shows another transport example of a simple railway system. A detector in the railway track detects the presence of a train and sends a signal to the signal box where a decision is made to stop the train or let it proceed on its journey. If the track ahead is clear the signal will be lowered which will allow the train to proceed. In addition to this there may be points to change and other signals to raise or lower. Hence such a control system can be quite complex.

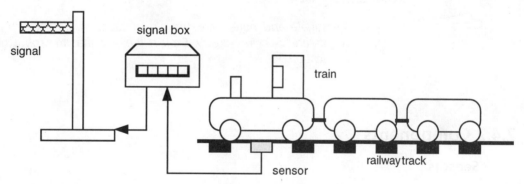

Figure 2.52 Sensor detects train

Robotic Production Systems

Robots are used in manufacturing systems in environments which are unsuitable for humans to work in. Typical examples would be in the manufacture of car bodies when spot welding parts together and paint spraying the car body. The advantage of using robots in this way is that they can do the same work repetitively with a great deal of accuracy. A typical example of a repetitive operation would be termed 'pick and place', where an object is picked up from location 'A' and then carried to location 'B' where it would be placed. Location 'A' could be a storage bay where components are stored and location 'B' could be a machine where the components are cut to size, the robot placing the component into the machine. Alternatively the location 'B' could be where the component is fitted together with other components.

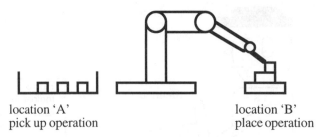

location 'A'
pick up operation

location 'B'
place operation

Figure 2.53 A Robotic production system – pick and place

When a robot is used to paint spray the body of a car the task is very repetitive. In addition, the environment created from the vapour given off by the paint spray is very unhealthy for human operators to work in. Health and Safety legislation would in fact prohibit human operators from working in such conditions. A robot, however, can work quite satisfactorily in such conditions. The only precaution that would have to be made is to cover up the robot's joints as paint would cause them to fail when it dried.

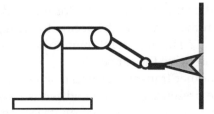

Figure 2.54 A robot spraying paint

Task 2.19 PC 1

Investigate and note, with the aid of diagrams, other applications where robots are used in industry. Explain the role that the robot has within that application.

2.4.2 Components

Sensors

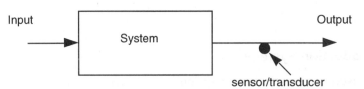

Figure 2.55 A block diagram of a simple control system

Sensors are devices which are usually positioned at the input or output of a system and used to sense something that is happening to the system. They are used to convert one form of energy into another, usually to electrical energy, which can then be easily passed to the input port of a computer. When the sensor is being used to convert energy in this way it is usually called a transducer. A sensor, or transducer is an essential part of a control system because it gives information about what is actually happening in the system. For example in some of the control systems quoted previously, the thermostat would be sensing the actual temperature of the room or boiler. The load cell would be sensing the actual weight of the contents in the tank.

❐ Heat sensors

Heat is a form of energy and the amount of energy in an object, body or material depends upon a number of factors. These factors are the mass of the object, the temperature and the type of material the body is made from. In the majority of cases the material and the mass of an object are constant. Hence, when a sensor is used to detect heat, it is actually measuring the temperature of the object. The problem with measuring temperature is that it is very subjective, since it is defined as ' the degree of hotness of a body '. So the effect of temperature on substances or materials is used as a feature that can be measured. Features that change in this way are called parameters of the substance. Indeed, anything that in some way changes with respect to temperature variation can be used to represent that variation in temperature.

For example, many materials expand when the temperature increases and this effect can be used as an indicator to measure that temperarure change. A very well known example of this is the thermometer. The type of liquid inside the thermometer dictates the temperature range over which it can be used.

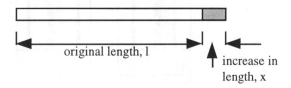

original length, l

increase in length, x

Figure 2.56 A metal bar which has increased in length due to temperature

When a metal undergoes a change in temperature it expands and increases in length as shown in figure 2.56. The increase in length, x, is proportional to the temperature change and the original length, l. This is given by:

$$x = l\, \alpha\, \Delta_t \text{ metres}$$

where l is the original length in metres, α is the coefficient of linear expansion in m per m °C, and Δ_t is the change in temperature in degrees Celsius, °C.

As an example, consider a steel rod with a length of 2 metres at a temperature of 15°C. The coefficient of linear expansion is 11.4×10^{-6} m per m°C. Determine the length at 65°C.

The increase in length, $x = l\, \alpha\, \Delta_t$ metres

$$\begin{aligned}
\text{therefore} \quad x &= 2 \times 11.4 \times 10^{-6} \times (65 - 15) \\
&= 2 \times 11.4 \times 10^{-6} \times 50 \\
&= 1.14 \times 10^{-3} \text{ metres or } 1.14 \text{ mm.}
\end{aligned}$$

Therefore the new length would be 2.00114 m.

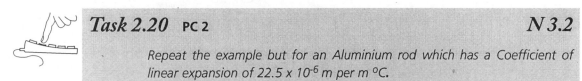

Task 2.20 **PC 2**   *N 3.2*

Repeat the example but for an Aluminium rod which has a Coefficient of linear expansion of 22.5 x 10⁻⁶ m per m °C.

Two different metals can be joined together to form a bi-metallic strip. When the temperature changes the two materials expand at a different rate causing the strip to bend. The rate at which it bends is proportional to the temperature increase and this change can be used to give an indication of the temperature. This is the principle behind the thermostat which we have already used a number of times.

two different metals

an increase in temperature causes the strip to bend

Figure 2.57 A bi-metallic strip

In the thermostat, the bi-metallic strip is used as the moving contact in a switch. At low temperatures the switch will be in the OFF position. At high temperatures the bi-metallic strip bends and moves from the OFF position to the ON position.

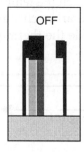

thermostat at low
temperature

thermostat at
high temperature

Figure 2.58 A thermostat – application of the bimetal strip

Task 2.21 PC 2

Take a glass thermometer and place it into a container of hot water and observe the expansion of the liquid in the column of the thermometer.

Task 2.22 PC 2

Heat the end of a bi-metallic strip and observe the expansion of the strip causing it to bend. Explain how a bi-metallic strip can be used in a thermostat as a 'heat switch'.

Heat also changes the electrical properties of materials. The two basic devices are the resistance thermometer and the thermistor.

❏ Light sensors

• Solar cells

These devices convert light into electrical energy.

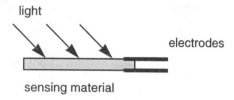

Figure 2.59 A solar cell

The sensing material in a solar cell is made from silicon, the same material used for semiconductors. When light shines onto the surface of the sensing device, the photons of light react with the atomic structure of the silicon converting the light's radiant energy into electrical energy. The electrodes are used to take the electrical energy out from the device to the control system.

Such devices are very common today and are used to power many electronic devices. These range from calculators and watches to telecommunication satellites in outer space. They are usually used in measurement and control to detect the presence or absence of light e.g. counting the number of people entering a building.

Task 2.23 PC 3   N 3.1

Draw a simple diagram to show how a solar cell and a light source can be used to detect and count the number of people entering a building.

• Light sensors

The solar cell is only one example of many types of light sensor. Any device or material which changes in some way when illuminated by light can be said to be a sensor. It is a sensor because the change can be seen or measured. For measurement and control we are largely interested in devices which will give an electrical output which can then be connected to a computer system. With the solar cell, a voltage is generated when light shines on the sensor. The voltage generated is of the order of one volt which is quite small, so a number of solar cells are combined to make up a solar array.

There are other types of device used for light sensors but instead of a voltage being generated the resistance of the device changes when light is shone on them. These devices effectively use this change in resistance to vary the electrical current in a detecting circuit. There are a number of light sensors which use this principle, including a semiconductor diode called a photodiode, a phototransistor and a light dependent resistor.

A photodiode is a diode fitted with a small lens so as to focus the incident light. When increasing levels of illumination falls on to the photodiode the resistance becomes proportionally reduced, allowing the electric current flow to increase through the diode.

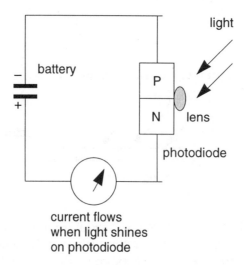

Figure 2.60 The light sensitive diode

The electrical symbol that is normally used for a photodiode is a variation on that used for a diode and is shown in figure 2.61.

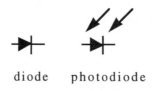

diode   photodiode

Figure 2.61 Symbol for the light sensitive diode

Task 2.24 PC 4, 5 & 6

Connect a multimeter (switched to milliamps) to a photodiode and a battery as shown in the circuit in figure 2.60, with the photodiode connected in the reverse bias mode. Measure the value of the current flowing in milliamps when:

❏ *the photodiode is covered;*

❏ *the photodiode is exposed to light.*

What happens when the diode is only partially covered?

A phototransistor is much more sensitive to changes in the level of light intensity than the photodiode. It is therefore far better for controlling the flow of current, just like a switch. This is because it effectively works as both a photoconductive device (i.e. a photodiode) and as an amplifier of the current generated by the incident light.

The electrical symbol that is normally used for a phototransistor is a variation on that used for a transistor and is shown in figure 2.62.

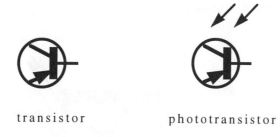

transistor   phototransistor

Figure 2.62 Symbol for a light sensitive transistor

❏ Video sensor

A video sensor or camera is a large number of photo-detectors. There are many types of video camera available, but basically they can be divided up into two categories, tube and solid state cameras. We shall only consider here the solid state camera as it is a follow on from the photo-diode and transistor that we have just considered.

The solid state camera consists of a matrix of solid state sensors where an image of the object being viewed is focused. The photodiodes react with the incident light producing an electrical reaction proportional to the brightness of the incident light. In order to obtain an electrical copy of the image on the matrix the sensor is scanned row by row by electronic circuitry and the information from each column of photodiodes is read serially.

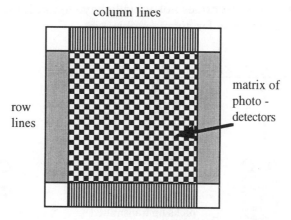

Figure 2.63 The matrix light sensor of a solid state camera

Task 2.25   PC 2 & 3   C 3.3

Investigate the basic construction of a video tube type camera. Draw a simple diagram and explain how it works.

❏ Sound sensor and Microphones

The most common form of sound sensor is the microphone. A microphone is found in the mouth-piece of a telephone, used in cassette tape recorders etc. The microphone converts sound waves into electrical signals which in the case of a telephone is ideal for transmitting through telephone wires. There are a number of ways in which sound waves can be converted into an electrical signal, but the majority of the devices include a diaphragm. The diaphragm is used to convert the sound waves into a movement and then this movement is detected and converted into an electrical signal.

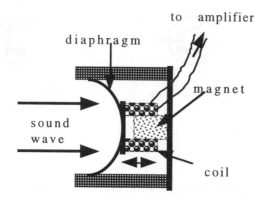

Figure 2.64 A microphone

In figure 2.64 the movement of the diaphragm is detected by a coil moving up and down a magnet. As this happens the coil 'cuts ' the lines of magnetic field causing a voltage to be generated. This voltage is then an electrical replica of the sound wave.

❏ Proximity sensor

Proximity sensors, as the name implies, detect the nearness or proximity of an object and are very useful because the sensor does not actually have to touch the object. Usually these devices rely on an echo to detect how far away an object is.

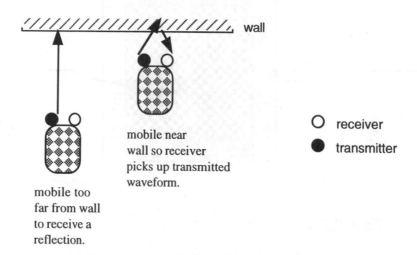

Figure 2.65 Mobiles using proximity detectors

The transmitter sends out a burst of signals which hit a surface and are reflected back to the mobile. The reflected signal is picked up by the receiver. The time it takes for the signal to travel to and from the wall is proportional to the distance the object is away from the wall. Hence this distance can be easily calculated. The type of signal transmitted depends upon the type of transmitter used and the types of surface used for the wall. If the wall is a smooth surface and white, or even better has a mirror type finish, light can be the transmitted signal and the detector a photodetector. Infrared light or ultra sound signals could also be used. Naturally a different sensor would have to be used for the receiver.

❏ Contact sensor

This type of sensor is the exact opposite to the proximity detector as it has to make physical contact with an object. The cheapest and simplest form of contact sensor would be a micro-switch.

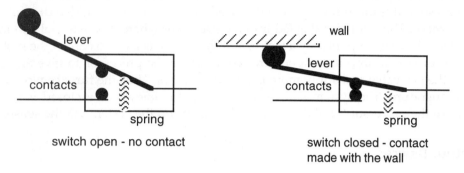

Figure 2.66 A micro-switch

When a force is applied to the lever of the micro-switch the contacts close. Such a force occurs when the end of the micro-switch hits the wall as shown. This can be used for the mobile as shown in figure 2.67.

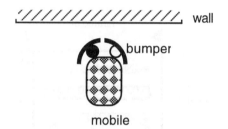

Figure 2.67 A micro-switch contact detector

The bumper is connected to the micro-switches, one for each half. If both switches are closed a signal will control the mobile so as to move back away from the wall. If the left hand bumper hits an object its micro-switch will close causing a control signal to move the mobile towards the right away from the object. On the other hand if the right hand bumper hits an object the resulting control will cause the mobile to move towards the left.

Processors

A processor is a device which can perform logical and arithmetical operations.

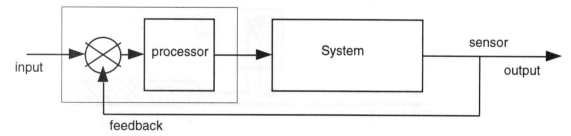

Figure 2.68 The processor as the brain of the system

The processor is an integral part of the control system. In addition to the logical and arithmetic operations, it outputs control signals to the system. The sensor monitors the system and feeds back a signal which is compared to the input signal. These two signals represent the actual condition and the desired condition respectively. The difference between the two is the error. In the case of the furnace which was annealing steel ingots the temperature of the furnace as measured by the sensor was the actual temperature but invariably when the door of the furnace opened it dropped below the desired temperature and an error, the difference between the two, was present. It is this error signal that is used to correct for this sudden drop of temperature in the furnace. The error signal is fed into the processor where it is manipulated in a mathematical algorithm e.g. amplified by a factor, and the output is used to correct the system. In the case of the furnace, a drop in temperature would cause the processor to give an output signal to open the gas valve and apply more gas to the burners. Thus the furnace would be brought up to temperature. The system shown in figure 2.68 is known as a closed loop control system because the processor 'sees' the effect of its actions on the system via the sensor.

Output Devices

❏ Heaters

A very simple but effective form of control is found in our convection heaters in the home. They are thermostatically controlled so as to control the temperature of the room in which they are placed.

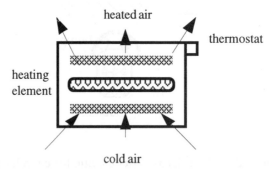

Figure 2.69 A thermostatically controlled heater

The warm air passes out of the top of the heater causing convection currents. These circulating currents heat the room. As the room warms up, the thermostat (which is preset to some value) turns off the electric current to the heating element and so the heater cools down. The room temperature falls, the thermostat comes into effect and turns on the current causing the heating element to heat up, thereby repeating the process. The circuit arrangement for the thermostat and heating element is shown in figure 2.70.

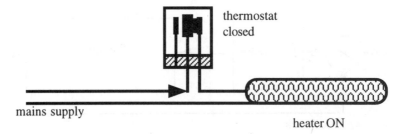

Figure 2.70 Electrical connection for a thermostatically controlled heater

❏ Sound

An example of an output device used to produce sound is a loudspeaker. A loudspeaker is very similar in structure to that of a microphone, the only difference is that it operates in reverse.

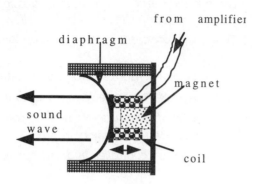

Figure 2.71 A loudspeaker

An electrical signal from the amplifier is sent to the coil of the speaker and energises it. The resulting magnetic field from the coil reacts with the magnet's magnetic field causing the coil to move. If the electrical signal from the amplifier represents music the resulting effect is to cause the coils to move back and forth in sympathy with the music. As the diaphragm is connected to the coil it will also move in the same way and pressure waves are set up in the air surrounding the cone. These pressure waves are the sound produced by the speaker.

Interconnecting Devices

In many cases the systems that we have been considering have signals associated with them that are varying or fluctuating with respect to time. Such a signal is called an analogue signal. The computer or microprocessor, on the other hand, can only handle digital signals. A digital signal is made up of bits and batched together to form bytes or words. A typical word could be 8, 16 or 32 bits depending upon the complexity of the computer. A bit itself has only two states, a '1' or a '0'. Therefore a computer has to be connected to a system via a special interface in order to control it. This interconnection is known as the I/O port, or Input/Output port. For example, the I/O port would have to have an analogue to digital convertor in the input port and a digital to analogue convertor in the output port for the computer to communicate with and control the system to which it is connected.

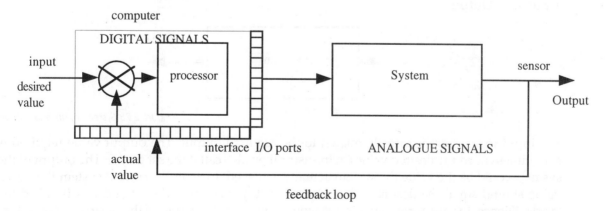

Figure 2.72 A system showing the I/O ports

Task 2.26 PC 2   *C 3.3, C 3.4*

Investigate the components used in a traffic light control system which controls the traffic and pedestrian crossing at a typical high street junction. Your investigation should cover the following points:

- ❐ *the type of sensor used in the road to detect traffic such as cars, lorries etc;*
- ❐ *the type of sensor used for the pedestrian crossing;*
- ❐ *the type of output device used to control the flow of traffic;*
- ❐ *the type of output device used to control pedestrians, assume that some of the pedestrians may be blind;*
- ❐ *the type of controller and interconnecting devices used to control the junction.*

2.4.3 Specification

To put together a system that is controlled, the appropriate devices have to be chosen and matched. This is done by examining each component by its specification. The most important component that dictates which other components are used is the SYSTEM. In other words the APPLICATION is the primary specification for the sensors, actuators and other devices to be used in the control system. For example, the furnace would be the system and the purpose for which the furnace is being used would be the application. For a furnace, temperature control components would be used e.g. thermometers and a temperature controller, which could be a simple thermostat. There are other factors which have to be considered e.g. the range over which the furnace is to be controlled, how quickly you want the control to occur, the cost of the control system, the type of processor i.e. 8 bit or 16 bit, the type of output device used and the type of control system used. The choice might look easy, but a number of the factors are conflicting. For example, the best control is not necessarily the cheapest to buy. The fastest response to control the system isn't necessarily the one that going to give you the best response. We shall now look briefly at each of these specifications and see how they react with each other.

Input and Output

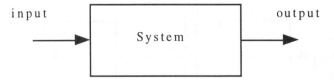

Figure 2.73 System inputs and outputs

The input to a system is directly related to the required output. The output value required is sometimes called the desired value (in industry they also call it the set point). The output of the system would be the value the system actually achieved. In a perfect control system the actual value should equal the desired value, but invariably they are different and this is called the 'error'. Hence, for our furnace the input would represent the value of the desired temperature of the furnace. This input value might be put into the system by means of the keyboard of the controlling computer and the value stored in memory. Alternatively a variable resistor based on a potential divider is used to represent the desired temperature.

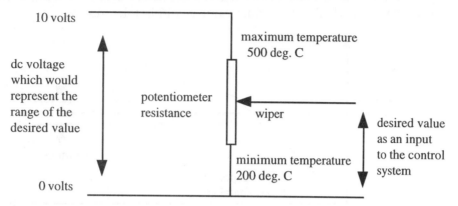

Figure 2.74 The potentiometer as a desired input

As the wiper moves up and down the potentiometer resistance, so the voltage for the desired value varies from 0 to 10 volts. This represents an input temperature change to the control system of 200°C to 500°C. This range of temperature is that expected for the type of furnace being considered. Normally the desired value of temperature for this situation would be somewhere in the middle of that range i.e. 350°C.

Question 2.24

What voltage from the potentiometer would be used to represent a temperature of 350°C?

Tolerances

To have perfect control would be very expensive and in the vast majority of applications this is not required anyway. Hence we say that adequate control has been achieved if the actual value is within a percentage of the desired value. This percentage is known as the tolerance. In the case of the furnace the desired temperature may be 500°C with a tolerance of ± 5°C. This would mean that the maximum temperature could vary in the range of 495°C to 505°C and would be satisfactorily within tolerance.

Question 2.25

What would be the acceptable range of values for a minimum temperature of 200°C for the furnace if the tolerance was (i) ± 5°C ; (ii) ± 2%?

The input device can also have a tolerance. For example, in the case of the thermostat the set level of temperature at which the room is to be controlled might be set at 20°C. However the heater will not turn off until it reaches a temperature of 24°C causing the room to cool down. The thermostat will turn the heater back on when the temperature has dropped to 16°C, i.e. it has initiated the control action. The thermostat has a tolerance of ± 4°C.

Responses

The output response is of interest since it gives an indication of how well the control system is being controlled and whether the actual value is within tolerance.

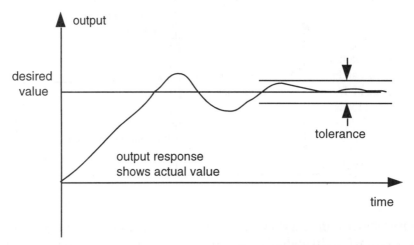

Figure 2.75 A typical output response for a control system

In the case of the temperature control of a furnace, the control has to be within tolerance so that the steel ingots are annealed correctly. The response shown in figure 2.75 shows the temperature of the furnace rising from room temperature to the required value once it is switched on.

Costs

In the preceding sections we have looked at a number of the components which make up a process control system. These components are sensors, actuators, processors and interconnecting devices. In each category we saw that there were many different types, especially in the area of sensors. For example, just for temperature sensors there are many different types depending on their principle of operation. In the section on heat the temperature sensors that we considered were the bi-metallic strip, mercury in glass thermometer, the resistance thermometer and the thermistor. However there are many more which are also used in industry very effectively in a process control system. Some of these are liquid-in-steel thermometer, gas thermometer, vapour thermometer, thermocouple, optical pyrometer and radiation pyrometer. To make matters worse in terms of selection of a particular sensor there are many different types of thermocouples, different types of resistance thermometers etc. and this doesn't take into account manufacturer and the different ranges over which they can be used. The choice is vast!

One important factor which helps us choose our sensor is cost. If we have an application requiring a sensor, we would use a process of elimination to arrive at the one sensor that will do the job. If we had three sensors that measured the variable within the range we wanted, gave the output signal required to the necessary accuracy and one was cheaper to buy than the other two, we would probably purchase the cheaper sensor.

Types of feedback

Feedback is the term used in a process control system where part (or all) of the output signal is fed back into the input of the system. Such a system is generally known as a 'closed-loop' system.

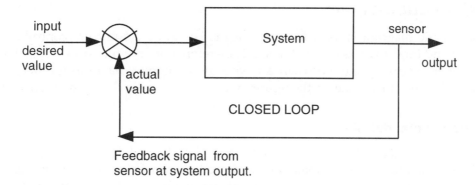

Figure 2.76 A simple closed-loop feedback control system

In figure 2.76 all the output signal from the sensor is fed back to the input of the system where it is compared as the actual value with the desired value. Ideally there will be no difference between the two values showing that we have 'good' control in our system. However if there is a difference between the actual and desired values this difference can be used as a signal to put things right. The difference or error signal can be used to correct the output to bring it into line with the desired value. The greater this error, the greater the correction required. So the error signal can be used in this way, we have to amplify it to give the signal power to drive the actuator in the control system. This can be achieved by using a servo amplifier. The type of feedback used here is called 'Negative Feedback' because the two signals are subtracted from each other. The difference is the error signal we use to put things right via the process control system.

When the desired value and actual value are added together we have 'positive' feedback and this will cause the output to further increase. Normally positive feedback is not used in control systems as it has the effect of causing instability.

However, not all systems require feedback since the output always responds in the way it is intended i.e. the actual value accurately follows the desired value so there is no error and as such there is no need for feedback. Such a system is known as an 'Open-Loop' control system.

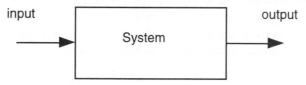

Figure 2.77 An Open-Loop control system

Task 2.27 PC 4 & 6   N 3.3

For the traffic light control system analysed in task 2.26, write down the sequence of operations that occur when :

☐ *a car approaches the junction;*

☐ *a pedestrian wants to cross the road.*

Making particular reference to order and time of each sequence repeat the exercise a number of times to determine the tolerance used by the system.

2.4.4 Schematic diagram

A schematic diagram is used to represent the layout of the process control system to help understand how it works or functions. It is therefore not drawn to scale nor is it a plan of how the system is actually laid out. There are other more complex diagrams for this purpose. In fact all the diagrams that make up the figures in this section are in the form of schematic diagrams.

Environmental definition

The environmental definition of a process control system relates to the physical and chemical reactions used to process or manufacture a product or reaction. In other words, what is happening in the process to make something happen that is desirable or required. In order to effectively control any process, a full understanding of what the process is doing, how it functions, what variables are measurable and what their effect is on the output product is all important. The whole purpose of the process is to produce as high a quality product as possible at the lowest cost and in order to achieve this goal effective control is necessary. Hence a full understanding of the process is very important in order to achieve effective control. It is very difficult to control the unknown – where do you start?

Analysis of such a situation would be necessary, and the following questions would be asked:

- ❐ What is the process manufacturing i.e. what is the output?
- ❐ What are the desired parameters of the output?
- ❐ How can the output parameters be controlled?
- ❐ What variables in the process directly or indirectly affect the output parameters?
- ❐ Can these variables be measured?
- ❐ What sensor/s can be used to achieve that measurement?
- ❐ What variable/s need to be controlled?
- ❐ What actuator is used to activate the control?

These are all questions related to the control in the environmental definition and are essential to the design of the components used to control the given process. It is important to realise that even if one process is very similar to another the environmental definition could dictate completely different components to be used on that 'similar' process.

2.4.5 Process Control Procedure

The process control procedure describes the way in which the whole system is supposed to perform under ideal control conditions. In order to write such a procedure there has to be a complete understanding of how the process to be controlled works and what is the ideal product or service that the process is going to produce. Once we know what we want and what the process is doing, we can then start to think about bringing the two together. In essence that is what control is all about, knowing what is desired and comparing it with the actual. The difference between the two can then be used to put things right.

Task 2.28   PC 3, 4, 5 & 6

The control of traffic lights at a road junction with a pedestrian crossing.

(i) Schematic Diagram

Draw a schematic diagram of the control system used for the traffic lights at a road junction which has a pedestrian crossing. Show clearly the output devices, sensors and processor with appropriate interconnections and feedback. The pedestrian crossing should be suitable for blind persons. Explain clearly the purpose of each device and how they interact with each.

(ii) Process Control Procedure

Write down the total sequence of events that occur when a car approaches a RED traffic light at a typical road junction developed in (i).

Write down the total sequence of events that occur when a pedestrian indicates that they wish to cross the road.

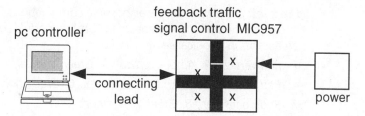

Figure 2.78 Layout of the Feedback traffic signal control system

Feedback's Micamaster MIC957 Traffic Signal Control module is a representation of the traffic and pedestrian control, with lamp signals at a crossroads and one pedestrian crossing. It is designed to be controlled by a range of microcomputers or Feedback's Microprocessor Applications Trainers, for the purpose of providing exercises on the use of a microprocessor to monitor and control objects external to itself.

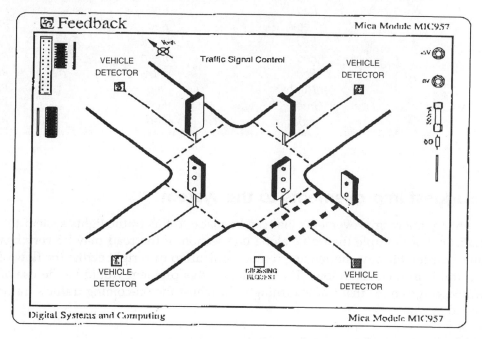

Figure 2.79 Feedback MIC957 Traffic Signal Control module

115

Question 2.26

Why do you think LED's are used in Feedback's Traffic Signal Control module rather than low voltage lamps?

2.4.6 Test the system for effectiveness

Feedback have provided a number of exercises which effectively test the system in a practical situation. They provide sample programs which can be used with their module or alternatively programs can be written by the teacher or the student. In the latter case these programs could act as evidence for an alternative unit and in this way integrate this unit with others.

Task 2.29 PC 6   N 3.2

Use a test program that sets all possible combinations for the eight lamps used to control the traffic and pedestrians on the module so that they are switched on and off in a logical sequence, i.e.

1. Red vertical, 2. Amber vertical, 3. Green vertical;

4. Red horizontal, 5. Amber horizontal, 6. Green horizontal;

7. Red pedestrian, 8. Green pedestrian.

Task 2.30 PC 6

Use a program to run the traffic lights to the following specification for a duration of 10 seconds:

Vertical lights	Horizontal lights	Pedestrian lights
Red	Red	Red
Red	Red	Green
Red	Red/Amber	Red
Red	Green	Red
Red	Amber	Red
Red/Amber	Red	Red
Green	Red	Red
Amber	Red	Red

2.4.7 Suggest improvements to the system

There are many improvements that can be made to this traffic lights system to make it more realistic. For example the traffic along one section of the road may be very heavy at certain times during the day and making it more difficult to turn right across the flow of the on-coming traffic in such conditions. The solution to this problem would be the use of a filter. This would be green for that traffic turning right whilst the on-coming traffic's traffic light would be red.

Task 2.31 PC 6

Use a program so as to run the traffic lights as for task 2.30 but with the addition of a filter so that traffic can safely turn right at the junction. Modify the specification shown in task 2.30 to incorporate the filter in the horizontal lights sequence so that it is on for a duration of 10 seconds.

Answers to questions in Unit 2

Answer 2.1   Your answer could be quite varied, but good examples include stationary for letters, invoices, purchase orders, message pads etc. Other examples could be equally valid.

Answer 2.2   If we look at the detail contained in the heading and the body of the agenda, it is all information that is needed before the meeting, especially the time, date and venue.

Answer 2.3   When the minutes are received, everyone can quickly scan the action column to identify those issues where they need to do something. It is a helpful way of reminding people of the agreed activities.

Answer 2.4   The width needs to sufficient to contain the names (or at least initials) of the actionees and wide enough to be recognised as the action column. Typically somewhere between 1 and 3 cms would be the norm.

Answer 2.5   No. The housestyle could be anything. The intention is to create a style that is recognisable and that may be a column or a zone across the top of the page or whatever is the best design for the organisation.

Answer 2.6   Some overhead slides with just a few bullet points look better on landscape than portrait layout. Your answer may have identified equally valid situations.

Answer 2.7   The layout of the document changes quite a lot. Widows and orphans may occur if the document hasn't requested their avoidance. Diagrams and text can get separated by page boundaries. Further proof reading will be required after the change to check for such detail.

Answer 2.8   A limited amount of font change is acceptable, although there are combinations that are good and equally mixtures that are bad. Fonts belong to fundamental types and mixing between types is bad practice. It may be better to emphasise with bold, italics and underlining at the outset.

Answer 2.9   It would look like the first diagram in figure 2.25 if filled with white or like the last diagram in figure 2.24 if filled with a colour (or other filler patterns).

Answer 2.10   Some words would be detected by spell checker: Thr, venew and noice. Other words that are incorrectly used but not incorrectly spelt need to be detected by proof reading. They are sea and two.

Answer 2.11   Yes, the word 'the' appears at the end of the first line and the beginning of the second. These are hard to spot when wrong.

Answer 2.12   This is a bit-map.

Answer 2.13   Each slide show can have the slides set up in the sequence required i.e. than can be re-sequenced from an earlier presentation. Once set, no accidents can happen, like a set of acetates falling on the floor and loosing their relative position. If automatic timing is used the presenter would not have to worry about changing the slides, they can concentrate on the speech or presentation.

Small changes to the content of an individual slide can be made without having to reprint an overhead. This is a helpful tool to businesses who make a lot of use of slide presentations.

Answer 2.14   A square is only a special case of a rectangle. Hence if we have a facility to draw a rectangle then we can always construct a square.

Answer 2.15   It is as important as the combination of clothes that you wear. The contrast between background and any detail needs to be sharp. E.g. orange on red would not show very clearly.

Answer 2.16   It is a few words that states the main point or heading of a section of the presentation. There is little or no detail provided but they provide a framework to the reader of how the topic is being introduced and the sequence in which points are being raised.

Answer 2.17   A bit-map.

Answer 2.18   Drawing clip art can be quite slow. If a good range can be supplied as part of the package, then these can be used in combinations to provide the impact you are seeking. Figure 2.39 was constructed from clip art provided within a package.

Answer 2.19   The user can see the relationship between the parts and the way in which they fit together should be easier to show in the diagram.

Answer 2.20   Your answer could be varied, e.g. you might have thought about modelling a wind tunnel so that the flow of air over a new car design can be determined without having to build a car shape.

Answer 2.21   Yes, this will tell us whether the network will handle all the traffic properly before we build it. This a good example of simulation software.

Answer 2.22

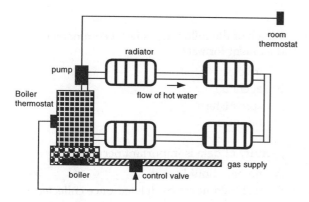

In this central heating system the room thermostat is used to control the pump. Hence when the temperature in the room where the thermostat is placed gets too hot the thermostat is adjusted so as to turn off the pump which stops the hot water circulating through the pipes and the radiators. However the gas supply is still on and continues to heat up the water in the boiler. The boiler thermostat is used to turn off the gas supply when the water in the boiler gets too hot and as the water is no longer circulating this happens very quickly. When the gas supply is cut off the temperature of the water begins to fall and when it falls too low the thermostat turns back on the gas supply to heat up the water. In the mean time the room temperature also falls and this is detected by the room thermostat and as it falls the thermostat turns back on the pump, circulating the water around the system. When hot water is drawn from the boiler it is replaced by colder water this being detected by the boiler thermostat which will turn on the gas supply. In effect in this system we have two control systems, one which maintains a reservoir of hot water in the boiler and the other which circulates hot water to keep the room temperature at a preset valve.

Answer 2.23 The operations involved are numerous and not always in the order given:

- slow down, take foot off accelerator;
- look in the mirror to make sure the road behind is safe to pull out into the middle of the road;
- indicate that you are about to turn right;
- change down in gear to 3rd keeping control of speed by sparingly using accelerator;
- keeping an eye on the mirror, if safe pull out into the middle of the road;
- look ahead at the on coming traffic if clear, change down to 2nd, make right turn, if not stop at junction, change down to 1st gear, release accelerator, break and wait;
- once the oncoming traffic has cleared, release break, accelerate and turn right;
- change up in gear to 4th or 5th if necessary;
- ensure that the indicator has turned itself off properly.

This list could be further amplified but it does illustrate how complex such a simple operation as turning right actually is.

Answer 2.24 This would best be solved by using ratios:

0 volts represents 200°C.

10 volts represents 500 °C. i.e. 10 volts represents a change of 300°C.

Therefore 1 volt represents a change of 30°C.

Now the desired temperature is 350°C. i.e. 150°C. above the minimum temperature.

$$\frac{150°C}{30°C} = 5 \text{ volts}$$

Answer 2.25 If the tolerance was expressed as ± 5°C, then the range is 195°C to 205°C.

For a 2% tolerance the range is 196°C to 204°C, since 2% of 200 is 4.

Answer 2.25 They take a lot less power and hence can be smaller in size and so a smaller power supply can be used.

Unit 2 Sample Test Paper

Questions 1 to 3 relate to the following information. A company uses a spreadsheet to record details of the weekly staff wages.

	A	B	C	D	E
	Name	Hours	Rate	Bonus	Total pay
	Fred	55	£ 4.00	£ 1.00	£ 275.00
	Jim	60	£ 4.50	£ 1.20	£ 342.00
	Doris	38	£ 5.00	£ 0.90	£ 224.20

1 Which of the following is a weekly VARIABLE?

A rate of pay
B bonus rates
C hours worked
D spreadsheet

2 Which of the following is an invalid entry for hours worked?

A 20 – 60
B 20 – 168
C 40 – 170
D 35 – 150

3 You have entered the data, but the total pay looks wrong. How would you check the validity?

A enter the data again
B set up a new spreadsheet
C work out the results by hand calculation
D assume everything was OK

4 Your sports club uses a spreadsheet to keep details of their membership subscriptions. Why would a spreadsheet be used?

A to avoid any calculation errors
B it is more accurate than manual records
C it is quicker than any other software package
D it produces the data quicker than other methods

5 The layout of text in a report has straight left-hand edges but a jagged right hand edge. Is this report:

A aligned to the left
B aligned to the right
C justified
D attributed

6 Which of the following is not a commercial document format?

A invoice
B agenda
C spreadsheet
D minutes

7 Security of data is important because:

A no one should see it
B it should never be deleted once collected
C you need instant access to information
D data is an important business asset

8 Data is best presented:

A in graphic format
B in table format
C in a format designed for the intended reader
D in text format

9 Which layout tool can be used as an in-text pointer to further detail?

A a header
B a footer
C a footnote
D a summary

10 Which layout style ensures that the contents can still be read when the document is placed and bound in a filing system?

A windows
B tabulation
C font size
D margins

11 Which software aid can be used to help a business presentation?

A a slide show
B a bit-map
C a vector
D a graphic image

12 Which type of software is most suitable for determining the queue length in a supermarket?

A a spreadsheet
B a database
C a modelling package
D a project evaluation package

13 A new row needs to be added to an existing spreadsheet. What do we need to do?

A   amend a formulae
B   change the column headings
C   edit the row
D   use longer stationary

14 Clip art is provided in many presentation software packages to enable one of the following to be provided.

A   documents can be enhanced with relevant graphics
B   diagrams may be included in the document
C   bit-map output is available
D   colour images are provided

15 Which of the following is not a relational operator?

A   =
B   AND
C   LESS THAN
D   <

16 Which of the following is not a logical operator?

A   AND
B   OR
C   IF
D   NOT

17 A model to determine the effects of change in fuel consumption, when a car is carrying different loads, would be run on which of the following provisions?

A   simulation
B   gaming
C   hypothesis testing
D   3-D representation

18 Which of the following does not provide part of a design specification for an image?

A   width
B   height
C   colour
D   none of the above

19 A bit-map graphic is which of the following?

A   a set of bits, where each bit represents a dot in the image
B   a file of bits which can be scaled down
C   a file of bits which is smaller than an equivalent vector graphic
D   a graphic showing how each bit can map into an image

20 An organisation may invest money in creating a corporate style for a range of reasons. Which of the following reasons would be true?

A   follow the styles available in the graphics package
B   to use bit-mapped graphics
C   create a recognisable image
D   separate the business documents into different groups

21 The input device you would use to detect a change in light level is a:

A   light bulb
B   LED
C   photo diode
D   IR transmitter

22 The output device which gives an audible warning is a:

A   microphone
B   solar cell
C   IR transmitter
D   loudspeaker

23 A temperature measuring device which gives a binary output is a:

A   thermostat
B   resistance thermometer
C   mercury in glass thermometer
D   thermocouple

24 An example of an actuator would be a:

A   thermometer
B   solenoid
C   IR receiver
D   microphone

The following figure relates to questions 25 to 27.

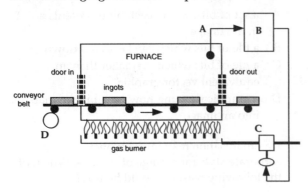

25 For the furnace in the above figure, the valve actuator would be the component marked:

A   A
B   B
C   C
D   D

26 Which component is the thermometer?

A   A
B   B
C   C
D   D

27 The type of control system used is known as:

A   a manual control system
B   an open loop control system
C   a closed loop control system
D   a closed loop manual system

28 A thermostat consists of a:

A   resistance element
B   bi-metallic strip
C   thermometer
D   heating element

29 An example of a proximity sensor would be a:

A   thermistor
B   lamp
C   actuator
D   micro-switch

30 The output device used to assist blind pedestrians use a crossing at a traffic light controlled road junction would be a:

A   loudspeaker
B   green light
C   red light
D   flashing amber light

31 The type of sensor used to detect the presence of a car at a set of traffic lights is a:

A   switch
B   microphone
C   loudspeaker
D   proximity

by **Dave Evans**

Organisations and Information Technology

Introduction

This unit explores how information technology is used in organisations. As a first step the structure and functioning of different types of organisations are outlined. Each have differing styles of management and structures to operate and function.

The flow of information around the organisation and the way in which the data handling systems operate will be investigated. The importance of data in organisations is emphasised, and so safety and security of information is covered in some detail.

There is an overlap of work needed to complete your portfolio with other units and whenever appropriate reference to those areas will be made. This hopefully will reduce the number of tasks needed in collecting the evidence.

Element 3.1

Investigate the flow of information in organisations

Introduction

The business world consists of organisations which exist in order to achieve some pre-determined purposes or goals. They may be profit-oriented or exist to achieve a non profit goal, e.g. social, medical. The setting of goals and the overall long term mission of organisations are the responsibility of the top management, e.g. the board of directors, the government etc.

What then is an organisation? Simply speaking, it is a combination of several elements which combine to support and further the mission of the organisation. An organisation can be pictured as seen in figure 3.1.

ENVIRONMENT

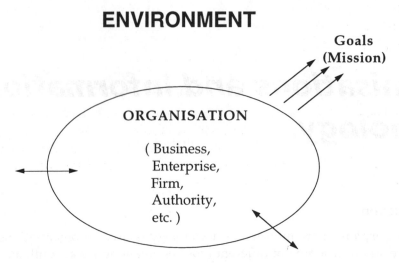

Figure 3.1 The Organisation

Figure 3.1 shows the other names commonly applied to an organisation or business system. There is a boundary or interface between the firm and its surroundings or environment. Interaction takes place between the firm and its environment, i.e. the firm reacts to changes in the environment which affects it.

The environment of an organisation has a major effect on the operations that the organisation carries out. Figure 3.2 shows the major players in the environment that affect a firm.

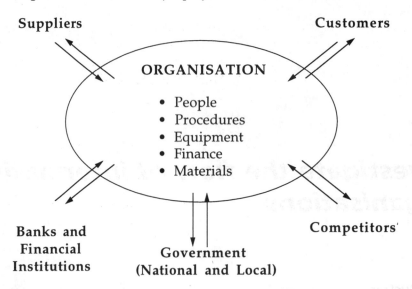

Figure 3.2 Major Players Influencing an Organisation

The arrows indicate activities (events) that could occur and which cause the firm to react, e.g.

- ❐ supplier delivers goods;
- ❐ customer cancels an order;
- ❐ bank demands overdraft charge payment;
- ❐ competitor brings out a new product.

The organisation consists of a number of identifiable elements:

❑ the **people** who work there;

❑ the **procedures** they use;

❑ the **equipment** they operate;

❑ the **materials** they use;

❑ the **money** necessary to fund the operations.

The **information** they produce and use to control the activities of the organisation are all termed the **resources** of the organisation. These resources are made (organised) to act or operate together to help achieve the goals of the firm. The operations of an organisation can be viewed from a systems point of view as a hierarchy of systems and sub-systems, each contributing to the overall functioning of the firm.

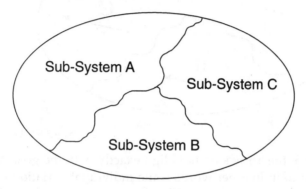

Figure 3.3 Sub-Systems making a Whole System

The sub-systems themselves decompose into lower level systems until a primary or elemental level is reached as shown in figure 3.4. The result is a hierarchy of systems in the organisation.

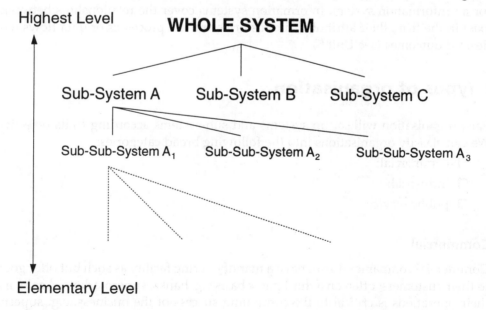

Figure 3.4 The Systems Hierarchy

Some systems will deal with physical events, e.g. making an item for a customer whilst others are more abstract in nature, e.g. recording the payment made by a customer in the customers' record and posting it to the accounts ledger. Systems dealing with data and its processing are termed **information systems** and form a critically important part of the resources of a firm. They enable the other resources to be organised and used to achieve the objectives of the firm.

The firm as a whole system is termed the corporate system and sub-systems etc. are set up according to the way in which the firm is organised. The corporate system can be thought of as the central, main purpose of the firm, fed and supported by the various sub-systems that exist.

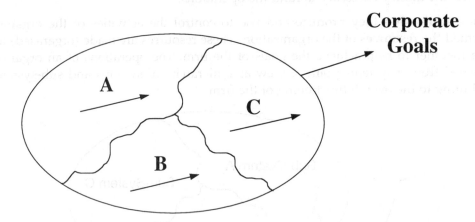

Figure 3.5 Sub-Systems supporting the Corporate Goals

Note in figure 3.5, the arrows do not align exactly with the goal direction, but neither should they be opposed to it. In other words some individual variation is to be expected (due to the nature of people and organisations). The sub-systems are polarised towards achieving the corporate goal (team effect).

All systems have events occurring to which they react. The capture and recording or posting of data on such events is called **transaction processing**. This is the basic procedural level for an information system. Information systems cover the relationships between entities that exist in the firm, their attributes, life histories and the processes or data flows required for the desired outcomes (see Unit 5).

3.1.1 Types of organisation

Each organisation will set up systems and sub-systems according to its objectives and goals. We can classify organisations into the following broad categories:

❐ commercial;

❐ industrial;

❐ public service.

Commercial

Commercial companies do not have a manufacturing facility as such but offer goods or services to their customers, often on a third party basis e.g. banks, supermarkets. Again, information on their operations is critical to the continuing success of the business, e.g. supermarket checkouts automated to provide more detailed information on sales. For banks, up-to-date information on customers, their balances etc. is crucial to their operation.

Commercial organisations still have a need for information flow. The units between which these flows occur will be closely linked to the specific commercial operation. Typically there will be strong marketing, financial and accounting management, service centres, corporate services.

As an example, a Building Society may have a simple organisational structure such as:

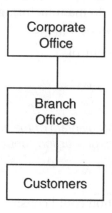

Figure 3.6 Simple Commercial Model

Of course this model can be expanded and the specific data flows added.

Task 3.1   PC 1   **C3.3**

Investigate how a Building Society is organised and draw a modified version of figure 3.6 to reflect the structure.

Question 3.1

What types of service would you expect to see offered by a Building Society at their branch office?

Task 3.2   PC 2   **C3.3**

The corporate office of the Building Society in Task 3.1 has just designed a new mortgage package for first time buyers. Show on your model how the information will flow between the operating units.

Industrial

These companies are generally involved in converting input materials into an intermediate or end products. To this end they have a manufacturing facility which may be primary, secondary or tertiary, or a combination of them.

- ❑ **Primary** processes convert raw materials into an intermediate (secondary) product or state, e.g. iron ore into steel slabs, silica and sand into glass;
- ❑ **Secondary** processes continue the development of the product, e.g. steel slabs into coil or sheet glass into glass panes;
- ❑ **Tertiary** processes produce a recognisable end product, e.g. sheet steel into saucepans, car bodies etc.

Within the manufacturing sector, information is needed from a number of sources:

- ❏ from 'engineering' – to manufacturing to state how to do it;
- ❏ from production control – to manufacturing stating when and how many to do;
- ❏ from customer to sales ordering items;
- ❏ from sales to production control.

Task 3.3   PC 3   C3.3

Draw a block diagram of the areas identified (customer, sales, manufacturing, engineering, production control etc.). Show the flow of information between these areas.

Typically an industrial organisation could consist of a number of small sub-systems, each with their own data flows. These sub-systems are then inter-related. Examples of data flows are:

timescale for availability

```
          ┌─────────────────────────────────────────┐
          │                                         │
          ▼                                         │
  ┌─────────────┐                        ┌──────────────────────┐
  │             │                        │                      │
  │    Sales    │──────────────────────► │  Production Control  │
  │             │      request           │                      │
  └─────────────┘                        └──────────────────────┘
```

Figure 3.7 Information Flow in a Sub-System

Question 3.2

Can you identify two more possible flows of information in an industrial organisation?

Public Service

Sometimes characterised by a bureaucratic image where the system is the important factor. These organisations have a prime function in the operation of the civil service, state funded institutions or local government, e.g. Local Authorities. Increasingly, market testing is seeking to impose the same conditions upon this sector as exist in the industrial and commercial area, i.e. introduction of the concept of competition. In all areas pressure exists to make it critical that information is available on all aspects of the organisations' operations. A further factor in the nature of organisations, as defined above, is size, i.e. whether they are localised, national or international in their operations and locations.

Hierarchical and Flat Organisations

People have a limited capacity to perform work, this is a human limitation and organisations reflect this in the way that personnel are distributed in an organisation.

Tasks and duties are divided or split such that they are delegated according to human capacity in general terms. (N.B. individuals can vary greatly in their own capacity).

A person generally can control 7-9 subordinates and so **levels** of organisation build up, typified by the pyramid representation. Some organisations are **flatter** in structure than others, i.e. they have less levels of control.

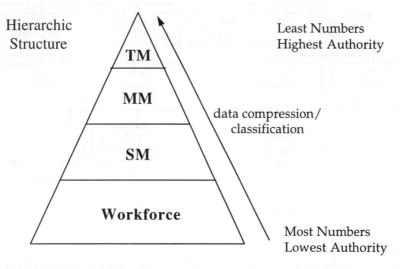

Most Events / Transactions

TM = top management
MM = middle management
SM = supervisory management

Figure 3.8 The Management Pyramid

Putting the business functions into the picture, we have:

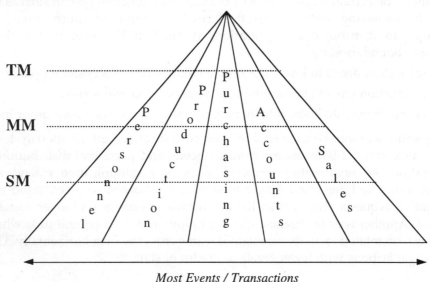

Most Events / Transactions

Figure 3.9 Business Functions in the Organisational Structure

Managers have a specific role in organisations including planning, organisation & resourcing. With each function, personnel will be distributed at various levels, according to the size of the functional department. Typically an **organisation chart** is used to show the personnel distribution in an organisation. The number of subordinates a person controls will result in a deeper or flatter structure.

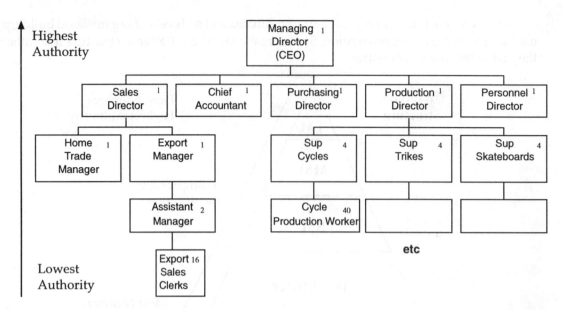

CEO = Chief Executive Officer
The numbers in the boxes indicate the number of persons employed at that level.

Figure 3.10 Organisation Chart

Managers need to control the receipt and issue of information into or from the department. This system, however, allows the suppression of information, is slow and can be unresponsive. Most organisations circumvent this formal flow by either allowing direct communication at lower levels on certain requirements or the use of an informal system such as the telephone. In organisations having electronic mail the formal flow can occur much faster.

People are distributed in organisations by function. However, information needs to cross functional boundaries, e.g.

☐ sales clerk needs to know up-to-date credit status of a customer placing a new order;

☐ production wish to know when supplies ordered will arrive;

☐ accounts need to know whether a customer has received their order in its entirety etc.

Such questions cannot be answered by their own **localised** information systems.

We have conflict between information needs and personnel distribution in a traditional organisation. As organisations expand, lines of communication extend and information requests can take longer and longer to service. Obviously, we need rapid response to most information requests. This means the old formal system is no longer suitable and must be replaced. Another way of organising is to employ the matrix organisation where project teams or process-orientated (activity orientated) teams cross the firm horizontally. These are generally flat organisations with fewer levels or grades of staff.

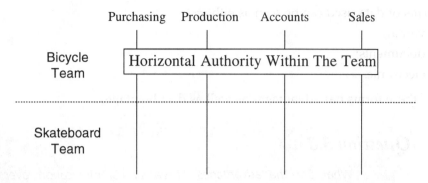

Figure 3.11 Matrix Organisation

This type of organisation can be supported by suitably designed information systems.

Task 3.4   **PC 1**

Investigate and report on the structure of three organisations. This must be one commercial, one industrial and one public service organisation.

3.1.2 Forms of information

Business information can have the following characteristics:

action	– upon receipt some action is immediately required;
non-action	– information from books etc. or confirmatory information of a previous action;
recurring	– at least once a year – reports etc;
non-recurring	– once-off information for studies etc;
documentary	– recorded in some permanent form;
non-documentary	– by word of mouth etc;
internal	– concerning events within the organisation;
external	– policies, plans of Government, status of orders on suppliers etc;
historical	– data on events that have occurred, e.g. sales analysis;
future projection	– predication of future events based on projections made from historical information, e.g. sales forecast.

Using these, several generalisations can be noted:

❏ Action recurring documentary, internal, historical information is the prime candidate for automation. In fact this classification will form the 'data base' for most automated information systems;

❏ The timing and accuracy of action information is usually important;

❏ Non-action information is a prime candidate for elimination;

❏ Non-documentary information is just about impossible to control;

❏ Non-recurring information is not usually subject to automation;

❏ The higher the management decisions the more important becomes external information and future projection.

The forms of data used can be seen as either:

- ❑ verbal;
- ❑ documents;
- ❑ electronic.

Each of these forms has advantages as well as disadvantages.

Question 3.3

What are the advantages of verbal communication over the other two approaches? What are the disadvantages of verbal data?

Electronic communication can also range from informal information using e-mail to formal data using EDI. Indeed many organisations now require their suppliers and sales outlets to communicate through EDI. This avoids any data re-entry and capture of data must be as accurate as that provided by the communication. Hence if 100 components are ordered via EDI, then 100 components are captured and no possibility of only 10 or 1000 being entered in error can occur. Element 1.1 includes further details of electronic communication, including transferring funds and point-of-sale.

3.1.3 Types of information

We have seen that three levels of management exist:

Top Management (TM)	– concerned with the future, long term;
Middle Management (MM)	– control of current performance and mid-term future plans to achieve objectives set by top management;
Supervisory Management (SM)	– control of day-to-day operations detailed data or information is very important.

The responsibility placed on management is to organise, direct, motivate and control their resources for the overall effective benefit of the organisation. In order to control, we need information on what is happening (principle of feed-back), and a previously prepared plan of what we intend doing. We compare information on events occurring against the plan and decide what action to take to maintain or re-direct performance to the plan.

To obtain information on events, we must capture data on events, process it to provide information and then use this information to compare with the plan. A decision can then be taken.

When many events occur, a need for processing a high volume of data results. To have tight control, data on events must be processed quickly to provide information for appraisal – the longer the delay, the longer the operation may be out of control. Thus we have a requirement for rapid processing of a high volume of data to provide information. This can only be done effectively using computer based systems.

Management require information to support them in decision making.

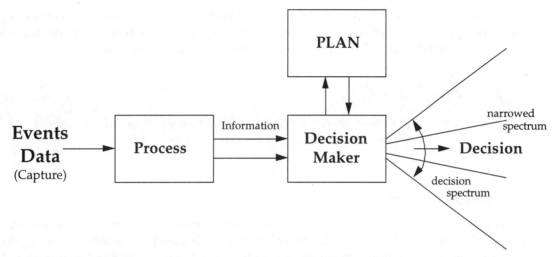

NB: For predictable outcomes we need to narrow the possible decision spectrum.

Figure 3.12 The Decision Making Process

Change is occurring ever more **rapidly** due to new materials, new manufacturing methods, new products, market pressure etc. Management are faced with the challenge of trying to exercise control in circumstances which may be completely new or about which there is little known knowledge. They, therefore, need help from tools such as modelling to support them in trying to understand the nature of problems and possible actions to take. Such help and support is provided by suitably designed computerised information systems, to handle the **volume** of transactions **rapidly, economically** and **accurately** and provide information in the **right format** at the **right time** to support decision making (or take decisions based on formalised decision rules).

The net effect of such systems should be to **reduce uncertainty** and **increase predictability** and, therefore, give more **effective control.**

This should be the objective of all information systems.

Sales and Marketing

The emphasis here is on the outside world, in particular customers, the market in general and competitors activities or performance. Good relations need to be built up with customers and their loyalty retained. Typical activities in this functional area are:

- ❑ taking customer orders and visiting customers;
- ❑ answering customer queries;
- ❑ sales promotion activities;
- ❑ preparing sales forecasts, setting targets for salespersons etc;
- ❑ gathering knowledge on competitors;
- ❑ carrying out market investigations and surveys etc.

The core activity here will be customer relations and order taking. (In some industries customers place enquiries which need to be examined, costed, planned etc., before firm orders are placed). There will need to be close liaison with all other functions to supply needed information for their planning and operations to obtain information to answer customers queries. The information flows are frequently based around two types of data; orders and invoices. Both of these are the formal triggers on which organisations will react.

Control information – cost of sales, distribution costs etc. External information plays a major part in the management function of marketing so that the firm can judge the adequacy of past performance as well as appraise the opportunities for new activity.

Question 3.4

In a travel agent's transaction, what type of detailed information is associated with a 'sale' that next gets transferred to the invoice?

Purchase information

Bearing in mind the detail outlined for production information, there is a requirement for purchasing to work closely with production planning and also to be able to react quickly to urgent requests for materials or components caused by spoiled work, amended customer orders etc. Good and close relationships need to be built up with the firm's suppliers and information kept and maintained with regard to a suppliers ability to provide goods at the:

- right time;
- right quality;
- right price.

Statistics will also need to be kept on their performance, alternative sources of supply may also be sought for critical parts – policy of multi-sourcing. Close attention and control will also need to be taken over production stock levels, the free, available materials (if any) and the net material requirements to meet the production plan.

The purchasing (or provisioning) function must not cause production to halt or customers to be dissatisfied due to lack of materials. Having said this, a large amount of money is tied up in stocks so it is important to keep them as low as possible (bank interest charges, warehousing costs, obsolescence, spoilage, theft etc.).

Just-in-Time ordering requires very close and good relationships with suppliers and long term contracts. Immediate response from suppliers is not always possible due to distance, i.e. location, so western firms tend to have a hybrid just-in-time approach. Electronic Data Interchange can reduce the order placing cycle time and effect savings in paperwork. Details of receipts against orders (goods inwards) need to be originated, the goods received and checked against the order so that when a subsequent suppliers invoice is received, the purchasing function can check it and authorise it for payment or otherwise. Thus the two formal information flows are based on orders and invoices.

Design and production information

There are three main issues which influence information in this area:

- Design specification;
- Production Planning;
- Production Control.

The design of new products, processes and operations will be carried out by product development, i.e. another function. Production planning will require full specification details on the design from all products that are made covering:

- materials used and parts made;
- components bought in;

❏ product structure;

❏ quantity measures of all parts used.

These are contained in the product Bill of Materials or BOM, i.e. the WHAT of manufacture. In addition they need to know the HOW, i.e. a full list and description of the **operations** and **processes** to be carried out on a product in order to convert it from an initial state into the finished product. Standard times and process or operation losses due to unavoidable scrap or a standard level of performance resulting in some spoiled work are also required for full requirements calculation and the effective scheduling of operations. The HOW of manufacture forms the standard product plan and consists of the product ROUTE and operational details and standards.

Production control has the responsibility for seeing that:

❏ manufacture starts on time;

❏ delays or problems are actioned;

❏ all operations on products are monitored;

❏ the status of all production orders is recorded for interrogation.

Question 3.5

For whom is the design specification written?

Bearing in mind how busy the shop floor is, this gives rise to an enormous amount of data to be captured. Much development of shop-floor data capture devices has taken place to automate the operation, reduce error and provide timely data, e.g.

❏ touch screen input systems;

❏ voice input systems;

❏ bar code systems;

❏ laser systems (supermarkets) etc.

Production control information (logistics) is concerned with information about the physical flow of goods through an organisation covering ordering, production and distribution and includes sub-systems such as inventory control, production planning, production control, scheduling and transportation (distribution). Because the quantities of data are so large and the timing of information so essential, the logistics systems will be the most adaptable to automation and is one in which the largest benefits may accrue in terms of solution of critical and costly problems.

The production or operations system, particularly in a manufacturing plant is unquestionably the most important from an operating stand point. It crosses all sub-system boundaries and has an effect throughout the company. Despite this importance, the production/operations area has had less management involvement and less development than the financial system. However, because of problems in the production area arising from growth and associated complexity, this area has received much attention and the 'Total Systems' doctrine stems from examination of production etc. problems. Their solution naturally leads to the design of integrated and inter-related sub-systems throughout the company.

Operational information

The type of information that an organisation may hold to provide a successful operation includes:

- ☐ instructions;
- ☐ decisions;
- ☐ responsibilities;
- ☐ holiday dates;
- ☐ opening times.

Question 3.6

Why would we need to include holiday dates in the operational information of an organisation?

Customer information

Information flow will revolve around the sales ledger. This includes billing and control of debtors. The credit rating and viability of customers may well be held. Much of the information flow with customers stems from the sales activity covered earlier.

Supplier information

Control of costs starts with the negotiation of purchasing covered earlier. Ideally a reliable supplier will always deliver goods at the requested time and at the right price and quality. The information held will reflect this requirement. E.g. what is the track record in keeping to delivery schedule, has the price fairly reflected the quality and service obtained. Suppliers can be given a ranked order against these attributes and become preferred suppliers or simply dropped depending on their performance.

Accounts information

Concerned with the flow of money in an organisation and its control viz:

- ☐ the payment of suppliers (purchase ledger);
- ☐ the billing of customers and control of debtors (sales ledger);
- ☐ the payment of employees (payroll);
- ☐ the monitoring of costs against pre-set budgets;
- ☐ preparing standard costs for new products;
- ☐ maintaining a set of accounts, normally controlled on a monthly basis – the nominal or general ledger;
- ☐ preparing new budgets for the next financial year;
- ☐ PAYE, VAT, COMPANIES HOUSE returns etc.

The above will require a great deal of information to support the operation and there needs to be very close contact between accounts and all the other business functions. The need is for data to flow in a controlled manner so that it is available when required.

Financial information

Typical examples are budgets, accounts, payment of creditors, invoice and debtor control, payroll etc. Although largely concerned with historical, recurring, documentary, internal information, it does provide for projections. By and large, the conversion of a manual financial system to a computer based system is subject to less improvement as a management device than other types of information systems. From a data handling point of view, financial systems are usually the first candidate for conversion, but there is less opportunity to improve the quality of the information system. Improvement is obtained by promptness and accuracy.

The financial system is probably the most important single management information system in companies and it is the oldest and best developed. The major problems are the necessary design actions that will make it a vital tool for operating and planning. There is a tendency among many managers to think of information systems almost exclusively in terms of their companies accounting system and reports. **This approach can be a serious deterrent to both the design and utilisation of an information system.**

3.1.4 Functions

Data are raw facts about an event we wish to record, and consists of a string of characters (group of non-random symbols) which have an inherent structure and meaning as perceived by the originator and future recipients. Information is data that has been processed to a wide variety of levels according to the requirements of the decision maker and the nature of the system being controlled. Apart from the above distinction, the terms data and information are used interchangeably.

Data or information can originate in two main areas:

❑ internally in the firm;

❑ externally in the environment.

It should always be possible to control the format, frequency, accuracy etc. of internal information. External information is more difficult to control.

Information, whether verbal or in other form, is more easily handled if it is formatted according to some laid down rules. Free form data, i.e. unstructured, is often difficult to comprehend, erratic in presentation and leaves the recipient somewhat uncertain.

If we structure information by laying down rules as to syntax and content, we can standardise the presentation and remove ambiguity, error and uncertainty.

Documents, e.g. customer orders, invoices, payslips, timetables etc. present information in a known and understood fashion. Communication is improved and enhanced by presenting information in a standardised form.

Information systems should, therefore, use and present information in standard and easily understood formats for maximum effect. NB: The purpose of information is to promote action! Within organisations, standards and conventions should be adopted with regard to the content and format of the information required for control.

Typically organisations have the following business functions which are major sub-sections of the operations and are aligned to serving the needs of the particular area. The major functions are:

Sales and Marketing – dealing with all matters relating to customers, e.g. taking orders, resolving queries, visiting customers, promoting products, awareness of competitors etc.

Purchasing	– responsible for provisioning all aspects of the activities of the organisation i.e. materials for production of products (direct materials) materials or supplies to support activities (consumables) outside consultancy, expertise, service etc.
Accounts	– controlling the flow of money in the organisation Paying suppliers Billing customers Collecting payments Monitoring costs/budgets etc.
Production	– planning the production, scheduling production, monitoring production for timeliness and quality etc.
Personnel	– ensuring all areas are provided with the staff and skills required, staff relations, contracts etc., payroll.

These functions can be represented in the organisation as shown in figure 3.13.

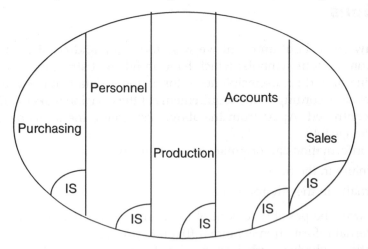

IS = Localised Information System

Figure 3.13 Typical Business Functions in the Organisation

Some points that may be noted about business functions are:
- ❐ They may have a localised information system (IS) to support their activities;
- ❐ They may be cellular and isolated in their operation;
- ❐ They can act in a sub-optimal way, i.e. in their **own** and not **corporate** interests;
- ❐ The information systems used may be disjointed, unco-ordinated and out-of-phase across the organisation (receiving information at different times, in different formats and with differing accuracy);
- ❐ Any disjointed, inconsistent information will lead to inconsistent decision making and loss of control;
- ❐ A major reason for dividing the organisation down into business functions is that it reduces a complex organisation into more manageable parts;
- ❐ By organising functionally, the sub-sections can concentrate on tasks within a limited boundary;
- ❐ However, communication becomes more difficult the more that sub-division occurs.

Question 3.7

If a company has many separate or localised information systems, how may they start to create a single information system?

External

The data held for external sources provides the basis for suppliers and customers. The issues here have been covered earlier in the element. There are statutory functions which include making returns to the Inland Revenue. This includes the personnel tax returns.

Data for the Health & Safety Executive will also be held. This will include risk assessments and the planning and control information required by this body.

Task 3.5   PC 2

Investigate and report on the information generated and used by two organisations. In the report you should cover the verbal, documentary and electronic forms that are used. At least four types of information must be considered such as sales (orders, invoices), market information, design specification, customer information etc. In the report distinguish between the internal and external format of sales information and design specifications. Explain why the sales orders and invoices used internally relate to their financial and marketing information systems.

Investigate data handling systems

Introduction

Historically, the processing of data has been carried out clerically using pen and paper with aids such as typewriters, calculators, copiers, carbon papers etc. Clerical processing is characterised by the following:

- ❐ it is generally slow and volume dependent;
- ❐ it is expensive;
- ❐ it is error prone.

Clerical operations tend to require extensive data manipulation and re-presentation of data which are difficult or complex and also slow and error prone. However, the main feature or advantage of clerical processing is that it is adaptive, people adapt to new situations in an ad-hoc fashion or can think out new procedures for new situations. This gives an inherent strength to the whole process but can suffer if ad-hoc procedures are badly thought out. A further advantage of clerical systems is that, in general, a record will exist, in hard copy form, of all events that have occurred in the system. This is vital for error or omission tracing etc.

In systems, events occur of which details need to be captured and processed to provide information for management to take action. Events in general will occur at random intervals in the outside world and similarly internally, but can be triggered or originated by other stimuli such as time of week (payroll), condition satisfaction (stock below re-order level) etc. Many events result from pre-planned activities such as a production schedule, end of month accounts processing etc. In all cases the events need to undergo the activity of **transaction processing** which basically should:

- ❐ validate the transaction, i.e. check it;
- ❐ post its effect to relevant files;
- ❐ log the transaction, i.e. record it for future reference/error tracking/audit.

In this element the various methods of processing and types of data handling systems will be reviewed. Two data handling systems need to be compared in terms of their objectives, methods of data capture and data handling processes employed so that the necessary requirements of the element can be satisfied.

3.2.1 Methods of Processing

We can either process events as they arise or if this is not possible use an alternative approach. The main processing methods used are:

- ❐ batch processing;
- ❐ on line real time processing.

Batch

Historically, all processing in early computers was carried out in batch mode. This involved collecting information on events that have occurred, normally by means of documents and then making up batches of documents to be input to the computer system. A schedule is usually created to process the batch in one complete session. The batches are subjected to clerical pre-processing involving the derivation of control totals in order to satisfy audit and reconciliation requirements.

Data entry normally takes place at the central collecting and data preparation facility. Disadvantages are that processing is time-removed from the originator of the information and this time gap can mean that error correction – by someone other than the originator – can take time and prove difficult. Indeed the user has very little interaction with the process. Batch processing, today, forms a relatively small percentage of the transaction processing scene.

Transaction

A transaction is the name given to an event that occurs in a system, e.g. a piece of work is completed; we need to enter such details into the system. Transactions are processed immediately they are entered into the system in on-line real time processing. The point of entry may be close to the event location, e.g. a data capture point on the shop floor of a factory or is at the point of receipt of documentation or phone call etc. relating to the transaction. The processing will include full validation of the transaction data, e.g. code values, identity certification via on line master files or data base. Any errors are signalled on the VDU screen and the entry operator can make the necessary changes to correct the entry. When satisfied, the operator can allow the transaction to be accepted and processing finished. This method of data entry requires the processing system to be available, via telecommunications, at all data entry points. All files etc. in the system must also be available for use in checking and updating. Once the transaction is accepted and processed, the system is in the updated state immediately. This type of system is required for situations where tight control is necessary and where the system events are high volume and dynamic in nature.

- ❐ production control;
- ❐ holiday bookings;
- ❐ airline seat reservations.

Again, in such systems, transaction logging is a necessary feature for purposes of reconciliation and to enable system recovery and reconstruction in the event of system failure due to error, accident or natural disaster. On the PC scene, real time processing is the norm but much of the software used does not have inbuilt audit facilities.

Single user on-line

The machine is totally dedicated to the requirements of the single user and all facilities attached to the configuration – printer, disks etc. are similarly dedicated. System response time will reflect the nature of the software used and the inherent speed of the processor, disks etc. The processing volume will be low and much of the power of the machine will be idle, waiting on the wishes of the user. At the PC level this is not considered a significant waste.

Multi-user on-line

This is the most common method on larger computer based systems, typically mainframes and networked PCs. Its use introduces several further problems which are not encountered in the single-user case. The general scenario is that many users share the resources of the mainframe or network including:

❐ the files and data storage available;

❐ the printing facilities.

Element 4.3 contains further details of the networked benefits.

Centralised system

In a mainframe system the normal configuration is a central system (based around a CPU) with users connected via dumb terminals. The central part of the system provides the processing power and supplies services to all users. Such services includes file handling services (via a file server or central storage) and print services. In this system all data flows into the centre for processing.

Distributed processing

This is a variation of a multi-user system where the user connections are typically PCs and workstations with local intelligence and processing power, rather than dumb terminals attached to a mainframe CPU. The same processing considerations apply with respect to conflict and queues. Each computer system adds to the overall processing capability of the system. Hence a job may be executed by several processors simultaneously, wherever there is spare capacity and parallel processing activities have been identified.

Processing overload does not occur since each PC has its own processing power. Some PCs may be slower than others or the software version used may be less efficient in time. The solution is to standardise software to the same version (held centrally on the file server), and where necessary to increase local processing power as required. Extra PCs may be added to the network to increase processing capacity.

As an example one machine could have details of e-mail addresses whilst another is constructing material for distribution over the network.

3.2.2 Types of data handling systems

Bookings

This kind of system offers customers the ability to go into a local outlet and make enquiries on the range of holidays on offer, the availability of holidays, special deals etc. They can then confirm a booking, pay the deposit and conclude the preliminaries all in one visit. The system requires that there exists only one copy of the availability for each holiday offered by a tour operator. Where more than one tour operator is franchised then the system must link to each operators' master files of holiday availability as required. The system is multi-user on line and has all the problems previously outlined. Typically, a booking system is as used for holiday bookings or reservations by a travel agent. The scenario is:

	Customer	Travel Agent	Tour Operator
↓	Arrives	Sign-on Screen & Selection Menu	
	Queries general availability/price of holiday	Select operators in turn as required	Holiday files availability
TIME	Reserve holiday Pay deposit	Reservation entry confirm booking Holiday costed Print confirmation slip	Holiday reserved on tour operators holiday file
↓	Receive confirmation slip		
	Receive final invoice		
	Make payment	Record payment	Finalise details
			Print tickets
↓		Receive tickets Inform customer	
	Receive tickets		Tour Reps Schedule sent to Resort

Figure 3.14 Typical Booking System

Task 3.6   PC 1

Visit a travel agent to observe and record their procedure.

Payroll

A typical chronology of main events for payroll will be as follows:

Daily   Receive employee amendments and post to the employee file, e.g. tax code changes, marital status, allowances, deductions, change of address, rate of pay, grade, etc. Verify changes made

Weekly   Receive and process time-sheets
File audit trail, generate controls
Calculate pre-payroll
Print exceptions list
Action exceptions
Calculate Payroll
Print Payslips
Print cheques
Prepare GIRO CREDIT TAPE/DISK
Print Coin analysis for cash payments
Print Allowances/deductions control list

Monthly	Enter sickness records
	Prepare pre-payroll with exceptions
	Action exceptions
	Print salary advices
	Prepare GIRO CREDIT tape/disk
	Print other reports
Yearly	Print P9/60 pay/tax records
(at year end)	Re-set employee record totals for new year
i.e. 5th April	Remove last year's 'leavers' records, i.e. employees who left during the year
	Print tax reconciliation list for year Prepare tax reconciliation tape for Inland Revenue
When National budget is activated	Change tax tables for new budget rates

Task 3.7   PC 1 & 2

Investigate some of the above activities to find out what data is used, what procedures are required, what controls and reconciliation is carried out. Contact a local firm, local authority or examine a comprehensive payroll package to see the options, features and functions provided.

Ordering and Invoicing

Here, a simplistic view is taken of a typical ordering system for sales where a firm supplies its customers with items that it holds in its warehouse. Customer orders are received by telephone, fax, etc. and entered onto an internal customer order form, item codes are added and the order entered into the computer system. The outline of events is then as follows:

	Event	Document	Dept.
	Customer places order	Customer Order Fax.........	Sales
	Check order for completeness and accuracy		
	Enter onto computer		
	Prepare internal order form	Internal Order	
	Send to warehouse		
	Prepare pick list	Pick List	Warehouse
	Pick the items for order	Annotated Pick List	
	Report Picking		
	Pack the order	*Consignment note (delivery note)	Despatch
TIME			
	Deliver the order	Consignment schedule	
	Receive proof-of-delivery	*POD note	Accounts
		Credit note	
	Invoice the customer	Invoice	
	Post the invoice to customer account in Sales Ledger	Sales Ledger posting print-out	
	Send statement to customer	Statement	
	Receive payment from customer	Cheque and statement	
	Allocate payment to customer account in Sales Ledger	Payment Posting print-outs	
	Clear closed items from Sales Ledger		
	Produce debtor analysis of Sales Ledger	Aged Debt Analysis	

Figure 3.15 Life Cycle of a Customer Order

Stock control

The warehouse will require periodic re-organising to facilitate picking according to item popularity thereby saving time, this often occurs on the 80/20 rule, i.e. 80% of transactions occur for only 20% of the range of items stocked. Full usage statistics of items must be maintained by the system to facilitate warehouse organisation and more importantly, being used to re-calculate stock maximum, minimum and re-order levels as well as re-order quantities. Inventory control is a complex activity and you might like to consider such requirements as:

❑ multi-warehousing;

❑ locating a stock item in more than one location;

❑ stock rotation – First in First out (FIFO) etc.

Personnel records

This is the people function of the firm and is, perhaps, the most variable. Group and individual considerations apply, e.g.

- ❏ trade union considerations;
- ❏ professional groups;
- ❏ individual staff records;
- ❏ needs of the various business functions.

Individual staff records need to be kept and maintained covering:

- ❏ personal details;
- ❏ education and courses;
- ❏ skills;
- ❏ experience;
- ❏ assessments;
- ❏ remuneration and contract details;
- ❏ medical details;
- ❏ accidents;
- ❏ statutory and legal.

The value of the above type of record in large firms is in the management of the personnel function, for example fitting the right people to the right jobs, fulfilling short term urgent needs due to illness, investigations etc. Recurring, documentary, internal historical classification. The purpose of the personnel system is to service the other major systems of marketing, production and finance. A systems approach to manpower management will integrate the personnel system with those areas of the business that will benefit most, for example planned training in conjunction with operational departments.

A very comprehensive record can be built up. In addition details may be kept of outside training agencies, courses offered etc. Multimedia training courses are becoming a feature of staff education programs as the technology becomes more readily available.

3.2.3 Objectives

Speed

The significant benefit in implementing a data handling system which is based on complete systems is the speed, accuracy and reliability issues. Once the system has been fully implemented and tested, the time to perform calculations and update records is a fraction of manual systems. We covered examples in Element 1.1 and noted that some systems could not function without a computerised system, e.g. banking.

Accuracy

Errors can arise at many points in computer based processing but mainly so at the data input stage. If allowed to go uncorrected, input errors will cost progressively more to correct the longer they remain undetected. In clerical systems, errors are treated on an ad-hoc basis as they are found, but for computer based processing we actively plan to detect and correct errors as soon as possible so as to minimise error and future cost. The major method of data input today is in real time mode, where conversational dialogue can take place between the system and the data entry operator (user). It is very worthwhile expending considerable effort on the system design to check input data for accuracy etc. In general the types of check that can be carried out are as follows:

- ❏ field size/length;
- ❏ format, e.g. numeric;
- ❏ sign of numeric field;
- ❏ value – is zero possible;
- ❏ presence or absence of field – mandatory?;
- ❏ justification of fields – i.e. left or right;
- ❏ validity of codes entered ;
- ❏ reasonableness checks;
- ❏ further checks.

Cost

Organisations are always striving to keep their operating costs under control. In many organisations it is the staff costs that are a significant part of the operating costs. By providing effective information system and data handling capabilities staff can be more effective in their role.

Other cost savings come from reduced storage space, since digitally held information requires significantly less space than paper copies of the same data.

Support Decision Making

We have already seen that systems can help us focus on solutions to problems. Figure 3.12 is indicative of the way in which information systems can be used to narrow the choice and help select options. They are able to model solutions and control systems as outlined in Element 1.2.

3.2.4 Methods of data capture

The methods used to capture data on events that occur have been fuelled by the increasing need for information, the need for accurate and fast processing and also the economics of the whole operation. To this end the data capture market has witnessed the pursuance of various technologies with the general aim of automating data capture as far as possible, removing or reducing the occurrence of error and providing the necessary resultant information at a competitive cost. The general trend has been to cut out manual operations wherever possible and replace them with alternative methods which are cheap, error free (or relatively so) and fast. Such systems generally require high initial investment to set up the information infrastructure to support the capture system. The general benefits are the reduced reliance on manual input, less errors, faster input and a tendency towards volume independence in the general costing of operations. For example this trend may be illustrated by the adoption of bar codes and laser reading technology by the retail (supermarket) trade. The start point is a hand-written bill and clerical (machine assisted) totalling, then in chronological order:

- ❏ operator entry and non-itemised priced bill;
- ❏ operator entry part itemised priced bill;
- ❏ operator controlled laser scanned fully itemised priced bill;
- ❏ user controlled scanned shopping trolley;
- ❏ where next? – 'cable' shopping at home?

What we see overall is an increase in the automated components of the capture and a very much reduced manual contribution. Note that totally automated systems will only gather what they are designed to gather and for real intelligence the **human** factor is of **overriding** importance.

Keyboard

With the proliferation of the PC we have seen the continued expansion of data entry via keyboards at the origin or point of receipt of event data. Such entry is not normally in stand-alone mode but connected, via networks, to a centralised or distributed file facility. For low-volume entry, the keyboard skill of the user is relatively unimportant but as volume of transactions rise the need for true keyboard skills emerges. Some people spending their working day in front of VDUs and data input via keyboards is now protected by law on various aspects and conditions of the job. **Repetitive strain injury** (RSI) and **VDU safety/operating recommendations** are just some of the considerations to be borne in mind. The overall observations to be made on keyboard entry of data are that:

- ❑ it is the most popular mode of entry;
- ❑ many operators are keyboard unskilled;
- ❑ manual operations are error prone and costly;
- ❑ physical injury can result from lack of or poor training (RSI).

Mouse

Although not directly associated with data entry, a mouse can be used to control a system. The point and click activity which replaces the requirement to enter commands at the keyboard is popular. This is particularly true for those users who are not regular system users and find the Graphical User Interface and a mouse more intuitive than issuing commands.

Keypad

This is a reduced keyboard in its functionality. Perhaps its most frequent use is to enter limited types of data at the point where the data is created, e.g. a factory floor directly on a numerically controlled machine or a hand-held electricity meter readers' unit.

Bar Code Reader

This method uses a combination of thick and thin lines interspersed with spaces to make up a coded representation of data. The bar codes are produced by bar code printers when required. The most common occurrence of such codes is on foodstuffs and other goods in the retail market sector. These codes are an integral part of the packaging of or the item itself (newspapers, magazines). In Europe articles are identified using the European Article Number which is an unique code formatted according to a standard laid down by the European Article Numbering Association. For private, internal use in an organisation, code design is at the discretion of the user, though many firms will choose to stay with standard codes where they exist.

Application areas are in supermarkets etc., i.e. the retail trade, libraries, shop floor reporting for manufacturing operations etc. The article can be identified by its bar code and also bar codes can be set up as standard transaction identifiers, e.g. issue of a book, return of a book, transfer of location etc. The operators use a wand reader to swipe across the transaction identifier and then the item identifier in order to capture event data. The readers are either of the wand type or are fixed as found in supermarket check-outs. The read error rate is extremely low and for the right applications bar codes are an extremely effective means of data capture.

Optical Mark Recognition

This method has been around for a long time but has never succeeded in achieving a high market penetration. Its major use has been in the areas of multiple-choice examination answer scripts and gas or electricity meter reading. The method requires the input document to be designed such that marks appearing in designated portions adopt a pre-assigned value when such forms are clerically entered. The resulting, completed document is read by the mark reader which scans the document and where marks are sensed, they are given the pre-assigned value. The method is limited in its application, is error prone and has generally been replaced by other technology.

Optical Character Recognition (OCR)

This again is not a new technology, but with the development of more powerful, cheaper electronics the method has become more widely used as the price of the system has fallen. Essentially the method relies on scanning text presented to the reader in document form and building up a pixel image of a character which is then compared to a stored set or sets of characters. In this way, characters can be interpreted and stored internally in the computer. It represents a reasonably cheap and fast way of getting data into computers but some problems may arise with errors on poor quality input documents. The user needs to be careful in adapting the technology to applications where accuracy needs are high.

Note, do not confuse this method with the technology of document image processing (DIP) which does **not** interpret documents but merely stores digitised images available for later recall.

Magnetic Character Reader (MICR)

The earliest attempt at automating data entry, this technology has remained firmly in a single application camp – that of banking. We are all familiar with the E13B font of stylised numbers at the bottom of our cheques. These characters are printed in an ink which has ferrous traces in it capable of being magnetised when put into an MICR reader (Magnetic Ink Character Recognition). The reader then 'recognises' the magnetic field associated with each character and converts it into the internal character code. The clearing banks would seem to be still using this technology for some time to come.

Voice

In 1994 IBM announced its Personal Dictation system, now called voice type dictation, which is able to accept vocal input and convert to text, which is then displayed on a VDU screen as for a word processor. The system operates in the following way:

❑ Upon receipt of the software, the **designated user** must spend about one hour customising the recognition function of the software to adjust to the personal intonation and pronunciation of the user. Subsequent to this, the package will statistically adjust its interpretation as both user and package 'learn' from one another;

❑ The user learns to speak discretely, i.e. with a slight pause between words, but this is not considered to be a handicap by users. The normal rated dictation speed is 70-100 words per minute.

To differentiate between like-sounding words the system builds up usage statistics and also uses the context of the sentence to interpret between e.g. to, too, two etc. Some of the uses of the system are:

☐ The system could have application to common and control situations where vocal input could cause the computer system to perform required actions;

☐ Doctors use it to dictate patients records, send letters etc;

☐ Lawyers use it to draft agreements, contracts. Because no keyboard skill is required it is well received, there is an increase in productivity and less time revising documents;

☐ Banks see a potential for great improvement, pre-defined paragraphs, letters to customers etc. Less secretarial support needed.

Touch-tone Telephone

The current range of telephones work on different tones for each key. Data entry can, therefore, be achieved using the limited range of keys on a standard touch-tone telephone.

Question 3.8

What benefits may voice input have for users with special needs?

Task 3.8   PC 3   *C3.2*

Investigate and report on the data capture method used for two systems with which you are familiar, e.g. library, supermarket checkouts, stock control.

Task 3.9   PC 5

How well do those two systems work and provide support for the systems in which they are working? Can you think of any ways in which improvements could be made?

3.2.5 Data Handling Processes

Data in computers is held as attributes of entities in formatted groups called records. The set of similar records containing individual attribute values for the whole set of entities is termed a file. Files are held in computer systems in two main ways – magnetic disk or magnetic tape, in addition archive files (read only) may be held, e.g. on EPROM disk. A database is a set of related files. Data is represented internally in computers by an eight-bit binary code, or two hexadecimal characters, giving 256 different combinations. These may be ranked in absolute value from 0000 0000 to 1111 1111, giving an ordered ranking of code (character) values called the collating sequence.

This ranking can be applied to any alpha-numeric string (data field) occurring in each record of a file, so that we can sequence records in a file. The main point to note is that we can sort, i.e. order or sequence all the records of a file into any sequence (ascending or descending) on a number of data fields, provided that the fields exist (or field space is reserved for them) in every record. The ability of the computer system to manipulate or sort data into different sequences is probably its major benefit for business use.

Calculating

For arithmetic calculation, the data must be held in true binary form and have a sign element attached. The CPU will perform arithmetic on **any** character string, so it is essential that programmers ensure only properly formatted arithmetic data is input to calculations. In most programming languages (assembler excepted) this is normally taken care of by the facilities embedded. In business processing, the typical calculations carried out are of the form:

$$A * (B + C)$$
$$A = \frac{B}{C}$$
$$A = B + C + D \dots$$
$$A = C - D \text{ etc.}$$

i.e. generally simplistic in nature.

Generally the programmer should always ensure that the result fields are large enough to hold the answers. Arithmetic overflow occurs on fields too small to hold results and can lead to processing errors if not adequately dealt with.

Sorting

The fields used in a sort are classed hierarchically from **major** to **minor**. The major control field has **most control** over the ultimate sequence obtained and the minor field has the **least control**. There may be any number of intermediate control fields, e.g. a file of sales records has the following data fields:

- ❏ Invoice number;
- ❏ Customer number;
- ❏ Agent number;
- ❏ Product number (item number);
- ❏ Quantity sold;
- ❏ Price each;
- ❏ Order date;
- ❏ Invoice date, etc.

The file is held in invoice number sequence. Suppose we want to know the total sales for each agent printed out as a report where there are sub-totals for each customer the agent deals with, i.e.

agent number	customer A	invoice	123
			456
			789
		Total	____
	customer B	invoice	366
			522
		Total	____
next agent number	customer G	invoice	911

151

The file would need to be sorted as follows in order to produce the correct sequence for the report:

Major field	Intermediate	Minor field
Agent Number/	Customer Number/	Invoice Number

N.B. The major field changes value **least frequently** in the sorted file, the minor field changes the **most frequently**.

The sorting methods fall into two categories:

❑ internal sorting of files held totally within CPU storage using exchange, bubble and shell techniques;

❑ sorting large files held externally on disk or tape using tag sorting or balanced merge sort.

Searching

Frequently it is required to examine data in files or indexes in order to extract some further required data for a particular entity, e.g. the disk address of a file record where the key is known. The tables to be searched are held internally in the CPU and will consist of two portions, a **search argument** and a **value**, e.g. record key and disk record address. Locating the one value enables extraction of the other. The table will consist of a series of consecutive entries which may be in random (unsequenced) order of search argument or may be collated on search argument (ascending or descending).

Search techniques will depend on the sequence of the table:

Linear search – for random sequence only a linear, entry by entry search is possible. The table is read until the required argument is located. On average this means half the table entries need to be read for every retrieval. This then can be a slow search method.

Where the table is sequenced, then we may still use the linear search above, but instead we can now use the embedded sequence of the entries to improve search time by using alternative strategies. Two cases arise:

❑ the input search arguments are sequenced;

❑ a random sequence.

For the first case we can progressively move forward on the table entries as each input search requirement is processed, i.e. there is no need to look at **earlier** table entries. This reduces the search time.

Binary search – for the second case we can use the **binary search** method whereby, knowing how many entries are in the table, our first look is **halfway** along the table. The result of this look is either our search argument is higher or lower than this midpoint value. We can now concentrate on only the portion of the table in which the sought entry is located. We look at the record halfway between the mid-point and table-end and depending on the result continue the search until equality is found.

Selecting

This procedure occurs when it is required to extract records from a set which satisfy certain criteria for selection, e.g. all customers who have placed orders for Product X in excess of £1000 value this year. In selection situations there is normally always a multiple response although generally we can have none, one or many records satisfying the criteria. The need for record selection can arise in two ways:

❐ an immediate, unforeseen need;

❐ a perceived or known need.

Unforeseen needs can only be serviced by a search of all records of the file, extracting the details of every record satisfying the criteria.

Foreseen needs could be serviced similarly but it is much more beneficial and often necessary that the response to such requests be immediate, i.e. in real time. In such situations linear searching is inappropriate and in order to satisfy such requests the file data must be indexed or referenced in such a way as to service the query quickly. This is termed **inverting** the file and is a basic feature of databases, e.g. a customer file is sequenced on customer number but management frequently wish to know what customers are located in certain regions of the country for delivery purposes. In this case a secondary index to the file could be set up having **customer number** and **region code** as its entries. The table would be maintained in **region code** sequence and of course could have many entries for each region code. The retrieval procedure would then involve locating the first occurrence of the region required in the table and then reading all successive entries until region code changes. This allows an almost immediate answer to the request. Unit 7 covers appropriate techniques in more detail.

Merging

When two or more files of information need to be assembled to form one file, the process is called merging. Generally the process of merging takes one of two forms:

❐ simple merging or append-at-end;

❐ the classical merge to produce an assembled, sequenced output file.

The simple merge may best be illustrated where event transaction files from different days need to be assembled into one file for archiving purposes. We start with day 1 transaction file and **append** at its end-of-file the transactions for day 2 (deleting the end of file in the process). Proceeding serially day-by-day, successive transaction files are appended at the **end** of the consolidated file. The resultant, completed file contains all the required transactions day-by-day. Contrast this merge with one where again all transactions need to be consolidated to one file. However this time it is required that during the period concerned all transactions relating to a particular entity be collated time-wise so that, if printed out, they would give a day-by-day, hour-by-hour etc. record of all transactions concerning that entity. This is a somewhat different problem, we can no longer append-at-end since this separates the entity data. Also entity data occurs at random during each day so even within a day the sequence is inappropriate to our needs. In this case we need to proceed by sorting each **day's** transactions to **entity/time** sequence.

We then merge day two with day one to give an output file sequenced as **entity/day/time**. Carrying on in this fashion we produce a final tape which is in **entity/day/time** sequence for the events that have occurred in the period covered. Note; we no longer append at end but in each merge we start off with the brought forward merged tape to day N. By processing the next day's transactions, i.e. (N + 1) against this tape we **slot in** or **merge** the relevant transactions for day N + 1 after the set of transactions for each entity up to day N. This means, after every merge, we produce a new, incrementally consolidated merged tape. This process will be far slower than the append-at-end but produces a result far more **useable** with respect to possible demands for information.

Use information technology for a data handling activity

Introduction

This element requires the practical activity of providing reports from a database. These reports should demonstrate the following activities have been completed:

- ❏ file maintenance;
- ❏ range of data handling processes;
- ❏ used accuracy and security checks.

The work may be coupled with work from Unit 7, in particular Elements 7.2 and 7.3 may be used to contribute to your portfolio of evidence for this element.

3.3.1 File maintenance

A file is a set of records having data fields whose values we need to use in controlling the system.

File maintenance consists of the following major activities:

- ❏ creation and entry of new records;
- ❏ amendment of details of existing records;
- ❏ extraction of details to be used elsewhere in further processing;
- ❏ removal of records which are no longer required, i.e. deletion.

The data entry to create or add new records could be manual activity. Increasingly attention is being given to automating this aspect of work. This would reduce the possibility of errors being introduced to the data entry stage and improve overall efficiency.

3.3.2 Data handling processes

The normal processing activities apply here. Typically they include:

- ❏ calculating (numerical fields, totals);
- ❏ converting (numbers, characters);
- ❏ sorting (one field, multiple fields);
- ❏ searching (=, <, >, AND, OR);
- ❏ selecting;
- ❏ merging;
- ❏ grouping.

Elements 6.2 and 3.2 have covered the issues. The detail of implementation will depend on the database you are using.

3.3.3 Database Reports

Unit 7 has a major section on database reports and may be read now. Reports may fall into one of several main categories:

❒ operational;

❒ summary;

❒ data grouping;

❒ exception.

Task 3.10 PC 2

Investigate what each of these report types should contain and write brief notes on their typical contents.

3.3.4 Accuracy Checks

Validation

This is the term applied to the checking of data input to the computer for accuracy, reasonableness and format as far as can be ascertained at the time of entry. The lengths to which one will go depends very much on the system application concerned and the **criticality** of the data being entered to the ultimate system performance, e.g.

❒ Rate of pay is very important to payroll;

❒ Employee grade is less so.

Check digits are often used to provide validation or a range check on the data to ensure it is within the expected range. Other checks ensure length and content are right.

Verification

This is normally a check made on the accuracy of data entry undertaken by the operator. This can involve either a read back of the data entered as a visual check or a double data entry to compare the two versions. Errors detected are then put right.

3.3.5 Security Checks

Confidentiality

Both passwords and non-disclosure fit this category and are covered in Unit 4, Elements 3 and 4. Passwords are sometimes ineffective because they are:

❒ simplistic passwords – FRED, JOE, USER1 etc;

❒ dates of birth or house number;

❒ pets name.

Each of these are things a serious hacker would not find difficult to determine. Quite often one sees lists of passwords pasted to VDUs, noticeboards etc., completely negating the level of security attempted. The general rule is to use non-simplistic but easily individually memorised passwords to provide a reasonable first hurdle to prevent entry, say six to ten characters in length. In addition, do not leave passwords lying around for others to see, log out if leaving a machine unattended, use physical keyboard locks etc. Each of these increases nuisance value as far as users are concerned, but security improvement is achieved. To go one stage further, a master matrix may be set up in the system which specifies exactly what files a user may access and in what mode (update, read only) and this may be further defined down to specific field rights in the files concerned. Encryption of sensitive data is another possibility, though this does carry an additional overhead for processing. The level of security obtained from a system is a function of:

❐ the security planning built into the original system design;

❐ the perceived satisfactory level for operation;

❐ the ability to pay for and monitor the security features installed.

For most users a reasonable balance between the level of security obtained with regard to its cost will be the norm. The determined hacker or criminal will always find ways to circumvent all but the most secure systems.

Regular File Saving and Back-up

Element 2.1 in Unit 2 fully covers these issues.

Theft

PCs, lap-tops etc. suffer from the disadvantage of being readily portable and also readily saleable. The wave of 'steal-to-order' crimes currently sweeping areas of the country is evidence of this. The aspects of such loss are the hardware loss, the software loss, and the data and information loss. Keeping a note (audit register) of all machines on site, all software licences etc. at least gives a basis for recovery should theft occur. In addition basic physical measures can deter the opportunist theft. In more critical situations much more attention, planning and money will need to be devoted to the physical security aspects.

At a minimum level, PCs should be physically secured to walls, desks, floors etc. allowing certain movement and adjustment but preventing removal without the necessary keys etc. All software should be recorded for audit purposes and for version control of the software implemented. The organisation is responsible for ensuring that all software used is legal, software piracy is ever increasing on a world-wide scale. In Britain, the Federation against Software Theft is policing the use of software in business and commerce and has powers to audit an organisations' use of software and if unlicensed (illegal) they can fine the offenders. In recent European surveys Britain tends to be one of the lesser perpetrators of software piracy.

Copyright and Access Rights

Element 2.1 fully covers the issues raised here. Unit 4 additionally covers the issues of access rights to files over a LAN.

3.3.6 Evaluate Effectiveness in Terms of Reliability

Unit 2 has already covered the issues of reliability, speed, cost, benefit and volume. When an information system is originally specified these issues of performance and effectiveness should be quantified. Once implemented, the system can be measured to evaluate its performance against the original specification.

In the following set of tasks a small system is created. Once you have completed the tasks you should be able to determine the effectiveness of your implementations and whether any change to the structure would have improved the overall performance.

Task 3.11 PC 1

Investigate the information normally held in a database implementation of a library loan system. Typically this will include:

❑ *user name;*
❑ *ISBN of book(s) on loan;*
❑ *date of return of book(s);*
❑ *loan entitlement (how many books the user may borrow);*
❑ *current overdue debt (if any);*
❑ *book reservation requests.*

Create a database, with these fields for 100 users. Assume each user has an initial loan entitlement of two books at a time.

Task 3.12 PC 1 & PC 2

Five of the users are now identified as staff and are entitled to borrow five books simultaneously. Change the entry in your database for the users identified as staff. Produce a report identifying the change made.

Task 3.13 PC 1 & PC 2

Five students withdraw from the course. Delete their entry from the database. Produce a report identifying the change made.

Task 3.14 PC 1 & PC 2

Update the database to append three new users to the system. Assume they are all students. Produce a report to identify the change made.
Assume that each day a book is returned late, a fine of five pence is imposed. No books may be taken out on loan if the user is already a debtor.

Task 3.15 PC 1 & PC 2 $\qquad$ N3.2

Enter operational data to the system to show multiple loans. Include an attempt to:

❑ *take out a book when entitlement is already taken;*
❑ *the user is a debtor.*

Provide a report to identify this activity.

Task 3.16 PC 2   N3.1, N3.3

Assume that each day a book is overdue a five pence fine is imposed. At the end of each day, calculate the new debt(s) by user(s). Print out an exception report of debtors' names.

Task 3.17 PC 2   N3.1

Sort the database on who has the most overdue books. Report, on this order of tardiness, for those users now overdue.

Task 3.18 PC 2   N3.3

Calculate the total debt now due to the library as a sum of all the fines. Produce a report of this amount.

Task 3.19 PC 2

Produce a report indicating the ISBNs of books on loan to staff.

Task 3.20 PC 2

Search the database for any staff members who have made a book reservation request. Produce a report on the outcome of the search.

Investigate the safety and security requirements of data handling activities

Introduction

In this element some of the information needed to prepare for a presentation covering the following topics will be given:

- ❏ protection of data held on individuals and organisation;
- ❏ health and safety issues for system users;
- ❏ obligations of system users;
- ❏ security checks.

3.4.1 Reasons for the Protection of Data

Data is an important asset to any organisation or a private issue to individuals. However, data is exposed to many threats and it is generally recognised that data needs protecting. The range of threats includes:

- ❏ computer crime and computer security;
- ❏ software theft and intellectual property rights;
- ❏ hacking, virus and worm invasion;
- ❏ computer unreliability and software quality;
- ❏ storage access – authorisation and privacy of data;
- ❏ social implications of AI and expert systems;
- ❏ problems arising from workplace computerisation and business process re-engineering (BPR).

Question 3.9

Has the common use of PCs, which hold corporate data, increased or decreased the problem of data protection?

Confidentiality

We must recognise the requirement to monitor privacy of information that arises from business relationships. It would be improper if information gathered from one client was passed to another client (who was a direct competitor of the first). Equally important is personal data that may have been acquired. The Data Protection Act gives individuals rights to access data held about them on computer systems.

Legal

The data held on individuals is also subject to legal requirements on how it is kept and how it is used. It may only be kept for specific purposes and generally requires the individuals agreement. Certainly the data held must be registered to comply with the legislation. Access to the information can only be made by authorised personnel and the subject has the right of access. The code of behaviour is subject to both EU and UK data protection legislation.

Moral

Society has become increasingly dependent on computer based systems. This puts an added responsibility on the system designers and operators to provide a secure environment, since we are all increasingly vulnerable to the consequences of breaches of confidentiality or system failure.

Apart from the above concerns, a more serious social concern is the possibility of **misuse** of information held on individuals with regard to its **privacy, security and confidentiality**, e.g:

- ❏ 'Data mining' is the trawling of different databases seeking relationships or correlation to uncover further facts about groups or individuals, e.g. multiple share applications.
- ❏ Cross correlation of separate databases particularly by government.
- ❏ The inspection of an individual's electronic post box by others (particularly management and employers).
- ❏ The legal status of electronic messages with respect to attribution, i.e. issues concerning the identity, authenticity and status of such communications. (Current law favours clerical authorisation or attribution).
- ❏ The effects of poorly designed, written or maintained systems on the users who operate them.
- ❏ Criminal use of information for blackmail, extortion etc. against individuals or companies.
- ❏ Copyright protection of software for developers, 'look and feel' litigation, piracy etc. Often viewed by perpetrators as a normal act and not seen as theft.
- ❏ Hacking and virus invasion can be benign, but where it is damaging or criminal in intent, what recourse or recompense can be gained by those affected?
- ❏ What demands and requirements be placed upon computer system designers to ensure (to a defined standard) the privacy, access authorisation and integrity of the data in the system, whether it concerns individuals or companies – personal or corporate?
- ❏ Desk top computing has distributed data in organisations and generally the quality of security and integrity has suffered.

3.4.2 Data held on Individuals

The data held on individuals must relate to the specific purpose for which it was collected. It must be relevant to that purpose and must be accurate. Examples of different categories of individuals on whom information may be collected are:

- ❏ criminal;
- ❏ educational;
- ❏ employment;
- ❏ financial;

❑ medical;

❑ social.

Question 3.10

Give examples of the type of financial information that may be held on an individual?

Question 3.11

Give examples of the type of educational information that may be held on an individual?

3.4.3 Data held on Organisations

Commercial

In most commercial organisation, their data is probably their most valuable asset. Hence the safety and security of this asset is paramount to the well-being of their future. The range of data held by a commercial organisation will include products, customers and suppliers. In many organisations exchange of information may only be via EDI and hence the whole of the information will be held in databases. The detail of each of these categories has been covered in Element 3.1.

Financial and Legal

Not only will financial details of an organisation be held by themselves, but many others will have an interest in the detail. Included in these interested parties will be the Inland Revenue, the suppliers, the shareholders, the bankers, the auditors etc. Each will have their sub-set of information that will be of interest to them. To meet legal obligations details of profit cannot be made public except at staged points throughout the year. Other confidential information includes payment to most employees (except to the tax authorities).

Question 3.12

What financial information about an organisation will be of interest to their suppliers of raw materials?

Companies have to make a number of statutory returns to government agencies such as Companies House, Central Statistics Office etc. Each of these will hold legal data on organisations. Other examples are charities making annual returns to the Charity Commissioners.

3.4.4 Authorisation Access to Data

Computer systems hold data which covers a wide spectrum of applications:

- ☐ public data which is available to anyone requiring it;
- ☐ corporate data;
- ☐ personal data.

The above classifications impose or require different procedures for the access and use of the data.

3.4.5 Health and Safety

Some very important considerations for employers and employees are the provision of a safe working environment and employees accepting responsibility for carrying out tasks in a safe manner that will not endanger others. The legislation concerning health and safety at work has grown over a long period of time and currently the Health & Safety at Work Act of 1974 attempted to provide a coherent framework for governing the actions of employers and employees. From time to time REGULATIONS (which are legally binding) can be introduced by government ministers, normally the Secretary of State for Employment. Regulations can be supplemented by CODES of PRACTICE which are not Statutory regulations.

Generally **employers** are required to:

- ☐ assess risks to the health and safety of their employees and others who may be affected and record the significant findings of the risk assessment;
- ☐ make arrangements to implement the health and safety measures as identified by the risk assessment;
- ☐ cover the issues of planning, organisation, control and review, also the measures to be implemented;
- ☐ set up emergency procedure provisions;
- ☐ provide employees with clear instructions as well as training where necessary.

The general issues of health and safety have been introduced earlier. In particular current issues of concern are:

- ☐ eye strain;
- ☐ radiation from VDU screens;
- ☐ stress;
- ☐ ergonomics (including environment, repetitive strain & physical stress);
- ☐ hazards (electrical, fire, obstruction).

Task 3.21 PC 2

Investigate and report on the range of health and safety issues listed above in Element 3.4.5 as it applies to your own place of study.

Electronic Equipment

The Display Screen Equipment (VDU) Directive covers the installation and operation of VDUs. The regulations cover the observance of minimum standards, e.g. screen design, keyboard, desk, chair, lighting, positioning etc., as well as other environmental factors. Workers may be entitled to have eye and eyesight tests before starting screen display work and at regular intervals afterwards and, if necessary, an opthamological examination and special spectacles.

General safety considerations:

❏ do not leave rubbish lying around;

❏ any lifting should be carried out properly, i.e. straight back, knees bent method;

❏ ensure cables etc. are not causing hazards, e.g. tripping people up;

❏ don't overload power outlets;

❏ ensure fire precautions are in force;

❏ ensure emergency procedures are in existence and all are aware of them;

❏ ensure that a member of staff is responsible for first-aid and has received appropriate training.

The main advice is that people should work and act sensibly and safely without endangering themselves or others.

3.4.6 Obligations of System Users

The issues addressed here are essentially the same as those presented in Elements 2.1 and 4.3 plus Unit 7. The major topics which should be reviewed by considering the appropriate text in these sections are:

❏ confidentiality of data;

❏ accuracy;

❏ right of individual to disclosure;

❏ copyright (data and software);

❏ responsible attitudes.

Task 3.22 PC 3

Investigate and report on four responsibilities you have as a system user at your centre of study. The responsibilities must be selected from the headings listed above in Element 3.4.6.

3.4.7 System Security Methods

The issues addressed here are essentially the same as those presented in Elements 2.1 and 4.3 plus Unit 7. The major topics which should be reviewed by considering the appropriate text in those sections are:

❏ control of access;

❏ forced recognition of security;

❏ virus checking;

❐ back-up procedures;

❐ audit trails.

Control of access

❐ It is necessary to define access privileges to information according to the user set. Some users are allowed unrestricted access, others limited access and unauthorised persons must be prevented from gaining access;

❐ As well as access rights it is usual to couple these with update rights, e.g. read only, read and amend, create etc;

❐ Within a data set, certain data may be in the public domain whilst some is of a confidential or restricted nature. In these cases differential access can be provided by encryption of sensitive data or by the software controlling what a user may see;

❐ It is usual to set up access control matrixes to define for each user which functions may be used and, at a lower level, which data fields may be viewed or operated upon;

❐ With data in the public domain it should not be possible to identify individuals details from the data set, i.e. identity must be **separated** from the attribute data.

The risks of **unauthorised access** are considerable and there needs to be sufficient investment in security and authorisation procedures to give individuals or companies **confidence** in the privacy and confidentiality of the data. For public information little protection is needed apart from data security considerations. Corporate data must be protected from:

❐ industrial espionage;

❐ deliberate acts of destruction;

❐ malicious interference and alteration.

Private data must be protected to prevent:

❐ blackmail, extortion etc. (malicious);

❐ unauthorised disclosure (accidental).

The consequences of breach of confidentiality or security can be:

❐ financial and cause disruption to business;

❐ personal health may suffer;

❐ personal privacy is breached;

❐ where information is held on behalf of the subjects, disclosure (accidental or not) can render the keeper liable to legal action;

❐ loss of commercially sensitive data and commercial confidentiality;

❐ personal or corporate embarrassment etc.

The threat to security takes two major forms:

❐ electronic surveillance (bugging);

❐ hacking or unauthorised access.

The first threat requires system operators to consider counter measures such as use of Faraday cages or screens, live monitoring etc., in general these will be hardware-based activities. The second threat causes much more serious concern:

❐ currently it is extremely difficult, if not impossible, to prevent determined hackers gaining access to systems;

- ❏ the Data Protection Act places obligations on keepers of data encryption techniques, have an associated cost overhead but can give the level of confidence and protection required, e.g. the Data Encryption Standard;
- ❏ the Computer Misuse Act offers litigation against hackers;
- ❏ viruses, worms etc. are a further hazard.

System security requires that system usage be closely monitored and any breaches dealt with quickly and effectively. In addition all users must be made aware of their obligations and basic security procedures be adopted, e.g.:

- ❏ not leaving equipment connected in open mode, i.e. logged on;
- ❏ not leaving passwords etc. lying around;
- ❏ no importing of games;
- ❏ not using simple construct passwords;
- ❏ shredding all unused or unwanted printer output;
- ❏ using only accredited software and disks;
- ❏ good security for locally held data;
- ❏ use of keyboard locks;
- ❏ vigilance against unauthorised visitors etc., i.e. physical access restriction;
- ❏ use of virus detection software.

It is to be hoped that future systems will address the issues of user identity to a much greater extent than currently possible, i.e. proof positive of identity.

In addition to the data access problem there is the problem of **data integrity**, i.e. how to ensure that the data held is a **true reflection** with regard to the subject of the data. The problem becomes exacerbated when distributed databases are used but in single-type database systems the factors to be considered are:

- ❏ sufficient testing of software to remove all significant bugs;
- ❏ maintenance of audit trail data and subsequent reconciliation procedures;
- ❏ periodic spot checks;
- ❏ alternative confirmation of sensitive and critical data.

This, of course, will take time and cost money but should be designed into the system from an early stage.

Forced recognition of security

Element 4.3.7 introduces this topic and provides the main emphasis. Additionally this topic is concerned with the protection of information in systems from accidental loss or damage arising from events such as:

- ❏ power loss;
- ❏ floods and fire;
- ❏ natural disaster;
- ❏ deliberate act of sabotage.

IT systems consists of four elements:

- ❏ hardware to run the system;
- ❏ software which executes the processing;

❑ data which is subjected to processing;

❑ people who use and operate the system.

In circumstances of disaster then it is evident that:

❑ new replacement hardware can be readily purchased, also new premises obtained;

❑ people can be replaced, but perhaps not quickly.

However, the situation regarding software is more complicated:

❑ packaged software of whatever nature can be replaced by purchase;

❑ bespoke software should be treated as data.

Back-up procedures

Data and information which form the final element of the IT system is much more difficult to protect and recover. Most systems having been in existence perhaps for a number of years will possess data and information of much more intrinsic value and certainly more **critical business** value than the cost of replacement premises and hardware. Loss of business data in circumstances where it cannot be easily recovered sounds the death knell for a business. It is, therefore, critically important that all data (including operating software) be subjected to procedures which assure the ability to recover from loss as easily, quickly and cheaply as possible, concomitant with its perceived value to the ongoing survival of the business. Premises etc. can be replaced by ad-hoc, previously unplanned actions, but this is not the case for data and software, for these prior procedures must have been planned and instituted such that:

❑ data is secured on a regular basis by copying and saving to media which is removable and held in safe locations;

❑ software versions are similarly secured but on a less frequent basis than for data. Procedures are devised for the recovery of the whole IT system from a disaster. Such procedures can cover:

- total loss of site;
- loss of equipment and data;
- loss of people;
- loss of data.

The planning against such eventualities will cover such considerations as having a mobile or tandem computer room, compatible in every way with the system destroyed to enable recovery of operations to ensue.

The recovery may be:

❑ cold start up where it will first be necessary to recover all the data;

❑ warm start up where the back-up installation has been mirroring the processing and can be switched in to full operational status fairly readily;

❑ have an agreement with a local business or user having similar equipment such that their spare capacity can be utilised. Not really suitable for real-time systems.

Total disaster is the **least likely** event to occur on a probabilistic basis and users generally give much more consideration to software or data protection from loss. Events which are more likely to occur are protected against in two ways:

❑ additive hardware or protective equipment;

❑ data security procedures;

❑ in addition, insurance against accident and particularly the **consequential loss** of business revenue arising from loss of hardware, data and software must be obtained.

Hardware considerations that can apply will depend on the effect a loss will have on the operations:

❐ installation of equipment to prevent power supply surges or spikes affecting computer equipment;

❐ installation of an uninterruptable power supply;

❐ tandem computer equipment in case of equipment breakdown;

❐ idle PCs held in readiness against breakdown or malfunction.

Task 3.23 PC 4

From the first list on security in Element 3.4.7, choose four issues to investigate in your own centre. Report on how well these security measures operate.

Answers to questions in Unit 3

Answer 3.1   This of course will vary depending on which Building Society you base your answers. However, we would expect a counter service providing deposit and withdrawal facilities on a range of accounts. The service may well look and feel like that of a bank and include foreign money transactions. We may also expect an advisory service handling loans, mortgage applications and insurance policies.

Answer 3.2   Your answer may be quite different but typically may have covered a flow of information from sales to production control, or production control to manufacturing (and vice versa), from engineering design to manufacturing, from manufacturing to despatch, from despatch to accounts.

Answer 3.3   Many activities and functions work successfully because people are adaptable and goodwill also makes a contribution. Part of establishing goodwill is culture of communication between people. If you 'know' someone who needs you to do something, you are most likely to be responsive to the exceptional request than a written input. There is also much more content in verbal communication that would not normally be in the written equivalent, e.g. an explanation of why the request is an exception. Of course, a telephone call is quick!

On the negative side, verbal communication can introduce inaccuracy. One end thinks it understood what the other was saying, and vice versa. Equally the personalities need not necessarily be on 'friendly' terms.

Answer 3.4   When you make a holiday reservation the detail of the sale will typically include information on the package or tour purchased, the date and flight details, the destination and accommodation arrangements, the names and details of members of the party etc.

This information together with the cost of the holiday will appear on the invoice.

Answer 3.5   The design specification is usually written to guide the manufacturing division on how to make the product. Of course the product could be software code in which case 'manufacturing' becomes the programmers to produce a software product. Hence we need to be a little flexible in our interpretation. Additionally marketing may well use the design specification, or at least parts of it, in their publicity material to create sales.

Answer 3.6   If we are supplying a service to other organisations, there must be an expectation of when they can contact us. Hence holiday dates must be published well in advance. In planning the production flows through a manufacturing plant to meet existing orders any scheduled plant closure for summer holidays must be considered.

Answer 3.7   The route to integration is via databases and networks which combine the existing information sources with one system. Ideally only one set of data should exist, rather than multiple occurrences. Hence if a customer changes their address only one update is needed.

Answer 3.8   Some special needs users have restricted mobility and are unable to use the traditional data entry mechanism such as a keyboard. The use of voice input to operate a system may well give them an opportunity to being normal users.

Answer 3.9   Unless care and attention is paid to file security, including the security of back-up copies, the introduction of PCs has considerably raised the problem of data security.

Answer 3.10   An individual may have the following financial information held on them by various systems:
- salary;
- tax paid;
- current overdraft or debt;
- mortgage details;
- insurance policy details;
- credit worthiness.

Answer 3.11   Educational data held may include:
- Establishments attended;
- Examinations passed;
- Awards made.

Answer 3.12   Suppliers are always keen to know whether the customer has the ability to pay for the goods or services supplied. Hence the credit rating of a new customer is important. This may include data on cash flow, and financial security.

Unit 3 Sample Test Paper

1 Your company is planning to hold information about the way in which their customers spend money. What must they do?

   A prevent viruses attacking people
   B delete the data immediately
   C register under the Data Protection Act
   D remove any references which identify the customer

2 You are concerned that data is being stolen from your system. What would you do?

   A take regular back-ups
   B keep an audit trail
   C only allow authorised access
   D arrange for some processing to undertaken on another site

3 Your GP needs to keep medical records private and confidential. However some details can be released for research purposes. Which items could be released whilst maintaining the confidentiality?

   A patient's name and illness
   B patient's address and illness
   C patient's illness and age
   D patient's name and age

4 To enable you to recover from a system crash when the information on the hard disk becomes corrupted you should:

   A change the passwords frequently
   B take regular back-ups
   C verify all data inputs
   D verify all data outputs

5 At your local travel agents, which information technology development has provided the most significant improvement?

   A better colour screens
   B smaller VDUs
   C access to on-line information
   D confidential service

6 Your company plans to give each salesperson a lap top computer and a modem. What will be the greatest benefit?

   A the sales force become familiar with PCs
   B the customers will be impressed
   C all orders could be formatted identically
   D the salesperson can electronically send the order rather than posting bits of paper

7 The introduction of IT into banking has enabled

   A higher bank charges to be levied
   B EFT
   C monthly statements to be produced
   D SCSI

8 What advantages are gained from using a bar code reader in a supermarket system?

   A the bills are now accurate
   B the equipment is cheap
   C the equipment is reliable
   D use is made of the product bar code labelling

9 Which is a breach of moral behaviour?

   A making back-up copies of personal data
   B selling a list of customers to a rival company
   C removing outdated information
   D leaving your VDU whilst still logged in

10 A high street bank is an example of

   A a public sector organisation
   B a public limited company
   C a sole trader
   D an industrial organisation

11 A hospital is an example of

   A a public sector organisation
   B a private sector organisation
   C local government
   D a flat organisation

12 When a company receives goods that it has ordered, a note is sent to

   A   sales
   B   personnel
   C   production control
   D   accounts

13 A catalogue company receives many hundreds of orders by post each day. Data entry clerks process this input through which type of system?

   A   batch processing
   B   transaction processing
   C   distributed processing
   D   real-time processing

14 A distributed processing system has which one of the following characteristics?

   A   processing is designed to have different local techniques
   B   all data is processed locally
   C   there is no head office system
   D   all processors in the system can contribute to the system

15 A large university is organised into 6 faculties, each with a faculty head or Dean. Each Dean reports to the Vice-Chancellor. Within each faculty there are 4 departments each with a small number of teaching and research teams, typically with 12 or more staff in each team. What type of organisational structure does this represent?

   A   hierarchical
   B   flat
   C   matrix
   D   centralised

16 An industrial company makes a range of products which a designed by a team of people within the organisation. Typically sales, design engineering, production and purchasing may all have an input. Once designed the product comes under a product line manager. What type of organisation structure does this represent?

   A   hierarchical
   B   flat
   C   matrix
   D   centralised

17 The check digit on an account number is used during data entry to provide

   A   validation
   B   verification
   C   information
   D   consolidation

18 If you don't protect important data, what may happen?

   A   data can be accessed from anywhere
   B   data will be lost
   C   data will be hidden
   D   the system will crash

19 A bank employee may be asked to sign a non-disclosure agreement. What does this achieve?

   A   copyright is enforced
   B   forced recognition of security
   C   data is censored
   D   theft is prevented

20 If a student gains access to the student record information system, what will be the result?

   A   the student gets a credit on the system security unit
   B   the confidentiality of the system is lost
   C   the student fails the database unit
   D   nothing

21 What is the best method of entering personal records into a computer system?

   A   mouse
   B   magnetic strip
   C   keyboard
   D   optical mark reader

22 A supermarket is conducting a survey using a questionnaire. What would be the best device for handling the data entry to a computer system?

   A   a bar code reader
   B   a digitiser
   C   a MICR reader
   D   an OMR

23 A service centre on a motorway provides a VDU display of traffic information in the surrounding areas. What will be the most suitable method to allow customers to quiz the system?

A   touch screen
B   mouse
C   voice
D   keypad

24 The car spares counter in a garage has a point-of-sales terminal and inputs the bar coded information using:

A   icons
B   keyboard
C   laser reader
D   mouse

25 A company want to reduce the stock levels on the number of widgets held in stores. Which type of report will assist.

A   tax return form
B   audit trail
C   just-in-time stock analysis
D   customer order file

by **Peter Hodson**

Communications and Networking

Introduction

The unit covers many terms used in data communications and networking. The range statements are extensive and hence the text here explains a lot of terminology. However the thrust of the unit is to help you understand the issues of data communications and is intended to be practical in nature. You will need a minimum of a personal computer, a modem, a telephone line and relevant software to complete this unit.

There are four elements in this unit which cover:

1   Investigate electronic communications;

2   Use electronic communications to transfer data;

3   Investigate computer networks;

4   Use a computer network.

Whilst Elements 4.1 and 4.3 have a requirement of reports as evidence indicators, Elements 4.2 and 4.4 have a higher practical flavour. Many centres will be well equipped to undertake the practical work. To help everyone (but especially those centres who are less well equipped) some network services have been set up at the University of Glamorgan to which you may connect. These services allow you to explore the internet and achieve some of the evidence indicators. The university will provide you with the evidence needed for your portfolio that certain tasks have been accomplished.

The text covers only the material needed for this GNVQ unit and does not explore the subject in detail. Other textbooks in the DPP series will provide a more detailed treatment.

Investigate data communications

Introduction

Electronic communications by its very nature consists of a number of separate devices which are frequently some distance apart. To achieve a connection and exchange data a few conventions have to be established and standard procedures used. If everybody observes those basic conventions, there is a reasonable chance that electronic communication can be achieved.

In this element we seek to explore some of the terms used and the network services available. Once these are understood, the reasons for using protocols and the options available will become more obvious. At the end of the element you should be able to:

❐ explain network services used for electronic communication;

❐ describe the system components and standards for electronic communication;

❐ explain protocol parameters and modes of electronic communications.

4.1.1 Network Services

The need to communicate and find different ways of enabling communication has been developing ever since civilisation began. Red Indians used smoke signals and reflective surfaces, Scouts have used semaphore flags and when The Spanish Armada was approaching the English used beacons to signal the arrival of the invading fleet. These are just a few examples of an enormous variety of approaches taken over the centuries. With the state of current technology and digital communication, the range of services is wide. For two or more devices to exchange a digital signal, there must be a link between them. It is easy to make a direct connection between two, three or maybe four devices. As soon as you add further devices, putting a direct physical link between each one of them gets more difficult. Each addition becomes a little more cumbersome.

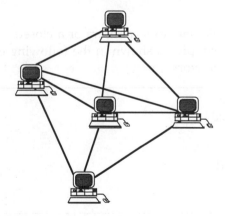

Figure 4.1 Interconnected devices

Now consider that the number of devices that are connected may be in the millions and could span across the whole of the earth. Clearly direct physical connections cannot be contemplated, hence the need to create a structured service to which individual devices can be connected. Networks are the basis of a structured service and may provide different service levels. At the simplest level they may offer a route across which bits can travel to the destination. However, a value added service can be provided on top of this basic functionality and users can connect to these services.

If we assumed a network to simply offer the ability to exchange raw bits without offering any software services or useful functions, then it is unlikely that much use will be made of it.

If the network now adds some functionality, then users may be attracted to using the service. If the additions were an e-mail or bulletin board service then potential users will be attracted to using such services provided by the network and it becomes a realistic or commercially viable facility. We will consider a number of **network services** from the element's range statement, but this is not exhaustive.

Electronic mail

This is frequently considered to be electronic messaging but we can exchange letters, numbers and images. Indeed anything that can be represented digitally could be part of an e-mail. The normal arrangement is for a user to have a unique mail box to which other users can send their communication. A user can then connect to their mail box and retrieve any communications sent to them. Examples of e-mail services are:

❏ BT Mailbox (formerly Telecom Gold);

❏ Microsoft Mail, cc-mail, Wordperfect mail or other proprietary products;

❏ SMTP (Simple Mail Transfer Protocol);

❏ Viewdata.

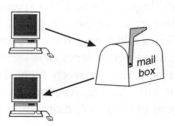

Figure 4.2 Electronic mail

If the mail box is available only to local users or a closed user group, then the format of the addressing can be quite simple, as shown in the following example of a Microsoft Mail message on a departmental network.

```
FROM: Hodson P J
DATE: 06/04/95 13:34
TO: Watkins M
CC:
SUBJECT: GNVQ IT
PRIORITY: R
ATTACHMENTS:
--------------------------------------------------------------------------------
Is the schedule for the GNVQ IT development on target with our project plan?
Peter.
```

Of course not everyone uses the same e-mail package. If worldwide e-mail communication is to achieved then either everyone must use the same package or we must be able to interconnect and convert between the various e-mail services. Given that the former won't happen then the provision of e-mail gateways, which provide the conversions, is inevitable. To send a message, it is relayed or routed through a switching node and the header is extended to show the path that the message has taken. Here is an example of a message that has been generated on one mail system, routed across JANET (the academic network) delivered to the University of Glamorgan's VAX mail system (called GENVAX) routed through to a departmental Microsoft Mail gateway (called msgate) and to my mailbox and ultimately read. The header shows a number of JANET switching nodes through which the mail has passed. Hence e-mail may not be delivered instantly but is delayed at each routing point.

```
Return-Path: <"CBS%UK.AC.KINGSTON.ISYS::XXXXX"@genvax.glam.ac.uk>
Received: from genvax by msgate.glam.ac.uk id <2EF74D6A@msgate.glam.ac.uk>;
 Tue, 20 Dec 94 13:32:26 PST
Date: Tue, 20 Dec 1994 13:40:41 +0100
Message-I
Sender: ZZZZZZ@uk.ac.ukc
d: <94122013404089@genvax.glam.ac.uk>
From: "CBS%UK.AC.KINGSTON.ISYS::XXXXX"@genvax.glam.ac.uk
To: PJHODSON@comp.glamorgan.ac.uk
Subject: 1996 Research Assessment Exercise
X-VMS-To: pjhodson
-------------------------------------------------------------------------------
Via: UK.AC.NSFNET-RELAY; Tue, 20 Dec 94 13:40 GMT
Received: from mercury.ukc.ac.uk by sun3.nsfnet-relay.ac.uk with JANET SMTP
 id <sg.04558-0@sun3.nsfnet-relay.ac.uk>;
 Tue, 20 Dec 1994 13:35:22 +0000
Received: from mail-relay.ja.net by mercury.ukc.ac.uk with SMTP (PP);
 Tue, 20 Dec 1994 13:32:20 +0000
Received: from mercury.kingston.ac.uk by mail-relay.ja.net with JANET SMTP
 id <sg.22186-0@mail-relay.ja.net>; Tue, 20 Dec 1994 13:32:13 +0000
Received: from isys.king.ac.uk by mercury with SMTP (PP);
 Tue, 20 Dec 1994 13:31:24 +0100
Date: 20 Dec 1994 13:22:50 -0300
From: XXXXX <XXXXX@uk.ac.kingston.isys>
Subject: 1996 Research Assessment Exercise
Return-receipt-to: "XXXXX" <XXXXX@isys.king.ac.uk>
To: YYYYYY <AAA@uk.ac.edinburgh.BBB>
Cc::ZZZZZZZ@uk.ac.ukc
```

Whilst many e-mail messages simply contain the text typed into the mail package, it is easy to attach an enclosure to the e-mail message. This attachment could be a wordprocessed document or a digital image, using the e-mail format as an envelope. The first e-mail example shows the attachments heading where the user simply specifies the name of the file to be 'attached' or enveloped.

Conferencing

The facilities for conferencing have been evolving for a number of years. Perhaps the earliest of the conferencing facilities were those offered by BT when the telephone operator could

175

interconnect a number of subscribers together to have a multiple-way conversation known as tele-conferencing. The evolution took us through a videoconferencing setup where centres with studio facilities could have visual and verbal contact, although the cost of setting up and operating such a system was and still is quite expensive.

The move to create a conferencing facility based on a central mini or mainframe for all users registered on such a multiuser system was a natural progression. The conference typically consists of one or more topic areas which people can read, add further data or comment on. Current developments involve PC conferencing where pairs of users can set up a conference. Each user's PC has a camera and conference board and is connected to others by a reasonably high speed communication link.

Bulletin Boards

Bulletin Board Systems (BBS) allow users to place messages etc. in a central server which can be accessed by others. Many BBSs look like electronic versions of newspapers. Others provide free software which can be downloaded, although this has been the source of some virus prone pieces of software in the past.

File Transfer

This facility is frequently provided in a network system and allows users to transfer files, programs or indeed any digital data from remote locations to their own machine. A variety of file transfer protocols (FTP) exist. At a very simple level, programs such as Kermit permit the exchange of information between two systems. Other products such as X-Modem provide more sophistication to remote transfers. The larger protocol suites have inbuilt capabilities which achieve transfers, without the user realising that it has been undertaken. Distributed File Systems such as Network File System (NFS) by SUN are indicative of the developments in this area. Typically the following information could be specified:

- □ source and destination information including file names;
- □ mode of transfer describing how files will be created, appended or deleted on completion of the transfer;
- □ the quality of service;
- □ any security levels to be observed.

Interacting with databases

It is common for interactive exchanges to occur which interrogate databases and update them when appropriate. For example, when you book a holiday at the travel agent, the normal activity is to query the travel company's database to check availability and costs. The database responds to the query with the current situation. A selection can be made and the database updated if a booking is confirmed. This is a typical example of an interactive session.

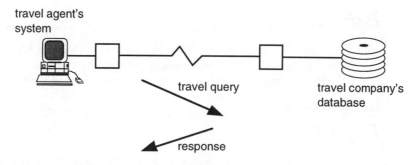

Figure 4.3 Interacting database

Question 4.1

Can you identify another typical interaction with a database?

Direct interaction

The telephone system has long been the primary means of exchanging voice 'traffic'. In the past this was conveyed across the network in analogue format. This meant that digital data had to be converted to an analogue format before it could be carried.

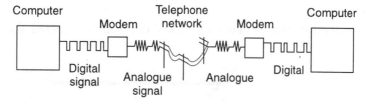

Figure 4.4 Analogue network carrying digital data

Voice is almost always carried in digital format nowadays with the traffic being converted from analogue format.

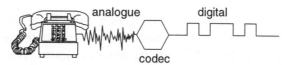

Figure 4.5 Digital network

The digital format permits us to use the same physical network to carry data without any significant reformatting. Each data element carried across the network is packaged to support the transfer. The format of the packet is known as the protocol and structures the communication in such a way that both the sender and the receiver know that the data transfer has been completed successfully.

It is also possible over data communication links to exchange video. An interesting development is video conferencing, where a camera can be mounted on the top of a PC. The PC has a special conference card slotted in, to which the camera is connected. When you connect your PC over a data communications link to another similarly equipped station, a window on both PCs can carry the video image of the other end, i.e. you can have a video link of direct interaction.

Task 4.1 PC 1   *C 3.4*

Examine the features of your electronic mail package and compare the structure with the two examples of e-mail shown earlier in this element. Are the structures easy to use? Are the features overly complex for a new user?

Task 4.2 PC 1   *C 3.1*

List the range of services you may find on a network. For each service identify one example implementation. Indicate why you would use your example in a daily situation.

4.1.2 System Components

To physically set up a network service requires a number of components to be connected. Rather than each manufacturer inventing their own rules or standards on how to achieve interconnection, a number of international standard interfaces have been agreed. If a manufacturer keeps to the standards then interconnection of their equipment should be easier. This allows a user in one country to communicate with another country's user, both using different equipment. In this section we will define a number of the major components needed to achieve communication.

In a simple arrangement where two local stations are connected, the physical structure may look like:

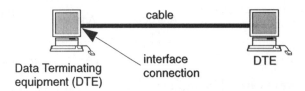

Figure 4.6 Adjacent DTEs

Of course communication frequently involves a little more complexity and is not simply a direct link. In this case the communication structures are extended to include a DCE (Data circuit terminating equipment) and the ability to communicate over long distances is available.

Figure 4.7 Remote DTE connection

Data Terminating Equipment & Data Circuit Terminating Equipment

The standard distinguishes between the terminal side which kicks off the transmission and the circuit or transmission side which handles the incoming data and passes it on. It calls the terminal side or end station a DTE and the transmission side or circuit interface device a DCE.

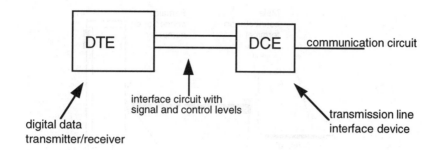

Figure 4.8 DTE and DCE Roles

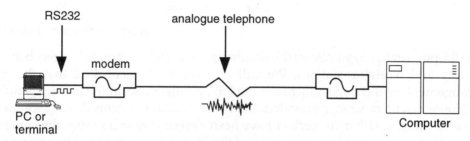

Figure 4.9 Remote connection with RS232

In the example shown here the DCE converts the digital signals from the RS232 interface to an analogue telephone network and vice-versa at the other end. The DCEs in this example are the modems and the DTEs are the PC and computer.

The interface has physical, electrical, functional and procedural characteristics. The connector and cabling provide the basic elements of these characteristics.

Connectors

A number of different connectors have been defined for a range of structures that can exist. By predefining a number of standard connectors between DTE and DCE or DTE and DTE devices, establishing communication is made somewhat easier. For example the communication link between a DTE and a modem was the original specification of the RS232 standard and was built around a 25-pin D connection.

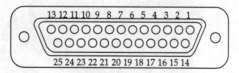

Figure 4.10 RS232 25-pin connector

The connector has both male and female arrangements with pins and sockets respectively. The standard defines that a DTE offers a male connector and a DCE offers a female connector. The cable layout for RS232 is shown in figure 4.34.

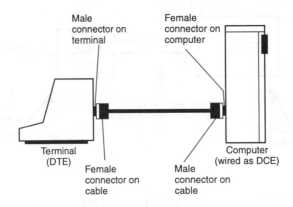

Figure 4.11 Male and female pin/socket convention

The 25-pin arrangement allows 25 simultaneous signals to be exchanged between the transmitting and receiving stations. We will also see in Element 4.2.1 that the pin connection arrangements will change if there is a modem, or otherwise, in the link e.g. a null modem connection when no modem is provided. Many connection protocols do not require as many as 25 separate circuits. Other connectors have been designed which reduce the complexity e.g. a 9-pin connector is a scaled down version of the 25-pin. A minimum of two wires would be used to transfer data (one data wire and one reference level), with the remaining wires available for control signals to manage the connection.

Where the distance between the stations is short (a few metres), the transfer of bits need not be a serial flow of bits. A number of bits can be sent in parallel across the connection, each bit needing its own wire or circuit. Typically 8 bits are sent in parallel allowing a byte to be transmitted as a single transfer. Since the connection still requires control signals, the cable (or ribbon) requires more than 8 wires.

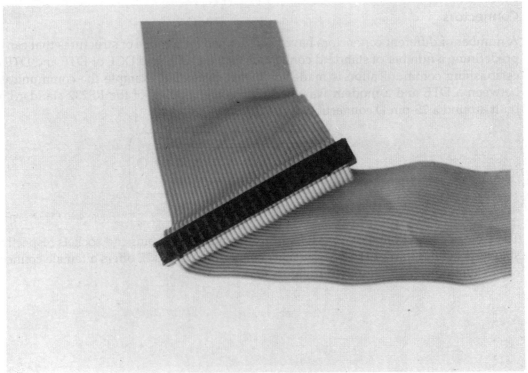

photo of parallel connector

Photograph 4.1 Parallel connector and ribbon

In local area networks the RJ-45 plug and connector are increasingly becoming the preferred arrangement. Hence we are likely to see further developments in using the RJ-45 plug in other structures in the future.

Software

Each interface is normally driven by software systems. Sometimes this is embedded in the hardware, having been developed in a low level language or with target hardware in mind. Typical of this approach would be the software embedded on the local area network card which connects a PC to the network.

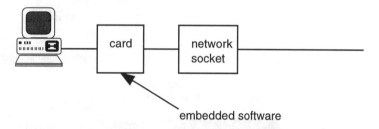

Figure 4.12 Embedded software on network card

The software on this interface card takes the data from the PC and formats the bits into the packet structures expected by the 'transmission'. On receipt of incoming data it is able to provide the reverse operation. For example, the interface card could be token ring or ethernet card creating or receiving token ring or ethernet packets.

At a higher level, the software loaded in the PC needs to direct data to the hardware interface. This could be part of the system software which would be servicing requests to do so from the application software. Software packages to send data across links include terminal emulation software e.g. Pacerterm. This allows the PC to look like any dumb terminal recognised by the computer system to which you are connected. Other examples of software that request transmission include internet software such as MOSAIC or electronic mail software. Software such as Terminal in Windows would be a good example of the interface for users of electronic communications.

Cabling

A range of cable exists, the majority of which provides a path for a one-way or two-way flow on a single serial stream basis. As we have already seen, parallel ribbon or cable allows a multiple stream of data to be sent. As the desire to achieve high speeds of transmission have developed, then the types of transmission media have also developed. Typical of the range are twisted pair, coaxial and fibre.

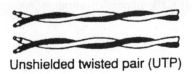

Unshielded twisted pair (UTP)

Figure 4.13 Twisted Pair

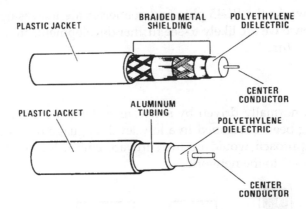

Figure 4.14 Coaxial cable
(Copyright Ungermann-Bass Reprinted with permission)

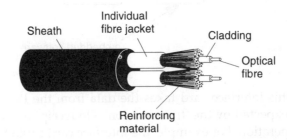

Figure 4.15 Fibre Optic
(Diagram courtesy of Cray Communications)

Such cable can provide transmission speeds in the Mega bits per second (Mbps or Mbit/s) range with some high quality fibre able to transmit at even higher speeds.

Where both ends of the transmission media are connected to equipment, there is a termination point. Typically coaxial cable is used in bus configurations where the devices are connected to points between the ends of the cable. To prevent signals reaching the cable ends and reflecting back, each cable end is terminated with a passive resistor (which matches the cables impedance).

All transmission media will normally have either equipment or terminators as their end points.

Task 4.3   PC 2   *C 3.4*

Check the DTE and DCE devices at your own location. Do they have male or female connectors?

What is the normal arrangement for a DTE, DCE and cable connection?

4.1.3 Standards for electronic communications

Data Representation

To carry data between two points we need to have a convention to represent each symbol. Semaphore flags and morse code are typical examples of representing each character in a unique way. In digital signalling we recognise bits as having a value of 0 or 1. If we group several bits together we can find unique patterns of bits to represent the range of characters or symbols. Of course the more symbols we want to uniquely represent, the more bits that need to be grouped. Typically there is a need to represent the characters of the alphabet in both upper and lower case (Aa,Bb,Cc,...), numeric characters (0,1,2..), control characters (Carriage Return(CR), Line Feed (LF), End of Text (ETX),....) and punctuation marks (!,?,",...). International standards have evolved which group 7 bits together to provide a sufficient range of different bit patterns to represent each possible symbol. The most commonly used data representation is ASCII (American Standards Committee for Information Interchange). Other standards exist such as the IBM standard EBCDIC (Extended Binary Coded Decimal Interchange Code).

Low 4 bits	High 3 bits							
	000	001	010	011	100	101	110	111
0000	NUL	DLE	SP	0	@	P	`	p
0001	SOH	DC1	!	1	A	Q	a	q
0010	STX	DC2	"	2	B	R	b	r
0011	ETX	DC3	#	3	C	S	c	s
0100	EOT	DC4	$	4	D	T	d	t
0101	ENQ	NAK	%	5	E	U	e	u
0110	ACK	SYN	&	6	F	V	f	v
0111	BEL	ETB	'	7	G	W	g	w
1000	BS	CAN	(	8	H	X	h	x
1001	HT	EM	)	9	I	Y	i	y
1010	LF	SUB	*	:	J	Z	j	z
1011	VT	ESC	+	;	K	[	k	{
1100	FF	FS	,	<	L	\	l	|
1101	CR	GS	-	=	M	]	m	}
1110	SO	RS	.	>	N	^	n	~
1111	SI	US	/	?	O	_	o	DEL

Table 4.1 ASCII codes

If we use the ASCII table, the representation for A is 1000001.

Question 4.2

What is the ASCII representation for d and E?

Data Circuit Connections

Each bit is usually represented on the copper wire as a voltage level. The normal arrangement is for a 'zero' to be represented by a positive voltage and a 'one' to be represented by a negative voltage. To ensure that each device is capable of sending to, or receiving from other devices, international standards have been established. This was intended to persuade designers not to create their own representations for their devices. This would have created havoc with possibly hundreds of different approaches and with little ability to connect devices which were supplied by different vendors. The interface standards, which include signalling conventions, that are most commonly found on devices are the RS232 or V.24 interface standards. The more recent X.21 standard has been in place for quite a while, but migration to this has been slow. Fortunately transition arrangements between X.21 and RS232 have been introduced to accommodate this slow migration.

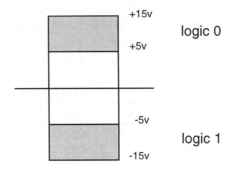

Figure 4.16 RS232 Voltage levels

Normally the voltage levels used in RS232 signalling are +12v or -12v, although voltage levels between +5v and +15v will be interpreted as a 'zero' and equally a 'one' will be interpreted by a signal in the -5v to -15v range. A voltage level in the shaded areas of figure 4.16 should be recognised as a signal representing a bit. Using this standard the bit stream 01010 may be represented by the signal levels in figure 4.17.

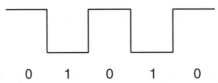

Figure 4.17 RS232 information coding

Question 4.3

How would you represent 10100 using RS232 signalling?

Task 4.4   PC 2   N 3.1

Identify four different standards for data representation, indicating which are still actively used.

Why do we use a standard such as ASCII?

Investigate how many different characters and symbols can be represented in ASCII?

Task 4.5   **PC 2**

Examine the interface(s) on at least four devices and list the type of connection ports that are available.

Identify the most common type of port connection and list five characteristics of the standard it adopts.

Are these characteristics mandatory or optional?

4.1.4 Protocol parameters

Transmission rates

It is evident that the faster you want to send data between two devices, the shorter the duration of each bit signalled on the transmission medium. A problem now arises at the receiving end of any data transfer. How does this receiver know when data is about to be sent and how will it know the rate at which the sending device will be transmitting? To recognise the incoming data and recover or record the data accurately, the receiver needs to read or sample the signal on the cable at a rate determined by the speed at which the data is being transmitted.

Typical transfer rates which are used and their respective character rates are:

Transfer Rate (bps)	Character Rate chars/sec
110	10
300	30
600	60
1200	120
2400	240
4800	480
9600	960
19200	1920

The odd entry in the table here is the first entry. That is because devices receiving data at the slow rate of 110 bps are those which need two stop bits (i.e. 11 bit characters).

To transfer data between two devices there are a few basic points to be examined. Let us consider the physical connection:

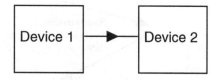

Figure 4.18 Simple Serial Connection

Assuming that the system components are compatible and the signalling conventions are the same at both ends, then we must ensure that the speed at which we send the data is acceptable and doesn't overwhelm the capabilities of the receiver. We also need to make sure that the receiver knows when to expect a data flow and that the data has arrived without error(s).

Flow Control

As we develop our data transfer concepts, we have assumed that the destination is capable of receiving the data at whatever rate it is sent. In reality of course, this may not be true. At a simple level, a personal computer is capable of generating and sending data much faster than a printer can handle it. For short bursts of data this can be managed by having a receiver memory or buffer to store incoming data until it can be handled. To prevent overflow occurring and the sender swamping the receiver by sending data faster than the handling capacity, we need to introduce the idea of flow control.

Consider the positive acknowledgement system where further data will only be sent on receipt of an ACK (acknowledgement) from the receiver.

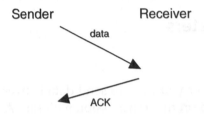

Figure 4.19 Positive Acknowledgement

If the receiver wants to exert flow control at this level, we need an additional response to indicate that the packet has been received O.K., but not to send any more packets until a future response indicates a state of readiness to receive more. RNR (Receiver Not Ready) is such a response.

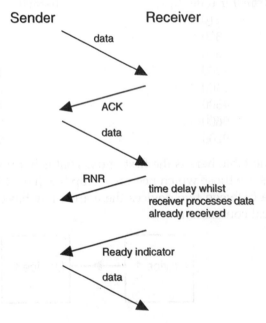

Figure 4.20 Flow Control

The ready indicator notifies the sender that the receiving device is now ready to continue and data flow can be resumed. At the receiving end the time delay between sending the RNR and the ready indicator permits the receiving device to 'catch up' with the processing of the information flow. Once it has emptied its buffers and is ready to resume receipt of the flow, it sends the ready indicator response.

Two fundamental approaches to flow control are frequently encountered. In the RS232 arrangement the Data Terminal Ready (DTR), Data Set Ready (DSR), Clear to Send (CTS) and Ready to Send (RTS) control signals provide a mechanism to allow data to flow or indicate that data is available to send. To establish a call the DTE device signals DTR to the other end, i.e. to the DCE. The DCE replies by raising DSR. The sender transmits data by raising RTS and the DCE indicates it ability to receive by raising CTS. If RTS or CTS are not present then the flow of data stops. On completion of the transfer DSR is lowered or switched off. This is known as hard handshaking or the DTR protocol.

Another approach is to use in-band signalling. Instead of using the control signals just seen, the transmit and receive lines (Tx/Rx) can be used to send X-on and X-off characters meaning Transmit on/Transmit off. Sending these characters on the same transmission line as the data to switch the data flow on and off means the flow control is in the same bandwidth as the data signalling. Hence the nomenclature of in-band signalling.

In higher level protocols, the Receiver Ready (RR) command and the Receiver Not Ready (RNR) command exist within the protocol suites such as HDLC. Other examples of flow control exist in these higher level protocols based on acknowledgements and window size.

It must be agreed in advance what the flow control mechanism will be between the two points.

Number of bits

It has already been shown that we need 7 bits to represent a range of characters and symbols. To provide a mechanism for checking that the data has been sent without an error, an eighth bit is added. This extra bit is known as the parity bit and will be covered in the next section of this element. The issue of alerting the receiver that data is about to arrive needs to be understood. Let us first look at the situation where everything is idle i.e. the quiescent state. To alert the receiver that a character (eight bits) of data is about to be transmitted, a start bit is sent at the front of it. Conventionally, we also send a stop bit at the end of the character. These start and stop bits also act as delimiters on the character so that the boundary points of any character being transmitted will be understood by the receiver. Thus, the stop bit is an important check for the receiver that the end boundary point of the character frame has been correctly reached. Hence, a typical transfer of a character in asynchronous mode would look like:

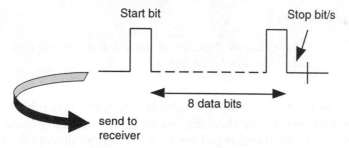

Figure 4.21 Asynchronous Character Transfer.

The detail of asynchronous mode is covered at the end of this element.

Some systems may need more than one stop bit and a character will be terminated by 1.5 or 2 stop bits. This is usually for slower devices, typically with slow mechanical components, and is becoming less common. If we send two stop bits to a receiving device that only requires one, it won't matter since the second stop bit will just appear to be the start of an idle signal level.

The first bit of the 8 bits transmitted is the least significant bit of the character representation and the last bit sent is the parity bit.

Parity

The eighth bit is used as a parity bit to help ensure the character transfer has been successful and provides a mechanism for us to detect when simple errors have occurred.

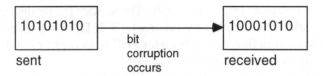

Figure 4.22 Serial bit corruption

On receipt of a character, a check is made to see if the correct parity is set. If it is incorrect, the character transfer is discarded and a retransmission of the corrupted character is required. The first step of this process is known as error detection and the second is known as error correction. Parity setting on a character is a simple technique, but unfortunately several variations of parity setting are in use. The most common of these are odd and even parity. In the case of odd parity, the parity bit is set to ensure that the total number of 'ones' including the parity bit itself is an odd number. Even parity ensures that the total number of 'ones' in a character is even. Both of these parity modes are common. The other methods, such as null parity, are less prevalent.

Consider the ASCII representation for A which is 1000001. Using odd parity this would be represented as 11000001. Using even parity it would be represented as 01000001.

The data communications installer would be responsible for ensuring that the correct parity setting was established between installed devices under his or her control. The suppliers or vendors of each item of equipment will identify the required parity setting for the individual interface. Of course it must be the same at both ends of the link!

Question 4.4

> *What would the parity bits be for the ASCII code of B and E using odd parity setting? What would they be for even parity setting?*

Question 4.5

> *If the character B is sent across a link using odd parity and one stop bit, what would the signal look like?*

This technique is good for detecting single bit errors, but if two bits were corrupted it would not detect the problem. Parity checking is also fine at detecting those error conditions where the number of bits that have changed are odd, but cannot detect the case where an even number of bits have changed.

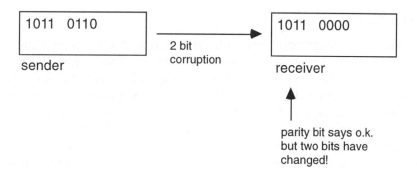

Figure 4.23 Multiple bit corruption

It will not surprise you to learn that more sophisticated techniques of error detection have been implemented. It is critical that corrupted or erroneous data be detected. We are slightly less concerned that data becomes corrupted than we are in making sure we know when it is wrong, although we clearly strive to achieve error free transfers. At least when we know it is wrong we can take action to put it right. Undetected errors can create enormous problems because we may believe the corrupted data is right and continue to use it afterwards in the context of it being accurate data.

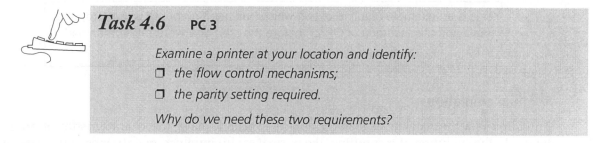

Task 4.6   **PC 3**

Examine a printer at your location and identify:
- ❏ *the flow control mechanisms;*
- ❏ *the parity setting required.*

Why do we need these two requirements?

4.1.5 Modes of electronic communications

Typically within this area we can separately establish modes for terminal operation and transmission modes. Issues relating to echo, wrap, CR/LF and terminal emulation are terminal mode. Transmission mode issues cover simplex, duplex, serial, parallel, synchronous and asynchronous approaches.

Echo

A useful check on any attempt to input or send data is the echo feature. The receiver sends back or echoes the data and the originating station compares what it sent with what it receives back. If all is OK, then we are fairly confident that it was received correctly. Sometimes the comparison is automatic and sometimes it is manual. An example of a manual check is data entry via a keyboard. The data is sent to the computer and then echoed back to the screen. The user performs a visual check on the screen display to confirm all is OK. By preventing the echo back at some fixed points, e.g when we are entering passwords, special features such as security can be introduced.

Wrap and CR/LF

Many devices, such as screens, have a fixed length of characters in a line. Once the maximum length is reached then some action needs to be taken. If we continued typing on a typewriter beyond the page width we would 'fall off' the edge of the paper and characters would be lost. On a typewriter the typist intervenes at the appropriate point and manually resets the next line by returning the carriage to the start of the next line. This action can be emulated on a computer by using two control characters, carriage return (CR) and line feed (LF). On encountering these two symbols the next line is commenced.

If you were entering characters through a keyboard and typed beyond the maximum length of a line on the screen, then the characters would wrap onto the next line. The appearance of such a wrap around is not very pleasing.

> This is an example of a line of text which has wrapped around onto the ne
> xt line.

Word processors and word processing packages have improved the situation enormously. If they detect that a word spans two lines they are able to insert CR and LF characters and automatically create a more pleasing appearance.

> This is an example of a line of text which has been prepared with Word, and
> has automatic insertion of CR/LF before the start of a word rather than mid
> word.

Terminal emulation

Emulation is a mechanism to make a device appear to have the characteristics of another device. In the evolution of computing, the normal set up involved mainframes with users connected to the system via dumb terminals. These terminals had particular features which were set in standards such as VT100 and VT240. It is relatively straight forward to write code to run in a PC to make the PC emulate one of these terminal standards. Such packages provide us with terminal emulation.

Question 4.6

Can you suggest another device that can be emulated?

Simplex

In all our considerations so far we have assumed transmission based on a single set of wires handling serial transmissions. Data only flows in only one direction and is known as a simplex system.

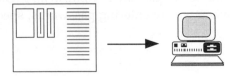

Figure 4.24 Simplex system

Half duplex

A slightly more sophisticated model, known as half duplex, will permit a flow of data in both directions, hence enabling the responses ACKs (acknowledgements) or NAKs (not acknowledgements i.e. not received o.k.) to be handled. But in the half-duplex arrangement the data flow is in either one direction or the other, but not in both directions simultaneously. Hence, we still only need a single set of copper wires (normally two wires) or uni-directional transmission media. This is analogous to a single lane stretch of road controlled by traffic lights allowing traffic through in one direction or the other, but not in both simultaneously - otherwise we have a conflict of interests or a crash! Another example is a radio link, where an ACK is the statement 'Roger' and the release of control in one direction to the other direction is the statement 'Over'.

Full duplex

We could introduce more than one circuit between the devices allowing data flow in both directions simultaneously. This mode of operation is known as full-duplex. Indeed, the RS232 interface which was introduced earlier, permits flow of data and signals in both directions simultaneously. In practice of course, we would need more than two sets of wires because we need to send control signals etc. However, for the sake of clarity on the diagrams it is represented as a two channel circuit. The connection cable used on systems frequently has 9, 15 or 25 separate wire circuits.

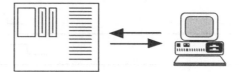

Figure 4.25 Duplex transmission

Asymmetric duplex

Within the full duplex range, the channel in one direction could be established at a different speed to the channel in the opposite direction. Such an arrangement is known as asymmetric duplex

Serial

The serial transmission approach is perhaps the most frequently used technique. The signal levels representing the data bits are sent one after another down the transmission media. At the receiving end the serial stream of bits is captured to form the transmitted data. Whilst it is simple, it does have the disadvantage that each byte of information or character takes eight time slots to be transmitted plus overheads for control bits (stop/start bits) or control characters (SYN chars).

Question 4.7

Why do we need these extra bits which create overheads and appear to contribute nothing to the contents of the information being transmitted?

Parallel

Over relatively short distances (e.g. between a PC and its attached printer) it is possible to have eight separate wires and to send each bit of a byte simultaneously. Each wire carries one bit of the character.

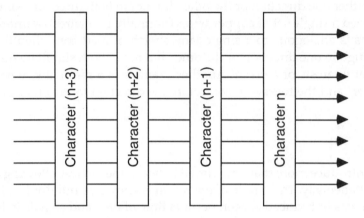

Figure 4.26 Parallel transmission

Because each wire has slightly different properties, there is a possibility that data could travel at marginally different speeds on each of the wires. This introduces the problem of skew, where the signal for each bit of the character arrives at the destination at a slightly different time.

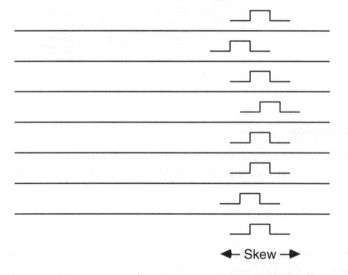

Figure 4.27 Skew

Ideally we need to clock all eight transmission lines at the receiving end simultaneously, so we cannot allow any significant skew to develop. Hence, we tend to keep the length of parallel transmission fairly short. This is coupled with the higher costs associated with the cabling and interfacing of the parallel approach. Consequently it is normally only used over short distances between two devices where the advantage of speed over the serial transmission technique may be desirable.

Question 4.8

If you assume that the transmission speed of a parallel connection is 800 bytes/sec, what is the shortest time taken to transmit 3200 bytes of data?

Question 4.9

What assumptions have you had to make in answering the previous question?

Asynchronous

The receiver needs to sample the line at the same rate as the sender is transmitting it. To achieve this, the transmission interface of each device has an internal clock which, within a reasonable level of accuracy, are both 'clocking' at the same rate. Devices sending data to each other know the data rate between themselves because the data communications designer will have pre-set the speeds at the same standard rates. The arrival of the start bit at the receiver starts the interface clock. It instructs the receiver's interface to sample the incoming signal i.e. the start bit provides a method of timing or alert signal to the receiver that a character transfer is commencing. Provided the sender and receiver clocks are running at the same rate, the data should be successfully received. As a check on the protocol, the receiver insists on seeing a stop bit in the tenth (and possibly eleventh) bit position. If that isn't present, there has been an error. In a typical character transfer, successive characters will have a short gap between them. It is possible for this inter-character time gap to be nothing or very small when the sender is transmitting at a maximum rate.

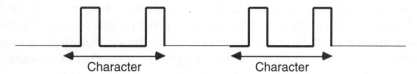

Figure 4.28 Character string

Consider a case where there is no 'lost' time between each character sent, i.e. a start bit for one character follows immediately behind the stop bit of the previous character. This would happen in any situation where characters had been buffered. If 200 characters are sent down a transmission line at a rate of 1200 bps we can now calculate the time to transfer the data.

200 characters = (200 × 10) bits to transmit (assuming 1 stop bit and 1 start bit).

$$\text{Time to transmit} = \frac{\text{Number of bits sent}}{\text{Speed of transmission}}$$

$$\text{Time to transmit} = \frac{(200 \times 10)}{1200} \text{ seconds} = 1.66 \text{ seconds}$$

Question 4.10

If we assume that each character could be sent without a delay between them, how long would it take to send 100 characters down a line at 2400 bps?

Synchronous

The approach to data transfer using serial lines with asynchronous transmission works well when the volume of data to be transferred is low. However, sending large volumes of data at low data rates is time consuming. To send data at higher rates we use a different technique known as synchronous transmission. The basis for this change stems from the difficulty we experience in keeping two clocks synchronised, i.e. the sending device's clock and the receiver's clock.

At low speeds this synchronisation isn't too critical given that the time cell or duration of the signal for each bit is reasonably wide and the total period for keeping it synchronised is only to 'clock' 10 bits across. After 10 bits the opportunity to re-synchronise clocks on receipt of the next start bit is available.

At higher speeds, the time cell for each bit obviously decreases. To speed up the effective transfer rate only the 8-bit ASCII (or equivalent) is sent, without the start/stop bit sequence. Characters are 'blocked' together to form a character sequence.

To permit the receiving device to synchronise its clock with the sender, each block of characters is preceded with a few synchronisation (SYN) characters.

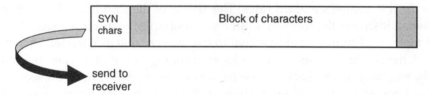

Figure 4.29 Synchronous transfer

When such a frame of information arrives at the receiving device, the receiver's clock uses the SYN characters to lock onto the sender's signal. Once this synchronisation has been achieved the remainder of the frame is sampled at the correct signalling rate and the data transfer completed. This approach to data transfer is called synchronous because the 'block' contains the timing information (in the SYN characters) to allow the synchronisation to occur.

Protocols exist where there is no fixed length to the number of characters in such a block. Hence, we need to be able to show where the start and end occur. Several ASCII characters are designated special control characters and two of these control characters are used to help define the boundary points. They are STX (start of text) and ETX (end of text). If we always indicate where the boundary points are, the flexibility of having variable length blocks readily exists. These control characters are often known as delimiters.

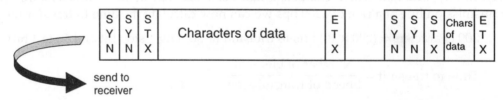

Figure 4.30 Example of long and short blocks

Question 4.11

Can you devise another technique to establish the exact length of a variable length block, other than the approach just outlined?

The exact structure of such a block and how many special characters are placed at the front and back is protocol dependent. Several different protocols exist and the variations within each of these protocols makes world-wide integration of all such systems just that little bit more difficult. At this stage we are not going to look at the detailed structure of a particular protocol standard.

Task 4.7   PC 3   N 3.1

Identify how many start and stop bits are sent under the following conditions:

- ❑ *A slow mechanical device (e.g a teletype);*
- ❑ *A VT100 terminal operating in asynchronous mode;*
- ❑ *In a synchronous transmission;*
- ❑ *In a multiplexer transfer.*

Why do we need or not need these bits and what use are they?

Task 4.8   PC 3   N 3.1

Check the transmission speed of your modem and/or network. If a 2 Kbyte file was sent through your modem or across your network, what would be the minimum time it would take to transfer it?

Task 4.9   PC 3

Examine your terminal and explain the terminal mode settings.

Task 4.10 PC 3   C 3.4

Briefly describe the six transmission modes covered in the last section.

Give an example situation where each one could be implemented

Use electronic communications to transfer data

Introduction

This is a practical element which, when tackled with Element 4.4, gives you the opportunity of setting up a data communication link and achieving a basic exchange of data.

To successfully transfer data between two stations we have already seen that a number of issues have to be determined. Normally, setting up the hardware and software to achieve such communication capability is a one-off activity that needs to be resolved. If the link is between two adjacent devices, identifying the two end points is easy.

Figure 4.31 Adjacent PCs

If however the devices are connected to an international network or a local network with multiple stations, then we have the added complexity of identifying with whom the exchange of data is required.

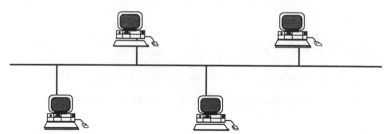

Figure 4.32 Multiple stations connected to a network

We need to set up the hardware and install software to achieve the data transfer. Accessing a remote station and undertaking a data file transfer is an opportunity to explore the principles of data communications. If you are able to do this without too much support that's fine. If you need a remote station to access, The University of Glamorgan will provide you with a facility. Instructions on how to do this are provided in the element.

4.2.1 Hardware

The hardware considered here can be at various levels of complexity. Perhaps the biggest challenge is setting up local systems that can connect to remote or distant systems. At a simple level we transfer data when a PC sends data to a printer.

Figure 4.33 PC connected to printer

Many of the issues involved in establishing the necessary controls and protocols such as flow control, parity setting etc., still have to be resolved in this simple model.

Data Terminal Equipment and Data Circuit Terminating Equipment

DTE and DCE devices have been outlined earlier in Element 4.1. Let's consider two PCs which could be directly connected. In this less complex arrangement both devices are DTEs, but some of the basic issues relating to communications have to be resolved. The major issue is the cable arrangement needed to make the connection.

Question 4.12

What concerns should we have over the cable used for direct connection?

Connecting Cable

The modem has already been seen as a basic DCE device. The cable to connect to the DCE from the DTE is a modem cable. Let's look at the standard arrangement for the pin connections. Pin 2 for a DTE says transmit from this end, whilst pin 2 for a DCE device says transmit from the other end and receive at this end. The opposite terminology applies to pin 3 at both ends.

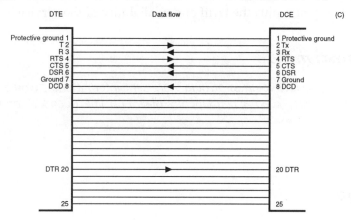

Figure 4.34 DTE to DCE cabling

Where two DTEs are directly connected, we cannot use a cable directly configured as a modem cable since the pins used to transmit at one end will arrive at the transmit pin and not the receive pin at the other end. Hence we have to set up a cross-over arrangement to ensure signals arrive at the right pin and the control signals work correctly. Such a cable is known as a null modem cable i.e. there is no modem in between.

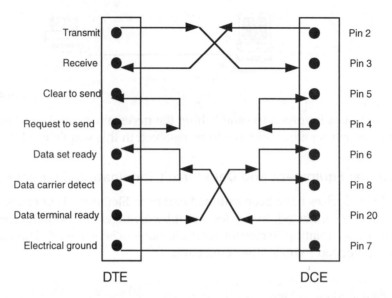

Figure 4.35 Null modem cable

Wide area network

To connect two or more devices which are distant from each other and typically beyond the immediate points of the building, we need to use the services of the Telecom companies such as BT or Mercury. They provide a range of connecting services such as dial-up facilities onto the public switched telephone network, switched data networks or dedicated services such as Telex. Each of these have a specified interface to which the user may connect. It is common to draw a wide area network (WAN) as a 'cloud'.

The type of service used and the connection made will depend on the volume and frequency of data transfer plus the tariff and availability of the service.

Question 4.13

If low volumes of data were sent intermittently, would it be sensible to lease a line, keep a permanently dialed-up line open or connect to a switched data network?

4.2.2 Software

Operating Systems

The operating system provides some routines to support data transfers. In the simple example of connecting to a printer then the print command will action the operating system into transferring the data to the printer. Of course the operating system will need to know what type of printer is attached so that the appropriate control signals are sent.

Within the communication software it is normal to see programs which are responsible for the secure delivery of data between the two end points. TCP is a commonly used transport protocol which runs in the host machines at both ends of the link to provide such a secure delivery. Many UNIX operating systems include TCP/IP as part of the system.

The TCP/IP environment offers a File Transport Protocol (FTP) which provides the internet standard capability. A user with a local FTP program can connect to a remote site also using FTP with the simple command:

ftp remote-host-address

Once connected the user ID and password is normally required, although general access as an anonymous user is frequently available as a means of supporting internet by the remote host. A prompt of FTP> should be seen now. A range of commands can now be actioned including:

- ❑ cd   change working directory;
- ❑ close   close the link;
- ❑ get   copy file from remote host to local system;
- ❑ help   display all client FTP commands.

Communication Systems

A range of public domain software (available on free distribution or for a nominal charge which is frequently an honour system of paying if you use it) and commercial software products are available to support data transfer. A popular public domain software file transfer protocol written by Colombia University is Kermit, named after the little green frog in the Muppets. Although it is slow and cumbersome it is readily available and many sites will have a copy. Other programs such as X-modem, Y-modem and Crosstalk provide file transfer capabilities. To transfer a file each computer must run a copy of the product. E.g. both running Kermit.

4.2.3 Controls

Binary Transfer

The format of the data transferred is important. It can be structured as a simple binary file with no implied structures or format. We are simply interested in transferring a copy of the file. However there may be a requirement to maintain a file structure. This structure may be maintaining the format of a word processed file or the structure of digital images. Each format may establish blocks of data which would become the element or size of the data transfer. If no such format is established, the file may be transferred as a simple binary file of 0's and 1's.

It is however usual to transfer blocks of data and we need a protocol to support such transfer. Where the contents of the block is simply a string of bits rather than a byte structure, the protocol is referred to as a binary transfer.

Modem Commands

There are a number of alternative arrangements that can be set up for a modem which can be sent from a PC using appropriate software. Some software packages permit a macro or script file to be written which will send a series of commands to the modem to establish a 'normal configuration' for a system. The following are examples of modem commands, but are not an exhaustive list. A full list will be available in your manufacturer's modem manual.

Command	Purpose
A	Puts the modem in answer mode;
AT	Alerts the modem that other commands follow;
E(0), E(1)	Disable/Enable echo printing of characters;
H	Hang up;
P	Pulse dialling;
T	Tone dialling.

Terminal Preferences

Terminal systems can be grouped into one of two types.

❏ An asynchronous terminal using start/stop and/or block mode transmissions. In block mode the terminal buffers the characters until a control character is typed. The buffer is then sent as a serial stream of bits, including the stop/start bits.

❏ A synchronous terminal using block mode transmission.

When connecting a terminal to the network, we must make the terminal communication channel and receiver compatible with each other. Hence the baud rate (signalling rate), flow control, parity setting etc. must be established. Some terminals can be configured to operate as one of a standard range of terminals (e.g VT240) in which case everyone knows the exact operation of the terminal.

NCSA Telnet uses a configuration file CONFIG.TEL to set up it's working environment. Most of the entries in config.tel can be left set to their default values. Listed below are some entries that you may need to change in your version of config.tel to customise telnet for your computer.

termtype="vt100"	# the type of terminal emulation, currently only vt100 # is supported
vtwrap=yes	# should VT100 be in wrap around mode or not?
myip=193.63.130.1	# the IP number of your computer which must be # unique. N.B the example is a University of Glamorgan # IP....not yours!
netmask=255.255.255.0	# subnetting mask
video=vga	# type of video screen e.g. CGA, EGA, VGA
ftp=yes	# do you want ftp enabled?
name=MyMainframe	# aliases that you can set up for commonly accessed # computers
hostip=193.63.130.2	

Figure 4.36 Example terminal setting

Terminal Emulation

We can make a PC look like a terminal of any major standard by running software to emulate the terminal required. We have seen examples of this in this unit where Kermit has been discussed. In the example of terminal preferences in figure 4.36, the telnet terminal specified is a VT100.

4.2.4 Protocols

Configuring the system such that we match the remote station is an essential element in achieving a successful data exchange. A check on the following features will help:

❏ data bits   ASCII or EBCDIC representation?
7 bits format?

❏ parity   Odd, even, space or mark parity setting?

❏ baud rate   Signalling rate; 300 bps, 1200 bps or higher?
(Note that baud rate is the signalling rate. Where only two signal levels are used, as in RS232, then the baud rate and the data rate are the same);

❏ flow control   In-band X-on/X-off or out of band signalling such as CTS/RTS?

❏ stop bits   One, one and a half, or two stop bits required?

Connection Port

Each device provides a mechanism for communication with other devices. This provision is frequently the RS232 or V24 port connection. RS232 was originally designed as the interface connection to a modem, but a null-modem connection has become the standard for local connection i.e. we directly connect two RS232 ports with no modem in between. Each device provides these connection port interfaces for external communication.

Carrier Detect

Data transfer between two modems is in the form of a modulated analogue signal or carrier. Devices would normally wait in a state that is activated by the detection of a carrier on the media. Whilst a carrier is present, the receiving device (typically a modem) maintains the connection and keeps the circuit open. Detection of a carrier by a modem changes the carrier detect from a negative voltage to a positive voltage on pin 8 in an RS232 system. Changes in the state of pin 8 are sometimes delayed, known as the carrier detect delay. This is deliberate, in case there is a temporary glitch or noise burst on the communication line. We don't want to close the link for each of these. Hence the carrier detect delay holds the line open for a reasonable period when the signal 'disappears' with such a problem.

4.2.5 Data file transfer

To exchange data between two devices, whether this be a file transfer or an interactive session, there are basic stages that are needed.

❏ establish the connection;

❏ exchange information;

❏ close the connection.

Other issues need to be resolved, but once these three stages are available, a basic service can be offered.

Data file identified

If a file exchange is to be achieved, you must know the name of that file and what you want it to be known as after the transfer.

Destination selected and communication link established

The location of the device with whom you want to exchange data must be known. It may be a local printer or a distant server. In the local case the link may be a direct wire connection or a local area network attachment. For more distant connections, you need to know the address. Examples of identifiers are a telephone number or an internet address.

Whatever the proposed connection method, the establishment of a connection is one of the primary stages in data exchange. For regular communication links and file transfers, this provision could be automatically set up on a user's menu.

Data file transfer undertaken and communication link closed

Perhaps the best way of looking at this topic is to do the work practically. Don't forget, at the end of the transfer to close the link. This avoids you having to carry on paying telephone line charges and it releases the facility for others to use. Of course you may have other facilities available to you and can use them instead. The University of Glamorgan has set up this mechanism with a certificate as evidence for your portfolio if you want to access a bigger network.

Practical session and Task 4.11 for this element   (all PCs)

NOTE: Messages in **bold** are those typed by the user. Messages that are *{italicised}* are additional comments to explain what is going on.

You need to configure your modem to 8 bits, 1 stop bit and no parity; commonly known as 8N1. The number for the University of Glamorgan is (01443) 482900 and there are four receiving modems which will handle up to 14,400 bits per second (bps)

{Local Messages and Commands for dialing to 01443 482900}

CONNECT 1200
<CR>
<CR>

DECserver 200 Terminal Server V3.0 (BL33F) - LAT V5.1
J152Q$70-A2

Please type HELP if you need assistance

Enter username> **gnvq**

Local> **connect a3500a** *{a3500a is an Alpha 3500 called "Alfi"}*
Local -010- Session 1 to A3500A established

{The following is is a start up message for all users of ALFI}

   Welcome to OpenVMS AXP (TM) Operating System, Version V1.5
    University Of Glamorgan / Prifysgol Morgannwg
    General Purpose System / System Aml Bwrpas

WARNING / RHYBUDD

The programs and data held on this system are lawfully available to authorised users for authorised purposes only. Access to any program or data must be authorised by the University Of Glamorgan.

It is a criminal offence to secure unauthorised access to any program or data on, or make unauthorised modification to the contents of, this computer system. Offenders are liable to criminal prosecution. If you are not an authorised user DISCONNECT IMMEDIATELY.

Mae'r rhaglenni a'r data a gedwir ar y system hon ar gael yn gyfreithlon i ddefnyddwyr ar gyfer dibenion trwyddedig yn unig. Rhaid cael caniatad Prifysgol Morgannwg i ddefnyddio unrhyw raglen neu ddata.

Gall unrhyw un sy'n mynedi, neu newid unrhyw ran o'r system yma yn anghyfreithlon wynebu erlyniad troseddol. Os nad ydych yn ddefnyddiwr cyfreithlon DATGYSYLLTWCH YN SYTH.

Username: **GNVQ**
Password: **GNVQ** *{This would not appear when typed}*

{The following is a start up message once a user logs on to ALFI}

Good Evening ! *{or other appropriate greeting}*

The IS Department is open during the following hours:

Monday to Thursday 08:15 to 21:30
Friday 08:15 to 21:00
Saturday & Sunday 09:30 to 12:30

NIGHTLINE is available from 8 pm to 8 am on 400333 if you're feeling stressed, upset or just want a chat.

Have you logged in to do work for private gain ?
Please answer Yes or No **n**

{GNVQ is a captive account which offers the following services}

1. TELNET to GNVQ
2. FTP to GNVQ
3. KERMIT
0. LOGOUT from this session
Option ?: **1**
GLAM*GLAM*GLAM*GLAM*GLAM*GLAM*GLAM*GLAM*GLAM*GLAM*GLAM*

Welcome to the Glamorgan Virtual Campus : a test Multi-User Domain (MUD) for the Department of Computer Studies at the University of Glamorgan, UK

THIS IS NOT A GAME - Rather it allows a textual tour of the Department. So what is going on here? Well, "GLAM" is an experiment in multi-user, consensual environment which will allow students and staff from all over to communicate in a completely controlled environment.

To log on, type "guest" if you want to look round, else type your name in a format which is all your initials followed by enough letters from your surname to make up to 8 characters. (e.g. Mike Reddy = mreddy, Charles Ludvig Dodgeson = cldodges, etc.)

For your password, type in something other than the password you may use normally; the Internet is not as secure as people might wish! When prompted for an e-mail address, enter your e-mail address. This will only be available to the Systems Administrator at Glamorgan. However, if you do not wish to give an address, type "none".

Finally, you will be asked what sex you are. Type in your own choice of gender, but don't assume that others will be what they appear either!

Version: 03.01.02

What is your name: **pjhodson** *{type in your own name here and in the next two entries}*
New character.
Password: **PJHODSON** *{This would not appear when typed}*
Password: (again) **PJHODSON** *{This would not appear when typed}*

You are now Pjhodson the visitor (level 1).
Please enter your e-mail address (or 'none'): **pjhodson@comp.glamorgan.ac.uk**

Are you, male, female or other: **male**
Welcome, Sir!

This is a test-only Multi-User Domain (MUD). For the purposes of this

demonstration you are in the fantasy world of GLAM. It works
like an adventure game; you type 'n' to go north, etc. Explore and have
fun! - Mike Reddy (MUD Administrator)

> look
This is a quadrangle with a central green. To the north is the front
entrance to J-Block. There is one obvious exit: north
> n
This is the front entrance to J-Block. Through the glass doors a Security
Reception Area can be seen.
There are two obvious exits: north and south
> n
This is the foyer to J-Block. To the south is the quadrangle, while the
north door leads to the back entrance. The Information Systems Department
(ISD) is through the west fire door. The Department of Computer Studies
is through the eastern fire door.
There are two obvious exits: south and east
> e
This is the western end of the first floor corridor of the Computer Studies Dept.
which stretches to the east. Staff and research student offices are dotted along the
northern wall. At the far end a fire door leads to the rest of the department.
There are two obvious exits: west and east
> e
This is the middle of the first floor corridor of the Computer Studies Department
stretches to the east and west. Staff and research student offices are dotted along the
northern wall. At the far end a fire door leads to the rest of the department.
There are two obvious exits: west and east
> e
This is the eastern end of the first floor corridor of the Computer Studies Dept.
which stretches to the west. Staff and research student offices are dotted along the
northern wall. To the east a fire door leads to the rest of the department, to
the north is the Departmental Office.
There are three obvious exits: north, west and east
> e
This is the north end of the first floor corridor that leads south towards the
computer labs. The General Office is to the north and a fire door leads west.
There is also a strange metallic door in the east wall, with a button beside it.
There are three obvious exits: north, west and south.
> press button
A little white lamp beside the button lights up.
> open door
Ok.
> e
This is the lift. On the wall are three buttons, numbered 0 (the ground floor),
1, 2 and 3. There is an open door to the west.
> press 0
Nothing happens.
> close door
Ok.
> press 0
The lift starts moving downward.
The lift continues...
The lift continues...
The lift slows down and stops
> open door
Ok.
> w
This is the ground floor corridor, leading to various lecture theatres. At the end of the Corridor to the south is
the Student Common Room. J11 is to the West,
J9 to the north east.

There are three obvious exits: west, northeast and south.
> **w**
This is the J11 lecture room. A lecture is in progress.
Lecturer is here.

{Students and staff from all over the world could give or listen to lectures and tutorials in any of these rooms}

> **examine lecturer**
He is writing something on the blackboard.
> **read blackboard**
The blackboard says "Don't forget to download the GNVQ certificate!"
Lecturer says: Hello Pjhodson.
> **say Byebye.**
You say: Byebye
> **wave lecturer**
Lecturer smiles
> **quit**
Saving Pjhodson

    1. TELNET to GNVQ
    2. FTP to GNVQ
    3. KERMIT
    0. LOGOUT from this session

  Option ?: **2**

220 Connected to www.comp.glam.ac.uk.
Name (GNVQ.COMP.GLAM.AC.UK:gnvq): **anonymous**
331 Guest log in, send E-mail address (user@host) as password.
Password: **mreddy@comp.glamorgan.ac.uk** *{type in your e-mail address}*

230-*<Log on message for the FTP Server>*
230 Anonymous login to 1 volumes. Access restrictions apply. "/pub".
FTP> **pwd** *{pwd = print working directory}*
257 "/pub" PWD command successful.
FTP> **ls** *{ls = list files}*
200 PORT command successful.
150 ASCII transfer started.
applications
incoming
publications
utilities
gnvq

226 Transfer complete.
49 bytes received in 00:00:00.03 seconds
FTP> **cd gnvq** *{cd = change directory}*

250 "/pub/gnvq" cd successful.
FTP> **ls**
200 PORT command successful.
150 ASCII transfer started.
gnvqcert.txt *{This is an ASCII text file which certifies that a file transfer was performed. Other files are not shown here for simplicity}*

226 Transfer complete.
63 bytes received in 00:00:00.08 seconds
FTP> **get gnvqcert.txt**
200 PORT command successful.
150 ASCII transfer started (34k).
226 Transfer complete.
local: GNVQCERT.TXT remote: gnvqcert.txt
33464 bytes received in 00:00:01.14 seconds

FTP> **quit**
221 Nice chatting with you.

  1. TELNET to GNVQ
  2. FTP to GNVQ
  3. KERMIT
  0. LOGOUT from this session

 Option ?: **3**

C-Kermit, 4E(070) 29 Jan 88, Vax/VMS

C-Kermit>**server**
C-Kermit server starting. Return to your local machine by typing
its escape sequence for closing the connection, and issue further
commands from there. To shut down the C-Kermit server, issue the
FINISH or BYE command and then re-connect.

*{On the local machine the user executes the following commands (The format for these commands may vary
for different machines:}*

Kermit> **dir**

Directory DISK$USER5:[COMP.MREDDY]

GNVQCERT.TXT;1 69 (RWED,RWED,RE,)
LOGIN.COM;16 3 (RWED,RWED,RE,)
MAIL.MAI;1 45 (RW,RW,,)
Total of 3 files, 117 blocks.

Kermit> **get gnvqcert.txt**
**

Receive (KERMIT) gnvqcert.txt: 33464 bytes, 5:14 elapsed, 106 cps, 88%

Kermit> **finish** *{This tells the remote machine to stop being a server}*

C-Kermit server done

C-Kermit>**quit**

  1. TELNET to GNVQ
  2. FTP to GNVQ
  3. KERMIT
  0. LOGOUT from this session

 Option ?: **0**
 GNVQ logged out at 12-JUN-1995 18:01:10.36
Local -011- Session 1 disconnected from A3500A
Local> **lo**

{Local messages about line disconnection}

Figure 4.37 Local messages and commands

4.2.6 Interactive electronic data communications

The principles of identifying the destination, establishing a connection, undertaking an interactive exchange and closing the link are the major issues. Indeed we have already seen in the last section that these principles also apply to file transfer. The practical work we undertook in section 4.2.5 also applies here. The difference is the new emphasis on the interactive nature of the communication, where the expectation is two operators or people are 'talking' to one another via the keyboard.

Perhaps the best way this can be demonstrated is using some local software which provides a 'talk' facility between two, or more, connected stations. The connection could be as simple as two connected PCs through to a full LAN. The principle is the same. Some of the office software on the market, such as Wordperfect Office, provide a talk facility in their product which is ideal for this purpose. You can see who is currently working at their stations and buzz them if you want to talk.

4.2.7 Communication activities log

This is often available as part of the communications software that you may be using and would automatically be set up. It is important that a log of accesses be maintained so that an effective audit may be undertaken if necessary. The basic elements we should expect to see in the log are likely to include:

- ❏ date of communication;
- ❏ time taken on line;
- ❏ amount of data transferred;
- ❏ names of files.

If you used the ftp facilities to access the University of Glamorgan in Element 4.2.5 then you already have an example of a communications log. The example shown in that element is also a communications log.

Investigate computer networks

Introduction

The performance criteria in this element are largely descriptive. Hence the text provides the detail behind the range statements. The element provides an underpining skill and knowledge to enable you to tackle the next element more effectively.

The types of networks and their components are considered along with the topologies available. The benefits of networking and media access control issues are explored. Given that networks are growing in size and becoming more complex, it is understandable that a greater emphasis on network management and security has been rising in importance. This element addresses some of the issues concerned.

4.3.1 Networks

Local Area Networks

Anyone can set up their own local area network (LAN). It requires the purchase of appropriate hardware and software, installation of the cable infrastructure and operation of the service. You own and operate the LAN over geographical distances that are constrained by both the size of your premises and the physical constraints of the LAN. A LAN can be as small as two users and as large as you wish within the physical constraints. Typical LANs have previously had a physical infrastructure of one of the following, but note there are very many other alternatives on the market. These represent the major approaches:

Ethernet – based on thick or thin coaxial, but has rapidly moved to twisted pair and fibre cable. Supports 10 Mbps;

Token Ring – based on twisted pair and operates at 16 Mbps (some old 4 Mbps versions may still exist);

Token Bus – based on coaxial cable and normally found in manufacturing environments;

Appletalk – based on Apple's own proprietary standards offering 230.4 Kbps and used to connect Apple products together.

Developments in LAN technologies include 100 Mbps ethernet and a LAN implementation of ATM (Asynchronous Transfer Mode). Resident on top of any LAN infrastructure is the Network Operating System (NOS). It is that level which provides the functionality and services whilst the infrastructure physically supports the NOS by providing a data transfer capability.

Wide Area Networks

We can think of a Wide Area Network (WAN) as simply a network 'cloud' to which we connect. The cloud takes data from the point of entry and delivers it to the destination point. How it achieves this is not considered our worry, we just use the service. The network may offer particular types of protocol connections.

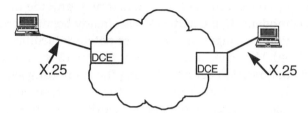

Figure 4.38 X.25 interface

For example X.25 is a typical protocol between DTE and DCE devices and British Telecom offers X.25 network connection. The WAN is able to transfer the data internally to the specified destination DCE. X.25 requires synchronous transmission and will not permit direct connection of asynchronous terminals.

Growth areas are the current developments of ATM networks, MANs (Metropolitan Area Networks), and Frame Relay Networks. The next few years will probably see a significant growth in the use of ATM.

Broadcast

Television providers offer a service which includes an information facility such as Ceefax and Oracle. These are broadcast networks.

Public Switched Data Network

This network is also represented as a 'cloud' on diagrams of networks. The data network interface accepts packets, frames or cells of information and switches them across the network to the destination. These data elements are often all referred to as packets which is a generic name to cover all the terminology used, although there is a distinction between them. The method of connection between the entry point and destination points of the PSDN may be virtual circuit or datagram.

Countries in Europe have been working together under the auspices of CCITT (Consultative Committee of the International Telegraph and Telephone), called the ITU (International Telecommunications Union). The standards which have become widely used are based on 64 Kbps channels and network user addresses are defined by X.121. This specifies a 12 decimal digits plus two optional digit format.

Digit	Purpose
1-4 (DNIC)	Three digits identifying the country;
	Digit 4 helps identify a network within a country;
5-12 (National Number)	Local area number and local number;
13/14 (Optional)	Subaddress where operated.

Other standards for PSDN networks include Frame Relay, ATM and MANs. In each case the original user data is routed across the network in packets which are normally smaller than the original component. At the destination, the fragmented packets are reassembled to form the complete data.

Public Switched Telephone Network

The PSTN is the general telephone network for voice traffic. Where data exchanges between two points are required for a limited duration, it may provide the ideal communication facility. Connection via modems to the network has already been covered earlier in the unit. Should we require connection for longer periods other network facilities such as leased line or PSDN should be considered. Hence we must consider the duration of connection, volume of data and the various tariffs in operation before selecting the connecting service.

Where the DTEs are distant from each other it is relatively simple to connect the two devices via the public switched telephone network. The modems provide a means of representing the digital signal as frequency tones. The basic idea behind this approach is similar to you whistling at different notes to signal the data. If two notes represent a 0 and 1 in one direction and another two notes represent a 0 and 1 in the opposite direction, then we can exchange data. All V.21 300 bps modems use this principle of using frequency shift keying to represent the data.

Modem A to B		Modem B to A	
0	1	0	1
980 Hz	1180 Hz	1650 Hz	1850 Hz

In this arrangement modem A is the originating modem (and therefore in originate mode) and modem B is in answer mode. Modems normally power up in the originate mode and switch to answer mode when they hear the ringing tone. The ITU V.21 standard operates at 300 bps, but higher speeds ranging from 1200 bps using V.22 modems through to 9600 bps using V.32 and 19200 bps using V.32 terbo are available.

The PSTN offers a 2-wire line and is the basic telephone network provided by British Telecom. Each country has its own services e.g. DDD in the USA. A 4-wire specification is also available. Most modems come with the standard telephone plug to connect to the telephone network. The various controls and protocols that need to be established are covered later in this section.

Integrated services data network

ISDN is a developing standard for digital communication allowing complete integration of voice, data, fax and video on a single system. In the basic format, it consists of two channels (B channels) of 64 Kbps and one 16 Kbps channel (D channel). This has developed into a megastream facility of 30 B channels and 1 D channel, making up a 2.048 Mbps system. Each of the B channels can carry voice or data. Larger capacity channels can be provided by combining a number of B channels together.

Private Wide Area Networks

Some WANs are established for the benefit of groups of people or organisations. Banks will have closed WANs for managing their business, including Automatic Telling Machines. The universities have a closed network called JANET and Hewlett Packard have HP Internet as a closed Internet which operates across all their organisation. There are a range of closed wide area networks to which connection can be made. Typical of such networks are:

❏ Compuserve   A commercial information service network. This is private in as much that it is a subscriber service, but public in as much that anyone can subscribe.

❏ Internet   A collection of many networks all running the TCP/IP suite. This can be run over X.25 dial up or any other connecting service. BT have just launched BTNet.

Task 4.12   PC 1

For each of the networks considered in section 4.3.1, note the major features associated with them. Investigate where each type of network may be used and note the key points of the application.

4.3.2 Components

Workstations

The workstation can be a dumb terminal, a PC or a powerful station such as a SUN micro-computer. The selection will depend on the funds available and the work to be carried out. Increasingly, to provide flexibility and allow for future developments, a PC or higher specification platform are normally selected for users. Remember, these are classed as DTE devices.

Data Transmission Media

To carry the signal from one point to another needs a transmission media to support the signalling approach taken. This could be anything from a piece of string or air waves to something more sophisticated. However we most commonly use different forms of copper wire and fibre optic cable. Infra-red and microwave links provide more specialist services. Recent developments with wireless networks using Spread Spectrum Transmission (SST) and microwave channels are appearing on the market place. The allocation of frequency channels which do not clash with the UK cellular operation of Cellnet and Vodafone has been problematic for the microwave developments. The physical appearance of the media were shown in figures 4.13 to 4.15.

Computer to Media Connectors

In Element 4.1.2 we introduced the 25-pin and 9-pin D connector which continue to provide the most popular general connection. For LAN installations, the RJ-45 plug and socket is emerging as the preferred connector.

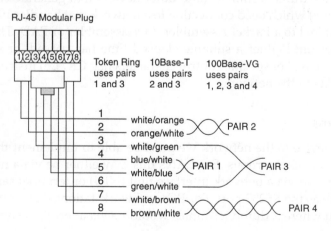

Figure 4.39 EIA/TIA 568B Specification

Previously the BNC connector and DIN plugs provided the connection facility.

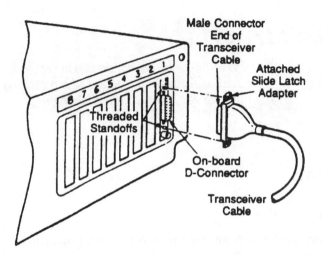

Figure 4.40 Ethernet card attachment
(Copyright Learning Group International Reprinted with permission)

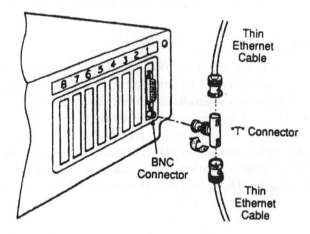

Figure 4.41 Example BNC connection
(Copyright Learning Group International Reprinted with permission)

Where the network card is for a token ring the card also acts as a repeater.

To accommodate dumb terminals (and other devices that generate characters for transmission relatively slowly) which need connection to a network that handles packets of data, we connect the dumb terminal to a Packet Assembler / Disassembler or PAD. This PAD stores the characters in a buffer until either a suitable elapsed time has passed, or sufficient characters have arrived or the arrival of specific control characters (e.g CR/LF) instructs it to forward the packet from the PAD to the network.

Network Cards

To connect a device to the network we must be able to implement that network's access technique and data packet formats. For LANs this may either be via a network card connected to the device's bus or via a network interface unit (NIU) or terminal server using existing device interfaces such as the RS232 port. For PCs and workstations this would normally be a network card approach whereas dumb terminals would be via a terminal server.

Photograph 4.2 Typical Ethernet card

Typically LAN cards provide either token ring or ethernet facilities. Photograph 4.2 shows an old ethernet card with a D connector and a BNC connector on the right hand edge. We would now expect an RJ-45 connector to be provided, the other connectors may be also provided, as in Photograph 4.3.

Photograph 4.3 RJ-45 connector on card

Task 4.13 — C 3.4

Investigate and record the major features provided by an ethernet card.

File and Print Servers

PC developments have created, and supported in some circumstances, an unprofessional approach to I.T. and companies in this situation frequently had no clear I.T. strategy. The introduction of LANs in the late 1980's as an interconnection mechanism supporting central facilities offered an opportunity for organisations to regain control. Data and software products could (and should) be organised or recognised at central points in the system and private copies of data ought to disappear. (By private data we simply mean data that has been collected by individuals to assist in their local environment. If correctly structured and stored this may be of benefit to others in the same organisation when made available. This is not normally confidential information and everyone should recognise that information is a corporate asset and should be shared). Typically, the central point in a networked solution to store both data and software is a fileserver.

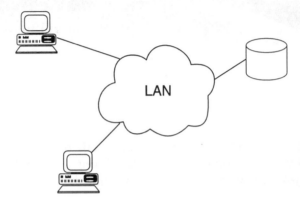

Figure 4.42 LAN support for fileserver

Question 4.14

In providing a fileserver approach, what benefits are gained by the organisation in controlling software? You may ignore the data issues just now and concentrate on the application software issues.

The central server approach clearly offers the organisation enormous benefits in creating genuine corporate data. Both data and application software can be accessed or downloaded to local workstations as appropriate by authorised users. It offers the organisation an opportunity of keeping control of software releases, exercising control to remain legal with the number of product licences purchased (and users attempting to use the product simultaneously) and can avoid too great a spread of products thus achieving greater data compatibility. The user gains by having access to a wider data source with better data integrity. The potential is available for a wider range of supported software products, which are release compatible across the organisation, and with access capability to other servers and services. The server is designed to give a wider access for users to share the resource offered by the server. In the case of the fileserver, this has been the application software and data.

Question 4.15

In addition to a fileserver, what other types of server might be helpful to the users?

Question 4.16

Are there any disadvantages to the server approach compared with individual workstations operating in isolation?

Question 4.17

The environment in which a fileserver can be used has been biased towards an office environment in the above text. Suggest one other environment in which a central fileserver may be helpful.

A typical network within an organisation is likely to provide access to its central computer facilities. This may be the repository for the main database and hold much of the corporate data. Indeed, the central mini or mainframe may even play the role of the fileserver in many installations. In such a situation, the network may have the following features.

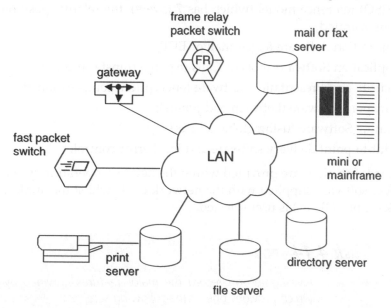

Figure 4.43 Examples of Servers

In many networks it is likely that a number of printers exist. If the user sends all printer requests to the print server, the option to select a specific print station for output exists. A default would normally operate if the user didn't specify or select a particular station.

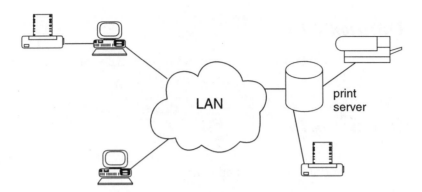

Figure 4.44 Shared print facilities

Control of the printer server will normally be a function of the network operating system. Equally, control of individual user access to a fileserver will be provided within the network operating system. Network management and security issues will be covered in Element 4.3.6 and are important issues, since we have to comply with legal requirements such as the Data Protection Act.

Software

We have already seen that software exists at many levels in data communications. If we show the relationships in a hierarchical model, which is based on the international standards organisation's (ISO) reference model (which has 7 layers), the relative position of different aspects can be demonstrated.

- ❐ Application Software (e.g. e-mail or EDI);
- ❐ Application Software Tools or Calls (e.g. file transfer routines);
- ❐ Security and Presentation Software (encryption, compression etc.);
- ❐ Transport Software (between end points);
- ❐ Routing Software (using global addresses);
- ❐ Point-to-point delivery software and local error control.

Some of these functions are provided within the network operating system, some with the network driver software supplied with the network cards whilst the application software (e.g. e-mail package or EDI etc.) is user selected.

Task 4.14 PC 2

Investigate and record the major features provided by a software package which provides one of the following services:

- ❐ *EDI;*
- ❐ *Security;*
- ❐ *Compression.*

Multiplexer

In the early days of computing there was little opportunity for users to 'talk' directly to the mainframe computers. Jobs were submitted in batch format which had been prepared on paper tape or punch cards and a relatively small range of peripheral devices existed which were directly connected to the host machine.

As systems evolved, the opportunity to permit direct terminal connection to the host machine was established. A greater need for terminal access developed and it was no longer feasible to provide each with a direct connection as in figure 4.45.

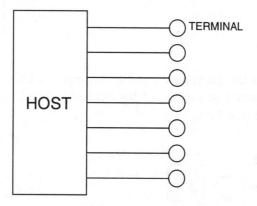

Figure 4.45 Direct Connection

Direct connections required individual ports on the host machine for each connected device and this became expensive both in terms of space and cost as the number of direct connection requirements grew. Equally, poor utilisation of the system for the volume of data carried by each connected station was experienced, especially when many of the terminals could be inactive for significant periods of time.

To overcome the problem of so many direct terminal connections, each carrying low volumes of traffic, the concept of channelling multiple data inputs into one connection was developed. Each input could be separately identified and handled on arrival.

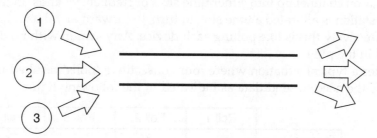

Figure 4.46 Channelling

At the host end of the connection or 'pipe' of mixed data inputs is a single connection, but each individual station's data flowing down the pipe must be separately identified and managed by routing it to the appropriate 'process' or 'operating system socket'.

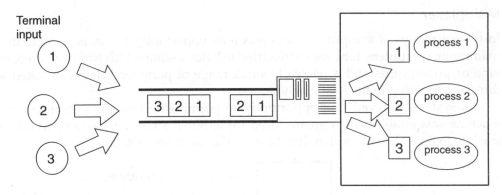

Figure 4.47 Data flow on a multiplexer

The clever bit of this design is how a particular input is identified and filtered through to the correct destination point or process at the host end. The intention is to emulate the original structure of direct connection.

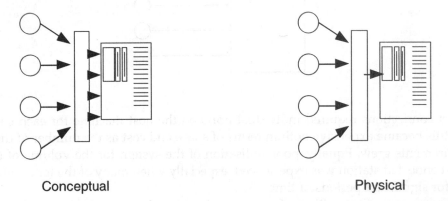

Conceptual   Physical

Figure 4.48 Conceptual and physical multiplexer arrangement

The approaches used to implement multiplexing were initially based on dividing the pipe or communication channel up into either time slots or frequency bands. In the first approach each connected station is allocated a time slot, in turn, to forward any data it has to send to the multiplexer. Effectively this is like polling each device. Any station with no data to send leaves an empty slot in the pipe.

Consider a typical situation where four consecutive 'polls' resulted in the attached terminals having the need to send data as indicated in the following figure.

	Poll 1	Poll 2	Poll 3	Poll 4
Terminal 1	✓	✓		✓
Terminal 2	✓		✓	✓
Terminal 3	✓	✓	✓	

Figure 4.49 Typical poll outcome

Such a poll outcome would result in the sequence of data flowing in our multiplexed channel as in figure 4.50. The data element, especially in the early range of Time Division Multiplexers (TDMs), could be either a bit or a character and is called bit or character interleaved channels.

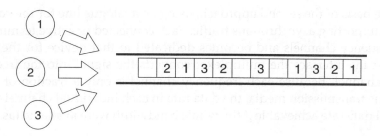

Figure 4.50 Typical multiplexed data flow

When a character is sent using asynchronous transmission, the start and stop bits are removed and only the eight bits are sent. These start and stop bits are of course restored at the receiving end.

Question 4.18

Why are there empty slots in figure 4.50? Why didn't we just bring forward the next active station's transmission into the empty slot space?

Question 4.19

If most of the time slots are not used, how could we ensure the receiving multiplexer stays in synchronisation with the sender when using asynchronous mode?

As the technology of TDMs has changed to utilise high speed digital links, we have seen the introduction of high speed TDMs linking over 50 channels or input devices. Each channel can support either asynchronous or synchronous protocols with V.24 or RS232 interfaces.

In the time slot or time division multiplexing arrangement, the data signal in each time slot occupies the full frequency range or capacity of the transmission media. Alternatively it is possible to divide the frequency range or spectrum of the cable up into a number of separate channels or ranges using the concept of frequency division multiplexing.

Question 4.20

If TDM is the acronym normally used for Time Division Multiplexing, what acronym is assigned to Frequency Division Multiplexing?

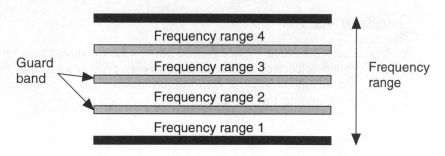

Figure 4.51 Frequency division of transmission medium

FDM is the basis of the second approach, using an analogue line for the connection and is most suited to supporting asynchronous traffic. Each connected or active terminal is allocated to one of the frequency channels and becomes dedicated to that device for the duration of the connection. At the interface the multiplexer converts the signal into the frequency range for the allocated channel. Because each frequency channel is only a fraction of the whole frequency range of the transmission media, the data rate in each individual channel will also be a fraction of the total data rate achievable if the whole bandwidth were available (as in time division multiplexing).

However the advantage to any terminal here is that the frequency channel is dedicated and always available to that station. There is no waiting 'your turn' to send. A small disadvantage is the loss of some of the frequency range to act as a guard band. These guard bands are necessary to ensure a clear separation of each of the frequency channels defined. The hardware at the receiving end has to pick out each frequency channel from the 'mixed' signal received and pass to the destination host the digital signal for each of the inputs.

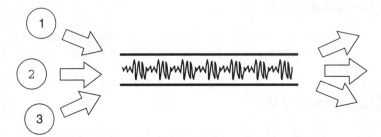

Figure 4.52 Signalling on FDM

Both the approaches have the disadvantage of wasted capacity whenever the input stations have nothing to send.

Question 4.21

How is wasted capacity in TDM and FDM seen on the transmission medium?

Question 4.22

A transmission medium has a fixed bandwidth of 3000 Hz and can carry 19200 bps using V.21 signalling. If we have 18 stations each sending 2 characters per second, what utilisation have we made of the link if TDM is operating in asynchronous mode?

Question 4.23

Using the same cable as in question 4.22 we now implement FDM with 18 channels (each of 120 Hz bandwidth) each providing a 110 bps capacity. What is the utilisation of the transmission medium in this arrangement assuming asynchronous transmission?

Auxiliary Storage

Any storage space which isn't central to the system (e.g. file server) may be considered to be auxiliary storage. Local disk space can be classified as auxiliary.

Repeater, Bridge, Router and Gateway

A local area network, owned and administered by an organisation, is frequently created on a small scale. A signal generated by one station clearly has a maximum distance it can travel before it degenerates in quality to such an extent that it is no longer recognisable. The maximum distance for a signal to travel is well established and known. If we want signals to travel further than these distances we need a relay device to boost or regenerate the signal. Such a device is a repeater.

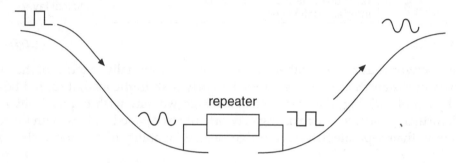

Figure 4.53 Repeater function

The connecting devices that we used to connect segments together in figure 4.53 are repeaters. In their simplest form they do nothing else but this regenerating process. More sophisticated models are able to provide some additional features such as isolating a faulty segment when error conditions in the signalling are detected. Each interface in a token ring network also has a repeater function in addition to its other functions. Typically repeaters delay the signal by just a few bits as they regenerate individual bits.

The international model provides a structure or framework for the design of networks based on a 7-layer model. This approach is helpful, since individual networks that conform to the standards created ought to be able to interconnect with each other without too much difficulty. The repeater works at the bottom layer of this 7-layer model, boosting or regenerating the signal.

Question 4.24

Consider a scenario where two companies have just merged. Both companies had previously installed their own networks which conformed with the international 7-layer model. Will the approach they had adopted be helpful as the newly formed organisation attempts to join the two separate networks together?

7	File Transfer, access and management document and message interchange etc	Application layer
6	Data representation transformation and security	Presentation layer
5	Dialogue and synchronisation control	Session layer
4	End-to-end transfer management (connections, error or flow control, segmentation)	Transport layer
3	Network routing and addressing	Network layer
2	Framing, data transparency, error control	Link layer
1	Mechanical and electrical network interface definitions	Physical layer

Figure 4.54 7-layer model

Once a network has reached either a maximum size (especially in terms of the number of users allowed or distances covered) or reached a fairly high traffic load, it cannot be expanded further by simply adding more repeaters. However, we may wish to physically extend our network further or partition our existing network into two joined 'halves' with the majority of traffic kept in their separate halves. A bridge has the capability of creating such a joined network.

Question 4.25

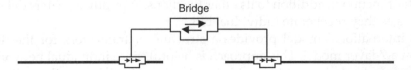

If the network traffic is fairly high, would the introduction of a bridge create two separate but joined halves with roughly split loading on each half?

Bridge

Figure 4.55 Bridged Network

Each half of the network can function independently of the other and data traffic is only passed through the bridge when the destination is not on the originating half of the network i.e. the bridge filters the traffic such that most of the traffic is retained in the originating half of the network and never seen on the other side. Slightly more robustness is built into a bridged configuration because of the filtering capabilities of the bridge. In the 7-layer model it operates at level 2. It is usually used to join two similar networks together, such as ethernet to ethernet. However, bridges to join two IEEE 802 conformant networks are available and we can bridge a token ring network and an ethernet network. The IEEE 802 series are a set of LAN standards and are widely used.

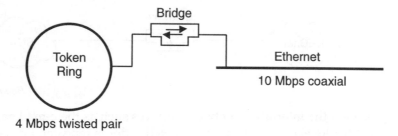

Figure 4.56 Permissible Bridged Networks

If we wish to join two dissimilar networks which are using the same protocols at the higher levels of the 7-layer model, we can use a router. The router operates on the international internet address which can be assigned to each station and encapsulates the data in the appropriate packet structure. Normally a router operates at layer 3 in the 7-layer model. Routers work on an internet address and local hardware addresses are only known within the LAN. Thus a router has created what can be simply regarded as administratively separate zone or LAN. Part of the internet address identifies the LAN and the other part of the address identifies an individual workstation on that LAN.

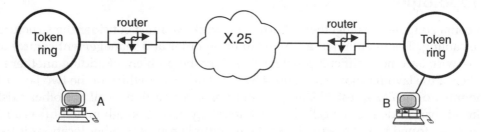

Figure 4.57 Typical Router Connection

A router makes decisions about forwarding packets based on the layer 3 internet address. Packets which have a final destination outside the immediate area are sent to a router by devices on the network. Thus the router is an addressable device. This is in contrast to a repeater and most bridges which are transparent to the devices on a network and where packets are sent directly to the hardware address of the destination. Thus a workstation on the LAN in figure 4.57 that wishes to talk to an equivalent workstation on the other LAN would send the packet with the destination's internet address wrapped up and then addressed locally to the hardware address of the local router. On receipt of a packet the local router unwraps it and examines the internet address of the destination. The router then forwards the packet by re-wrapping it and sending onwards. Finally on arrival at the destination LAN's router it recognises the local internet address and translates this to the destination workstation's local hardware address. The packet is then sent on the last leg of the transfer to the intended receiver.

Question 4.26

How does the router attached to the destination network know that a packet just received is for this LAN and shouldn't be routed onwards?

If the protocols are completely different between the two environments we are seeking to connect, then the connecting relay is a gateway. This may operate at layer 7 of the model.

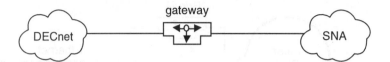

Figure 4.58 Gateway Connection

A gateway is often the interface to network services such as the e-mail gateway.

In terms of the level of complexity the ranked order is repeater, bridge, router, gateway. A repeater is the cheapest in the range, does little more than regenerate the signal but works at the speed of the network. At the other end of the range the most expensive device is a gateway. It does a lot of conversion work and is not capable of working at the maximum speed of the network. It can only process at a lower rate. Fortunately in the majority of networks only a subset of the traffic on a network is directed at the gateway, hence it can keep up with the performance demands made of it. As long as each of the devices can keep up with the performance of the slowest of the connected networks, it will not be a constraint on overall performance.

4.3.3 Topologies

In connecting devices together to form a network we must consider the structure or layout of the cabling. The intention of a LAN is to bring order and management control to what could otherwise become a difficult problem. Consider the problem of adding another node or PC to either of the layouts shown in figure 4.59. It is fairly clear which of the two layouts will give us the most difficulty in establishing an additional connection to all the other existing stations. The left hand side is often called a **mesh** topology and although unhelpful as a LAN structure it is often found in WAN situations where multiple routes to other locations is useful.

Question 4.27

In the unstructured topology of figure 4.59 what do you see as the major problem of adding more nodes?

Question 4.28

Why do you think the structured version is better?

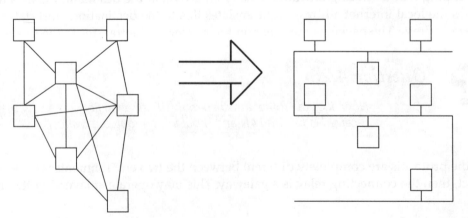

Figure 4.59 Cable structures

Cable structure is very important and its logical layout is a key element in supporting the different LAN approaches such as ethernet and token ring. The physical installation of the cable which represents the logical layout has been changing quite significantly over recent years. A structured cabling approach is now commonly implemented which may not resemble the layout we are fundamentally trying to create. Since it is important that the fundamental structures are understood, we'll use that as a starting point.

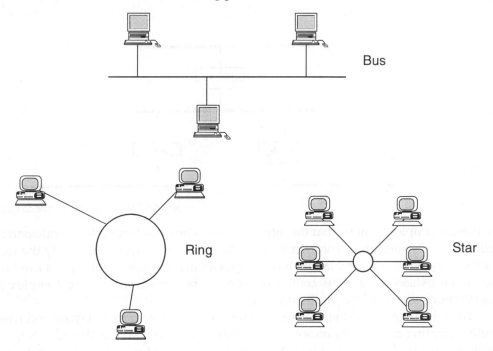

Figure 4.60 Typical topologies

Bus

A bus topology consists of a 'single' communication channel. Each connected device is attached to the media at an interface point and has its own unique hardware address. Data transfers between the interfaces or nodes take place using these hardware addresses.

Question 4.29

Why does each node have a hardware address which is unique as far as that LAN is concerned?

The maximum permitted length of the cable depends upon a number of factors:

- ❏ signalling methods   (e.g. digital, analogue)
- ❏ access method   (how we share access to the shared transmission system)
- ❏ speed of signalling   (data rates)
- ❏ cable type used   (physical properties)

Although we have represented the bus topology as a single cable run, in all but the simplest of installations the bus will have more complex arrangements with several interconnected segments. There are precise rules on how the interconnection of segments is arranged.

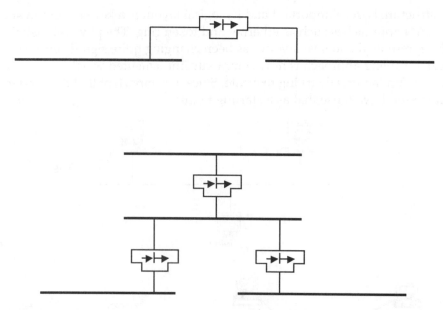

Figure 4.61 Two examples of more complex bus structures

In these examples, assume that the interconnection box is intended to be transparent. It may be difficult to visualise these configurations as single bus structures, especially the second configuration. Indeed the second layout has the appearance of a tree topology but can logically operate as an extended bus. Bus configurations can be significantly more complex in large site installations than the layouts shown here.

The advantages of using the bus structure include simplicity of layout and ease of connectivity. Locating cable faults on such a topology is also relatively easy and this is an important issue for network maintainability. The topology is ideal for one-to-many data transmissions since all connected devices 'hear' the traffic on the cable. This is achieved because signalling on the cable is normally bi-directional and the signal reaches all stations regardless of their position on the bus. There is a security disadvantage arising here since eavesdropping on other station's traffic is relatively easy. Also there is no automatic acknowledgement of receipt by virtue of the topology i.e. the 'signals' stop when they reach the end of the cable and do not return by default to the sender. However, higher level protocols exist which can ensure that data is successfully exchanged.

Question 4.30

Can a bus topology easily handle broadcast messages where all stations hear the data transfer?

Question 4.31

Why might significant volumes of broadcast messages to all stations be a nuisance?

Ring

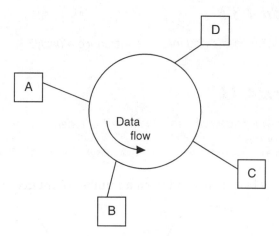

Figure 4.62 Simple ring topology

In contrast to the bus, it is normal in a ring configuration for the data transmission to be uni-directional. Of course, there are exceptions to this when dual cable rings are operating, but the simple arrangement is uni-directional. Data transmissions are received by each station's inter-face as the data passes through the interface connection. As in the bus topology, each interface only copies the data from the network and passes it to the device it connects to the network when it recognises the packet's destination address as its own. Each network interface connection has its own hardware address for identification.

There are several local area network standards based on a ring topology. Dominant in the U.K. during the 1980's was the Cambridge Ring implementation, but this has largely disappeared. Currently both token ring and larger networks such as Fibre Distributed Data Interface (FDDI) and Metropolitan Area Networks (MANs) are based on a ring topology.

There is one important concept which applies to most ring implementations. Each interface station allows data transmissions to pass through the interface with only a few bits delay. So, for example, in a data packet structure of say 64 bytes, the start of the data packet may well have circulated around the ring and arrived back at the originating station before the end of the packet has left it. In this mode there is only one circulating data packet on the ring.

This will not be true in all ring based implementations and they may support one or more complete packets in circulation. This area is quite complex, with FDDI imposing different criteria to the token ring. But, for the ubiquitous token ring, the concept that any station is only 'holding' a few of the circulating bits at any instant is an important one to recognise. The token ring is so named because a station cannot talk (or transmit) until it notionaly holds a token which is circulating around the ring.

Normally each node or interface on a ring has a signal regeneration capability. Hence to ensure the quality of the signal at any point on the ring, the critical factor is the distance between any two nodes. Additionally, overall performance will be coupled to how many nodes play an active role in the network. Clearly there can be no routing problems since everyone on the ring will get the data, with the addressed node being able to copy the data. Because the sender sees the packet it generated eventually returned to itself (by virtue of the data completing a lap around the ring) the opportunity to implement automatic acknowledgements can be in-built.

Question 4.32

Why does a ring interface introduce a delay?

Question 4.33

Why is overall performance of a token ring coupled to the number of active nodes?

Larger networks may be constructed from a number of interconnected rings.

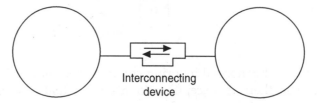

Figure 4.63 Interconnected rings

Star

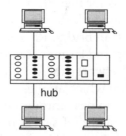

Figure 4.64 Star Configuration

The normal arrangement for a star topology includes a central switching system or hub. In the figure shown, if station D wishes to talk to station B, it does so via the hub. Implementations based on this topology include systems using PABX (Private Automatic Branch Exchange). In the basic form shown here, the medium is not really shared and each new device requiring connection will result in another cable run to the central point or hub. If the hub was physically close to its connected devices then the individual cable runs would not be problematic.

Provided the central point which is switching data through to the destination is robust, this topology gives better overall reliability against cable faults etc. than either of the previous two approaches. Only a single node will be unavailable in the event of a cable failure. LANs implementing the star as their logical topology are sometimes based on existing telephone wiring in the building and do not normally have high data transfer rates.

There are not many implementations of LANs which have a star topology as its logical structure. However, the physical layout of most other LANs looks very much like a star topology even though they are considered to be some other topology. Structured cable systems make the physical appearance of ethernet and token ring systems appear as star topologies. The hub component is then a specially designed 'box' to maintain the original logical features of the LANs.

Task 4.15 PC 3   *C 3.4*

For each network topology described in section 4.3.3, note the major features associated with them. Investigate where each topology is typically used and note the key points of each application.

4.3.4 Benefits

Shared benefits

Before the PC became a popular workplace tool in the early 1980's, computer systems usually consisted of central mainframes. Suites of programs were written to handle particular applications and this often resulted in multiple occurrences of data. E.g. a customer's name and address might exist in several application program suites. Amendment of data required multiple updating and this frequently led to discrepancies between the various occurrences of the data. This problem led to the central database developments that we now see as the appropriate approach. But PC's introduced another problem in the 1980's with 'private' user developments including applications programs and data. Hence, we re-introduced the problem that multiple data sets may co-exist which were not compatible with each other. Data was created and existed within organisations that possibly only one or two individuals knew existed. Applications were developed that were locally produced, frequently undocumented and did not conform to organisational standards. These systems may have used a range of different software across the organisation (e.g. LOTUS 123, Excel, Quattro etc.) and were frequently at different product version levels. These incompatible standards reduce the ability to easily move the data between one PC and another.

Typically, the central point in a networked solution to store both data and software is a file-server.

In setting up a LAN with many users sharing a central disk facility or file server, the network manager must assign areas on the disk for users' private data. These might simply be areas of workspace or areas where a user may store data. Indeed, in an ideal world, the server provision should be transparent to the user and simply be seen as another local disk drive. It is simply that this extra disk drive isn't on the users' own local workstation but provided on the server. By controlling logins to the network, this data is protected from other users.

Equally there will be some files, typically system files, holding copies of application programs such as editors, spreadsheets, compilers etc. These system files should ideally be held as a single network copy on the server and any user wishing to use a specific application program would download a copy to their workstation. Hence, the network copy of each application program will need to have sufficient numbers of user licences for the predicted number of simultaneous users. Fortunately, network software exists which can control the number of copies which have been downloaded and are in active use at any one time. This will prevent illegal use of software.

In figure 4.43 and in answering question 4.15 we introduced the concept that it is not only data that may be centrally kept and provided on a server basis. There are other types of device which an organisation is unlikely to provide separately to each individual station. For example, it is unlikely that every user would have their own laser printer, at least not a quality laser with a variety of paper trays holding company headed stationary and blank paper of both A3 and A4 size. Nor is it likely that each station would have its own FAX, modem link or scanner.

In these cases, the organisation need only buy sufficient numbers of each type to satisfy the shared demand. Indeed, one of the benefits of installing a network is to provide the capability of sharing devices. In accepting that shared access is beneficial and is a correct implementation approach, we need to resolve the problem of contention where two or more stations require simultaneous access to a shared device. What isn't really acceptable to an individual station is to find that on one attempt to use the shared facility it is seen to be available, yet on a subsequent attempt it is seen to be unavailable and the user has to manually intervene to delay access until a re-attempt some time later. The server approach overcomes this difficulty by accepting the requests for service from stations and queueing these requests up for action on a 'first come first served' basis (or whatever other algorithm is selected). To the user such access is seen to be successful but actually the action may have been slightly delayed until the request gets to the front of the queue.

Question 4.34

If we examine the services that could be available on a FAX server, what facilities might optionally, or additionally, be provided?

Hence the benefits may be summarised as the sharing of software, hardware, resources and data.

Central services

The issues of security, support and maintenance may be viewed as problematic. The wider the geographic distribution of access points, the greater the potential security risk. However, with a corporate approach to security, the system can potentially be established with greater security compared to multiple freestanding devices, each relying on the measures introduced by their users. Sensitive data can now be held at a central point with appropriate access controls.

Users can also specify their own data as available for access to others using the access control fields seen earlier. Hence, data created and saved from a database application by one user can be made readily available for other users to read. It is this aspect of data sharing capability that is attractive to organisations and achieves some of the objectives

When computer installations comprised of mainframes, the opportunities for incremental growth and system evolution were sometimes restricting. The introduction of PCs allowed additional resources to be easily purchased, but frequently lacked integration into the corporate information system. LANs provided a technical capability of integrating the PC based software developments back into a corporate entity. The network also provided end users with improved local performance and better response time whilst providing the system integration capability. Additional benefits of a distributed computer system over a highly centralised approach include better overall reliability figures and a multivendor selection option, since purchasing need not be restricted to mainframe suppliers.

The support and maintenance can be centrally organised to cover the issues that are unique to a distributed system.

Efficiency

Keeping only one set of data up-to-date and holding single network copies of application software on servers adds an efficiency level to the network system. Upgrades of application software can easily be achieved without having to locate each copy. Equally, the whole organisation upgrades at the same time which reduces any potential conflicts of exchanging non-compatible information.

Team working

Where data is held on a central facility the opportunity for people to work together on the same information (albeit with suitable updating and access control procedures) becomes available. It is common to see teams of people in a common project or area working on the same data and files, allowing easy and rapid sharing rather than relying on sneakernet to transport data around. Sneakernet is an American expression where a user puts on their trainers (sneakers) and walks with a disk to another location!

Task 4.16 PC 4

For each of the benefits identified in section 4.3.4, abstract the key points associated with them.

4.3.5 Media Access Control (Data flow control methods)

Although the GNVQ unit definition calls this element **data flow control**, at this level of range statements we are really considering **media access control** techniques. Within the definition of the unit, the classification distinguishes between the reservation approach (token ring, time slots and polling) and the contention approach (collision avoidance). Within this section we will discuss each of these approaches.

One of the important issues that needs to be emphasised are the methods of achieving efficiency and good utilisation of the network capacity. The installed transmission media needs to be effectively used since it represents a high proportion of the network costs. LANs were originally designed on the basis of sharing the transmission media amongst all the connected stations and the access techniques that have been designed are based on this premise. Hence, if we have shared transmission media and multiple stations capable of placing data on the media, we must control each stations access capability to prevent multiple occurrences of data corrupting each other. For a LAN environment the basic access methods fit into the following model, but a range of other access techniques have evolved for other environments and are considered here also.

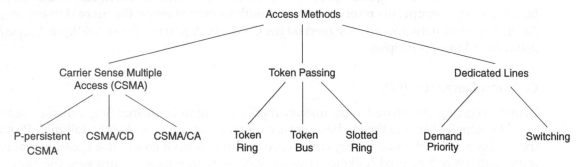

Figure 4.65 Access methods

231

Token Ring and Token Passing

Within this sub group, the basic approach is simply that before a station is allowed to transmit, it must hold the permission to do so. Generally this takes the form of a token which is passed between stations. A station wishing to transmit must be in possession of the token before transmitting. A token is typically a 3 byte data structure of a unique format. Token passing is effectively a speedy form of time division multiplexing without allocating time to stations that have nothing to say. The slotted ring is a derivative in so much as the circulating token also contains a pre-established data field. All forms are logical rings as shown in figure 4.66, but may physically look like stars.

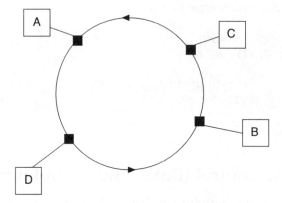

Figure 4.66 Logical Ring Layout

Time slots and polling

We have already seen time slots being used as a control approach when we examined multiplexers. Time Division Multiplexing effectively polled the connected stations and allocated a time slot to each. Polling is simply asking each device, in some predetermined order, if they have data to transfer. Frequently the predetermined order is a simple round robin, but more sophisticated approaches can be undertaken.

Collision Avoidance (CA)

This approach tries to avoid a collision occurring rather than detecting it and taking corrective action. There are a variety of implementation approaches taken which include sending a reservation signal which is long enough for everyone to hear before the particular station begins to talk. If anyone corrupts the reservation signal with its own attempt, the process re-commences. Apple Localtalk networks are designed on the CSMA/CA (Carrier Sense Multiple Access/Collision Avoidance) principles.

Collision Detection (CD)

Before accessing the shared transmission media a station implementing collision detection would normally listen to the media to ensure no other station was already 'talking'. Providing the media is quiet, the station may commence transmission. Of course it is possible that two or more stations commenced 'talking' at what was, to all intents and purposes, the same time. Clearly the data on the media gets corrupted. Rather than waste time by completing a transmission, each station will give up its attempt. Each will have detected the collision with the other stations by undertaking a 'listen while you talk' capability. Each compares what it heard with what it was transmitting and any differences indicate a collision has occurred. This is the collision detection element. Each station would re-attempt access using a clever back off algorithm implemented in ethernet networks. The whole ethernet access technique is known as CSMA/CD (Carrier Sense Multiple Access/Collision Detection).

Task 4.17 PC 5

Describe reservation and contention resolution techniques.

4.3.6 Management activities

Check network activity levels and System Reporting

In any well managed LAN it is essential that an active maintenance policy is pursued using some of the network management tools now available. It is in this area that the fastest developments have occurred in the past few years. Vendors have been striving to make their systems more attractive by offering the 'best' range of facilities in this area. Most networks do not operate independently, with interconnection and interoperability increasingly being a requirement. This has dictated that network management systems ought to be able to report on the integrated installation, hence the requirement for standards in this area. Unfortunately at this moment more than one standard exists, and this is likely to be the situation for some time to come. Having said that, there are some clear market leaders and it is on these standards that we will concentrate.

Simple Network Management Protocol (SNMP) has gained rapid widespread acceptance and become a de facto standard with support from over 250 different vendors. An attraction for SNMP vendors is the implementation cost, since MIB-1 agents are in the public domain. It is the ability to maintain such a Management Information Base (MIB) that is critical and this is maintained at the Application Layer.

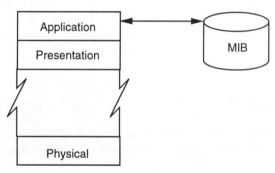

Figure 4.67 MIB

The result is no licence fees when developing a system. SNMP is based on a limited number of primitives Get, Set and Trap.

All devices which can be managed by SNMP are able to provide operational data when polled or requested for by the network management centre, e.g. how many transfers were sucessful since the last poll. Typical of devices in this category are bridges. The code is referred to as the agent in the management station and in the end station is called the client. The agent information is in the form of counters or parameters, known as objects. Hence the client retrieves these objects in order to configure, report faults or gather statistics of the device being managed.

There are some limitations with SNMP, e.g. a client cannot make a single poll request to an agent, but has to maintain a whole sequence of polls. Hence polling frequencies have to be thoughtful, otherwise over polling and too much data will be collected over the network.

The OSI offering is Common Management Information Service and Protocol (CMIS/CMIP). CMIP is a comprehensive network service and protocol tool supporting what has become accepted as the major features required to maintain and operate an enterprise wide network:

❏ accounting management;

❏ configuration management;

❏ fault management;

❏ performance management;

❏ security management.

The MIB created is then controlled by a number of well defined primitives such as 'get' and 'create'. The result hopefully will allow the integration of individual network management systems to be seen as a whole.

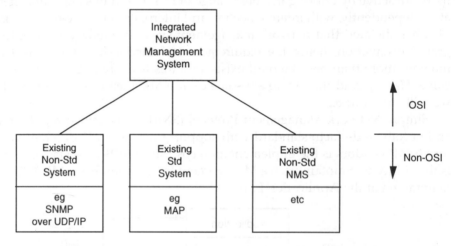

Figure 4.68 Integrating Capability of CMIP

Question 4.35

If all the LANs in an enterprise wide network use SNMP, does this make it easier to create an integrated network management system?

Just to give an outline of the existing range of network management systems currently available, a list of just a few of the vendors products is given:

BT	CIMS
HP	Openview
IBM	Netview
Novell	NMS
Spider	Spider Sentinel
SUN	SunNet Manager
SynOptics	SNMP Lattisnet

A number of features may be considered particularly relevant when selecting a network management system:

☐ graphical interface (including network maps);

☐ remote control;

☐ visual (colour coded/audible alarms);

☐ auto-discovery;

☐ monitor and analysis.

Security

We have seen already that security issues have been raised and various technical aspects addressed. At a management level we have statutory responsibilities defined under the Data Protection Act. Additionally, copyright and licence arrangements have to be observed. Management procedures to ensure compliance via the technical approaches need to be in place. Regular audit of procedures will give confidence that compliance is being achieved.

Storage

The concept of a fileserver providing a major storage facility has previously been introduced. Auxiliary storage may be provided locally. In a fully distributed model, all hard disks could be part of the central storage facility. Where multiple users share storage space it is important that each file created is associated with the owning user.

As management issues, we would want to resolve:

☐ how much disk space can be allocated to a user;

☐ who is responsible for managing the space and backups;

☐ what protection/access mechanisms should apply;

☐ how long should files be kept online before archiving or purging
(this is important where multiple versions have been created).

System Configuration

The configuration of any system will depend on a range of issues including:

☐ the size and complexity of the system;

☐ the topology or architecture;

☐ the level of security needed.

Depending on the system there will be service queues available to users. E.g in many systems if a user issues a print command, the output will be placed on a printer queue and printed when it reaches the front of the queue. Some systems will have multiple print queues. Each queue will be associated with the physical location of a printer or printer quality. Each station will have an associated default printer defined to which print will be directed unless instructed differently.

Each service may be provided with access rights and possible password controls. E.g students may be denied access to the colour printer queue or external resources.

235

Task 4.18 PC 6   *C 3.4*

Investigate one of the common network management tools and report on the key features of the product.

4.3.7 System Security Methods

The security level implemented will need to reflect the value of the information or system that is being protected. In a commercially sensitive environment (i.e. the stock exchange) the extent of the security will be different from a local college or school network where breaches of security, although unwelcome, ought not to end in the collapse of the organisation. Sensitive data may be encrypted to prevent recognition of content by unauthorised readers. This is particularly useful during transmission.

Control of access

Early computer systems housed in computer centres were able to control access almost completely by controlling physical access to the building. Access controls could be categorised as something you own, something you know or something you are. Typical controls include:

- identity cards;
- pass cards;
- control doors with security staff;
- coded locks with security code or simple swipe card;
- special devices e.g retina scanners, palm/finger print readers.

Each of these have advantages and disadvantages.

Question 4.36

List a possible advantage and disadvantage for each of the control approaches given above.

Question 4.37

Which category (own, know, are) do each of the above controls fit?

Of course, communication systems have changed the security requirements, since personnel may be located outside the central office suite. Staff may be working from home, sales staff may connect in from remote locations and sales orders may be received via EDI. Hence a logical access control, in addition to the physical access, is required to support the security.

Security breaches are often caused by staff not following procedures. Raising the awareness of security amongst all users is important if systems are to be well protected. Leaving passwords written on 'post-it' stickers on the side of workstations is not unknown! Since there are statutory obligations to protect data, the security procedures will be the focus on meeting such legal requirements. The logical access controls may be implemented by software or hardware controls. They can specify the various levels of access in terms of the range or permitted penetration into the system or in terms of the read, write, execute and delete permissions at any level.

Forced recognition of security

Many organisations require staff to sign non-disclosure agreements as a condition of employment. Government Agencies may demand all staff working within the agency, or on contracts placed by government, to sign the Official Secrets Act. Various levels of security vetting will be undertaken on staff signing the Official Secrets Act. Bringing a disk into some organisations and potentially introducing a virus is a sackable offence. Equally the unauthorised removal of data from organisations can result in the same outcome!

Task 4.19 PC 6   C 3.4

Investigate the security measures at two types of installation e.g. a low security installation such as your own school or college and that of a major installation. Report on the different security approaches taken.

Use a computer network

Introduction

This is really the element to put into practice issues of establishing and managing a network. The approach you will be able to take will depend entirely on the network(s) that are available within your own school, college or organisation. Since there are very many network operating systems on the market it is not possible to cover each possibility here. Novell currently has a significant market penetration of the PC installations and many systems look like figure 4.69.

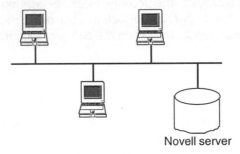

Novell server

Figure 4.69 Typical network server configuration

Another popular route may be the use of a UNIX host to provide services to other client machines.

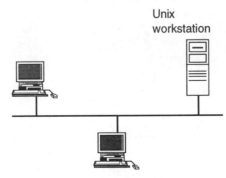

Unix
workstation

Figure 4.70 Networked UNIX environment

4.4.1 Access

In this section you are required to perform the following activities:

- ☐ login;
- ☐ display files;
- ☐ access files;
- ☐ display applications;
- ☐ access applications.

If you have already accessed the University of Glamorgan's system in Element 4.2.5, you will have already collected the evidence needed.

4.4.2 Organisation's Standards

The relevant issues here are:

- ❏ User identification;
- ❏ security convention;
- ❏ copyright requirements;
- ❏ procedural requirements;
- ❏ allocated workspace.

The information in Element 4.2.4 on accessing the University of Glamorgan's system shows the user I.D. and security conventions used. Any user, by proceeding beyond login, accepts the standards of behaviour and security requirements set. Taking material that is copyright protected is illegal. This includes copying software as well as books and music recordings, even if it is for private use.

In a LAN, users may be allocated their own disk space on a server. You can check how much you have used e.g **ls -l** on a Unix system. You need to check out the option on your own system.

4.4.3 Data file processes

Accessing data is a routine activity on any network. Existing data needs to be retrieved, frequently updated with the amend routine and the updated copy saved. Creating original data and deleting obsolete data are the extreme ends of this activity. For each set of data, a decision should be made about the level of file protection that should be set up.

On your LAN, most of the activities needed as evidence can be undertaken using your local editor or wordprocessing package. Indeed the work you did in Element 2.2 would be fine if was completed on a LAN based system.

4.4.4 File management and access rights

A range of file management facilities should exist on any networked system. They will include copy, rename, delete, move, list files, create and modify directory structures and set rights to directory structures. How you are able to do this will depend on the facilities you are able to access.

Task 4.20 PC 1, 2 & 3

On your network, investigate the file management facilities and access rights. You should be able to set access rights to your own files and the sub-directories for other users.

Task 4.21 PC 5

One of the performance criteria in this element requires you to undertake an e-mail activity. The concept was covered in Element 4.1.1. If you wish, you may exchange e-mail with:

gnvq@ comp.glamorgan.ac.uk

Otherwise, send e-mail to a friend on your installation, requesting a reply.

4.4.5 Install

This activity is associated with setting up users on a network. The activities would include:

- ❏ access server;
- ❏ create user name;
- ❏ give initial password;
- ❏ set initial access rights.

How you can achieve ths will depend on your own LAN.

Task 4.22 PC 6

Investigate how to install a new user on a LAN available to you. Once you have this information, install a new user on the system.

Answers to questions in Unit 4

Answer 4.1   Your answer will reflect your own experiences. It could be an example such as the Gas Board looking up details of your account or a query on account details at the bank or building society. Whatever your specific example it should involve a two way flow of data, typically where you pose a question to the database and it responds with the information. There may of course have been an update to the database if you had supplied information.

Answer 4.2   d is 1100100
E is 1000101

Answer 4.3

1 0 1 0 0

Answer 4.4
B is 42H or   11000010 with odd parity
01000010 with even parity
E is 45H or   01000101 with odd parity
11000101 with even parity

Answer 4.5   We are representing B with the following ASCII code... 11000010
Remember that the least significant bit is sent first. Hence the signal will look like:

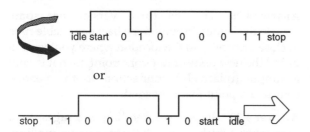

or

It is the order in which the bits are seen at the remote end that is important. Both of these give the same order, but you may see them drawn in either format in other texts.

Answer 4.6   Just about any device could be emulated including the CPU, which can be made to look like another type of architecture. Hence your answer could be varied.

Answer 4.7   The extra bits are needed to keep the the data in a recognisable format which can be delivered. It is an envelop for the data. You wouldn't send pieces of paper through the post without an envelop!

Answer 4.8   In parallel transmission we transmit one byte at a time. In this case 800 bytes/sec. To transmit 3200 bytes will take 4 secs.

Answer 4.9   There has been no delay between each byte and no error(s) which need retransmission have occurred.

Answer 4.10   100 characters is 1000 bits, assuming 1 start and 1 stop bit.
To send this at 2400 bps will take (1000/2400) seconds = 0.416 s

Answer 4.11   Other than using fixed length blocks, a variable block length could have a field at the front of the block which states how long this block will be. Of course this is another overhead in controlling the format.

Answer 4.12   How are the wires in the cable connected to the connector plug pins? Is everything a straight through connection from one end to the other or do some of the wires need to cross over in the cable? Is the specification of the cable at a sufficiently high level to support the data rates proposed? Is the distance between the two stations short enough to allow the signal to travel from one end to the other without loss of strength? There are other concerns but these probably represent major points.

Answer 4.13   Leased lines are fixed price tariffs for handling constant flows of data and would not be the best solution. Neither would the idea of keeping open a dial up line for long durations. A data switching network will accept packets of data as they are generated and probably represents the cheapest way of managing low volume intermittent data.

Answer 4.14   All users can download the same version of any application software. This should remove the complication of creating incompatible data or data that cannot be readily exchanged. By having centrally controlled software on a server, we are also able to make sure that only legal software is being used within the number of licences purchased.

Answer 4.15   Your answer may include:
print server, directory server, fax server, mail server etc.

Answer 4.16 When working in isolation, any connected devices to that free-standing system are dedicated and instantly available. On a server basis, the devices are shared and this has inherent delays in access. There are less connection or network contention problems to create potential problems in a free-standing system. It is also possible that the number of software licences for a particular application were insufficient for the organisation at large and if (at any given instant in time) they are all in use, then additional users attempting to access the application should be denied.

Answer 4.17 Your answer may be varied here, but could be a hotel or holiday reservation system, stock control, banking or finance sector etc.

Answer 4.18 The algorithm used to send the data by polling around the stations (round robin), is also used at the receiving end to separate the "mixed" data into the original inputs. If we avoid sending empty slots by filling them with the next data to send, the receiving end would have difficulty in identifying which traffic was which. If such a modification were to be preferred then we would have to send some form of ID with each slot. This wouldn't be simple TDM, but a more complex approach which is introduced later.

Answer 4.19 In asynchronous mode we send the data between the multiplexer without the start bits because they are 'stripped off'. To ensure there is synchronisation between the two, it is common to send null or synchronisation characters in empty slot positions to retain a data flow.

Answer 4.20 It is known as FDM.

Answer 4.21 In TDM, wasted capacity is seen as empty slots. In FDM wasted capacity is seen as an idle channel.

Answer 4.22 1 station sends 2 chars/sec or 16 bps
18 stations send 18 * 16 bps = 288 bps
Hence utilisation 288/19200 * 100% = 1.5%

Answer 4.23 If we ignore the lost capacity of the guard bands and have all 18 channels working at a rate of 16 bps over the 110 bps channels, then the utilisation of each channel is
Utilisation = 16/110 * 100% = 14.5%
Of course the overall utilisation of the transmission medium, is the same as in answer 4.22.

Answer 4.24 Hopefully, if both organisations had been fully compliant with the OSI standards, then integration of the two networks should be seamless. However it is more likely that both networks followed the structure of the 7 layer model and adopted different routes through the standards. Hence there may well be some work to do in achieving the integration of the two networks.

Answer 4.25 Hopefully yes. If the position of the bridge within the network was correct we should be able to create the two separate but joined networks with about half of the traffic on both sides. Hence the traffic levels seen by any side will only be that created on that side plus traffic from the other side that has a destination address on this side of the bridge. Reducing traffic levels by placing a bridge in a LAN is one of the options open to network designers when the traffic levels start to rise and the efficiency of the network looks as though it may begin to suffer.

Answer 4.26 Each LAN will have its own internet address. When a packet arrives at this LAN's router then it recognises that this is the destination LAN from the internet address. The router then puts the packet out on this network addressed to the device represented by the other half of the internet address.

Answer 4.27 If we add another node to the unstructured topology on the left of figure 4.59 there is a major amount of extra cabling required. In addition the routing of data to the new node needs careful management.

Answer 4.28 The structured version has some logic to the layout. Provided the backbone cable runs in close proximity to the location where you want to install the new node or network point, then it is only a simple (relatively) connection to the nearest connection point that is needed.

Answer 4.29 If we are sending messages to a destination which shares the transmission medium with other stations, it is important that we can uniquely identify each station.

Answer 4.30 Since a station connected to a bus structure normally puts the signal out on to the transmission medium and it is sent bi-directionally, then every station hears the message. Normally only the network card whose address is is the destination address will pass the data to the station it attaches to the network. Hence it is relatively easy to specify a special address which every network card responds to called a broadcast message. If we broadcast a message asking each station if they were "fred", everyone would hear the message and hopefully "fred" would respond. We could therefore use this idea to locate particular addresses.

Answer 4.31 When we pass a broadcast from the network card to the station, it interrupts the current processes to determine what action is appropriate. This may be nothing or it may require the station to do something. If we had a lot of broadcasts, then each connected station would be slowed down whilst it handled all the interrupts.

Answer 4.32 Each ring interface normally regenerates the signal. To do this, a whole bit (at least) must be held in the ring interface to permit the regenerating logic to work. So there is at least one bit delay in each ring interface and probably more (usually 2 or 3 bits delay).

Answer 4.33 The more active nodes in a ring, the longer the delay in the ring as we add up the delay in each of the stations. Equally important is the simple fact that the greater the number of stations in a ring, the greater the probability of someone else holding the token when you want access. This causes a short delay before access can be granted.

Answer 4.34 Possible options are:

❐ automatic retry if busy;

❐ delay sending overseas until a cheaper time tariff is available.

Answer 4.35 Yes. If everyone is collecting performance data from network devices in exactly the same format, then integrating each of the separate systems into a single enterprise wide management system will be a lot easier.

Answer 4.36

❐ Identity cards are cheap to produce and can hold a photo. They can however be lost and potentially abused;

❐ Pass cards may be quite sophisticated with magnetic strips to swipe through controlled access doors. Of course they can be lost and used by others;

❐ Control doors with staff are expensive to maintain, since staff costs are relatively expensive. Unless the security person is insistent on passes or whatever, a cosy relationship can develop and security procedures become less effective;

❐ Coded locks are OK until the control code becomes too widespread. Codes need to be changed regularly and careful mechanisms set up to disseminate new codes;

❐ The special devices like retina scans are really expensive, but normally very secure. Finger print readers cannot read cut fingers though!

Answer 4.37
ID cards are owned
Pass cards are owned and possibly know
Control doors with security staff could be any or all of the three
Coded locks are what you know
Special devices are typically what you are.

Unit 4 Sample Test Paper

1 A file of 200 characters is sent asynchronously to a serial printer. How many bits will be transmitted?

   A 2000 bits
   B 16000 bits
   C 20,000 bits
   D 200,000 bits

2 2000 characters are transmitted on a line operating at 200 bps. How long will it take to transmit these characters?

   A 10 secs
   B 16 secs
   C 100 secs
   D 160 secs

3 A special sensor device requires an asynchronous transmission with one and a half stop bits. If the data is 8 bit ASCII format, what is the maximum effective data rate across a 2400 bps connection?

   A 2000 bps
   B 1920 bps
   C 1829 bps
   D 1745 bps

4 How would you represent the character A using ASCII representation with even parity?

   A 01000001
   B 11000001
   C 01001001
   D 00010100

5 If even parity has been specified, which of the following characters has an error?

   A 01000010
   B 11000010
   C 11000110
   D 01000100

6 Synchronisation characters (SYNs) are used to:

   A tell the sender there has been an error
   B allow the receiver to synchronise with the transmission
   C allow the sender to synchronise with the transmission
   D ensure asynchronous techniques are used

7 The ETX character is sent to

   A close down a connection
   B end a character transfer
   C release synchronisation of a transmission
   D indicate the last character in a block

8 A synchronous protocol has two SYN and one STX character at the front of every block. Each block is terminated with one ETX character and has a maximum size of 200 data characters. What is the shortest time it would take to transmit 4000 characters over a transmission line whose speed is 9600 bps?

   A 3.4 secs
   B 4.25 secs
   C 33.3 secs
   D 4 secs

9 Communication designers determine the maximum block size for a protocol based upon:

   A the balance between line speed and overheads
   B the efficiency between error recovery and overhead ratio
   C the efficiency of the protocol code
   D the maximum size packet the transmission line can hold

10 Checksums are used to
   A add value to the data
   B add up the number of characters sent
   C provide a check on the accuracy of data sent
   D check the speed of the data transmission

11 Which of the following cables will not support signalling using voltages?

   A shielded twisted pair
   B unshielded twisted pair
   C coaxial cable
   D fibre optic

12 Asynchronous transmission is used when
   A blocks of data are transmitted
   B characters are separately transmitted
   C there are millions of bytes of data to transfer
   D a synchronous link is maintained

13 A NAK indicates

   A   data is not received correctly
   B   no data has arrived
   C   the device has just got the hang of how to send data
   D   all data has been received OK

14 Serial transmission is used when

   A   its breakfast time
   B   bytes of data are transferred simultaneously
   C   a single stream of bits needs transferring
   D   parallel connections are required

15 A communications log is unlikely to contain

   A   a date or time stamp of the communication
   B   the names of the files transferred
   C   the speed of the link opened
   D   the amount of data transferred

16 Which of the following may not be a benefit to an organisation?

   A   establishing a fileserver to share data
   B   installing a network to establish data communication
   C   sharing access to any special hardware e.g. scanners
   D   keeping multiple copies of all data on the system

17 Simplex transmission is used because

   A   it is simply the best
   B   only traffic in one direction is transmitted
   C   traffic in both directions occurs simultaneously
   D   duplex is not sophisticated enough

18 Parallel transmission requires cable consisting of

   A   only one wire
   B   only two wires
   C   multiple wires
   D   a skewed wire

19 Flow control is used to

   A   allow the sender to control the speed
   B   ensure data flows in the right direction
   C   control the rate at which responses are generated
   D   ensure the transfer rate is acceptable to the receiver

20 A modem is used whenever

   A   digital data is sent on a digital network
   B   a digital device is connected to an analogue network
   C   data is to be scrambled for security
   D   data is transmitted over long distances

21 Media access control may be handled by

   A   collision detection techniques
   B   synchronising users
   C   structured cabling
   D   management information base.

22 Which of the following devices do not provide a network service?

   A   fileservers
   B   a printer
   C   e-mail software e.g., cc-mail
   D   a diskette

23 The function of a print server is to

   A   provide an intelligent switch to a printer
   B   service the printer
   C   allow any network user to print immediately
   D   provide an orderly buffer queue between users and the printer

24 A topology not commonly used is

   A   star
   B   bus
   C   direct
   D   structured

25 FDDI is what type of topology?

   A   star
   B   ring
   C   bus
   D   mesh

26 Token passing techniques are not implemented on

   A   token ring
   B   token bus
   C   slotted ring
   D   collision detection

27 A device whose primary function is to regenerate a signal is a

   A gateway

   B bridge

   C repeater

   D router

28 The number of layers in the international standard's reference model for networking is

   A 6

   B 7

   C 8

   D 9

29 A bridge cannot be used to

   A connect a LAN to a WAN

   B extend the size of a LAN

   C filter traffic between two LANs

   D join two IEEE 802 conformant networks together

30 A modem is classed as which one of the following types of devices

   A DCE

   B DTE

   C CTS

   D DTR

31 A password should preferably be

   A a person's first name so it can easily be remembered

   B your cars' index number to mix alpha and numeric characters

   C a complex combination of letters and numbers which are recorded on a piece of paper in case you forget

   D changed regularly

32 Encryption is used

   A to prevent data from being accessed

   B to protect data from unauthorised use

   C to make it easier to transmit

   D to make the system fault tolerant

by **Tim Hutchings**

Systems Analysis

Introduction

In today's cut-throat business environment where organisations, large and small, survive only by providing superior services to their customers, the use of Information Technology (IT) to support business activities is essential. In this unit we will cover the analysis and design of Information Systems. Systems which support the administration of business activities.

The range of administrative business activities which can be streamlined by using IT is vast including:

- ❒ Individuals using 'Microsoft Money' to manage their finances;
- ❒ Local shops using accounting packages like 'SAGE';
- ❒ Office workers, using office packages like 'Microsoft Office' and 'Lotus SmartSuite' (typically including a Word Processor and/or Desk Top Publishing package, a Spreadsheet, a Database, a Slide Preparation package and some Time Management software) to improve their productivity;
- ❒ Medium sized organisations using DBASE for order processing and an off-the-shelf payroll system;
- ❒ Multi-national organisations using Relational Database Systems (RDBMS), such as 'ORACLE', 'INGRES' and 'DB2' on mainframe computers to manage enormous networked databases.

Office packages, in particular office database packages such as Lotus' 'APPROACH', Borland's 'PARADOX' and Microsoft's 'ACCESS' are very easy to use for creating simple databases, e.g. telephone directories. However, when using these packages it is easy to fall into the trap of not carrying out a detailed investigation into exactly what is required before building screens and reports. The main objective of this unit is to describe how to identify and model what is required from an information system before you waste time building the wrong system. In other words it describes the basic tools, techniques and skills required of a systems analyst.

A systems analyst is a skilled communicator who can speak the language of business people, e.g. sales personnel, engineers, designers, mathematicians, doctors, managers, clerks, teachers, lawyers, accountants and personnel experts, but who also understands what computers and the associated packages can do. Figure 5.1 shows how a systems analyst interfaces with business and computer experts. A systems analyst should be able to establish business information system requirements using a variety of techniques and be able to communicate these requirements to computer experts who will subsequently build the system.

The Systems Analyst speaks the language of both business experts and computer experts.

Figure 5.1 The Role of the Systems Analyst

Question 5.1

The profession of systems analyst is a relatively new one. Why do you think the role evolved?

Two case studies will be used throughout the following elements, the first concerns the 'Ashgrove Surgery', the second concerns 'Dragon Video Rental'.

Case Study 1:   Ashgrove Surgery

The Ashgrove Surgery serves a busy market town, it has 9 General Practitioners (GPs) and approximately 15,000 patients. It has 5 reception staff, a number of nursing staff who carry out minor procedures at the surgery and a team of district nurses who visit patients at their homes. When patients join the surgery they are allocated to one of the GPs, however they may make an appointment to see any of the GPs. At an appointment the GP may prescribe many treatments for the patient. The surgery also processes repeat prescriptions and runs a number of clinics, such as Baby Care, Asthma and Diabetes. At present the surgery doesn't use computers, but due to the high volume of paperwork involved in scheduling appointments the surgery would like to develop a computer system to cover this part of its operation.

Case Study 2:   *Dragon Video Rental*

Dragon Video is a small but busy video rental club it has premises in a suburb of a big city. It has roughly 2,000 members and keeps a stock of approximately 3,000 titles. When joining the club prospective members have to provide two forms of identification showing their name and address. If the application is successful the member pays a £5.00 membership fee and £5.00 insurance. Members can borrow any number of films per day. The length of hire for films is always one day, films have to be returned by 18:30 hours on the day after hire. The fee for hire ranges from £3.00 for new films, down to £1.00 for older films. Members can also reserve films. At present this is the major business activity of Dragon Video. However Dragon Video has recently started hiring out music CD's and computer games, the only difference being that the length of hire for these items is 7 days.

Analysis and design materials from the Ashgrove Surgery Case Study will be developed through the following units. The Dragon Video Case Study will form the basis of many questions and tasks with some suggested solutions appearing at the end of the unit.

Element 5.1

Investigate Principles of Systems Analysis and Specification

Introduction

In this element we will be looking at the following areas:

- ❑ *Processing Activities*: We will discuss a number of different data processing activities and begin to classify them as control, repetition, interrogation, calculation, manipulation (sorting, selecting, merging) and communication;

- ❑ *Information Technology Methods*: We will discuss program design, coding and testing and their place in the systems analysis lifecycle, and the use of application software facilities, e.g. Application/Report generators, the use of macros in spreadsheets and databases, and various data capture techniques;

❏ *User Information*: We will discuss the purpose of information systems, descriptions of current systems (whether manual or computerised) in terms of their inputs, outputs and processing activities, expectations of proposed information systems and finally the constraints imposed on the development of information systems such as timescales and costs;

❏ *Stages of Systems Analysis*: We will cover the whole of the systems development lifecycle beginning with Strategic Information Technology Planning, moving through feasibility, analysis (the problem statement, investigation, recording, modelling and reporting), design or specification, development, testing, implementation and maintenance;

❏ *Analysis Documentation*: We will discuss the major structured analysis techniques, i.e. Data Flow Diagrams and Data Models together with their supporting documentation requirements – typically held in a data dictionary) as an introduction to Element 5.2 and briefly discuss some other techniques such as system flowcharts, process specifications and program flowcharts (these techniques are discussed in more detail in Element 5.3);

❏ *Elements of System Specification*: As an introduction to Element 5.3 we will briefly describe the components of a system specification including detailed data models, input specifications (capture methods, screens), output specifications (screens, printed reports), process specifications (structured English, structure diagrams, decision tables and program flowcharts), resource implications (hardware, software, people) and the constraints on the systems development process.

5.1.1 Processing Activities

Financial and Cost Accounting

All organisations are required to produce two key business statements at the end of each tax year, these are the profit and loss statement and the balance sheet. The profit and loss statement describes the income the organisation has generated and the expenses they have incurred. In order to produce the profit and loss account the organisation has to keep detailed records of all financial transactions including payments received from customers and payments made to suppliers. The balance sheet describes the value of the assets and liabilities the organisation is responsible for, again careful records have to be maintained. The process of maintaining these records and of producing the profit and loss statement and balance sheet is called financial accounting.

Cost Accounting involves the internal analysis and planning of expenditure within the organisation. Cost Accounting is largely concerned with *control*, i.e. the control of an organisations financial resources and Financial Accounting with *communication*. The profit and loss statement and balance sheets are very important communication tools, e.g. from the organisation to the Inland Revenue (to calculate how much tax is due) and from the organisation to its shareholders.

In the past these activities would have been carried out manually using ledgers. Currently these activities, in all but the smallest organisations, are carried out using computerised information systems.

Calculating Bills

One of the key activities engaged in by almost all commercial organisations is customer billing, accuracy of billing is essential for all organisations especially large companies like British Gas, British Telecom and the power and water companies. (How would a customer feel if their telephone bill had been calculated incorrectly?).

Billing typically involves:

❑ Measuring and recording how much of a particular product or service you have used in a given period of time;

❑ Charging, i.e. multiplying the number of units used by the cost per unit and possibly adding a standing charge, VAT and any outstanding balance from previous time periods;

❑ Sending out bills;

❑ Processing and chasing up payments.

Large organisations count their customers in millions. Consider a huge army of clerks using calculators to produce bills in a large organisation like British Telecom. The idea is clearly ridiculous. Issues like this were in the past major driving forces for the development of Information Technology.

Essentially producing bills involves *calculation* and *repetition*, i.e. the same calculation has to be repeated for each bill.

Task 5.1   PC 1 & 2

Collect examples of gas, electric, water, and telephone bills and identify the kinds of calculations involved and the similarities and differences between them. (Please remember that personal information such as name, address, telephone and account number should be removed).

Producing Payslips

Another common processing activity is the production of payslips. Again there is a high volume of data to be processed and accuracy is essential. (If you worked 4 hours overtime, you wouldn't like to be paid for only 3 hours or at the wrong rate).

Producing payslips is also a repetitive, calculation activity, involving:

❑ Calculating basic gross pay (based on a salary scale);

❑ Adding any gross additions (e.g. overtime);

❑ Subtracting income tax, national insurance and pension contributions to work out net pay.

Many organisations pay their employees via a system known as BACS (Bankers Automated Clearing System). Using this system an employees net pay is electronically sent (via BACS) directly to their bank account. Thus payroll processing also involves *communications*, though clearly this is electronic communication across a network as opposed to communications in relation to the financial statements described earlier.

Forecasting

Many organisation attempt to forecast information such as interest rates, levels of unemployment and other indicators of economic performance. Using a spreadsheet to answer 'what if' questions, (e.g. what impact will an interest rate rise of 0.5% have on our repayments) is an example of forecasting (or guessing!). Forecasting is essentially a data *manipulation* activity involving *searching* (reading through data and extracting useful information), *sorting* (ordering data according to some criteria, e.g. ascending data order) and *merging* (bringing data from separate sources together) data from many sources.

Summary

There are hundreds of other data processing activities:

- ❏ Banking systems record details of all the transactions you carry out, such as writing a cheque, withdrawing cash from a till, enquiries on account balances (an example of an *interrogation* activity) and the production of monthly statements (an example of a reporting activity);
- ❏ NHS and Doctors Surgery systems which enable you to book appointments;
- ❏ Library/Video Rental systems which enable you to reserve and subsequently borrow, books, videos, CD's, computer games etc.;
- ❏ Stock Control Systems, recording issues from and receipts into stock.

Clearly there are many others, all of which may be assisted by the intelligent use of IT.

Task 5.2   PC 1 & 2

*Make a list of other data processing activities carried out by typical organisations and classify the various parts of these activities as **control**, **repetition**, **interrogation**, **calculation**, **manipulation** or **communication**.*

5.1.2 Information Technology Methods

Programming Languages

It is common for people to view programming as the process of coding and testing computer programs using languages such as Pascal, Basic or Cobol (Cobol being widely used as a business programming language particularly in well established systems). This however is a very narrow and dangerous view to take. A more professional view is that coding has to be preceded by program design which itself should be derived from a systems analysis and design exercise and that ad hoc testing isn't good enough (a formal test plan being required). The place of programming in the Systems Development Lifecycle can be seen in figure 5.2.

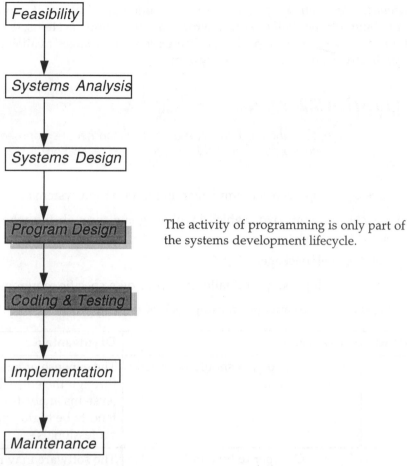

The activity of programming is only part of the systems development lifecycle.

Figure 5.2 Programming in the Systems Development Lifecycle

Application Software Facilities

You should be aware that various tools are available which reduce the amount of programming that has to be carried out:

❑ *Application/Report Generators* can be primed with requirements and used to produce skeleton applications including screen and report layouts and update logic;

❑ *Macros;* Many of the currently available Database and Spreadsheet tools offer the user a kind of mini-programming language which can be used to add extra functionality to their applications;

❑ *Data Capture Methods;* In the past the commonest approach to data capture was the use of data preparation staff, people who's job is to key bulk data into computer systems, typically taken from hand written sheets (obviously a time consuming and error prone task). This data would be saved onto a file and then processed overnight by a batch program. In this day and age where many systems are on-line users key their own data directly into transaction type programs which answer any queries or process any updates on the spot. We now also have available high quality scanners and associated software which can be used to scan tables of data into databases and spreadsheets. Another common approach is to purchase files of information on CD-ROM, e.g. the Post Office provides a file of all known addresses in the UK;

❑ *Automated Application Software;* In some common applications it is possible to purchase ready built (off the shelf or shrink wrapped) information systems, (SAGE' is an example of a common accounting package). There are also packages available for stock control, payroll and addressing/mailshot systems.

Question 5.2

What are the advantages of using a spreadsheet as opposed to a calculator or writing a program to carry out a repetitive calculation?

There are three basic approaches to implementing information systems:

1. Build a system of your own, which involves going through the whole of the Software Development Lifecycle;

2. Buy an off the shelf package;

3. Buy an off the shelf package and tailor it to your own specific requirements.

The advantages and disadvantages in using each of these approaches are:

Approach	Advantages	Disadvantages
1	The system you get should be exactly what you want	The expense of having to go through the entire lifecycle (systems analysts and designers tend to be highly paid professionals)
2	Usually Cheaper to buy and maintain	The software may not meet all your requirements
3	Tailoring an existing package should be cheaper than building your own system from scratch and should give you the system you want.	The manufacturer of the software may not be prepared to tailor the software or allow you to tailor it yourself

Task 5.3   PC 3

Suggest some further advantages and disadvantages for each of the approaches 1, 2 and 3.

5.1.3 User Information

In this section we describe the user information needed to initiate a feasibility Study.

Purpose

The first stage of systems analysis is to establish why the user wants the system, in other words to identify the purpose and main objectives of the system. The result should be a concise, accurate document describing in business (not computer) terms, the purpose and objectives of the system.

Description of Present System

Typically the present system is described in terms of its inputs, processes and outputs regardless of whether the system is manual (e.g. held on card indexes) or computerised. For example a gas billing system could be described in terms of its inputs (meter reading + outstanding balance), processes (subtract the lower meter reading from the higher, multiply the result by the price per unit, add on the standing charge and VAT) and finally outputs (a gas bill).

Expectations:

- ❑ *Functionality*: Once the overall purpose and objectives of the system have been clarified it is possible to identify in more detail the functional requirements of the system. The result should be a numbered list of the functional requirements of the system, ideally in priority order;

- ❑ *Output Requirements*: This activity builds on the functional requirements by identifying exactly what the system has to produce, i.e. what printed reports/documents, screen output and output required to be electronically transmitted, e.g. across a network;

- ❑ *Processing Requirements*: What processing is required in order to produce the necessary output, i.e. what algorithms, calculations, coding and decoding, reformatting, summaries, averages etc. are required;

- ❑ *Input Requirements*: What does the end user need to put in to the system in order to produce the required output;

- ❑ *Data Structure Requirements*: What data needs to be stored to enable the processing described above. Considering data structure requirements can result in more stable systems, since data structures tend to be more stable than processing requirements. For example British gas may change the way they bill customers but it will always have to bill its customers and therefore require information like name, address and account balance to be stored.

Constraints:

- ❑ *Timescales*: The analyst must identify the timescale over which the system should be developed. It doesn't matter how good a system is if it arrives too late for use;

- ❑ *Costs*: The analyst must also identify any costs incurred in building a system. A system which saves an organisation £20,000 is of no use if has cost the organisation £50,000 to build;

- ❑ *Resource Constraints*: These include hardware/software availability and the availability of people with the right skills.

Task 5.4   PC 4   **C 3.1**

Role play an end user with an information systems requirement using any business scenario or processing activity. Draw up your requirements under the following headings: • purpose • description of the current system • expectations • resource constraints.

5.1.4 Stages of Systems Analysis & Specification

In this section we discuss the nature of the project lifecycle and the phases involved from Strategic IT Planning (SITP) through analysis and design, to coding, implementation and maintenance. The stages of the project lifecycle range from high level strategic decision making, i.e. which systems are required by the organisation over a 3 – 5 year period to enable it to achieve its business objectives, down to low level detailed programming decision, i.e. what algorithms are required to solve this particular problem. Figure 5.3 illustrates the steps in a typical systems development lifecycle although you will see many variations on this theme in different text books.

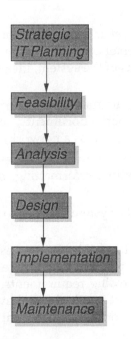

Strategic IT Planning; High level decision making regarding which systems an organisation requires.

Feasibility; Can the systems required by the Strategic IT Plan be implemented cost effectively.

Analysis; Detailed identification of what is required of the system, using techniques such as interviews and questionnaires and subsequently the use of modelling techniques such as Data Flow Modelling (i.e. Data Flow Diagrams and associated documentation) and Data Modelling (Entity-Relationship Diagrams and associated documentation in a data dictionary).

Design; This determines how the requirements are to be implemented. Sometimes design is broken down into logical (hardware/software independent) and physical (hardware/software dependent) design. In logical design DFDs and E-RDs are checked, refined and cross validated. In physical design various techniques are used to create database definitions and detailed process specifications.

Implementation & Maintenance; During these stages programs and systems are built and tested prior to their introduction to live running and then monitored, tuned and adjusted.

Figure 5.3 The Systems Development Lifecycle

Figure 5.3 is an overview of the whole process, a more detailed description follows. We will take this opportunity to discuss the whole of the systems development lifecycle, not just those involved in systems analysis, beginning with strategic planning and moving through analysis and design to software development, implementation and maintenance. Including all the information at this stage should give you an opportunity to see the whole picture.

Strategic IT Planning

Unfortunately, but perhaps unavoidably, many large organisations use of IT is uncoordinated with many different kinds of hardware and software used by different parts of the organisation with no overall control. The result is overlapping coverage with duplicated data and no real way of making effective use of the total corporate data resource. In an attempt to overcome this problem some organisations have tried to use Strategic IT Planning (SITP). SITP is an attempt to control the development of information systems such that the organisation gets the maximum return on its IT investment.

Question 5.3

Why do you think the use of IT is so uncoordinated in many large organisation?

Typically there are three main elements in a SITP exercise:

❏ The identification of what the organisation already has;

❏ The identification of what the organisation requires;

❏ The comparison of what's available against what's required.

The outcome of a SITP exercise is a series of development projects to be implemented over a fairly long time period, e.g. 3–5 years. Since the SITP covers such a long period it isn't in enough detail to be used as a working plan. The next step is Tactical Information Technology Planning (TITP). This plan goes into more detail, defining which projects are to be implemented in a shorter timescale, e.g. 1–2 years. Again the TITP isn't in enough detail to be used as a working document by a project manager.

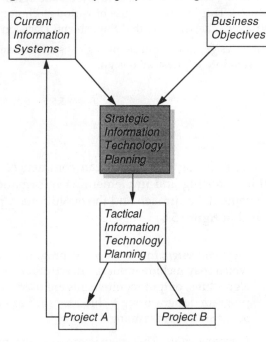

The Strategic Information Technology Planning exercise must be driven by the need to satisfy business objectives.

The whole process is circular and never ending because implemented systems become part of the current information systems and because business objectives change over the years.

Figure 5.4 Strategic Information Technology Planning

Feasibility, Analysis & Design

Some IT projects have timescales of up to 1 year and may involve many staff. In order to plan and control a project of this size it has to broken down into suitable chunks. The analysis and design stages of the project lifecycle, through the development of analysis and design methodologies such as SSADM (Structured Systems Analysis & Design Methodology), have become fairly well defined. SSADM consists of 5 phases (modules in SSADM terminology). The SSADM modules are summarised in figure 5.5, SSADM has been chosen as a vehicle for this unit for two reasons, the first is that it revolves around the use of Data Flow Diagrams and Data Models and the second is that it has become the standard methodology in the UK and is supported by the Government and other National bodies such as the NCC (National Computer Centre) and the BCS (British Computer Society).

257

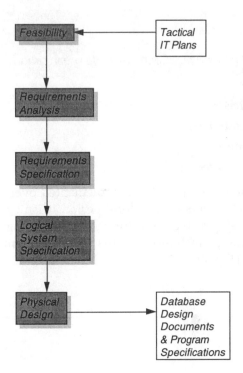

Feasibility; Is the System likely to be cost effective?

Requirements Analysis; The identification of requirements, using various *investigation* techniques, such as interviews, questionnaires, observation and document inspection, the *recording* of the results of the investigation and the production of a *problem statement* – a formal document agreed between end-users and systems analysts and ratified by senior management. At this stage the requirements are modelled using structured techniques such as Data Flow Diagrams and Data Models. Also at this stage various system options are prepared and presented to management. One of these options is selected and carried forward.

Requirements Specification; In this phase the chosen option is further refined to provide input to the forthcoming design phases.

Logical System Specification; During this phase a 'logical' (hardware/software independent) system design is produced. This involves the use of various techniques such as structure charts, structured English and Decision Tables.

Physical Design; In this phase the logical system design is converted into a 'physical' design.

Figure 5.5 Systems Analysis & Design

System Building

Once physical design has been completed, building the system can commence. There are a number of different approaches to building, testing and implementing information systems, including, the waterfall approach, the incremental approach and the evolutionary prototyping approach. The waterfall model is described in figure 5.6.

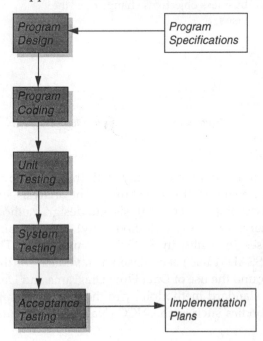

Program Design; In this stage the program specifications, which may include input file descriptions, key algorithms, output requirements are used to produce program designs using techniques such as Jackson Structured Programming.

Program Coding; This stage involves translating a program design into a working program written in either a 3GL such as Cobol or a 4GL such as ORACLE.

Unit Testing; In this stage each individual program or module is tested to ensure that it conforms to specification.

System Testing; In this stage suites of programs are tested to ensure that they interact with each other correctly.

Acceptance Testing; In this stage the system is tested in a simulated 'live' environment prior to actual implementation.

Figure 5.6 The Waterfall Model

The reason for the name 'waterfall' is that each phase takes as input the results of the previous phase and like a real waterfall the flow of control cannot go back up

A variation on the waterfall theme is incremental delivery, in which the waterfall model is used to deliver sub-systems one by one until the full system is delivered, rather than delivering a whole system in a single attempt.

A further alternative is the use of evolutionary prototyping. In this approach demonstration versions of a system are produced initially to ensure that the analysts and designers have correctly identified the users requirements, and subsequently to use as a baseline for the development of the finished system. In this model backtracking is allowed and even expected. The prototyping model is illustrated in figure 5.7.

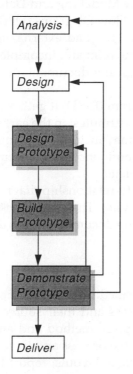

Design & Build Prototype; During this stage a working version of the system is created, typically using some application generation or 4GL tool.

Demonstrate Prototype; At this stage the end-users are invited to see a demonstration of the system and asked to comment on its functionality and appearance. The result of the demonstration could indicate that the analysis or design work may have to be revisited or may simply involve modifying the prototype.

Delivery; Following a controlled number of iterations the prototype goes through final quality assurance checks before being delivered as the completed system.

Figure 5.7 Evolutionary Prototyping

Task 5.5   PC 3   *C 3.2*

Describe in your own words the 'waterfall' and 'evolutionary prototyping' approaches to Information Systems Development. What are the advantages of the 'evolutionary prototyping' approach over the 'waterfall' approach.

Implementation and Maintenance

Implementation is an often neglected part of the systems development lifecycle. The typical approach is to implement the system and let the users get on with it. This is an unprofessional approach which ignores the psychology of the people likely to be using the system. It is essential that adequate training is carried out and that if necessary a period of dual running is introduced where the existing (computerised or manual) system is run alongside the new system until the users are happy that the system is suitable.

Following implementation there is bound to be some maintenance of the system to fix minor problems or to add new or changed requirements. Implementation brings the project lifecycle full circle because newly implemented systems become part of the current information systems which feed into the ongoing Strategic Information Technology Planning exercise.

5.1.5 Analysis Documentation & Elements of System Specification

Structured Analysis Techniques

The two key structured analysis techniques are Data Flow Modelling and Data Modelling.

A Data Flow Model consists of a hierarchic set of Data Flow Diagrams (DFDs) and the associated documentation of processes and data stores, data flows and external entities in a data dictionary. In the early stages the documentation is likely to brief and incomplete, as the analysis exercise proceeds and moves into specification/design the documentation is checked for accuracy and completeness.

A Data Model consists of an Entity-Relationship Diagram (E-RD) together with supporting documentation of the entity types, relationship types and attributes. In the early stages both the diagram and the documentation will be incomplete and may include some unresolved issues. As the analysis proceeds and moves into specification confidence in the accuracy of the diagrams and documentation grows and they become complete.

The construction of the Data Flow Diagrams and Entity-relationship diagrams is discussed in more detail in Element 5.2 (Undertake a Systems Analysis). The cross checking and validation of these diagrams and the completion of the supporting documentation is discussed in Element 5.3. Produce a System Specification.

Process Specifications

The processes in a data flow model form the basis of detailed process specifications. The diagram will indicate which data flows come into the process and their sources (each of these requires an input specification consisting of the data capture method and any screen or file descriptions). It also indicates which data flows go out of the process and their recipients (each of these requires an output specification consisting of screen layouts, report layouts and any data formats for messages to be transmitted electronically across a network).

Once these have been established it becomes possible to create detailed process descriptions using various techniques such as:

❏ *Structured English;*

❏ *Structure Charts;*

❏ *Decision Tables;*

❏ *Flowcharts;*

A further technique is the use of System Flowcharts, however this technique is more relevant to older batch oriented systems and is only occasionally used in modern on-line environments. These techniques will be more fully covered in Element 5.3.

Task 5.6   PC 1, 2, 3, 4 & 5   *C 3.1, C 3.2*

During the course of this element you should produce an investigative report which covers the following areas:

- ❑ *Processing activities and the IT methods used to implement them.*
- ❑ *User Information Needed to Initiate a Feasibility Study.*
- ❑ *Stages of Systems Analysis.*
- ❑ *Analysis Documentation*
- ❑ *Elements of System Specification*

1. *Background Reading; Visit your school/college library, there should be a number of textbooks on systems analysis and design and some useful articles in computer magazines such as Computer Weekly. A quick look at the material in Elements 5.2 and 5.3 would also be useful.*

2. *Interviews; An effective way to appreciate real data processing problems would be to visit an organisation and interview/observe people who face these problems, it would be very useful if your tutor could arrange some visits of this nature.*

Undertake a Systems Analysis

Introduction

In this element we will concentrate in more detail on the analysis stages of the project lifecycle looking at the following areas:

- ❑ Establishing the *purpose* and use of information systems in Organisations;
- ❑ The use of analysis techniques for investigating *information* systems requirements;
- ❑ Using structured analysis techniques;
- ❑ Producing *systems analysis reports*;
- ❑ Reviewing Systems Analysis in the light of user feedback.

5.2.1. Establishing the Purpose of a New System

This is a very important area of systems analysis since it sets the scene for all the following stages, it is important from the outset that everyone involved in an information systems project is clear about the purpose and objectives of the system. At this stage the analyst is trying to identify why the user wants the system and what benefits the system will bring to the organisation, i.e. the purpose and objectives of the system.

The analyst needs to investigate what business activities are currently carried out and how they work, the problems involved and the users expectations of the new system. The result should be a concise statement in business terms (not computer terms) of the purpose and main objectives of the proposed system. The purpose and objectives of a system can include improving quality, increasing speed of processing, reducing costs and improving efficiency.

5.2.2 Information

Prior to discussing the techniques available for identifying and recording information a brief description of the nature of organisational information will be useful.

Flow of Information

Information is the life blood of many organisations. Information flows into and out of organisations and between the different levels in an organisation. Typically at the lower levels of an organisation, information is very detailed, e.g. relating to individual customers, orders, suppliers, invoices etc. As information flows up the hierarchy of an organisation it tends to become summarised. As an example consider a banking environment. A teller is interested in the specific information about the account they are currently dealing with, such as account number and balance. At the end of each day the branch manager may receive a summary report showing the total of all balances of accounts at that branch, together with a short list of those individual customers with balances of less than –£500 or greater than £5,000 (an example of exception reporting). At the end of each week the area manager or director may receive a list of customers with balances of greater than £10,000. The flow of information in an organisation is described in more detail in Unit 3 (Organisations and Information technology). It is important in this context because much of the work of the systems analyst/designer is concerned with identifying the flow and structure of information within an organisation.

Different Types and Levels of Data/Information

There is a distinction between data and information which can be simply described by the statement 'information is data which has been processed such that it becomes meaningful'. In other words information is data which has been placed in a specific context. Consider the number 153. On its own this is meaningless data. When placed in a particular context, e.g. £153, the number becomes more meaningful because we now know that we are referring to 153 pounds. However this is still data rather than information. £153 only becomes information when you find out that it is the balance of account number 01234567.

Uses of Information

There are many uses of information:

- ❐ To fulfil legal requirements;
- ❐ To provide background knowledge;
- ❐ Decision support (better information results in better decisions);
- ❐ Enquiry processing;
- ❐ Analysis of trends (forecasting).

Standard Documents & Sources of Data/Information

There are many standard documents commonly in use in organisations, some have been mentioned already, e.g. profit and loss statements, balance sheets, bills, payslips. Others include order forms, application forms, delivery notes, invoices, business letters etc. These can provide very useful information to the systems analyst. Other sources of data include existing computer systems and their documentation, the internet, tables of data in magazines and newspapers

Information Gathering Techniques

■ Interviews

The purpose of an interview is to identify, how a person currently does their job (how the existing system works), the problems they face (what is wrong with the existing system) and how they would like to do their job (what is required of the new system).

A major factor in conducting interviews are the attitudes of the interviewee and interviewer. Remember that your not there to impress the interviewee with your knowledge of computers, so don't talk about megabytes, hard disk sizes and processor speeds.

Q. Who uses computers?
A. Mothers, Fathers, Aunts, Uncles, Brothers, Sisters etc.

Think of your friends and relations, what is their range of computing experience? The people you interview may be experts or complete novices, but they are likely to be apprehensive about the impact that a new computer system will have on their jobs (will I still have a job?, will I have to learn new skills? will I have to change the way I work?). As a systems analyst you have to build trusting relationships with these people in order to get the best information from them. An open, friendly, reassuring attitude is required.

Interview essentials:

❑ *Preparation* You need to be well prepared, you have to inspire the confidence of the people you interview by demonstrating that you can understand what they do and appreciate the problems they face. Some detailed background reading is advisable;

❑ *Convenience* A further point is that you should interview people at their convenience, at their place of work. Don't expect to get very far if you summon people to your office at short notice;

❑ *Dress Code* Respect the dress code of the people you are interviewing, don't expect to inspire confidence if you are interviewing a suit while dressed in tee-shirt, jeans and trainers. Not that dressing smartly will automatically inspire confidence or that it is impossible to inspire confidence if you are dressed casually, just that dressing casually in a semi-formal environment puts you at a disadvantage and you will have to work harder in order to inspire confidence

❑ *Body Language* How many of you have felt uncomfortable when a relative stranger sits too close and invades your space or when someone won't look you in the eye (or indeed when someone looks into your eyes too much). Try not to use threatening body language when interviewing, a useful tip is not to sit across a table from someone (this is uncomfortably reminiscent of helping the police with their enquiries). On the other hand don't sit right next to someone since you can get too close and it is difficult then to have eye contact. The ideal position to sit is at right angles to someone, this isn't threatening or too close, allows eye contact but also allows eye contact to be broken comfortably.

When conducting interviews there are different types of question which can be asked and it is important to know which kinds to use:

❑ *Open Ended* Questions avoiding terse replies and inviting the interviewee to develop their opinions. These tend to start: who, where, what, when, why, e.g. 'What does your job involve?';

❑ *Closed* Questions seeking precise information, e.g. 'Do you have...?' or 'Have you done...?';

❑ *Rhetorical* Questions which do not require an answer, e.g. 'We all want to improve productivity, don't we?';

❑ *Leading or Loaded Questions* Questions that suggest the answer, e.g. 'I believe in the strict control of expenditure and debtors, what about you?'. Sometimes loaded questions can put people in a no win situation, e.g. 'When did you stop beating your husband?'.

Try to avoid using loaded or rhetorical questions since they serve no useful purpose. Loaded questions in particular may cause offence because they imply that you already know the answer and will stick to it regardless of what the person actually says. It is also important that you avoid answering your own questions, bite your tongue! A useful approach is to use open questions to get the big picture and progressively move towards closed questions as more detail is uncovered.

So much for questioning, the next step is listening to the answers. You need to show the interviewee that you are listening to their answers and that you are interested by:

❑ *Making eye contact* when speaking and listening (but don't overdo it);

❑ *Adopting a relaxed posture* (leaning slightly forward conveys interest, leaning back conveys boredom);

❑ *Using verbal reassurance*, e.g. 'I see what you mean' but again don't overdo it as the same phrase used repeatedly can become aggravating;

❑ *Paraphrasing*, this is a method which involves restating in summary format your understanding of what the interviewee has said;

❑ *Clarifying*, don't be afraid to tell the interviewee that you don't understand something but be careful how you say it, e.g. 'I'm sorry but I didn't quite understand the last part, could you take me through it again' is obviously preferable to 'You didn't explain that very clearly can you say it again'.

Task 5.7 PC 1 & 2

Work in pairs and interview each other about hobbies or interests, give each other feedback on how the interview went. It would be very useful if some of these interviews could be video taped and played back to the class.

Task 5.8 PC 1 & 2

Role play a systems analyst preparing to interview the owner/manager of Dragon Video Rental. Prepare a suitable list of questions.

■ Questionnaires

Questionnaires can be useful if a proposed information system is likely to affect a large number of people doing the same or similar job and you wish to get an overview of their feelings, perceptions, computer experience, requirements etc. Remember that in general the response rates to questionnaires is quite low (20% is typical). You can however improve response rates by following a few simple rules:

❑ *Brevity* Make sure that the questionnaire can be filled in quickly, using check boxes, lists of alternatives etc.;

❑ *Simplicity* Make sure all the questions are brief and clear, don't expect people to write you an essay. However you should also include an 'any other comments' box so that people who have specific things to say can do so;

❑ *Anonymity;* Don't ask respondents to include their name, address, or telephone number. You are more likely to get truthful answers if people do not have to identify themselves;

❑ *Return Instructions* Make sure respondents know where to send their completed questionnaires, include a stamped addressed envelope if necessary.

Task 5.9 PC 1 & 2

Devise a questionnaire for use in your school or college to identify how widely computers are used in the home, covering issues like, type of computer (e.g. IBM Compatible PC, Acorn, BBC, Mac, SNES, ATARI etc.), usage (e.g. work or leisure), popular software, processor speed etc. Use the questionnaire at your school or college and analyse the results.

■ Document Inspection

Document inspection is an important activity in the initial stages of analysis to set the scene and to gain some useful background knowledge prior to interviewing. Useful documents include:

❑ *Organisation Charts;*

❑ *Company Reports;*

❑ *Policy/Procedure Manuals;*

❑ *Job Descriptions;*

❑ *Standard Documents* (those defined previously in the section on information);

❑ *Systems Analysis/Design Documents* The results of previous analysis/design exercises give useful insights.

NB Don't be surprised if what you find in practice is slightly or even greatly different from what you expected as result of reading documents.

Task 5.10 PC 1 & 2

The most useful activity you can carry out is to get hold of some of these documents, read through them and discuss your findings with your tutor or fellow students.

A portfolio containing examples and descriptions of these documents together with a list of common features would be useful evidence of completing this task.

❑ Observation

This can be a very useful technique, seeing people in action can be more revealing than reading documents or even interviewing, because as well as finding out what people do you see the prevailing conditions and problems faced. Observation can be misleading, it is possible that the fact that you are there observing people will cause them to act differently.

Task 5.11 PC 1 & 2

Fill in the table describing the advantages and disadvantages of the different investigation methods.

Technique	Advantages	Disadvantages
Interviewing		
Questionnaire		
Document Inspection		
Observation		

> ## *Question 5.4*
>
> *Which of these techniques would be most useful and which least useful if you were building a stock control system for a corner shop keeper?*

5.2.3 Structured Analysis Techniques

Data Flow Modelling

A Data Flow Model (DFM) defines the passage of data through a system. The DFM comprises:

❐ A consistent set of Hierarchic Data Flow Diagrams (DFD)

❐ Associated documentation

- ■ *External Entities*

- ■ *Data Flows*

- ■ *Processes*

- ■ *Data Stores*

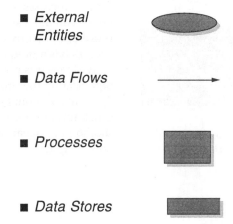

Figure 5.8 Components of Data Flow Diagrams

- ■ *Sends data into or receives data from a system*

External Entities; An external entity is a person, organisation, department, computer system or anything else which either sends data into a system (sometimes called a source) or which receives data from a system (sometimes called a sink) but which for the purposes of the project in question are outside the scope of the system itself. External entities (in the SSADM scheme) are represented as ovals containing the name of the external entity and a unique alphabetic identifier.

Figure 5.9 External Entities

■ *A route by which data can flow from one element of a DFD to another*

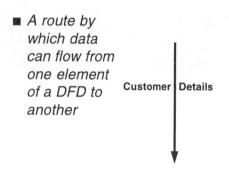

Customer | Details

Data Flows; A data flow is a route by which data may travel from one element of a DFD to another. Data Flows are represented by arrows which are labelled with a simple meaningful name.

Figure 5.10 Data Flows

■ *Transformations which change incoming data flows to outgoing data flows*

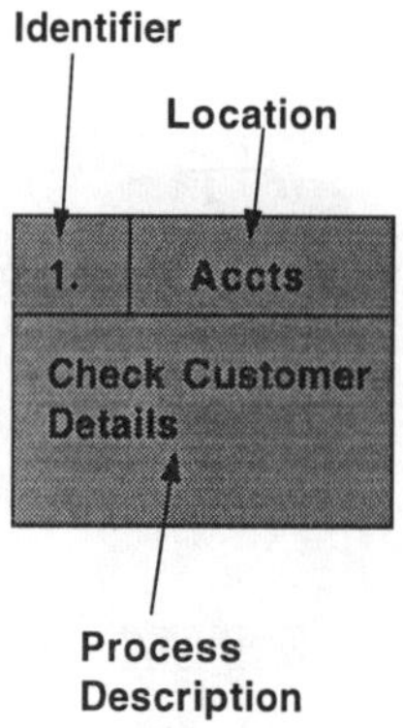

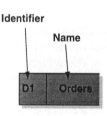

Identifier

Location

1. | Accts

Check Customer Details

Process Description

Processes; Processes are transformations which change incoming data flows into outgoing data flows. Processes are represented as rectangles which contain a simple description of the process, e.g. verify customer details. Each process has a unique reference number. In the early stages it is possible to show where in the organisation the process takes place, e.g. Accounts Section, however this is a physical constraint imposed by the existing system and should not appear in a completed 'logical' data flow diagram.

Figure 5.11 Processes

■ *A repository for data*

Identifier

Name

D1 | Orders

Data Stores; A data store is a repository for data. A data store is represented by an open ended rectangle containing the name of the data store (usually a plural noun such as customers), each data store has a unique reference number prefixed by the letter D.

Figure 5.12 Data Stores

Having described the basic components of DFDs the next stage is to explain how the components can be fitted together to form a complete DFD. Essentially the External Entity, Process and Data Store components can be interlinked using certain valid data Flows.

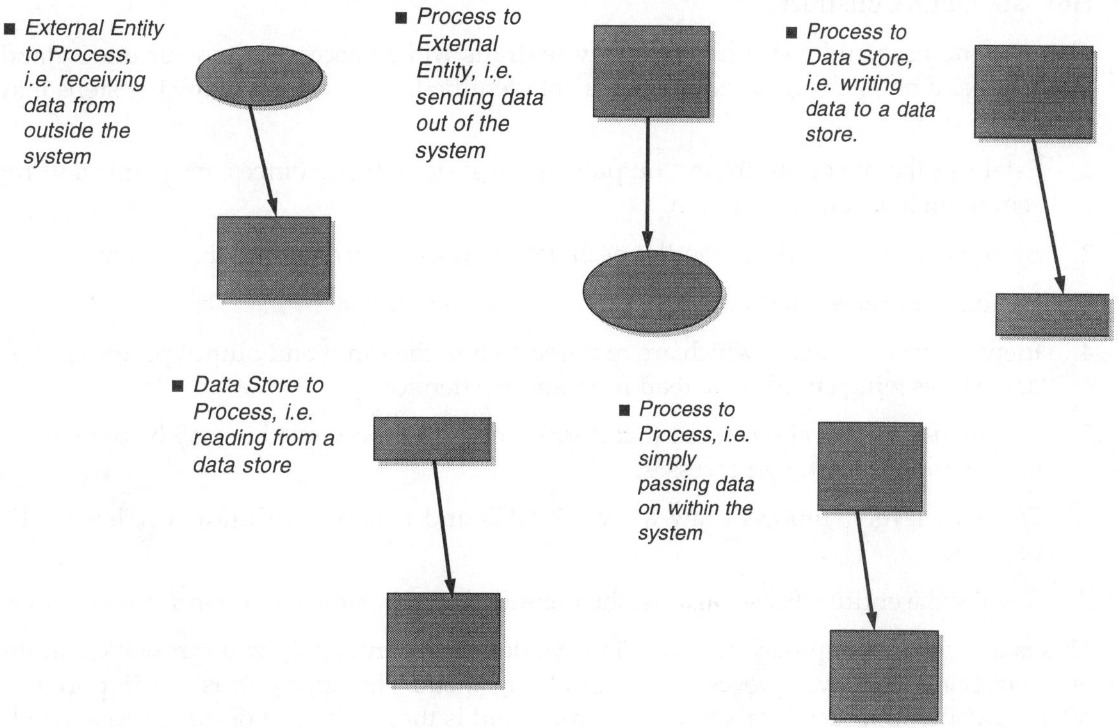

■ *External Entity to Process, i.e. receiving data from outside the system*

■ *Process to External Entity, i.e. sending data out of the system*

■ *Process to Data Store, i.e. writing data to a data store.*

■ *Data Store to Process, i.e. reading from a data store*

■ *Process to Process, i.e. simply passing data on within the system*

Figure 5.13 Valid data Flows

■ *External Entity to Data Store*

■ *Data Store to External Entity*

■ *Data Store to Data Store*

This is the logical equivalent of giving customers and suppliers direct access to update/delete your files, e.g. using an editor. There has to be a process to transfer data from external entity to data store

This is the logical equivalent of giving customers and suppliers direct access to read your files, e.g. using an editor.

In this case even a direct file to file copy is considered to be carried out by a process.

Figure 5.14 Invalid Data Flows

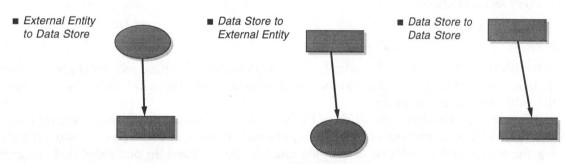

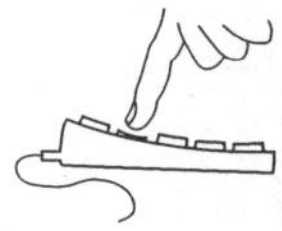

Task 5.12   PC 3

Redraw each of the above diagrams such that they only contain valid data flows

How are DFDs Constructed?

There are no hard and fast rules and many re-drafts will be necessary as your understanding improves and new/changed requirements are identified, however the following steps may be useful:

1. Establish the major inputs and outputs of the system, their sources, recipients and represent them in a context diagram;

2. Establish a process which handles each data flow on its arrival into the system;

3. Establish a process that generates each output data flow;

4. Identify the data stores which are required to link the input and output processes, i.e. the data stores which need to be read from and written to;

5. Rationalise the Level 1 DFD so that it includes 6–10 processes (this may be done by combining and/or splitting processes;

6. For each level 1 process draw a level 2 DFD and if necessary draw any level 3 DFDs required;

7. Review the entire DFD set against the identified requirements and re-draft if necessary.

This is a top down approach to Data Flow Modelling, alternatively you can work bottom up by identifying low level processes and grouping them. The approach is not important and often a hybrid approach is taken, what is important is that at the end of the exercise you have a consistent set of DFDs.

Each of the steps described above will now be explained in detail using the Ashgrove Surgery as an example.

Step 1

Establish the major inputs and outputs of the system, their sources, recipients and represent them in a context diagram (a context diagram is simply a very high level DFD which represents the entire system as one process).

The first steps in the construction of DFDs involve identifying the major information flows into (system inputs) and out of (system outputs) the system and in the case of inputs identifying the source and in the case of outputs identify the recipient. In our simplified Ashgrove Surgery Case study, the major inputs are as follows:

Input Description	Comments	Source
(1) New or Changed GP Details	This occurs when a new GP joins the practice or an existing GP changes their name (e.g. through marriage), address or telephone number	GP
(2) New or Changed Patient details	This occurs when a new patient joins the practice or an existing patient changes some of their personal details	Patient
(3) Appointment Requests	This flow is initiated when a Patient asks for an appointment	Patient
(4) Appointment Arrival	This flow occurs when a patient appears at the Surgery ready for a scheduled appointment	Patient
(5) Appointment Start/ End Times	The management of the Ashgrove Surgery want a report which shows the average length of appointments for each GP, to provide the data for this report GPs need to provide the actual start and end times of each appointment	GP

The major outputs of the system are as follows;

Output Description	Comments	Recipient
(6) Appointment Date, Time, GP	This information received by the patient following negotiation with a receptionist, e.g. "I'd like to see Dr. Philips tomorrow morning if possible.", "I'm sorry Dr. Philips isn't free until 2:00, but Dr. Jones is free at 10:30", "Okay I'll see Dr. Jones".	Patient
(7) Daily Appointment List	At the start of each working day each GP receives a list of their planned appointments for the day.	GP
(8) Average Length of Appointment Report	At the end of each week this report is produced and sent to the management of the Surgery.	Surgery Management

In reality of course there would be far more input and output flows but the list provided above is sufficient to explain the concepts of Data Flow Modelling. We will simplify the process yet further by only considering inputs (2) & (3) and outputs (6) & (7). Once the inputs and outputs have been identified they can be easily represented in a very simple DFD called a Context Diagram. A context diagram represents the whole of the system as one process box. In some books you may find that a context diagram is called a 'Level 0 DFD'.

An example context diagram appear in figure 5.15.

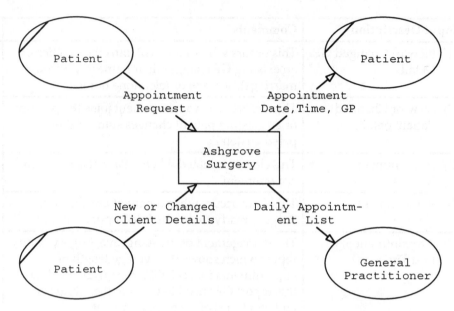

Figure 5.15 Ashgrove Surgery Context Diagram

Step 2 & 3

The second and third steps begin construction of the Level 1 DFD by creating a process to handle each incoming data flow and a process to generate each output data flow. These steps are illustrated in figure 5.16.

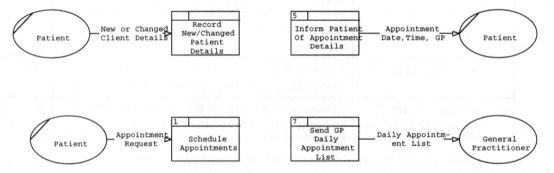

Figure 5.16 Ashgrove Surgery 1st Draft level 1 DFD

Step 4

Steps 2 and 3 are mechanical, step 4 requires a bit more thought. Essentially step 4 involves looking at each process in turn and identifying what information is required to be read in (input data flows) and what information needs to be created, updated or deleted (output data flows), figure 5.17 illustrates this process in action.

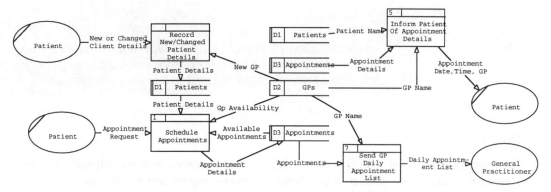

Figure 5.17 Ashgrove Surgery 2nd Draft level 1 DFD

Step 5

This step involves rationalising or simplifying the diagram such that there is no unnecessary duplication and that the diagram contains between 6 and 10 processes. There is a reason for the 6 – 10 processes guideline. The purpose of a Level 1 DFD is to provide a simple overview of the whole system on a single sheet of A4 paper. If you attempt to cram more than 10 processes onto a single sheet of A4 the diagram becomes too complex to comprehend in one go and thus loses its purpose. The simplest way to rationalise a level 1 DFD is to combine processes, for example process 'Inform Client of Appointment Details' will almost always take place immediately after an occurrence of process 'Schedule Appointment' and the processes share the Appointments Data Store. It would therefore be reasonable to combine these into a single process.

Having combined any appropriate processes the next step would be to remove any other unnecessarily duplicated components. Look at the left side of figure 5.17 there are two occurrences of the 'Patient' external entity (duplication being shown by the bar in the top left of the oval). Only one of these is actually required.

The result is shown in the figure 5.18.

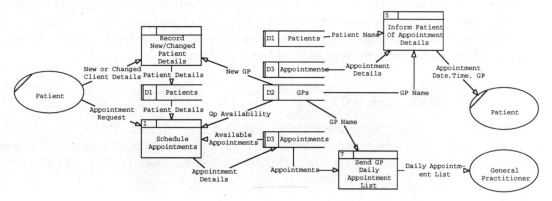

Figure 5.18 Ashgrove Surgery 3rd Draft level 1 DFD

As you can see drawing DFDs can be a repetitive job with many redrafts being necessary. The final step in the production of a level 1 DFD is a check for completeness. Each data store must have at least one data flow in and one data flow out. If a data store has no incoming data flows then no data can ever get into the data store. If a data store has no outgoing data flows then the data store stored can never be used. If either of these cases arise then the likelihood is that you have missed something during the analysis process.

Task 5.13 PC 3

Examine the completed Level 1 DFD shown in figure 5.18. See if there are any data stores which either have no incoming or no outgoing data flows. Suggest what extra components are required to complete the diagram

Step 6

The purpose of a level 1 DFD is to provide a simple overview of a complete system. Data Flow Diagrams can also be used to show detailed processing requirements. To show this detail each process in a level 1 DFD has its own Level 2 DFD. A example of a Level 2 DFD is shown in the figure 5.19.

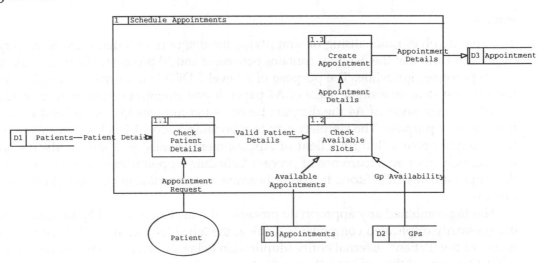

Figure 5.19 Ashgrove Surgery level 2 DFD (Process 1 Schedule Appointments)

When drawing level 2 DFDs it is quite normal to realise that you have missed things from the level 1 DFD. If this is the case then you need to backtrack and make any necessary corrections. A further point is that some very complex systems require the level 3 DFDs. These are constructed in exactly the same way as level 1 and 2 DFDs.

Task 5.14 PC 3   *C 3.1*

Select one other process from the level 1 DFD and draw a level 2 DFD. It may be useful to go through a class exercise with your tutor before starting to work individually. Then work in pairs, swap diagrams and give each other some feedback.

Step 7

The final step is to review the entire DFD set against the documented requirements and make any last minute adjustments.

At this stage the documentation is likely to consist of fairly simple text descriptions of processes, data stores, externals and data flows. The documentation becomes more refined as analysis proceeds into design/specification.

When the process is complete the nest step is to document the lowest level process using Input, Output, Process Specifications, thus the use of techniques like structure charts decision tables tends to cross the border between analysis and design (in ill-defined border in any case). The use of these specification techniques is described in more detail in Element 5.3.

Task 5.15 PC 3

Work through steps 1 to 7 as described above for the Dragon Video Case Study. Your DFD together with its supporting documentation could be used as part of your evidence for this element.

Data Models in Analysis

You should note that the following material is simply an introduction to a complex area of analysis and design. The material covered here is built upon in Element 5.3. and is described in more detail in Unit 7 (Database Development). Data Models are introduced here because they are an established systems analysis tool and because their use is not limited to database environments.

What is a Data Model?

A Data Model is a representation of the data used by a system. It shows how the data is logically grouped and the relationships between these groupings as defined by the business requirements of the system You may well find that other terms such as Logical Data Structure (LDS) and Entity-Relationship Model are used in place of Data Model in some books.

A Data Model comprises:

❏ A diagram called an Entity-Relationship Diagram (E-RD)

❏ Associated documentation of entities, attributes and relationships, usually held in a data dictionary system.

What do Entity-Relationship Diagrams Consist of?

Entity-Relationship Diagrams consist of representations of entity types and relationship types:

Entity Types

An entity type is a logical grouping of data which is relevant to the application in question. The entity type must be relevant, e.g. an information system specifically for the Ashgrove Surgery would not hold information about Clients cars, since this is not relevant. An entity type is an identifiable object, classification, concept, activity, event or thing concerning the application. The thing must be identifiable since if it cannot be identified no information can be recorded about it in a database, e.g. a particular bottle of medicine cannot be identified by the Ashgrove Surgery and would not therefore be an entity type (however in a pharmacy system a particular bottle of medicine could well be an entity). In other words there are no hard and fast rules about what is and isn't an entity It depends on the requirements of the application in question.

An entity is an occurrence of an entity type. The terms entity type and entity are often used interchangeably, the context usually defines what is actually meant. There must be the possibility of an entity type having more than one occurrence. A common mistake is to include one 'super' entity type in the E-RD representing the company , the garage the library or the surgery or whatever. For example The E-RD for the Ashgrove Surgery should not contain the Ashgrove Surgery itself as an entity type, since there is only one occurrence. However if you were to

275

develop a system for a network of practices then Practice becomes an entity type. Further examples of typical entities are Customer, Order, Part, Invoice, Delivery, Location, Supplier, Department.

Question 5.5

Should an E-RD for Dragon Video Rental include an entity type called 'Dragon Video Rental'?

Entity types are represented as soft rectangles containing the name of the entity. Naming of entities is critical, especially when groups of people are working together. An agreed definition of what is actually meant by an entity name will avoid a lot of confusion and pointless discussion.

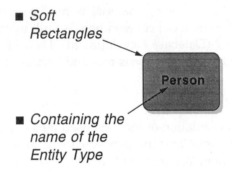

Figure 5.20 Representation of Entity Types

Relationship Types

A relationship type (again the terms relationship and relationship type are used interchangeably) is a relevant business association between two entity types (or in other words a relationship is a relevant business association between one entity of one type and 0, 1 or many occurrences of another entity type).

A relationship type is drawn as a line with a so called crows foot at the many or member end of the relationship. There are three different kinds of relationship shown in figure 5.21.

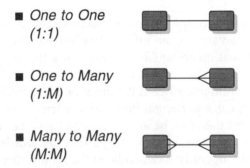

Figure 5.21 Different Relationship Types

In a completed E-RD all relationships are 1:M. 1:1 relationships are typically removed by combining the entities. M:M relationships are broken down into two 1:M relationships with the 2 original entities owning a 'link' entity. This technique is shown in figure 5.22.

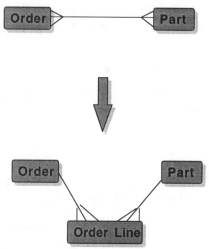

Typically the presence of a M:M relationship signifies that the analysis in this area is incomplete. The model shows that each order is for many parts and that a part appears on many orders.

The attribute Order_Date clearly belongs with the Order entity. The attribute part description clearly belongs with the Part entity.

What about the quantity ordered of a particular part on a particular order? This attribute doesn't quite fit into the order or part entities. In fact it belongs in the Order_Line entity

Figure 5.22 Resolving M:M Relationships

Each end of each relationship must be optional or mandatory. If a relationship end is optional (shown by using a broken line) the entity at that end of the relationship can exist without taking part in the relationship. If a relationship end is mandatory (shown using a solid line) the entity at that end of the relationship must take part in the relationship. Each relationship has two ends, each end can either be optional or mandatory, this gives rise to four types of 1:M relationship:

Owner Optional : Member Mandatory

- *A Customer can exist without placing an orders*
- *An Order must have been placed by one and only one Customer*

Owner Mandatory : Member Mandatory

- *An Order must consist of at least one Order Line*
- *An Order Line must appear on one and only one Order*

Owner Optional : Member Optional

- *A Employee may negotiate Orders if their job type is Salesperson*
- *An Order may be received directly from a customer and could thus exist independently of Employees*

Owner Mandatory : Member Optional

- *A Commission Plan will only exist if at least one Employee is being paid via that plan*
- *An Employee who is not a Salesperson doesn't get commission*

Figure 5.23 Different Kinds of 1:M Relationships

Relationships are named at both ends, the names chosen should be such that meaningful sentences can be constructed describing the nature of the relationship using the entity names and the relationship names.

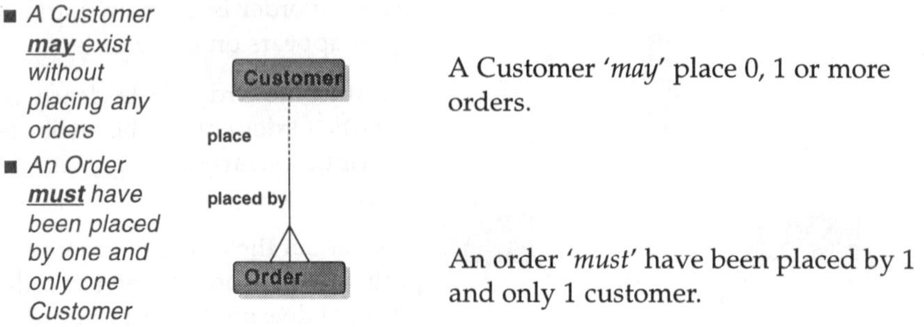

- A Customer **may** exist without placing any orders
- An Order **must** have been placed by one and only one Customer

A Customer '*may*' place 0, 1 or more orders.

An order '*must*' have been placed by 1 and only 1 customer.

Figure 5.24 Relationship Names

How are Data Models Created?

The following steps may be helpful but there really are no hard and fast rules. As the analysis and design exercise proceeds the E-RD will evolve and many re-drafts may be necessary as the analysts understanding of the application improves:

1. Identify an initial list of entities

2. Using an Entity/Relationship cross reference identify the initial relationships

3. Create a first draft E-RD

Each of the steps described above will now be discussed in the light of the Ashgrove Surgery Case Study.

Step 1

Identify an initial list of entity types.

On reading through the Ashgrove Surgery Case Study, the following are candidates for being entity types:

- ❏ GP
- ❏ Client
- ❏ Reception Staff
- ❏ Nursing Staff
- ❏ District Nurse
- ❏ Appointment
- ❏ Prescription
- ❏ Treatment
- ❏ Clinic

This list can be rationalised by combining GP, Reception Staff, Nursing Staff and District Nurse into a single entity type called Employee, this is possible because the entries in the database for the different types of employee will be very similar, e.g. Name, Address and Home Telephone Number. Resulting in the following list:

Entity Type	Example
Employee	A person who is employed by the Surgery, e.g. a GP, Receptionist or Nurse.
Client	A person who has registered with the practice and has been allocated to a GP.
Appointment	A scheduled meeting between a GP and a Client.
Prescription	A prescription form
Treatment	A drug which can be prescribed by the GPs of the practice e.g. Ventolin, Penicillin.
Clinic	An occurrence of a clinic e.g. Asthma Clinic on 10th July at 19:00.

The use of example tables such as the one shown above is very useful, they provide a baseline of agreed definitions, from which a team of people can work.

Step 2

An Entity/Relationship cross reference chart is simply a matrix which can be used to assist with the identification of relationships between entity types.

	Emp.	Clnt.	Appt.	Pres.	Treat.	Clin.
Employee	X	1:M (1)	1:M (2)	1:M (3)	X (4)	1:M (5)
Client		X	1:M (5)	1:M (6)	X	M:M (7)
Appointment			X	1:M (8)	X	X
Prescription				X	M:M (9)	X
Treatment					X	X
Clinic						X

Key	Description
	No need to consider (the shaded cells are the mirror image of the top right area of the matrix)
X	Possibility considered – no relationship (you may find it odd that the employee/emp. cell contains an X, in some more advanced situations it is possible for an entity type to take part in a relationship with another entity of the same type, e.g. an employee 'manages' another employee. The use of 'X' is preferable to leaving the cell blank, since a blank could imply that the possibility had not yet been considered.
1:1	1:1 Relationship exists
1:M	1:M Relationship exists, consider the cell labelled (1), in this case the 1 referes to employee and the M refers to Client.
M:M	M:M Relationship exists

Notes

1. Each GP is allocated many Clients, each Client is allocated to only one GP.

2. Each GP conducts many Appointments, each Appointment is conducted by only 1 GP.

3. Each GP signs many Prescriptions either as the result of an Appointment or a repeat prescription.

4. There is no direct relationship between GP and Treatment, there is however an indirect relationship between GP and Treatment via the Prescription.

5. Each Client attends many Appointments, each Appointment is attended by only 1 Client.

6. Each Client receives many Prescriptions, each Prescription is for only 1 Client.

7. Each Client may attend many Clinics and each Clinic may be attended by many Clients.

8. Each Appointment may cause many Prescriptions to be created.

9. Each Prescription may contain many treatments and a Treatment may appear on many Prescriptions.

The first step in the drawing of the E-RD is the mechanical representation of the relationships shown in the cross reference table. The result is shown in figure 5.25.

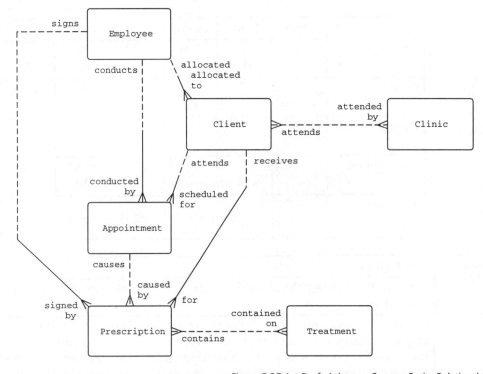

Figure 5.25 1st Draft Ashgrove Surgery Entity-Relationship Diagram

The next step is to remove the M:M relationships. The result is shown in figure 5.26.

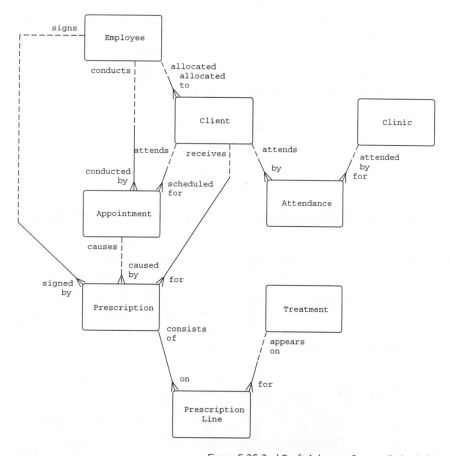

Figure 5.26 2nd Draft Ashgrove Surgery Entity-Relationship Diagram

Task 5.16

Work through each of the steps described above for the Dragon Video Rental Case Study.

At this stage the documentation is likely to consist of brief text descriptions of each entity type and relationship type. The becomes more detailed and complete until eventually the documentation serves as a detailed database definition. This is another area where the boundary between analysis and design/specification is crossed. Data Model documentation is described in more detail in the next element.

5.2.4 Systems Analysis Reports

A systems analysis report draws together all the information collected and presents it in a standard format. The format will typically be pre-defined, i.e. there will be an organisational standard for systems analysis reports, however as a minimum it should consist of;

❑ *Introduction;* describing the background, terms of reference, purpose & objectives of the system.

❏ *Problem Statement;* A description of the agreed requirements of the system presented in business terminology. This section could be supported by a appendices which contain interview notes, questionnaires used, documents read and observations carried out..

❏ *System Models;* This section should contain all your Diagrams (i.e. Data Flow Diagrams and Entity-Relationship Diagrams together with their supporting documentation.

❏ *Process Specifications;* This section should contain any preliminary specification work you have completed (e.g. Structure charts, decision tables, screen/report layouts), although it should be understood that at this stage these are still subject to validation and agreement.

5.2.5 Review of Systems Analysis Work in the Light of User Feedback

At this stage it is useful to carry out a semi-formal presentation of the analysis work you have done so far to the end-users (informal reviews of small items of work should occur regularly between analysts and end-users). Don't expect to get it right first time, some time spent explaining your modelling work to end-users will be repaid many times over in the errors and omissions they point out to you. Accept this feedback gracefully, remember they are criticising your work not you individually. Accept their criticisms (they know more about the business than you) and rework your models accordingly.

Task 5.17 PC 1, 2, 3, 4 & 5

In this element you are required to deliver three evidence indicators;

❏ *A Systems Analysis Report*

❏ *A Data Flow Diagram*

❏ *A set of notes showing the information collected, use of standard techniques and a review of systems analysis in the light of user comments*

The following activities may help you in the preparation of your evidence;

❏ *Role Playing; It would be helpful if your tutors could role play characters from various business scenarios and allow you to interview them. You can use the Dragon Video Club Case Study or any other scenarios you and your tutors can imagine, e.g. a library, a mail order catalogue, a sports centre booking system or a sporting league such as the F.A. Carling Premiership.*

❏ *Practice; In reality the only way to learn how to produce DFDs and E-RDs is to practice producing them over and over again and to discuss your results with your colleagues and tutors in order to obtain feedback, in other words to learn by doing and making mistakes.*

Produce a System Specification

Introduction

In this element we will look in some detail at the process of creating a System Specification or Design and at the main techniques involved. Two main areas will be covered;

❏ *Data Definition*
❏ *Process Specification*

5.3.1 Data Definition

The key activity at this stage is to ensure that the data model contains all the data required by the processes defined in the Data Flow Diagrams and to ensure that the model is in *first normal form* (1NF). 1NF is the first step in a technique called normalisation which will be covered in detail in Unit 7.

The first step is to conduct a more detailed analysis of the contents of data stores and data flows. At this stage 'client details' isn't enough, a database designer needs to know what 'client details' consists of, e.g.

❏ Name (which in turn consists of Title, Forename, Middle Initial and Surname),

❏ Address (Street/Road Address, District, Postal Town, County & Postcode),

❏ Telephone (Country Code, STD Code, Number, Extension)

The database designer needs to know what format these details have e.g. character, numeric, date, time, etc. and how long they are, to enable the database to be accurately sized.

Each data flow in the DFDs has to be described in this fashion and we have to ensure that the data stores themselves contain all these fields. Once this detail has been established the fields in the data stores should be mapped onto the attributes in the entity types of the data model.

A good rule of thumb is try to establish a 1:1 mapping between data stores and entity types, although in practice items such as order/order_line and invoice/invoice_line (which in a data model would appear as two entity types joined by a 1:M relationship) tend to appear as single data stores. Example mappings appear in figure 5.27.

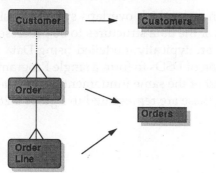

Figure 5.27 Mapping Entity Types and Data Stores

A useful techniques for achieving a good mapping between attributes of entity types and fields in data stores and for creating efficient database designs is normalisation which is covered in Unit 7.

The results of this detailed investigation are typical held in a *data dictionary*. A data dictionary can be manual or computerised and typically allows the following items to be defined:

- ❑ *Entity Types* Text Description, Primary Key, Foreign Keys & Other Attributes, Current Volume, Estimated Growth Rate, Entity Type/Data Store Cross Reference,

- ❑ *Relationship Types* Text Description, Owner Entity, Owner Optionality, Member Entity, Member Optionality, Relationship Names, Average Number of Members,

- ❑ *Attributes* Text Description, Where and How Used e.g. Customer_Number Primary key in Customer Entity Type, Foreign Key in Order Entity Type,

- ❑ *External Entities* Text Description, Originator Of, Recipient Of,

- ❑ *Processes* various process specification entries including inputs & outputs, algorithms,

- ❑ *Data Stores* Contents, i.e. fields, Data Store/Entity Type Cross Reference,

- ❑ *Data Flow* Contents, i.e. fields, Source & Destination,

- ❑ *Fields* Format, Length., How Used.

As can be seen there are many links and cross references, which tend to make manual data dictionaries unwieldy and difficult to control. Computerised data dictionaries are therefore more common and in many cases data dictionaries are integral parts of CASE (Computer Aided Software/Systems Engineering) tools.

Question 5.6

Why are manual data dictionaries unwieldy?

5.3.2 Process Specification

Structure Diagrams

Structure Diagrams are routinely used in the systems design and programming phases of systems development. In systems design a technique called Entity/Event Modelling is used to describe how entities behave during their lifecycle, i.e. under what circumstances they are created and deleted and how they can be updated between birth and death. Entity/Event Modelling involves the production of Entity Life History Diagrams which are specialised forms of structure diagrams.

In program design (an area which overlaps systems design and programming) often the first step is the modelling of the data structures to be processed and created by the program in question. Data structures are typically modelled using Data Structure Diagrams (DSDs). The next step is the combination of DSDs to form a single Program Structure Diagram (PSD). ELHs and DSDs/PSDs all consist of the same fundamental constructs, i.e. Sequence (SEQ), Selection (SEL) and Iteration (ITR), these are represented in figures 5.28, 5.29 and 5.30.

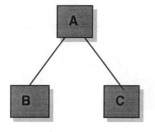

'A' is defined as a SEQ of exactly 1 occurrence of 'B' followed by exactly 1 occurrence of 'C'.

Figure 5.28 Sequence

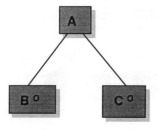

'A' is defined as a SEL of *either* exactly 1 occurrence of 'B' *or* exactly 1 occurrence of 'C' *but* not both.

Figure 5.29 Selection

A common mistake in describing these structure diagrams is to say that 'B' is a SEL because it has the ^{O} symbol in its box, this is not the case, 'A' is the SEL 'B' & 'C' are the selected components.

'A' is defined as an ITR of 0, 1 or more occurrences of 'B'

Figure 5.30 Iteration

Again a common mistake when describing these diagrams is to say that 'B' is an ITR because it has the * symbol in its box, this is not the case, 'A' is the ITR, 'B' is the iterated component.

Task 5.18 PC 2, 3 & 4

Examine figure 5.31 and decide whether each box is a SEQ, SEL, or an ITR. Remember that each box can only be defined by what appears below it in the structure and that any box which isn't broken down any further is by definition a SEQ

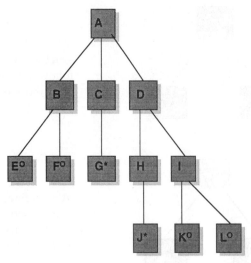

Figure 5.31 Data Structure Diagram

The basic constructs of SEQ, SEL and ITR may only be combined in certain ways, e.g. the diagram in figure 5.31 contains only valid constructs.

 Question 5.7

The combinations in figure 5.34 are invalid do you have any ideas why?

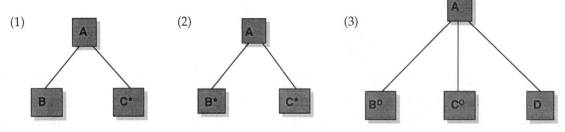

(1) (2) (3)

Figure 5.32 Invalid Structures

Hint

The important thing to remember is that each box can only be defined by what appears below it. In each of the examples above 'A' cannot be defined by what appears below it, e.g. in (1) above, is 'A' a SEQ or an ITR?

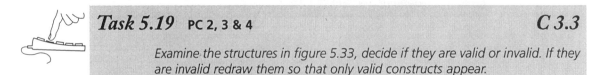 **Task 5.19** PC 2, 3 & 4   *C 3.3*

Examine the structures in figure 5.33, decide if they are valid or invalid. If they are invalid redraw them so that only valid constructs appear.

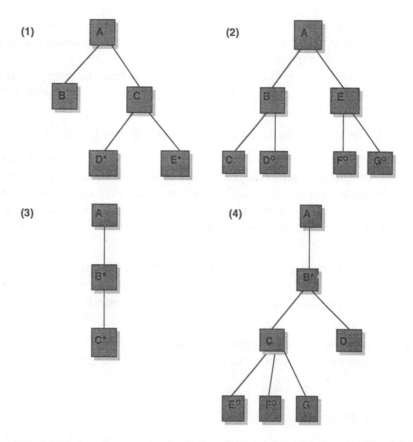

Figure 5.33 Valid or Invalid?

Entity Life Histories

Entity/Event Modelling is considered a fairly advanced design technique and does not appear in the GNVQ definition for this unit. For this reason the construction of Entity Life Histories will not be discussed in any detail, however a simple example appears in figure 5.34, based on the Ashgrove Surgery:

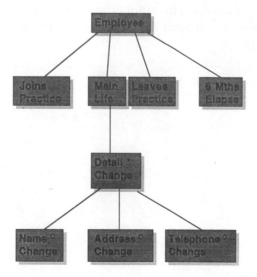

Figure 5.34 Example Entity Life History

The purpose of an ELH is to describe the events which cause a new occurrence of the entity concerned to be created, an old occurrence of the entity to be deleted and an existing occurrence of the entity to be updated

The sequence for reading ELHs (and any other structure diagram) is left to right and top to bottom. From figure 5.34 it can be seen that each Employee passes through 4 distinct phases so far as the Ashgrove Surgery is concerned.

1. A new occurrence of Employee is created when a new Employee joins the practice.

2. Each Employee then enters the main life cycle during which they conduct appointments, prescribe treatments, carry out procedures or work behind the reception desk. Please note that no information regarding appointments, treatments etc. appear on the Employee ELH since appointment and treatment will have their own ELHs. During the main life cycle the Employee may change either their name, address or telephone number on any number of occasions (including 0).

3. When the Employee leaves the practice their main life cycle ends and their record in the Ashgrove Surgeries database is updated to show that they no longer work at the Ashgrove. Their record is not deleted at this point in case any queries arise about their recent activities.

4. Once 6 months have elapsed following leaving the practice all details of the Employee are archived onto microfiche prior to actually deleting the Employee's record from the database.

Data Structure Diagrams

Consider the Employee and Appointment entities in the E-RD in Element 5.2. The management of the Ashgrove Surgery require a report to be produced which shows the average length of appointment for each GP within a specified date range. We can assume that each appointment has the following attributes:

- ❏ Date,
- ❏ Start-Time,
- ❏ Duration.

The Ashgrove Surgery's database (the input data structure) has to be processed in order to produce the printed report (the output data structure). The first step is to model the input data structure using a DSD.

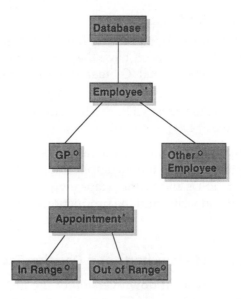

Figure 5.35 Input Data Structure

The database (for the purposes of this program) consists of an ITR of Employees, each of which either a GP or not, each GP consists of an ITR of appointments each of which is either within or without the specified date range.

The next step is to produce a DSD for the output data structure. The report simply consist of an ITR of lines, one for each GP on the database.

Figure 5.36 Output Data Structure

We would then combine the input and output data structures to form a Program Structure Diagram (PSD).

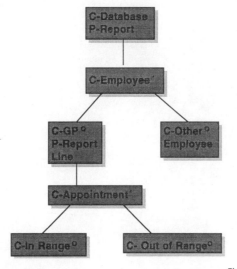

Figure 5.37 Program Structure Diagram

289

The DSDs have been combined as follows:

- Initially the program has to read through the database to produce the report. The components 'Database' and 'Report' have therefore been combined into a single box in the PSD. The convention being that 'C-' means *consume*, i.e. process and that 'P-' means *produce*, i.e. create;

- Each GP in the database causes a line to be printed on the report , so these boxes can also be combined in the PSD.

This is a brief summary of a program design methodology called Jackson Structured Programming (JSP). In reality the steps are more complicated, with rules for the ways in which DSDs can be combined to form PSDs and further steps involving the addition of operations (program statements such as read and write) and the production of Pseudocode, prior to coding and testing.

Structured English, Use of Flowcharts and Decision Tables

Structured English is simply a cut down version of the English Language which only allows certain basic constructs (SEQ, SEL, CASE and ITR), the use of strong active verbs (e.g. create, calculate, delete, add, archive, update etc., nothing meaningless like 'process' thank you very much) and the use of terms which have already been defined in DFDs and E-RDs, e.g. names of data flows and entity types. These however are not definite rules, so use your common sense and remember that the whole point of structured English is to avoid ambiguity. The purpose of Structured English is to describe fairly detailed programming requirements, whereas Structure Diagrams are more concerned with fairly static structural requirements. In fact Structure Diagrams and Structured English can be used together to provide detailed program specifications.

A Flowchart is a diagram which represents the flow of control in a system or program. A Program Flowchart it shows the sequences, selections (and CASE structures) and iterations necessary for a program or complete its actions. However Program Flowcharts have now largely given way to structure diagrams as tools for program design.

Figures 5.38 and 5.39 compare a Structured English approach with a Program Flowchart approach. The techniques are fairly straightforward and will not be described in any further detail.

Structured English
(1) Prepare DATABASE for use.
(2) Print Page Headings.
(3) Read first Employee.
(4) For Each Employee
    If Employee-Type = 'GP'
    then
        Initialise APPT-COUNT, SUM-APPT-TIME, APPT-AVERAGE.
        Read first APPOINTMENT
        For each APPOINTMENT
            If APPOINTMENT-DATE >= START-DATE
                and APPOINTMENT-DATE <= END-DATE
            then
                Add 1 to APPT-COUNT
                Add APPOINTMENT-DURATION to
                    SUM-APPT-TIME
            else
                Do nothing
            end if.
            Read next APPOINTMENT.
        Divide SUM-APPT-TIME by APPT-COUNT giving
            APPT-AVERAGE.
        Print GP-NAME, APPT-COUNT, SUM-APPT-TIMES,
            APPT-AVERAGE.
    Else
        Do Nothing.
    End if.
    (5)Read next GP.
(6) Close Database

Figure 5.38 Structured English

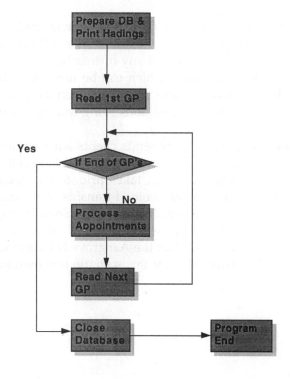

Figure 5.39 Program Flowchart

System Flowcharts show the sequence of events at a system level, i.e. the fact that program 1 precedes program 2, as opposed to the flow of control within a single program. Various symbols can be used in system flowcharts:

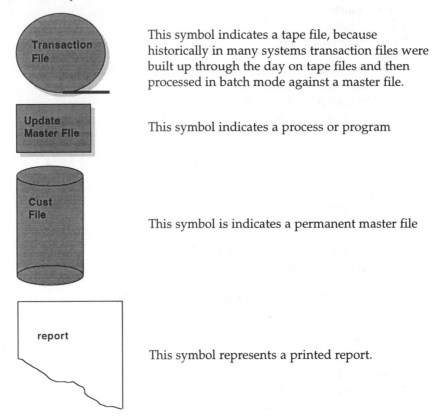

This symbol indicates a tape file, because historically in many systems transaction files were built up through the day on tape files and then processed in batch mode against a master file.

This symbol indicates a process or program

This symbol is indicates a permanent master file

This symbol represents a printed report.

Figure 5.40 System Flowchart Symbols

Currently, where most systems work in on-line mode with end-users running transaction programs directly against a large database, the use of system flowcharts has become unnecessary. For this reason they will not be discussed any further here.

There are many other techniques which can be used in systems specification, including decision trees and decision tables. These are of use when there are a number of different choices to be made as a result of certain conditions being true or untrue. An example of a decision table follows.

Occasionally the Ashgrove Surgery sends clients with certain ailments to a local hospital for blood tests. The blood test results consists of a red blood cell count and a white blood cell count, also the clients temperature will be taken prior to the blood test.

If the red cell count is less than 800 a blood transfusion is necessary. If the white cell count is less than 500 a course of GCSF (Granulocyte Colony Stimulating Factor, this drug helps bone marrow to produce white cells) injections is required. If the white cell count is less than 500 and the Clients temperature is over 38° then the Ashgrove is informed who then prescribe Antibiotics for the client. The decision table for this scenario is shown in figure 5.40.

Conditions	(1)	(2)	(3)	(4)	(5)	(6)	(7)	(8)
Red Cells < 800	T	T	T	T	F	F	F	F
White Cells < 500	T	T	F	F	T	T	F	F
Temperature > 38°	T	F	T	F	T	F	T	F
Actions								
Blood Transfusion	X	X	X	X				
GCSF Injections	X	X			X	X		
Antibiotics	X				X			
Do Nothing							X	X

Figure 5.41 Example Decision Table

The 8 conditions across the top of the table show all the possible combinations of the three conditions. The X's indicate that the action should be carried out, e.g. if all three conditions are true (1) then Blood Transfusion, GCSF Injections and Antibiotics are in order. If however the red cells are less than 800 and temperature > 38° (3) then only a Blood Transfusion is necessary, since antibiotics are only given if in addition to the temperature being high the white cells are low.

This could readily be transformed into a CASE structure (often used in programming languages instead of multiple if-then-else constructs) in Structured English as shown in figure 5.42.

```
Structured English
(1) CASE TEST RESULTS
        CASE (Red Cells < 800) & (White Cells <500) & (Temp > 38)
                Do Blood Transfusion
                Do GCSF Injections
                Do Prescribe Antibiotics
        CASE (Red Cells < 800) & (White Cells < 500) & (Temp <= 38)
                Do Blood Transfusions
                Do GCSF Injections
        CASE (Red Cells < 800) & (White Cells >= 500) & (Temp > 38)
                Do Blood Transfusion
        CASE (Red Cells < 800) & (White Cells >= 500) & (Temp <= 38)
                Do Blood Transfusion
        CASE (Red Cells >= 800) & (White Cells < 500) & (Temp > 38)
                Do GCSF Injections
                Do Prescribe Antibiotics
        CASE (Red Cells >= 800) & (White Cells < 500) & (Temp <= 38)
                Do GCSF Injections
        CASE (Red Cells >= 800) & (White Cells >= 500) & (Temp > 38)
                Do Nothing
        CASE (Red Cells >= 800) & (White Cells >= 500) & (Temp < 38)
                Do Nothing
```

Figure 5.42 CASE Structures in Structured English

5.3.3 Input Specifications & Output Specifications

Input and Output Specification can be considered as subsidiary parts of the Process Specifications described above.

The Input Specification for a process describes the data source, the relevant data capture methods, (e.g. direct keyboard input, received as a file across a network, retrieved from CD-ROM) Screen Layouts, Validation Rules, (e.g. Uppercase Only, Default Value, Range of Values, Use of Check Digits) and Verification (e.g. Security Checks).

The Output Specification simply consists of Screen, Report and File Layouts.

5.3.4 Resource Implications

It is very difficult in the early stages of analysis to provide accurate estimates of how long the programming stages of a project will take, since the exact requirements are often unclear at the start of a project. However by the time that the database definition and process specifications have been written the project manager should be able to provide an accurate estimate of the resource requirements of the project in terms of the number of staff required to build and test the system, the timescales, costs and constraints and the hardware/software platform. In many cases the environment is predefined, e.g. an existing PC Network running DBASE or a mainframe computer running ORACLE (a widely used Relational Database Management System), however at this stage the project manager should have an accurate idea of the system resources required such as disk space and memory requirements.

Task 5.20 PC 1, 2, 3, 4 & 5   *C 3.3*

In this element you are required to produce a system specification including the following;

❑ *A refined DFD (a DFD which you have 'improved' in the light of more detailed information).*

❑ *A set of data definitions in a data dictionary covering, Entity Types, relationship Types, Attributes, External Entities, Processes, Data Stores, Data Flows, Fields (elements of data stores) and very importantly the links between them.*

❑ *Process Specifications.*

❑ *Input Specifications*

❑ *Output Specifications.*

❑ *Resource Implications.*

An essential activity is for you to consider the Dragon Video environment and identify areas in which the different techniques described in this element could be used (as important as knowing how to use tools is knowing when to use them) and then to use the techniques and discuss the results with your colleagues and tutors. (Learning by doing and making mistakes is the most effective method.)

Summary & Conclusions

In this unit we have covered many concepts and techniques. I would like to summarise by picking out a key feature from each of the elements:

☐ *Investigate Principles of Systems Analysis & Specification* This element addressed the processing activities carried out by commercial organisations and the different Information Technology methods which can be used to implement them, e.g. programming and the use of application generators. It then described the nature of the user information required to initiate a feasibility study covering input, output and process specifications. *The key feature of the element was the description of the different stages of systems analysis.* There are many variations of the systems development lifecycle. You shouldn't worry too much that what one text book calls 'Requirements Analysis' may be called 'Systems Analysis' in another and 'Logical Analysis' elsewhere. The important thing is that large scale information systems projects have to be managed and thus have to be broken down into meaningful phases. The exact nature of the breakdown may vary from project to project. The element ended with a brief introduction to the following elements.

☐ *Undertake a Systems Analysis* This element began with a discussion of establishing the purpose of a new information system and with a discussion of the nature of data and information and their uses in organisations. *The key features of the element were the discussions of interviewing techniques and the production of Data Flow Diagrams.* Interviewing is probably the most important tool in the systems analysts toolkit as a means of identifying requirements and of building a trusting, supportive relationship with the end-users. Subsequently Data Flow Diagrams are a very useful tool for modelling the requirements established during interviews. The element ended with a brief description of systems analysis reports and of how the results of a systems analysis exercise can change in the light of feedback from end-users.

☐ *Produce a System Specification* This element began with a description of how to refine Data Flow Diagrams and E-RDs and the different items of information which could be held in a data dictionary. *The key feature of the element was the description of the different process specification techniques.* The important thing to note is that none of these techniques are inherently superior to any of the others. Each have their role to play, your task as a systems analyst is to use the right tools for the job in hand. So don't battle on with structured english because its your favourite if a decision table is more appropriate. The unit ended with a brief description of input and output specifications and finally with a discussion of resource implications.

In conclusion the role of systems analyst can be very challenging and rewarding as I found out while working as a systems analyst in a large organisation. It is quite possible to interview the director of marketing in the morning and spend the afternoon explaining a detailed technical specification to a trainee programmer. As a systems analyst you get to meet a lot of interesting people. I would advise you that personal skills, e.g. communication, report writing and giving presentations, are at least as important as technical skills.

Answers to questions in Unit 5

Answer 5.1 The role evolved because of communications problems between computer experts and business experts. In the early days of computer usage much more technical expertise was required from the average programmer, than is required today, giving rise to jargon.

Answer 5.2 Using a spreadsheet is less error prone than using a calculator, consider having to carry out a complex calculation many times with only one variable changing, e.g. (a + b + c * d), followed by (a + b + c * e), (a + b + c * f) etc. Using a spreadsheet a, b and c would only have to be entered once.

A spreadsheet is more flexible than a specific computer program. If the calculation changed to (a + b – c * d) a program would have to be edited and re-compiled, in a spreadsheet it would simply be a matter of changing the '+' to a '–' and carrying on.

Answer 5.3 The main reason is the rapid development of computers and their facilities.

Organisations obviously like to use the newer and more efficient machines but unfortunately do not have the time or resources to convert all of their existing systems to use the new technology.

Answer 5.4 Most Useful – Interview.
Least Useful – Questionnaire.

Answer 5.5 No! There is only one occurrence of Dragon Video Rental.

Answer 5.6 The difficulties involved are (a) maintaining the accuracy of paper documents and (b) extracting information.

Answer 5.7 (1) is invalid because it is impossible to describe 'A' as either a SEQ or an ITR.
(2) is invalid for the same reason.
(3) is invalid because it is impossible to describe 'A' as either a SEL or a SEQ.

The correct representations appear in figure 5.33.

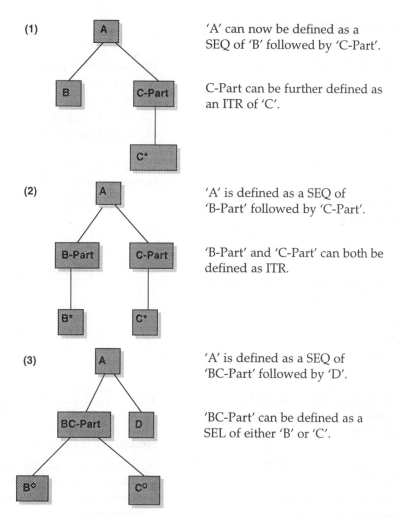

(1) 'A' can now be defined as a SEQ of 'B' followed by 'C-Part'.

C-Part can be further defined as an ITR of 'C'.

(2) 'A' is defined as a SEQ of 'B-Part' followed by 'C-Part'.

'B-Part' and 'C-Part' can both be defined as ITR.

(3) 'A' is defined as a SEQ of 'BC-Part' followed by 'D'.

'BC-Part' can be defined as a SEL of either 'B' or 'C'.

Figure 5.33 Correctly Drawn Structures

Unit 5 Sample Test Paper

1   In Large Organisations the use of IT is:

   A   Irrelevant
   B   Essential
   C   Useful
   D   A waste of time

2   The most important skill a Systems Analyst should possess is:

   A   Project Management
   B   Building Computers
   C   Accountancy
   D   Interviewing

3   The best software package for holding a list of names and addresses would be:

   A   A database
   B   A word processor
   C   A spreadsheet
   D   Graphics

Questions 4 – 13 are based on the material in Element 5.1 (Investigate Principles of Systems Analysis & Specification).

4   Calculating Bills, e.g. Gas, Telephone, essentially involves:

   A   Interrogation and Manipulation
   B   Calculation and Control
   C   Repetition and Calculation
   D   Communications

5   Which is a 'professional' definition of programming:

   A   Writing BASIC or PASCAL code
   B   Writing and then testing a program
   C   Clarifying requirements with a systems analyst, designing, coding and testing programs
   D   Writing a subsequently amending a program until it conforms to specification

6   What kind of application software facility would best satisfy a standard information systems requirement such as the maintenance of accounting data:

   A   Application generator
   B   Spreadsheet with macros
   C   Automated application software
   D   Database

7   An algorithm is part of:

   A   Output requirements
   B   Processing requirements
   C   Input requirements
   D   Data Structure requirements

8   Which of the following diagrams shows the correct sequence:

   A)

   B)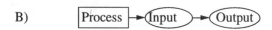

   C)

   D)

9   Strategic IT Planning involves:

   A   Maintaining current information systems
   B   Planning future information systems
   C   Decide which information systems to discontinue
   D   Comparing current information systems against business requirements and planning future information systems

10   What is the correct order of the SSADM modules:

   A   Feasibility, Requirements Analysis, Requirements Specification, Logical System Specification, Physical Design
   B   Requirements Analysis, feasibility, Requirements Specification, Logical System Specification, Physical Design
   C   Physical Design, Logical System Specification, Requirements Specification, Requirements Analysis, Feasibility
   D   Logical System Specification, Requirements Specification, Requirements Analysis, feasibility, Physical Design

11 Which model describes the approach where an initial version of a system gradually becomes the finished version:

A   Waterfall
B   Incremental Delivery
C   Evolutionary Prototyping
D   SSADM

12 Which of the following techniques would *not* normally be used in a process specification:

A   Structured English
B   Structure Charts
C   Flowcharts
D   Program testing

13 What does a data model consist of:

A   An Entity-Relationship Diagram plus supporting documentation
B   A Data Flow Diagram
C   A list of processes carried out by a system
D   An Entity Life History Diagram

Questions 14 – 23 Relate to Element 5.2 (Undertake a Systems Analysis).

14 Establishing the purpose and main objectives of a system should be carried out when:

A   At the end of a project
B   Prior to coding
C   At the start of a project
D   After coding and testing but before implementation

15 Why is exception reporting a useful management tool:

A   It ensures that managers receive all the information they need
B   It ensures that data is accurate
C   It increases the amount of information available
D   It lets the manager concentrate on important issues

16 Which of the following is best described as information:

A   1.9
B   Tim Hutchings is 1.9 metres tall
C   1.9 metres
D   190 centimetres

17 What information gathering technique is most appropriate for a systems analyst trying to discover how an end-user actually does their job:

A   Interview
B   Questionnaire
C   Observation
D   Document inspection

18 Which symbol would not appear in a data flow diagram:

A)

B)

C)

D)

19 Which is the correct definition of the term external entity:

A   A route by which data can flow from one component of a DFD to another
B   Something which either sends data into a system or receives data from a system
C   A repository for data
D   A relationship between 2 entity types

20 Which of the following is a valid data flow:

A)

B)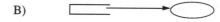

C)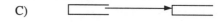

D)

21 Which of the following represents a process which checks customer credit information and then creates a customer order:

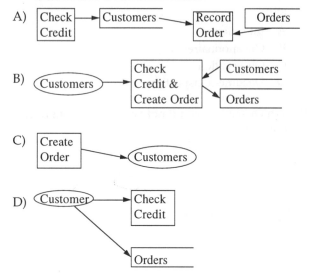

22 What is the purpose of a systems analysis report:

   A   To describe the problems encountered during systems analysis

   B   A document which describes how to carry out systems analysis

   C   To enable a systems analysis exercise to be planned

   D   To collect the results of a systems analysis exercise and present them in a standard format

23 Why is it important to show end-users the results of systems analysis:

   A   To prove that you have done the work

   B   To give the end-user the opportunity to identify errors and omissions

   C   To enable the end-user to work more effectively

   D   To show off your report writing skills

Questions 24 – 33 relate to Element 5.3 (Produce a System Specification)

24 Which Entity Type pair would typically appear in a single data store:

   A   Customer & Order

   B   Doctor & Appointment

   C   Order & Order_Line

   D   Book & Loan

25 Which of the following would *not* appear in the data dictionary definition of a data flow:

   A   Process Description

   B   Fields Contained

   C   Source

   D   Destination

26 Which of the following structure charts is valid:

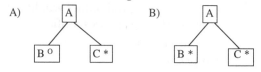

27 Which set of constructs are allowed in Structured English:

   A   Sequence, Selection, Iteration

   B   Sequence, Selection, CASE, Iteration

   C   Selection, Iteration, CASE, 1:M Relationships

   D   Iteration, Sequence, Selection, 1:M Relationships, CASE

28 The Symbol ◊ in a program flowchart represents what:

   A   A Sequence

   B   A Selection

   C   An Iteration

   D   A Decision

29 Decision tables are most effective in what circumstances:

   A   When there are only 1 or 2 conditions and actions

   B   When there a number of different possible actions depending on the outcomes of certain conditions

   C   When processing requirements are reasonably straightforward

   D   When the outcomes of certain conditions are unknown

30 Which of the following is normally part of an
input specification:

A   Output screen layouts
B   Validation rules
C   Algorithms
D   Structure Charts

31 When is a project manager in a position to
provide detailed accurate estimates of the
resources required to complete a project:

A   At the start of a project
B   After the feasibility study
C   When database definitions have been agreed
and program specifications written
D   At the end of the project

Software

Introduction

Software is the term used to collectively represent all the programs that may be used on a computer system.

This unit describes the software elements associated with a computer system through:

❏ an investigation of the different types of software package and their purpose;

❏ an examination of software production, both how this is achieved and the features/ characteristics associated with differing programming languages;

❏ an investigation of the techniques associated with the production of automated procedures.

Element 6.1

Investigate Software

Introduction

An investigation into the software elements associated with a computer system will provide an ability to:

❏ describe the categories of software and their purposes;

❏ explain the purpose of application software packages;

❏ explain the features of a computer program;

❏ describe the different modes of operation of software.

6.1.1 Categories of Software

Historically or even generally, software may be classified in two forms:

❏ Systems software;

❏ Applications software.

Systems software

Systems software represents the body of programs available to the computer user which provide the means to control and manage the computer. Development of software in this area requires the developer to possess the necessary technical understanding of the computer. Examples of system software include:

- ❏ Operating System;
- ❏ Utilities;
- ❏ Program Development Tools;
- ❏ Compilers;
- ❏ Assemblers;
- ❏ Linkers.

Question 6.1

Why does the systems software developer need to understand the technical aspects of the system?

Generally, *Program Development Tools, Compilers, Assemblers* and *Linkers* collectively provide a user with the facilities to develop further programs. *Utilities* include software such as text editors, sort packages and file management facilities.

Applications software

Applications software generally represents any software which isn't part of the overall control of the computer. Application software packages take various, diverse forms which permit the end-user to process information in some manner and produce a desired result. Generally, the less a program requires of the end-user in technically understanding the computer, the more the program may be viewed as being an application program. Examples of application software include:

- ❏ Word Processors
- ❏ Desk Top Publishing (DTP)
- ❏ Spreadsheet Managers
- ❏ Database Managers
- ❏ Payroll programs
- ❏ Stock Control
- ❏ Electronic mail
- ❏ Leisure software (Games)

Question 6.2

Define the term 'Applications software'.

It should be noted that some software may be regarded as belonging to both categories. A compiler may be viewed as belonging to both as it represents a piece of systems software but is also an application. Such a facility aids the user in developing their own programs possibly using technical system elements but still also represents an application because they are processing a document in some manner. It is processing readable text in the form of a programming language and converting it into a form more applicable to the computer known as machine code.

Question 6.3

Why may some packages be regarded both as systems software and applications software?

Task 6.1   PC 1

Using a typical PC system of your own, in your place of work or where you study, using the traditional software classifications presented, categorise the main software packages installed on the hard disk.

With such a vast pool of diverse software presently available, it is possibly better to categorise software in the following alternative manner:

- ❏ Applications software;
- ❏ Operating Systems;
- ❏ Utilities;
- ❏ User Interface Software;
- ❏ Languages;
- ❏ Program Generators;
- ❏ Database Management Systems.

Operating Systems

An operating system is a collection or suite of programs which controls the operation of the computer and the flow of information around the computer in order to execute further applications. It is the interface between user written or purchased software and the hardware. It provides the user with the range of commands to 'drive' the system. Each computer has associated with it at least one operating system permitting the user to easily operate the computer in some manner. It is possible that a computer may use alternative operating systems although normally only one is active at any time. The exception to this is the new Power MAC which has separate processors, one for the MAC operating system and one for the DOS operating system. In this case, both operating systems can run simultaneously. The IBM PC and it's compatibles may instead of the usual MS-DOS operating system, use a UNIX derivative operating system called LINUX.

Question 6.4

What is the main purpose of an operating system?

Utilities

The utilities category is concerned with the processing of routine tasks providing the user with various aids to generally administer the system through facilities such as disk formatting, back-up procedures, file maintenance, file copying, sorting and text editors. Some examples may be regarded as providing a systems software capability.

User interface software

This category of software includes procedures to manage the way in which information is presented to the user and user responses obtained. We frequently call this type of software the *Human Computer Interface*. Much emphasis is placed on the *'User Friendliness'* aspect of a program, that is, the flexibility and ease with which the user interacts with the running application. This includes both the actions associated with input and the format with which the output is presented.

User Interface Software includes Command Driven Interfaces such as that used in MS-DOS, Menu Driven Interfaces which are typically provided by applications running under MS-DOS and User Interface Management Systems. The latter is usually provided by means of a window based interface, the purpose of which is to provide a consistent interface across numerous applications. Such applications use the same standard input and output interface routines to accomplish this goal. This approach aids program development by eliminating the need for different developers to re-invent such routines. Figure 6.4 shows a typical screen used in word processing with a menu bar at the top giving the user a range of the commands to use. The package provides further button facilities to assist the user.

Question 6.5

Much emphasis is placed on the 'User Friendliness' aspect of a program. Briefly explain the reason for this.

Languages

We need to provide program developers with the correct tools to help them produce further programs. A programming language is such a tool. It permits the easy definition of the instructions and the order in which such instructions are to be executed to derive a desired outcome.

Although programs run in a computer in a numeric format, normally no programs are written in this form. Instead, development tools permit the program developer to set down a solution in a more human readable form, that is the *Programming Language*. This must then be translated into a form more easily understood and processed by the computer. Each programming language has associated with it a set of rules formally defining the permitted structure any program written in the programming language must take.

Although there appears to be an almost unlimited pool of programming languages in which to develop a solution to a programming problem, the developer should use the programming language most suited to the task to be accomplished. There exist languages more applicable to developing applications software and those more applicable to the area of systems software.

Question 6.6

Define the term 'Programming Language'. Why do so many languages exist?

Program generators

This category of software provides for the automated generation of parameterised program code. The user specifies what is required and is not concerned with how it is to be achieved. The code generated provides a working solution based on a collection of standard code segments. A program generator is designed to provide a solution to a specific type of task. It cannot be asked to do something it was not designed to do. An example of a program generator is a 4GL. The user defines the format of the information to be stored and following entry of the information, queries can be made upon it. How the queries are accomplished is of little importance to the user, the importance is the retrieval of information satisfying the request.

Question 6.7

Briefly identify how programming languages differ to the information submitted to program generators.

Database management systems

The Database management systems (DBMS) category of software represents software packages which provide for the management of structured data in the form of databases. The management functions provide the user with the ability to:

- ☐ define the structure of entities associated with a stored database;
- ☐ identify relationships and cross-references between database entities;
- ☐ enter new information into a pre-defined database;
- ☐ amend information stored in a database;
- ☐ query the stored information;
- ☐ re-organise the database, amending the pre-defined structures;
- ☐ control the operational characteristics of the database management software;
- ☐ generate applications to process the stored database(s).

Unit 7 further details the management functions associated with a DBMS.

Task 6.2   PC 1

Using a typical PC based system of your own, in your place of work or where you study and using the software categories just covered:

- ☐ *describe the categories associated with the software packages on your hard disk;*
- ☐ *identify the category to which each software package belongs.*

306

6.1.2 Purpose of categories of software

Having identified the basic categories software falls within, we'll continue by explaining the purpose associated with this software:

- ❏ Use for common data processing tasks;
- ❏ System control;
- ❏ Simplification of user interface;
- ❏ Creation and conversion of code;
- ❏ Management of shared data.

Use for common data processing tasks

If a user wants to perform a task or operation just once, it would be inefficient to put much effort into fully developing the software to provide this task. The simpler the solution the better, provided it achieves the desired result. However, whether the software is systems or applications based, it should usually provide the user with the ability to perform a range of common tasks. It would be inefficient to develop one program to do one explicit task and yet another to provide for a variation of it. Consider the following scenarios:

- ❏ Calculating the monthly repayments on a loan. What is required is a single program to forecast the repayment amounts for user-entered loan amounts and not a separate program for each possible loan amount.
- ❏ The procedures associated with file maintenance. Irrespective of the file contents, whether it be textual or executable programs, the user has a need to perform file operations such as create, copy, delete, backup and even format a disk.
- ❏ A text editor whether it be a simple version or even a comprehensive word processor allows the user to produce a textual document. The text may represent one of many diverse forms such as correspondence or even a program's source code.

System control

The system needs precise instructions to complete any activity correctly. The operating system is an example of system control. It controls the various attached devices and central system organising the way in which the whole system runs.

Both the applications user and the program developer need the ability to manage the system productively. The configuration of the system must be set up to manage areas such as memory and resource allocation. Such software permits the user to tailor the system to their own needs and those of the applications they run.

Simplification of user interface

It is essential to simplify the user interface for any software package so the user may run the package in as productive a manner as possible. However, the needs of the developer and those of the end-user differ.

- ❏ The developer's needs:
  - Early PC based applications ran on standalone machines and the software such machines could run was limited due to numerous hardware limitations. Few software packages existed and those available were generally inflexible and consisted of many different styles to display the information or obtain information from the user. The emphasis was placed upon providing a solution and not the ease of use to the

end-user. Different developers used differing standards of interface mechanisms. Eventually, developers recognised this limitation and started evaluating the different interface styles used in the marketplace and included the better methods in their own products.

• Developing and re-inventing procedures to make the product easy to use required considerable effort and time, resources which could be better spent developing the functionality of the package. What was required was a standard that developers could use, permitting them to concentrate on the functionality of the package. With the availability of more powerful micro-processors came the ability to provide comprehensive window based interfaces which provided the developer with a suitable standard user interface mechanism. The Windows standard provides the user with a view that looks similar for each different package that is run.

• There was a price to be paid by developers. To use early window based development facilities, developers had to understand the considerable technical issues and produce very complex program code. The necessary development tools to simplify this task did not exist to support their demands.

• Current development tools for window based applications allow the easier definition of window zones for differing purposes. Standard formats and areas for displaying messages and obtaining user responses are well defined. Thus the application developer is able to concentrate on the function of the application rather than develop their own interface handling routines.

Question 6.8

What is an application developer able to concentrate on and why?

❏ The end-user's needs – The first personal computers required the user to enter a range of commands to run the system. With the availability of more powerful micro-processors came the ability to provide comprehensive window based interfaces which removed the need for the end-user's technical awareness. Instead of complex commands, the system could be driven simply using point-and-click techniques to select and reflect their individual needs. We still need a basic computing awareness, but the available applications permitted the system to be used by more people.

Consider the two window extracts contained in figure 6.1. Each extract represents a displayable window containing a title, message and two user-selectable option buttons. The precise manner in which these are handled is controlled by standard software procedures, the developer specifies the form of the window, it's title, the displayable message and the button details whilst the end-user can easily select a button in some manner.

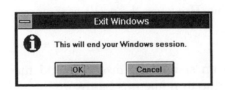
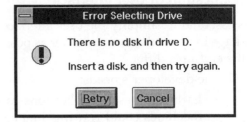

Figure 6.1 Example window extracts

Question 6.9

Generally, how do a developer's and end-user's needs differ in relation to the simplification of a user interface?

Creation and conversion of code

Programmers have to develop code that the micro-processor of the computer can understand. Ultimately, such code must exist in a numeric form or machine code. A major purpose of a large amount of software is concerned with aiding the production of further software packages. To this end, the developer needs to be able to:

❑ create their program solution in a readable textual form. This is achieved through the use of some form of text editor;

❑ convert the stored human readable form into a form understood by the computer. This is achieved through the use of suitable Program Development Tools such as compilers, assemblers and linkers as appropriate.

Question 6.10

What is a major purpose of development software and how does it ease the process for the developer?

Management of shared data

Data requiring processing may take many forms including text, program code, structured data (database information) or some other data form applicable to an individual application. Generally, such data must be stored on some form of secondary storage such as disks in the form of files. Early computer systems, generally mainframes, provided computing facilities which were shared by a large number of users. The associated operating system had to provide complex file management facilities to share the stored files amongst the various users authorised to access individual files. Such accesses could even be required to occur simultaneously.

With the advent of stand-alone personal computers came the distribution of both processing power and information, stored information being processed uniquely by a single application. The availability of more powerful micro-processors, operating systems, control software, communication software and networking software created the need to again provide multi-user access to shared information.

Many data sharing techniques and associated software based on such techniques have been developed to cater for the many different ways both users and applications need to gain access to stored data simultaneously.

Consider the software necessary to manage files in a multi-user or networked environment. The software must be able to determine those users authorised access to individual files (and the disk area they are stored in) to:

❑ read and copy the file;

❑ execute the program stored in the file;

❑ delete the file;

❑ amend the contents of the file.

Many users may be permitted simultaneous access to read or execute a file but facilities must exist to prevent authorised deletion or amendment when a file is already in use by other users. Furthermore, if a user or application is presently amending an entry in a sharable file, it is not productive to prohibit other users performing a similar task on another part of the file. This is a problem faced by both file management software and database management systems (DBMS). A DBMS contains structured data (records) which must possibly be shared simultaneously amongst many users. Software exists to provide for the management of shared data through the use of one or more of the following techniques:

❑ Authorisation details;

❑ File locks;

❑ Write locks;

❑ Read locks;

❑ Record locks.

Task 6.3   PC 1

Using your software package listing produced for Task 6.2, describe the purpose of each software category identified.

6.1.3 Purpose of applications software packages

Processing

A computer and any programs run upon it provide the user with the ability to process information in some manner. The information when handled by the program is referred to as data. The computer manipulates this data in an internal numeric form. The original information may represent:

❑ Textual documents;

❑ Numbers;

❑ Graphical information;

❑ Structured data.

or even:

❑ Sound;

❑ Video images.

Question 6.11

What name is generally given to information handled by a program?

Many software packages exist to process each of the above information forms. These titles embody a vast pool of application packages but traditionally, the office administrative processing of these forms was undertaken by individual packages as depicted in figure 6.2. Generally, the separate packages were developed independently of one another and consisted of data formats unique to each package. Such packages provided the following facilities:

❏ Textual documents were processed by text editors, word processors and desk top publishing packages;

❏ Numerical/statistical information was processed by spreadsheet packages;

❏ Graphical information was processed by a drawing package or presentation manager;

❏ Structured data was processed by a database package.

Question 6.12

Traditionally, textual documents were processed by what type of software packages?

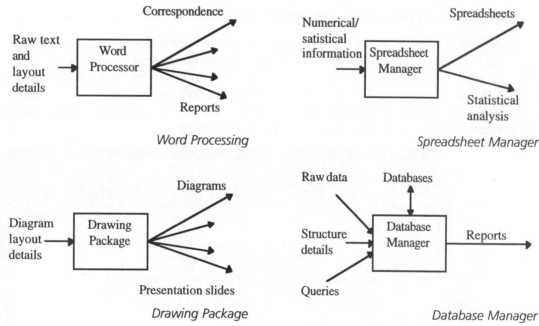

Figure 6.2 Traditional Office Administration Packages

The current trends of application developers is to provide fully-integrated office administration systems embodying all these facilities. This permits the easy transfer and consolidation of information between each representation or format of the data. Figure 6.3 shows such an alternative solution.

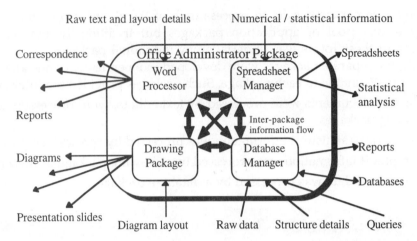

Figure 6.3 An Integrated Office Administration System

An example of one such integrated office system is Microsoft's Office. This suite includes the following window based programs to cater for the office administration:

❒ Document processing – Microsoft Word

A comprehensive word processor and desk-top publishing package to produce high-quality finish comprising both text and graphical images. It permits the user to import information from associated packages such as the spreadsheet manager, database manager and import text, graphical and statistical information of various forms from packages produced by alternative suppliers. Figure 6.4 shows a run-time snapshot of the Microsoft Word screen during the production of this text.

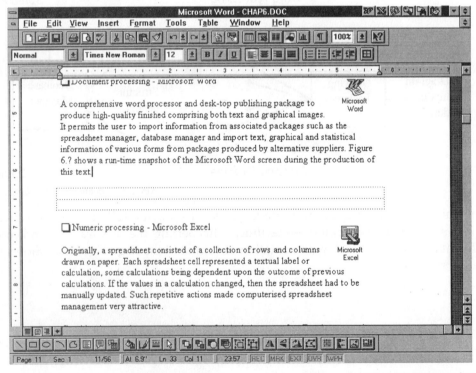

Figure 6.4 A Microsoft Word screen

❐ Numeric processing – Microsoft Excel

Microsoft
Excel

Originally, a spreadsheet consisted of a collection of rows and columns drawn on paper. Each spreadsheet cell represented a textual label or calculation, some calculations being dependent upon the outcome of previous calculations. If the values in a calculation changed, then the spreadsheet had to be manually updated. Such repetitive actions made computerised spreadsheet management very attractive.

Consider the partial run-time snapshot presented in figure 6.5 showing part of a Microsoft Excel screen and spreadsheet.

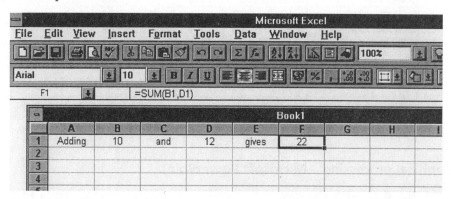

Figure 6.5 A Microsoft Excel screen and spreadsheet

Generally, each cell can denote some text (heading in a report), numeric information (original input to perform calculations upon) or the formula associated with a calculation. Here, the cells A1, C1 and E1 contain textual information whilst B1 and D1 contain the values 10 and 12 respectively. The cell F1 contains the formula =SUM(B1,D1) but is automatically displayed as the result of the summation. Any cell text starting with an = indicates that the text represents a formula for processing. Should the user amend B1 or D1 to contain alternative values, then the value displayed as F1 is automatically updated. Any cell which is dependent upon numeric information or outcomes of previous calculations is automatically updated whenever an amendment occurs to any cell the calculation depends upon.

Present window-based spreadsheet managers additionally provide the user with comprehensive editing, statistical analysis tools and the ability to include additional information such as diagrams developed in other packages. The editing facilities also permit the user to edit whole rows or columns, automatically updating any cell declared as being a formula. Figure 6.6 shows another example of a spreadsheet. Here, the user defining the structure of the spreadsheet has instructed the spreadsheet manager to display the formulas associated with cells instead of the results of the formulas.

	A	B	C	D	E	F	G	H
1	RUGBY LEAGUE							
2	COUNTY							
3			GAMES	GAMES	GAMES	TRIES	TRIES	
4		POINTS	PLAYED	WON	DRAWN	FOR	AGAINST	RATIO
5								
6	GLAMORGAN	=3*D6+E6	6	3	1	8	11	=F6/G6
7	GWENT	=3*D7+E7	6	6	0	15	4	=F7/G7
8	POWYS	=3*D8+E8	6	3	1	5	3	=F8/G8
9	CLWYD	=3*D9+E9	7	2	1	5	7	=F9/G9
10	YORKSHIRE	=3*D10+E10	7	2	2	5	6	=F10/G10
11	LANCASHIRE	=3*D11+E11	6	1	1	8	11	=F11/G11
12	WEST MIDLANDS	=3*D12+E12	7	2	1	4	7	=F12/G12
13	BERKSHIRE	=3*D13+E13	5	3	1	7	9	=F13/G13
14								
15								
16								

Figure 6.6 A spreadsheet example showing cell formulas

❏ Graphical processing – Microsoft PowerPoint

Microsoft
PowerPoint

Provides the user with the means to create and manage amendments to diagrammatic information. This information represents a collection of drawing
objects such as lines, boxes, circles, arcs, text and pictures. In essence, it provides for
diagram editing in the same manner as a word processor does for text editing. However, additional features permit the user to develop a presentation where each diagram represents a slide
within a collection of slides constituting a slide show. Figure 6.7 shows a run-time snapshot of
an example Microsoft PowerPoint screen.

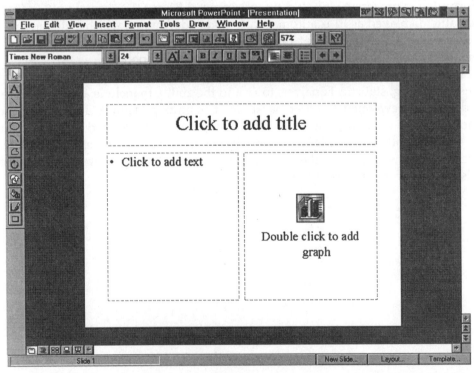

Figure 6.7 A Microsoft PowerPoint screen

❑ Structured data processing – Microsoft Access

This is a database manager permitting the storage of information in a logical manner for subsequent querying. Firstly, the user must design and declare the format with which data is to be stored. Subsequently, the user may interrogate this information via a query upon the data stored in the database. As with the other packages in the Office suite, as well as providing the usual database design and query facilities, this package provides additional facilities permitting the stored information to be integrated into the other packages. Figure 6.8 shows a run-time snapshot of an example Microsoft Access screen.

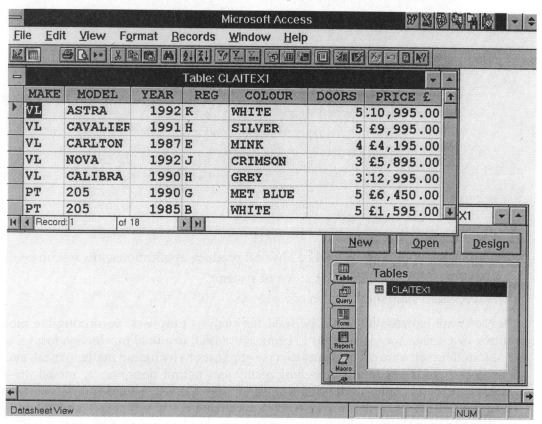

Figure 6.8 A Microsoft Access screen

Other applications included in the Microsoft Office suite are:

❑ Word Dialog Editor;

❑ Microsoft Query;

❑ Graph AutoConvert;

❑ PowerPoint Viewer;

❑ MS Access Workgroup Administrator.

315

Question 6.13

What Microsoft Office packages provide for the processing of the following forms of information?

☐ *Textual documents;*

☐ *Numbers;*

☐ *Graphical information;*

☐ *Structured Data.*

Task 6.4   PC 2

Using a typical PC based system of your own, in your place of work or where you study:

☐ *Identify the common application software packages used;*

☐ *Describe the main facilities provided by each package identified;*

☐ *Describe in detail the particular usage made of each identified package.*

Modelling

Without having to produce a final or physical product, application software can be used to:

☐ model or simulate a real situation or system;

☐ provide a simplified version of a process.

This software representation can be used for analysis purposes, permitting the model to be refined to a satisfactory form prior to being committed to a final production form.

Modelling software covers many diverse applications including mathematical, medical and solid object modelling. Solid modelling techniques permit designers to model three dimensional objects and scenes under differing conditions. Consider wind-tunnel testing of aircraft wing components or car bodies. Instead of producing costly prototypes and submitting them to testing in specialised facilities, a software model can be produced to represent the process.

Question 6.14

Briefly explain how solid modelling software may be used.

Virtual Reality techniques permit the user to explore modelled scenes. Such scenes may actually exist, represent imaginary locations or even in-accessible locations (possibly too hazardous to support human life or medical images of the inside of a human body).

Controlling

Any piece of software which controls the management of a device falls into this category. Although the central intelligence and overall system management of a computer is provided by the computer's processor, a system will invariably include devices such as a hard-disk and a display screen. Through the use of the operating system software, the processor controls the flow of information around the system between the various attached sub-components. Any peripheral or supporting device will ultimately be attached to the computer system by an interfacing controller. Such controllers derive their 'intelligence' by the logic programmed into them and/or software associated with them. Figure 6.9 depicts the layout of such a system.

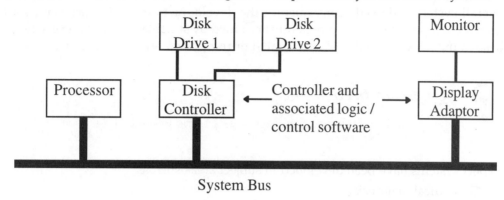

Figure 6.9 The logical structure of a computer system

Domestic automatic washing machines may include micro-processor based control software managing such functions as water levels during wash cycles, water temperatures during wash cycles, wash function times and the management of the spin speed depending upon the drum loading.

Question 6.15

How may control devices be used in one example of a domestic appliance?

Other devices using control software include:

- ❒ Audio CD-ROM players;
- ❒ Laser printers;
- ❒ Photocopiers;
- ❒ Programmable Microwave ovens;
- ❒ Electronic gaming machines;
- ❒ Lift or elevator management;
- ❒ Televisions and Video Cassette Recorders.

Expert Systems

An Expert System is a software package providing the end-user with access to a computerised form of the human expert to obtain a solution to a specific problem. Generally, for a given field of expertise, the package represents both the knowledge base of the equivalent human expert and a set of decision making procedures used by the equivalent human expert, that is, it tries to copy the thinking process using the same information as a human.

When the package is run, it can act out the decision making process of the human expert and draw conclusions based upon the answers supplied in response to a consultation or question and answer session. Each user response causes the expert system to re-evaluate it's decision making process in order that a subsequent question reflects those answers previously provided. Ultimately, a point is reached by the expert system whereby it is able to make an assessment of the problem.

It should be remembered that an expert system is only as good as the knowledge base and decision making rules it is provided with. Should there be a flaw in this information, then the overall system is flawed. Consequently, the development is not undertaken by a typical program developer. The development must be aided by suitable human experts whose knowledge base in the relevant field is of an accepted or recognised level of expertise.

Question 6.16

What represents an Expert System and why may it be flawed?

Expert systems have been developed in subject areas such as:

❒ Medical diagnosis;

❒ Law;

❒ Financial investment.

6.1.4 Features Of Computer Programs

Code

A computer program is a set of instructions written in a form that a computer will understand. The instructions are selected and ordered in a manner which when performed by the computer will undertake a required task. Such instructions are more commonly referred to as the *code* of the computer program. Computer programs are generally used to process information of some form. Typically a program:

❒ obtains a piece of information and stores it for later use;

❒ performs computations, usually upon previously stored information storing the result for later use;

❒ reports the outcome of computations by referencing stored information;

❒ performs a set of instructions in a sequential order;

❒ performs a set of instructions only when a specific condition prevails;

❒ performs a set of instructions repeatedly depending upon a specific prevailing condition.

Consider a program which calculates and reports a simple interest amount when an amount of money is invested for a number of years at a known interest rate. The program would need to know the amount to be invested, the number of years of investment and the interest rate. Having obtained this information, the program can compute the interest and report this to the user in a meaningful format. This solution, depicted in figure 6.10, represents a program which can compute the interest for various differing (variable) input values provided when the program is run.

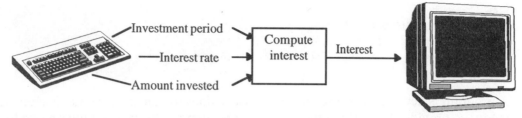

Figure 6.10 Simple interest example

A solution, as presented in figure 6.11, which always computes the interest for three fixed values such as 2 years, 5% and £10 is of little use, there can only ever be one answer, why compute it? If the interest rate changed, the program would become redundant and need updating. The better approach which allows the user to enter the three run-time values is much more flexible.

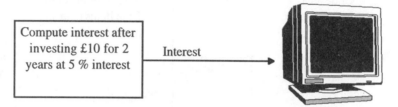

Figure 6.11 Poor simple interest example

Question 6.17

Why can a program, which processes data entered at run-time be regarded as being more useful than one which processes fixed information?

A calculator provides a simplified numeric capability similar to that of a program. Here, the operator acts as the program deciding what instruction or operation is to be done next and upon what data or values. Most calculators provide at least one memory store in which a value may be held or stored for future reference. Other calculators provide multiple memory stores which can be used to store individual single values, the operator stipulating precisely which store to use.

Data Types and Data Structures

Programs comprise definitions of both the *code* to perform and the *data* upon which to perform the code.

The individual data elements may take various forms:

❑ A whole number, such as, 12, -6 and 1234;

❑ A floating-point number, such as 12.534, -67.12 and 12345.67;

❑ A single character, such as, A, a, ? or %;

❑ A string representing a collection of characters in a sequential order, such as *This string contains 34 characters*;

❑ A composite structure, also known as a **Data Structure**, consisting of various occurrences (a set) of the previous individual forms. Data structures are further detailed in element 6.2.5.

Question 6.18

What forms may individual data elements take?

A program is developed as a set of coded instructions to manipulate data. Each programming language provides **Data Types** to permit the programmer to stipulate the precise form a piece of data (also known as a **data item** or **identifier**) is to take. When a program is executed, a representation of it's instructions is loaded into a free area of memory and additional memory allocated to hold the various pre-defined data items as shown in figure 6.12.

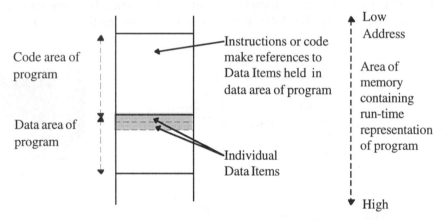

Figure 6.12 Program's run-time memory usage

Ultimately, a program references such elements by their run-time address, that is the address at which the data item is stored in memory. Again, consider the technique associated with a calculator. At an appropriate point in a calculation, the operator may reference a memory store possibly M or even M1, M2 or even M3 but not as an entity such as InterestRate. Such mnemonics aid the programmer in the development of the code but are not easily processed by the machine.

Data elements may represent simple individual entities such as a whole number for a person's age, a floating-point number to represent a monetary amount or a string of characters to represent a person's surname, address or telephone number.

Question 6.19

What data element forms would be best suited to define the following:
- *Person's salary;*
- *Car Registration Number;*
- *Stock Quantity;*
- *Average value;*
- *Post code.*

Unlike natural language which has inherent ambiguity, programming languages are formal in nature and must be set-out with strict regard to the pre-defined rules defining the language. The forms which program language instructions or code may take may be represented by a layered model as shown in figure 6.13. Those categories nearer the top of the model are closer to human language whilst those towards the lower end are close to machine code.

Example

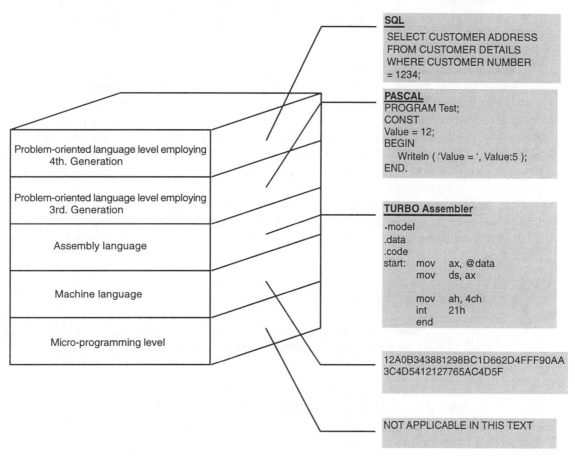

SQL

SELECT CUSTOMER ADDRESS
FROM CUSTOMER DETAILS
WHERE CUSTOMER NUMBER
= 1234;

PASCAL
PROGRAM Test;
CONST
Value = 12;
BEGIN
    Writeln ('Value = ', Value:5);
END.

TURBO Assembler

.model
.data
.code
start: mov   ax, @data
         mov   ds, ax

         mov   ah, 4ch
         int   21h
         end

12A0B343881298BC1D662D4FFF90AA
3C4D5412127765AC4D5F

NOT APPLICABLE IN THIS TEXT

Problem-oriented language level employing
4th. Generation

Problem-oriented language level employing
3rd. Generation

Assembly language

Machine language

Micro-programming level

Figure 6.13 Languages layered model

4th generation languages – such a high-level language permits the user to define the required task without having to detail how to do it, for example, selecting an entry within a data base in which a specified data element matches a specified value. The programmer need not concern themselves as to how the task is to be accomplished and wants the associated data returned or to be notified that no such entry exists. Such requests may be acted upon (*interpreted*) when a single query is made at the keyboard, submitted for processing as a script of associated queries or even embedded within a program written using a 3rd generation programming language.

3rd generation languages are those used by application programmers. A solution written in this form describes how a required task is to be accomplished. The source code of the solution must normally be translated into a machine-language form. This translation process is known as *Compilation*. This level includes many differing languages. Each language is specifically applicable to the required task. One such language, COBOL is a language applicable to commercial applications such as payroll production or stock control. Another language, C, is more applicable to applications concerning system management routines. PASCAL was developed as an educational block-structured language but has found favour in the production of solutions in various areas. Other popular languages include ADA, FORTRAN, BASIC and LISP. Each programming language is suited to developing a program solution in a specific area. It would not be appropriate to use COBOL based program code to handle image processing.

Question 6.20

Generally, how do 3rd and 4th generation language code differ?

The assembly language level provides the means to write source code applicable to the micro-processor of the target machine. Each micro-processor has associated with it a set of instructions specific to the micro-processor and known as an **Instruction Set**. An assembler program must be translated to a machine code representation through a process known as **Assembly**. Historically, programs were normally written in this form but with the development of high-level languages and the need for large complex solutions rapidly reduced the need to program at this level. Adequate solutions can now be generated using 3rd generation programming languages.

The machine code level is the form other languages are usually translated into by means of **Compilation** or **Assembly**. At this level, the form is numeric, the processing of which is accomplished through the interpretation of the number representation by the machine's micro-processor.

Question 6.21

What is the main difference between the code of a 3rd. generation language representation and a machine language representation?

The lowest level concerning us at this point is that of the micro-code level. Within the micro-processor exists segments of micro-code whose sole responsibility is to perform the operations associated with each machine code instruction. The numeric machine code representation is interpreted by the micro-processor by the micro-code program.

Method of translation

Translation, whether it be via Compilation or Assembly, is simply the analysis of the original source code to determine it's validity. The source code is represented by text which is read and processed in order to construct another form more easily processed by the computer.

Question 6.22

Identify the two forms of translation briefly identifying the need for each.

Usually, this translation represents the first part of the whole process. Following a successful Compilation or Assembly the output, known as an **Object Module**, must be **Linked** to other code elements in order to produce a final executable form of the solution. This process is illustrated in figure 6.14.

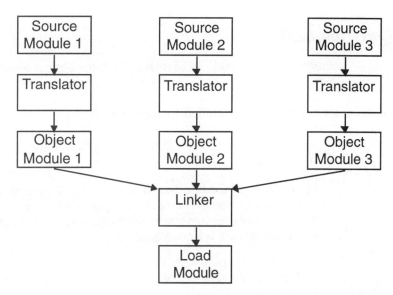

Figure 6.14 Translation and linking

Constructs

The order in which the program instructions are performed by a computer must be in a specific order to accomplish the required task. All programming languages provide basic control structures to achieve this:

- ❏ Sequence;
- ❏ Selection;
- ❏ Iteration (also known as repetitions).

Using these basic control structures, any programming problem may be refined into a collection of simpler problems, the processing of which culminates in the required overall task.

Question 6.23

By what names are the three basic program control structures known?

No solution to a non-trivial programming problem comprises just sequences, selections or iterations. A solution will comprise a nested structure of all three program constructs.

Sequences – Generally, program statements are executed in the sequential order they appear within the program source code.

Selections – Useful programs are not constructed using only sequence control structures. Selections permit the natural statement sequence order to be adjusted and thus permit alternative actions to be undertaken.

Iterations – Iterations provide the third basic program control construct and permits the solution to repeat a specific set of instructions a number of times.

Question 6.24

Briefly, outline the purpose of each of the three basic program control structures?

The control structure constructs are detailed further in 6.2.3

Task 6.5   PC 3

Using a typical PC based system of your own, in your place of work or where you study, describe the computer program features associated with (provided by) a resident development language. Your description should where applicable detail the following points:

❑ *Code;*

❑ *Data types and data structures;*

❑ *Method of translation;*

❑ *Constructs.*

6.1.5 Modes of operation

The *modes of operation* of a piece of software are managed by the use of:

❑ Commands;

❑ Menu;

❑ Graphic interface.

The text of this element collectively describes the range of such modes of operation. Most application packages give the user the means of interactive control using commands. The user is invited at the appropriate time to make selections in some manner. The way in which the user makes a selection falls into one or more of the following categories:

❑ function key (command mode of operation);

❑ character key (command mode of operation);

❑ multiple key combinations (command mode of operation);

❑ menu;

❑ object and icon selection (graphical interface mode of operation).

A typical keyboard provides the standard printable character keys together with function keys (possibly labelled F1, F2..) and other specialised keys such as ESC, RETURN or ENTER, Page-Up, Left-arrow, Home.

Question 6.25

A program may invite the user to make a selection in one of many ways. Identify the categories associated with these selection forms.

Any entered keystroke transfers the information associated with the key to the system for processing. The keystroke may instruct the system to perform a specific system task such as print the contents of the screen upon an attached printer or even re-boot the system. If the key is not for the system management, then it is passed to the running application. The application may be a system application such as a command interpreter or a user application such as a word-processor. The information associated with the keystroke is interpreted by the application as necessary. It may possibly represent a single character of some text or a character which selects a function of the application. The former represents character keys (including shift key combinations to attain uppercase characters) whilst the latter includes function keys and additional multiple key combinations.

Depressing a function key may initiate some help text, the subject reflecting the current point or operation within the application that the user is undertaking. Thus any such key may under application control, trigger the occurrence of some action.

Often keyboards include other special keys. When the user depresses a combination of keys the system processes this as necessary. The depressions may represent erroneous entries such as depressing many alphabetic characters simultaneously. They may however generate information to be interpreted by the application. The information may be the same as that associated with a function key. Consider the application interpreting function key F12 or the key combination (simultaneous depression) Control and Q to indicate the user's wish to quit or terminate the application. These key-strokes may represent one way in which the user selects the actions to be undertaken by the application.

The selection of a desired application function may alternatively be selected via a menu. Invariably a list is displayed to the user giving an invitation to make a selection. Some entries may not be presently available depending on the state of the application. The list may be:

- ❑ displayed as a drop-down menu which appears hanging down as the expansion of an option previously visible upon the screen;

- ❑ displayed as a list at a specific point upon the screen alongside an associated entity, possibly a sub-menu following previous menu option selection;

- ❑ displayed centrally upon the screen.

Question 6.26

Briefly, how may a list of menu options be displayed?

Consider an application which provides a menu driven interface together with shorthand-keys. These keys permit the user to immediately select a function without searching through a hierarchy of menus to locate and select the desired function. Irrespective of the manner in which a menu is displayed, the user is required to select an option of those presently depicted. This selection may be made by:

- ❑ moving a scrolling-bar up and down using the keyboard arrow keys until the desired option is highlighted and then selected by depressing the return key;

- ❑ entering a character identified as uniquely associated with a displayed option such as x or X for eXit. The associated character may be a key combination. Selection may occur immediately the key(s) are depressed or require confirmation using the return key;

- ❑ placing a mouse pointer or cursor over an option and confirming the selection or clicking (or double-clicking) one of the mouse keys.

Figure 6.15 shows a screen snapshot representing a typical windows based environment which uses many various forms of user selection. The application interface has been designed in a manner to make selection as convenient possible to the user.

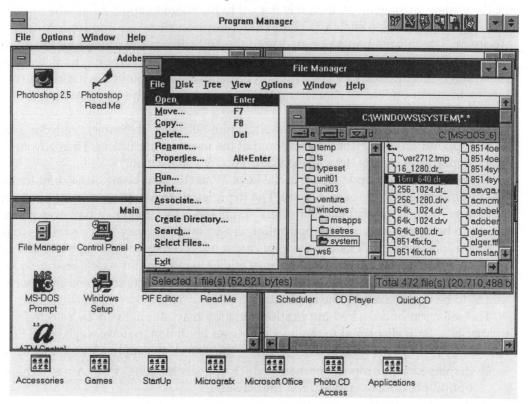

Figure 6.15 Window based screen snapshot

The screen presently consists of:

❑ a main/base window depicting various further icons;

❑ five application windows, the File manager being the currently active window;

❑ a Drop-down menu depicting the options associated with the File Manager's File Option;

❑ a directory listing of part of the hard-disk.

The application is presently waiting for the user to enter some form of input. The input may represent a selection from the File Manager's – File option menu made via:

❑ Enter key – depressing the Enter key to select the default *Open* option;

❑ Pointer device – placing the pointer device over the desired option and confirming it's selection be depressing the Enter key;

❑ Option letter – Each option depicted in the menu has one letter of the option text underlined. Entering this letter as some form of key combination (ALT/Letter) selects the associated option. ALT/O will presently select the *Open* option;

❑ Arrow keys – Move the scroll-bar highlighting the current option vertically using the Up-Arrow and Down-Arrow keys. When the desired option is highlighted, the option is confirmed by depressing the Enter key;

❑ Shorthand-keys – where applicable, the option text has associated with it a shorthand key. This may take the form of a single key or combination of keys as displayed. In turn, these keys may represent special keys such as function keys and PageDown. Enter will select the **Open** option whilst, F7 will select the **Move** option, F8 will select the **Copy** option, Del will select the **Delete** option and ALT/Enter will select the **Properties** option.

Question 6.27

Why were short-hand keys introduced?

Alternatively, the input may represent the user's wish to:

❏ swap to the alternative neighbouring File Manager options through the use of the Left-Arrow and Right-Arrow keys;

❏ swap to another window by using the pointer device or further key combinations;

❏ initiate another application by selecting one of the visible icons again by use of the pointer device or further key combinations;

❏ make use of the various buttons visible to scroll about the active window and even exit the window or even the environment entirely.

The above description details a window based environment. However, any non-window based application may make use of these facilities or techniques and tailor their management accordingly.

Task 6.6   PC 4

*Using a typical PC based system of your own, in your place of work or where you study, select one **window** based program.*

❏ *Describe the different modes of operation the program uses.*

❏ *Produce a user's option reference indicating the different ways a user may choose specific individual user selectable options of the program's options with which you are familiar.*

Task 6.7   PC 4

*Using a typical PC based system of your own, in your place of work or where you study, select one non-**window** based program.*

❏ *Describe the different modes of operation the program uses.*

❏ *Produce a user's option reference indicating the different ways a user may choose specific individual user selectable options of the program's options with which you are familiar.*

Examine software production

Introduction

An examination of software production techniques will provide an ability to:

- ❏ describe types of programming environments;
- ❏ describe features of program execution;
- ❏ explain what is meant by program constructs;
- ❏ describe types of data and structures;
- ❏ describe the expressions and operators used in software production.

6.2.1 Programming Environment

Programming language

A programmer should develop a working solution using the programming language most applicable to the area of the desired application. The programming language statements reflect the design algorithm or approach to solve the problem. These statements are known as the source code. Traditionally, programs were developed using the following program development tools:

- ❏ Text editors;
- ❏ Translators (Compilers and/or Assemblers);
- ❏ Linkers.

A program would frequently be implemented taking the following steps:

Step 1 – The text representing the source code of a program was entered and stored using a text editor. Such text editors were used to handle textual information for many reasons and had no prior knowledge of the usage of the source code or even it's formal structure.

Step 2 – The stored progam source code was passed to a *translator* for checking and if valid the associated object module was produced. A suitable report was generated detailing as far as possible any errors. No object module was produced. After making the necessary corrections steps 1 and 2 were repeated until the program translated successfully. This step checks the source code to ensure it follows the formal definition and has followed the rules laid down by the syntax of the language. The source code may still remain logically flawed in some manner.

Step 3 – Link the object module with others to produce an executable load module. Reported errors would indicate the failure to include or declare all object modules which collectively form a complete working program.

Question 6.28

What programs generally provide for program development?

The working program may ultimately represent application software or system software as previously outlined in Element 6.1.

The development tools used during these steps were stand-alone programs. The developer had to repeatedly run the programs associated with each step until the program was successfully implemented.

During the last decade, there has been a trend towards producing Independent Development Environments (IDE). Such environments embody all the tools necessary to develop a working program in one package and usually provide facilities to compile high-level languages as well as assemble lower-level languages, ultimately producing an executable load module. An IDE can increase the efficiency with which an experienced programmer develops a program. Such environments make it easier and require less detailed programming skills. This can also be the failing for many less able programmers because the environment's emphasis is on translating programs as quickly as possible. It is all to easy to hack code around hoping that a small change here or there will ultimately make a flawed program function correctly. Perhaps we are in danger of creating two types of people, programmers and hackers!

The time delays associated with the manner in which programs were traditionally developed provided the developer with time to consider the function of the program. Because each amendment cycle took so long, it was important to think carefully about the changes and make a major effort to get it right.

There is presently another trend emerging in which PC based applications can more easily be developed using a windows based environment or interface. Such tools are generally used in the areas of Database and Spreadsheet managers rather than in the production of system software. System software is associated with the overall control and performance management of the system and continues to be developed using 3rd generation languages to optimise the processing requirements.

Question 6.29

How do many present-day development packages differ from the more traditional development packages. Briefly identify the advantages and disadvantages associated with each.

Programming languages provide the programmer with the ability to define an action to be undertaken by the system. Each language has a formal definition consisting of two aspects:

- ❑ Syntax – a set of grammatical rules defining how keywords, symbols, expressions and statements may be structured and combined;
- ❑ Semantics – a set of rules that define the meaning of the language's constituent parts, that is what actually occurs when such elements are executed.

The syntax and semantics defining a programming language is highly independent.

Question 6.30

What two elements constitute the formal definition of a program language? Briefly identify the purpose of each element.

It is easier to consider the structure of any solution to a programming problem in a language-free manner. Pseudo code is a Program Development Language (PDL) tool representing a syntax free language form. This permits the programmer to specify the structure of a program solution without unnecessary concern to the rigour of the syntax of the eventual program language. Such statements mirror the three basic control structures through the use of Structured English or Natural Language.

Question 6.31

What role does Pseudo code play in program development?

Translators

These are described in Element 6.1.4.

Special programming languages

Unlike the typical programming language, it is possible to identify Special Programming Languages which act as application generators. High-level design tools (textual or diagrammatic) are used to define the user's requirements. Subsequent processing of which generates a valid representation of the original requirements in the form of a valid series of statements.

Automated application software routines

Many applications whether they are concerned with program development, document production, spreadsheet management or another application area invariably provide some form of support to cater for repetitive tasks. Such facilities provide the user with the ability to define their own short-hand instructions. Usually a macro represents a series of user entered keystrokes or actions which can be initiated by entering a key or selecting a window button which the user has previously defined as representing the macro.

Different applications permit the user to define macros in different ways:

- ❐ The user is required to produce a keystroke script representing the macro;
- ❐ The user is provided with a macro record facility. Here the user initiates the recording of the macro, steps through the actions the macro is to represent and then subsequently terminates the actions.

Each requires the user to indicate how the macro is to be initiated. Provided the macro details are valid, the user is able to undertake complex repetitive tasks with ease.

Question 6.32

Briefly define the usage made of macros.

Task 6.8 PC 1

Using a typical PC based system of your own, in your place of work or where you study, describe two types of programming environments available:

❑ *Programming languages – including support of 3rd generation language(s), Assembler(s), Operating System(s), Interpreter(s) and Compiler(s);*

❑ *Special Programming Languages – including support of application generators (form generators);*

❑ *Automated application software routines.*

Provide practical examples of each where applicable.

6.2.2 Features of Program Execution

A computer program is a set of instructions written in a form that a computer will understand. The instructions are selected and ordered in a manner which when performed (also termed *program execution*) by the computer will undertake a required task. The features of program execution can be represented by the terms:

❑ Run-time system;
❑ Executable file.

Run-time system

A *Run-time system* is represented by the complete system hardware (including central processing unit and all attached operational devices irrespective of their purpose) and the running software representing an active system. It represents the environment in which further programs are executed. The MS-DOS command MEM/D can be used to obtain details about the software element of an operational MS-DOS system, the output would report how memory was presently being used. The report would include information about all running device drivers, such as a mouse driver, memory management, CD-ROM driver, keyboard driver, serial ports and parallel ports together with details of other running software programs. Collectively all running software at such an instance defines a run-time system.

Executable file

An *Executable file* specifies a file containing information representing an executable program (also known as *executable load module*) and is the result of *linking* as described in Element 6.1.4. The file contains a description of the numeric representation of the program. The description simply specifies both where to load the program and the numbers representing the program. MS-DOS programs may be represented as .COM and .EXE files. Simply changing a file's extension to .COM or .EXE does not make it executable. Such files must be produced by suitable development tools. If you were to check the size of such files using the MS-DOS DIR command and were able to detect the amount of memory used to store and run the associated program, you would see that the stored file size was smaller than the run-time memory representation. Remember, the executable file contains information about what to load into memory and where to load it and does not represent a complete run-time snapshot of the program. A program which requires 5 Kbytes of file storage may need 50 Kbytes or more of memory during execution. The actual MS-DOS executable file formats associated with .COM and .EXE files do not concern us at this point.

Task 6.9 PC 2

Using a typical PC based system of your own, in your place of work or where you study, describe the methods provided to enable program execution.

6.2.3 Program Constructs

No solution to a non-trivial program will comprise just sequences, selections or iterations. The following details the three basic Program Control Structures using Pseudo-code.

Sequence

A sequence represents the most basic program construct and may be represented as:

> Statement 1
> Statement 2
> …
> Statement n

Here, execution begins with the first statement. When complete, execution proceeds with the second statement and so on until statement n is completed. Consider obtaining two keyboard entered numbers and displaying their sum and average upon the monitor.

A typical pseudo-code solution could be:

> Sequence Example
> Obtain two values from the keyboard
> Add the first value and the second value giving a total
> Deduce the average of the two values
> Display the total and average upon the monitor

Execution begins with the first statement and then progresses to the next and so on. However, the overall sequence of these statements is critical. It is not logically correct to attempt to display the eventual total and average without first deducing them. In turn, these values cannot be deduced without first obtaining the two values.

Question 6.33

Why is it not permissible to arrange the statements in the Sequence Example in a different order?

Selection

Generally, programs do not only consist of sequences. Selections permit the natural statement sequence order to be adjusted permitting alternative actions to be undertaken depending upon a prevailing condition. The selection construct exists in various forms.

❏ IF-THEN – Only if a particular condition prevails is the bounded statement sequence performed.

```
IF Condition
THEN
    Statement sequence
END-IF
```

❒ IF-THEN-ELSE – Provides the means to perform one statement sequence or an alternative statement sequence depending upon the prevailing condition but not both.

```
IF Condition
THEN
    Statement sequence 1
ELSE
    Statement sequence 2
END-IF
```

Consider obtaining two keyboard entered numbers representing a running total of a set of numbers and a count (possibly zero) of the numbers and displaying their average upon the monitor.

<u>Selection example 1</u>
```
Obtain the running total from the keyboard
Obtain the count of numbers constituting the running total from the keyboard
IF count of numbers is zero
THEN
    Display "No numbers available"
ELSE
    Divide running total by count of numbers giving an average
    Display the average
END-IF
```

More complex forms exist allowing multiple-choice based on *CASE* statements. Such structures are language dependent.

Question 6.34

How may multiple-choice selections be catered for?

Iteration (Repetition)

The Iteration construct provides the means to repeat a specific set of statements a number of times. The construct has three variations, namely, FOR, WHILE and REPEAT-UNTIL.

❒ FOR – The FOR iteration repeats a group of sequence statements a known number of times. The general form of the FOR iteration is:

```
FOR Something
DO
    Statement sequence
END-FOR
```

Consider displaying "HELLO" ten times on separate monitor lines.

<u>Iteration Example 1</u>
```
FOR ten times
DO
    Display "HELLO" upon the monitor
    Move cursor to next line on monitor
END-FOR
```

❒ WHILE – The WHILE iteration repeats a group of sequence statements whilst a condition prevails. The iteration occurs zero or more times because the condition is evaluated at start of each iteration. The general form of the WHILE construct is:

```
WHILE Condition
DO
    Statement sequence
END-WHILE
```

Consider deducing the sum of a set of positive numbers where the size of the list is not known in advance and is terminated by a value of -1.

Iteration Example 2
```
Set running total to zero
Obtain one value from keyboard
WHILE entered value not equal to -1
DO
    Add value to running total
    Obtain one value from keyboard
END-WHILE
Display running total upon monitor
```

❒ REPEAT-UNTIL – The REPEAT-UNTIL iteration repeats a group of sequence statements until a condition prevails. The iteration occurs one or more times because the condition is evaluated upon the completion of each iteration The general form of the REPEAT-UNTIL construct is:

```
REPEAT
    Statement sequence
UNTIL Condition
```

Question 6.35

What iteration construct should be used when:
❒ *the number of iterations is known?*
❒ *the number of iterations is variable?*

Task 6.10 PC 3

Using a typical PC based system of your own, in your place of work or where you study, a program development tool and associated programming language, describe:
❒ *in your own words what is meant by program constructs;*
❒ *how each program construct is provided by the programming language, giving one example of each.*

334

6.2.4 Types of data

Element 6.1 introduced the basic data type forms a data item may take. Any of a programming language needs to define the valid data types as well as the range of values such forms may take. Data types may take many forms:

- ❑ Integer numbers;
- ❑ Real numbers;
- ❑ Characters;
- ❑ Strings;
- ❑ Booleans;
- ❑ Constants;
- ❑ Variables.

Integers

Many programming languages define a whole number data item as an *integer* which has both a minimum and a maximum value as shown in figure 6.16.

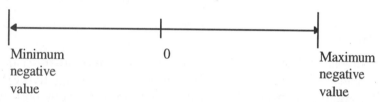

Minimum negative value   0   Maximum negative value

Figure 6.16 The integer range

This limits the values the data item may take within a range of positive and negative numbers because a computer cannot generally handle numbers with an infinite number of digits. This can be demonstrated when you use a calculator. It is easy to try to get a result of a calculation which the calculator cannot handle, the error being reported in some simple manner. A computer evaluates computations in a similar manner.

The actual minimum and maximum integer values are determined by the implementation of the programming language. Some state integers represent whole numbers in the range –32,768 to 32,767 accommodating 65,536 possible values. Some programming languages (as shown in figure 6.17):

- ❑ permit programmers to specify subsets of the integer range limiting the values data items may take, such as 0 to 100;
- ❑ provide alternative integer ranges other than the default integer form. Such additional forms provide for larger (-2,147,483,648 to 2,147,483,647) and smaller (-128 to 127) range values and are generally used to control the amount of memory required to store data items of these types;
- ❑ differentiate between signed integers (integers which may take both positive and negative values) and unsigned integers which may only represent positive / natural / cardinal numbers including zero. Thus an integer representing just positive values could have a minimum value of zero and a maximum value of 65,535 still providing a range of 65,536 possible values.

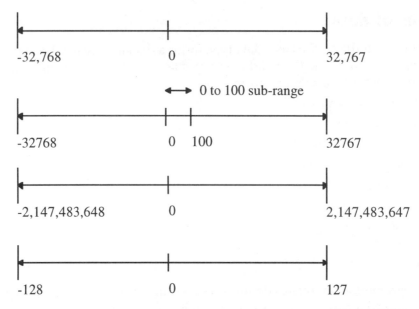

Figure 6.17 Integer range variations

Real numbers

When real numbers or floating-point numbers, as they are frequently called, are handled by a computer, they also have associated with them a minimum negative value and a maximum positive value. Again, the extent of the range is determined by the implementation of the programming language. The range provides the means to specify real versions of whole numbers. Real values are stored and processed by a computer in a different manner to integer values. Although the integer value 10 and the real value 10.0 represent the same value, they are stored and processed differently. Some programming languages again provide alternative ranges other than the default real form. Such additional forms provide for larger and smaller range values and are again generally used to limit the amount of memory required to store data items of this form.

Question 6.36

Some programming languages provide differing ranges for numeric data types such as integer and real data types. What are the reasons for this?

Character

A *character* data type is one which can represent at most a single character. Programming language implementations usually stipulate that a character is stored in a single byte of memory and therefore can represent 1 of 256 possible characters. Such characters include printable characters and non-printable control characters such as the Carriage-Return, Line-Feed or the ESCape character. Computers use numeric methods to process information. Consequently, character information is stored using an internal numeric form. There are several representations of characters using standards such as *ASCII* and *EBCDIC* as shown in Element 4.1.3.

String

A *String* is a sequential collection of individual characters. The mechanisms used to represent data items of this form is detailed in Element 6.2.5.

Boolean

The *boolean* data type not previously mentioned may not be provided or may not be necessarily applicable to many programming languages. The previous data types denoted information more applicable in the real world. Booleans represent logical values and are more applicable to the control structures within a program. A boolean value may take one of two values, TRUE and FALSE and generally represent the result generated when evaluating relational and logical expressions. They may also be used within a program to denote a two-state flag.

Question 6.37

Briefly describe the type of information associated with:
- ❑ *Integer numbers;*
- ❑ *Real numbers;*
- ❑ *Characters;*
- ❑ *Strings;*
- ❑ *Booleans.*

The data type definitions provided above briefly describe some of the data type forms a program may use to represent data items. The data items themselves are the actual instances of such data types. Lets look again at the Simple Interest example of the Element 6.1. The code would require at least three instances of data items:
- ❑ a real value to represent the interest rate;
- ❑ a real value to represent the amount invested;
- ❑ an integer value to represent the investment period in years (possibly real if fractional time periods required).

The solution program may also use a fourth data item to represent the final return amount. The form would again be a real value.

Question 6.38

Briefly define the difference between data types and data items.

At run-time, the data items would require memory to store their current values. Data Items are more commonly referred to as *Identifiers*, that is, the name given them during development by the programmer as a means of remembering their purpose and uniquely identifying them when referenced. Any data item forming part of the data processed by a program must be stored in some manner and exist within a program in one of two forms, namely:
- ❑ Constant;
- ❑ Variable.

Constant

A *Constant* defines a fixed value which during the program execution never varies. Consider a program which computes values based upon the prevailing Value Added Tax (VAT) rate. Such a program would best be developed having a constant represent the VAT rate. All other calculations could then reference this constant and thus the rate contained. Should the rate change, then the definition of the constant is amended. Any calculation dependent upon the value contained in the rate constant will function correctly. Alternatively, if the rate was explicitly written into each separate calculation, then a rate amendment would require the locating of each and every occurrence in order to amend the rate. The obvious flaw in this method is that of human error in identifying each and every code statement using this explicit value.

Question 6.39

What would be the data type of a constant representing VAT in a program?

Variable

A *Variable* represents a run-time data value which as it's name implies, the program during execution may amend for subsequent re-use. Consider the program solution to the Simple Interest example. Variables are user to store the information to be processed permitting the program to derive the outcome for differing input values.

6.2.5 Data Structures

A Data Structure is a collection of individual data items grouped together providing a new composite form. Such forms denote:

- ❐ Arrays;
- ❐ Strings;
- ❐ Records;
- ❐ Tables.

Arrays

The simplest form of data structure is that of an *array* which permits the definition of a data item as many occurrences of the same data type. Some languages such as the COBOL programming language identify such structures as *tables* instead of arrays. This should not be confused with tables as used by 4GLs.

Consider a program which processes exam results for up to 100 candidates. Assume it calculates various statistical information, such as the average mark attained, minimum mark attained, maximum mark attained and subsequently the deviations of each mark from the average. The solution program could not use one data item to store the first mark and then replace it's contents by the second mark and so on as the overall processing requires all the exam results to be available for later processing. The program could identify an exam mark data item as being an array of 100 identical elements as shown in figure 6.18. Here, when referencing individual array elements, the program code must identify precisely which individual element is being referenced by the use of a subscript.

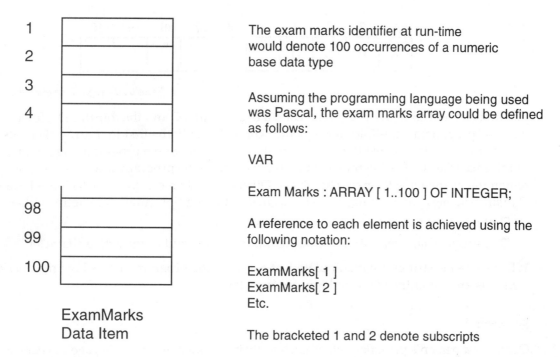

The exam marks identifier at run-time would denote 100 occurrences of a numeric base data type

Assuming the programming language being used was Pascal, the exam marks array could be defined as follows:

VAR

Exam Marks : ARRAY [1..100] OF INTEGER;

A reference to each element is achieved using the following notation:

ExamMarks[1]
ExamMarks[2]
Etc.

The bracketed 1 and 2 denote subscripts

Figure 6.18 Exam mark array

Programming languages usually provide facilities to handle both individual array elements and the whole array, such as, copying a whole array representing one identifier to another provided the data items represent exactly the same array structure.

Question 6.40

*Define the term **array**.*

Strings

A *String* was previously defined as a sequential collection of individual characters. The general data structure associated with strings is simply that of an array of characters. Figure 6.19 represents a ten element array denoting a string in which each subscripted base element denotes a single character of the string.

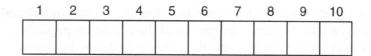

Figure 6.19 Ten element string array

Prior to any information being placed in the string, the array may be assumed to be unassigned, the contents must represent something but it does not represent any meaningful value. Assuming the string is then assigned the letters ABCD, the string array would then be represented as in figure 6.20.

339

1	2	3	4	5	6	7	8	9	10
A	B	C	D						

Figure 6.20 Assigned ten element string array

The first element contains an A, the second a B, the third a C and the fourth a D. However, how does the program at run-time subsequently know that only the first four array elements represent valid characters whilst the others remain unassigned. Some programming languages permit this basic form of string representation but demand the program at run-time to pad-out the remaining elements with space characters. Others provide more complex facilities based upon *Dynamic-Strings*. Such strings have associated with them information denoting either:

❏ the current number of active characters;

❏ a special character within the string indicating the end of the active character.

When dynamic-strings are manipulated, at run-time the program knows how many character elements are presently active and ignores any others.

Records

Consider a person's personal details such as their surname, initials, title, age in years, address, home telephone number, work's number, salary. Each individual piece of information may be represented by separate data items of differing data types. When the data elements being processed are strongly related as in the above personal details, it is better to use some form of more composite data structure to define them and indicate the association which naturally binds them together. Thus a single record may represent a person's personal details in which individual fields are used to denote the separate pieces of information about the person.

Unlike an array which comprises many occurrences of the same base data type, a record comprises a group of associated data elements each denoting a *field* within the record.

Question 6.41

How do arrays and records differ?

Usually, record usage comprises two parts:

❏ a description of the format of the record;

❏ definitions of data items/identifiers/variables which are of this form.

Consider a program managing the personal details of many individuals. The data definition would need to be that of many occurrences of the definition pertinent to one person's personal details. Each entry in turn contains the previously defined personal detail fields. It is possible to define an array of such records to denote the personal details of many individuals.

Task 6.11 PC 4

Using a typical PC based system of your own, in your place of work or where you study, a program development tool and associated programming language, describe how data types and structures are provided by the programming language. Give one example of each.

Tables

4GLs provide facilities to query and manipulate information in some form. The information is usually stored as a relational database using *Tables*. A single entry in such a table is logically similar to a single record. The table itself may be viewed as a collection of such records. Each entry is known as a row in the table and even more traditionally by the term *Tuple*. The 4GL will provide facilities to query the rows in the tables and additionally insertion, deletion and amendment facilities. Generally, unlike arrays, the processing of such tables is not concerned with the ordering or position of the individual table rows. More important is their existence or non-existence within the table.

The logical ordering or processing of table rows is defined through the use of key fields and indexes. Indexes may either represent *primary keys* where the contents of the relevant field in each row must be unique or *secondary keys* where the relevant field of one row may contain the same information as the same field in another row.

Consider the following:

❐ Each person in the country will be assigned a unique national insurance number identifying an individual, thus a primary key;

❐ A private telephone number represents the telephone number of a person with a particular surname and initials. However, many people may have the same surname and initials and even live in the same telephone district, thus a secondary key.

Question 6.42

How do primary and secondary keys differ?

It can easily be seen that the separation of the storage mechanism associated with tables away from the processing requirements of the application permit the 4GL programmer to concentrate on the processing task without the distraction of how each entry must be retrieved or stored.

6.2.6 Expressions and operators

A mathematical expression may be defined as *'a collection of symbols expressing a quantity'*. A programming language usually provides for three basic classifications to specify expressions:

❐ Arithmetic;

❐ Relational;

❐ Logical.

An operator not concerned with these expressions is *concatenation* which is associated with strings manipulation, in particular, the *joining* of more than one string to produce another string. The storage method associated with strings was detailed in Element 6.2.5. The run-time concatenation of strings is only successful if the identifier which is to accept the outcome is large enough to accommodate all the characters resulting from the operation. Consider the concatenation of *ABC* and *DEF*. The resultant string would be *ABCDEF*. The facilities provided by individual programming languages concerning concatenation are unique to each language.

The operators associated with such expressions provide the programming language with the means to define expressions with unique meanings through the use of predefined rules governing both the precedence and the associations between elements of the expression. As an introduction, consider the arithmetic expression:

2+3*4

Does this arithmetic expression represent *multiply 5 (the result of adding 2 and 3) by 4 giving 20* or *add 2 to 12 (the result of multiplying 3 by 4) giving 14.*

The alternative computations are represented diagramatically in figure 6.21.

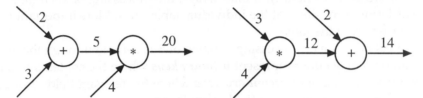

Figure 6.21 2+3*4

When deriving any required expression in the programming language being used, it is essential to know how each class of expression is processed so that the desired outcome is achieved.

Arithmetic

This class of expression provides for a basic set of operators (+, -, /, * and ^) to perform arithmetic evaluations.

The formal definition of the programming language will determine the precise precedence ordering of the basic operators, that is, the order in which they are evaluated. Generally, the ordering identifies ^ to have the greatest precedence, / and * to have the next greatest precedence (weighted equally) and + and – to have the least importance (again weighted equally). Consider the following arithmetic expressions in figure 6.22 and 6.23.

Expression	Equivalence	Result
3*6-5	18-5	13
2+8/2	2+4	6
10/5-5*4	2-20	-18

Figure 6.22 Arithmetic expressions

Particularly note the last example. The natural precedence in any of these expressions could have been changed through the use of brackets or parentheses.

Expression	Equivalence	Result
3*(6-5)	3*1	3
(2+8)/2	10/2	5
10/((7-5)*4)	10/(2*4) => 10/8	1.25

Figure 6.23 Arithmetic expressions using parentheses

Returning to the arithmetic expression 2+3*4. Enter this into two forms of electronic calculator, one providing complex mathematical functions and a simpler one providing the basic operators +, -, /, * and possibly %. It is possible that each deduces a different answer.

Consider the following expression:

10/5*8/4/4*10*5

Where the operators of an expression are of equal precedence, the expression is evaluated in a left to right manner. The above expression is therefore evaluated as shown in figure 6.24.

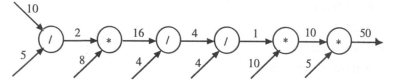

Figure 6.24 10/5*8/4/4*10*5

Now consider the expression:

$$10/5*8/4+4*10*5$$

This expression comprises two sub-expressions which contain operators of equal precedence (diagrammatically shown in figure 6.25):

10/5*8/4 added to 4*10*5

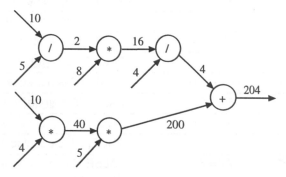

Figure 6.25 10/5*8/4+4*10*5 giving 10/5*8/4 added to 4*10*5

Each sub-expression is separately evaluated in a strict left to right ordering before the lower precedence operator, namely, + is evaluated. The evaluation is therefore the addition of 4 (result derived from 10/5*8/4) and 200 (result derived from 4*10*5) giving 204. Such precedence rules may be over-ridden through the use of parentheses. Finally, it should be noted that any precedence and associative rules are only concerned with expressions consisting of more than one operator.

Question 6.43

Evaluate the arithmetic expressions:

4*6-3*7

100/4*3/5

Relational

This class of expression provides a set of operators defining the relationships between sub-expressions (=, >, <, <>, <=, and >=). These operators provide the means to enquire how one sub-expression relates to the other. The simple relational expression:

$$4 < 5$$

This evaluates to a TRUE outcome because numerically 4 is less than 5.

The operators provide the following relational associations:

- ❏ = Equal to;
- ❏ > Greater than;
- ❏ < Less than;
- ❏ <> Not equal to;
- ❏ <= Less than or equal to;
- ❏ >= Greater than or equal to.

Relational sub-expressions may be represented by arithmetic expressions. Consider the relational expressions shown in figure 6.26.

Expression	Equivalence	Evaluation/Outcome
6 = 4+2	6 = 6	TRUE
10*4 = 2+3*5	40 = 17	FALSE, 40 is **not** equal to 17
2+2+5 > 3*2	9 > 6	TRUE, 9 is greater than 6
2+3 > 2*3	5 > 6	FALSE, 5 is **not** greater than 6
3*4 < 2+4*3	12 < 14	TRUE, 12 is less than 14
15 < 2*2+4	15 < 8	FALSE, 15 is **not** less than 8
12*4-5 <> 6*9/3	43 <> 18	TRUE, 43 is not equal 18
2+3 <> 3+2	5 <> 5	FALSE, 5 is **equal** to 5
2+3 <= 3*7	5 <= 21	TRUE, 5 is less than 21
2+3*4 <= 4*3+2	14 <= 14	TRUE, 14 is equal to 14
3+4 <= 2*3	7 <= 6	FALSE, 7 is **not** less than or equal to 67 is greater than 6
15 >= 3*1+2+1	15 >= 6	TRUE, 15 is greater than 6
2+3 >= 1+2+2	5 >= 5	TRUE, 5 is equal to 5
5*5 >= 4*5+6	25 >= 26	FALSE, 25 is **not** greater than or equal to 26 25 is less than 26

Figure 6.26 Relational expressions

Notice the structure of the relational expressions presented here only consist of a single relational operator between each arithmetic sub-expression.

Question 6.44

Evaluate the relational expressions:
20>19
20<=19
20<>19

Logical

This class of expression provides a set of operators defining the logical relationships between sub-expressions (AND, OR and NOT). The operators provide the means to construct compound relational expressions. The use of logical relationship expressions is best introduced through the use of the AND operator. Consider the logical expression:

2*3-4 >= 0 AND 2*13-4 <= 100 *or alternatively* (2*3-4 >= 0) AND (2*13-4 <= 100)

Each arithmetic sub-expression is first evaluated and the logical expression becomes:

2 >= 0 AND 22 <= 100

The evaluation of the logical expression is TRUE because both the left-hand and right-hand expressions evaluate to TRUE. Generally, the AND operator determines the existence of multiple conditions. If *a* is regarded as the left-hand relational expression and *b* as the right-hand relational expression, the overall outcomes for each permutation of inputs would be as shown in figure 6.27.

a	b	a AND b (i.e. both a = TRUE and b = TRUE?)
FALSE	FALSE	FALSE
FALSE	FALSE	FALSE
TRUE	FALSE	FALSE
TRUE	TRUE	TRUE

Figure 6.27 The AND operator

The OR operator provides the means to ascertain the existence of one or more conditions. Consider the logical expression:

(2*3-4 >= 0) OR (2+3*40 <= 100)

The overall evaluation is TRUE because the left-hand relational expression evaluated to TRUE even though the right-hand relational expression evaluated to FALSE. Provided one of the relational expressions evaluates to a TRUE, then so to does the overall logical expression. If *a* is regarded as the left-hand relational expression and *b* as the right-hand relational expression, the overall outcomes for each permutation of inputs would be as shown in figure 6.28.

a	b	a OR b (i.e. a = TRUE or b = TRUE?)
FALSE	FALSE	FALSE
FALSE	TRUE	TRUE
TRUE	FALSE	TRUE
TRUE	TRUE	TRUE

Figure 6.28 The OR operator

The final operator in this class is the NOT. This swaps or toggles the present TRUE/FALSE evaluation. Consider the left-hand relational expression of the above example:

2*3-4 >= 0

This evaluates to a TRUE outcome. Performing a NOT operation upon it:

NOT 2*3-4 >= 0 *or alternatively* NOT (2*3-4 >= 0)

would reverse the evaluation and so TRUE becomes FALSE. Consider the following expression:

NOT (2*3-4 >= 0) OR (2+3*40 <= 100)

The NOT operator reverses the evaluation of the first or left-hand relational expression and only then ORs this outcome with the second or right-hand relational expression. To achieve the NOT operation of the overall OR expression would require the expression to be presented in the form:

$$NOT ((2*3-4 >= 0) OR (2+3*40 <= 100))$$

It should be noted that as each expression class was presented above, it made use of the previous class(es) and their operators. Programming solutions generally use expressions consisting of various forms of all three classes of expression. All the above examples used fixed numerical values. A program solution would not be so rigid. There is only one predefined outcome to the examples presented previously. A program solution processes information in some required manner and uses variables or identifiers to do so. Such variables as their name suggests provide at run-time a variable piece of information which can be evaluated accordingly. Expressions would typically be of the form:

$$(ExamResult >= 0) AND (ExamResult <= 100)$$

Due to inherent accuracy problems due to rounding errors, it is not recommended to attempt equivalence tests upon floating-point values. If X represents a floating-point variable, the following forms of expression should be avoided:

- $X = 0.0$;
- $X <> 0.5$.

Question 6.45

Evaluate the relational expressions:

- (10<=12) AND (99<100);
- (9>=33)OR(45>=40)OR(34>30);
- NOT((2=3)AND(45>23)).

Task 6.12   PC 5

Using a typical PC based system of your own, in your place of work or where you study, a program development tool and associated programming language, describe how arithmetic, relational and logical expressions and their associated operators are provided by the programming language. Give one example of each.

Investigate the production of automated procedures

Introduction

An investigation into the production of automated procedures will provide an ability to:

- describe the purposes of using automated procedures;
- describe facilities available for creating automated procedures;
- produce a specification for automated procedures;
- create automated procedures to meet the specification;
- evaluate automated procedures.

6.3.1 Purposes

It is beneficial to use automated procedures representing the processing of some required task to:

- Reduce input error;
- Speed up processing;
- Standardise procedures.

Question 6.46

Why is it beneficial to use automated procedures?

Reduce input error

Any manual entering of the text representing a command or set of commands to be processed is prone to some form of human error. Consider loading a typical CD-ROM driver under MS-DOS using the following commands:

LH /L:1,19664 C:\CDROMDRV\OPTI-CD\CDCACHE /H:LASERWAV /K /DC /X:512
LH /L:1,32096 C:\CDROMDRV\MSCDEX.EXE /D:$cdcache /M:8 /V /E

If the commands were to be entered manually, each command must be entered both in the correct format and order. This inevitably provides many opportunities for incorrect entry in either case especially with long commands and/or a greater number of commands constituting the command script.

Specifying commands as some form of ordered script, such as a command or batch file, simply requires verification that the format of the commands has been specified correctly, the order of the commands is correct and that the functionality of the command set is correct. Subsequent re-use of the ordered script will minimise the possibility of errors occurring. Macros provide a similar function within an application.

Speed up processing

Automated procedures speed up processing because the text depicting each command to be undertaken is immediately available following the completion of the preceding command. This assumes that the text of the command script has already been verified to be correct. Manually entering such commands causes delays during which the system is waiting for the user to complete the entry (including possibly typing corrections) prior to processing it.

Question 6.47

Why do automated procedures speed up processing.

Standardise procedures

Standardising procedures permits the setting up of procedures, the format and function of which follow an agreed standard. Irrespective of the originator of a procedure, any user familiar with the adopted standards is able to interpret and use it. Correctly applied standards provide the ability to re-use a procedure with the minimum of re-development. Such standards also improve the development process because any re-used procedure should have already been verified to function correctly.

Task 6.13 PC 1 & 2

Using a typical PC based system of your own, in your place of work or where you study, the stored program development tools and any associated programming languages, produce notes describing:

❏ *in your own words the purposes of using automated procedures. Give one example of each available (used) on your selected system;*

❏ *the facilities available for creating automated procedures on your selected system.*

6.3.2 Automated procedures

Element 6.3.1 indicated that it is beneficial to use automated procedures for various purposes. Such procedures cater for:

❏ Repetitive routines;
❏ Templates;
❏ Calculations;
❏ File management activities;
❏ User menus.

Repetitive routines

Any repetitive task is well suited to being provided as an automated procedure in order that the task can possibly be incorporated into other procedures.

Templates

Any software package which invites the user to enter a set of associated information such as a customer's details or order details may do so through the use of a data entry screen. Such screens use templates for:

❑ positioning for input of data – this template would simply represent a screen containing the headings and labels identifying the relevant data fields and their positions upon the screen. The template code may also clear the screen areas at which responses to the headings will be later displayed;

❑ entry of commonly used variable data – this template is used to obtain and display user entered keyboard data at the appropriate screen positions for each relevant field.

A third template is generally necessary to clear the screen areas associated with user entered responses. Consider a program which accepts a set of associated information, subsequently saves the information and then repeats the process. The above templates may be used as follows:

❑ Step 1 – the program executes a set of instructions to display the headings and labels template;

❑ Step 2 – the program executes a set of instructions (a data entry clearing template) to clear the areas representing the user entered responses for each field;

❑ Step 3 – the program executes a set of instructions (a data entry template) accepting user responses representing one set of associated information. As entered, the responses are displayed at particular screen positions thus associating them with the previously displayed headings;

❑ Step 4 – the program executes the necessary instructions to save the entered set of associated information;

❑ execution continues with repetitions of steps 2, 3 and 4 as required.

Calculations

A procedure may represent the computation associated with a calculation. Providing the calculation as an automated procedure is only useful if it can be applied to differing inputs to derive an output. Element 6.1.4 discussed the merits associated with reusable calculations based on interest calculations. The more complex the calculation and common it's usage, the more desirable it is to provide it in a reusable form both reducing possible errors re-writing the associated code and development time.

File management activities

Such activities lend themselves well to automated procedures. Generally, a user needs to perform activities such as backing-up information. Such tasks need not always be undertaken by a person familiar with the technicalities associated with file naming, directory and sub-directory conventions. Providing file management activities in the form of reusable automated procedures invites the user to use them more regularly. In the case of automated backing-up, it is important that any necessary recovery or restoring of information provides that most recently saved.

Question 6.48

Identify one benefit associated with using automated procedures to provide file management activities.

User menus

User menus represent the displaying of various available options and the retrieving of the user selection. However, menus may take many forms including drop-down menus and pop-up menus. The way the user subsequently selects an option may be undertaken in many ways as detailed in Element 6.1.5. It is essential to provide reusable code of this form wherever possibly. Providing user menus through the use of automated procedures also provides a standardised form of display. Irrespective of which menu is being presented to the user, they recognise the menu style and know how to easily select an option.

6.3.3 Facilities

Automated procedures may be made available through the use of:

- ❑ Macros – processed directly by individual applications;
- ❑ Batch files – processed by operating system's command interpreter;
- ❑ Programs – processed by processor.

Macros

Element 6.3.1 specified that many applications provide some form of macro support to cater for repetitive tasks whilst using the application. Such facilities provide the user with the ability to define their own short-hand instructions. Usually a macro represents a series of possible user entered key-strokes or actions which can be initiated by entering a key or selecting a window button which the user has previously defined as representing the macro. Instead of entering individual key-strokes or actions, the user simply initiates the macro via the selected mechanism. Example macros include:

- ❑ a word processing macro which automatically searches for a specific string and replaces it by another;
- ❑ those associated with a window based application used by various people. Individual users may prefer different features to be turned on or off, such as toolbars. The application may provide different macros to adjust such features automatically irrespective of the complexity of the adjustment;
- ❑ a drawing package macro which automatically places specific boxes and text at relevant positions within the drawing;
- ❑ a text editor macro used to enter program skeleton source-code. Here a macro may be used to automatically place documentary information at the start of an associated text file each time a new program is created.

Question 6.49

What does a macro represent?

In any of the above cases, the macro facility provided must allow the user to record the key-strokes and actions to be associated with the macro together with the means to associate a name with the macro for subsequent selection. Many applications also provide the ability to use variables within a macro and even prompt the user for some information. Consider word processing macros to:

☐ delete a user specified number of text lines. The user must be prompted for the number of lines to delete;

☐ include the text of a user specified file. The user must be prompted for the name of the file.

Question 6.50

Identify one example of a macro which uses user entered information.

In the normal process of entering key-strokes and actions, the user may make an error such as attempting to include a text file into a document when the file does not exist. The user corrects their mistake and continues. When specifying the key-strokes and actions to be associated with macros, the user should note that the occurrence of some errors will make subsequent key-strokes and actions irrelevant and possible harmful to the information already stored.

Batch files

Unlike macros provided through and processed within a specific application, batch files represent command scripts which are submitted to the operating system for processing. The batch file may contain a collection of any commands normally entered at the keyboard for processing. Generally such commands are processed as a command sequence. The operating system usually provides additional facilities only available in batch file scripts catering for:

☐ Selections;

☐ Iterations (also known as repetitions);

☐ Variables;

☐ Parameter passing;

☐ Labels and GOTOs;

☐ Calling other batch files, returning to next statement in current script;

☐ Transfer of control to an alternative script without the ability to return.

Batch file processing has been developed to a point where they represent simple programming languages providing the three basic program constructs. Some batch file processors do not provide facilities to obtain user input. Such a facility can be provided by running an executable program within the script and returning the entered value in some way to the script for processing.

351

Question 6.51

Generally, how do macros and batch files differ?

Programs

Programs may be regarded as automated procedures which are directly executed or interpreted by the processor in some manner. The text representing such automated procedures must be submitted to a translator for verification and conversion into an executable form whereas macros and batch files are usually interpreted step-by-step to confirm the correct format of the contained instructions. Executable program code may be assumed to provide the fastest of automated procedures.

6.3.4 Specification

The specification of an automated procedure must be developed as for any other application. The specification will define the following details associated with the automated procedure:

- ❑ Purpose – as detailed in Element 5.3;
- ❑ Facility to be used – as detailed in Element 5.3;
- ❑ Type of automated procedure as detailed in Element 6.3.3:
  - macro – best suited to simplifying user interaction within a particular application;
  - batch file – best suited to simplifying user interaction with the operating system;
  - program – best suited to providing automated procedures not suitable for implementation as macros or batch files.
- ❑ Types of data – the data forms, such as integer, real, character and string associated with the information to be processed. These data types are detailed in Element 6.2;
- ❑ Structures – the data structures to be processed. data structures are detailed in Element 6.2;
- ❑ Program constructs – identifies the sequences, selections and iterations usually in the form of pseudo-code representing the automated procedure. Sequences, selections and iterations are detailed in Element 6.2;
- ❑ Expressions and operators – identifies the expressions and operators to be used by the automated procedure in it's operation usually in the form of pseudo-code. Expressions and operators are detailed in Element 6.2.

Question 6.52

Identify the three types of automated procedure and the role each is best suited to.

Task 6.14 PC 3 & 4

Using a typical PC based system of your own, in your place of work or where you study, the stored program development tools, available programming languages and associated documentation produce specifications for two automated procedures each of which uses a different facility and which together cover each of the following specification points:

- ❑ *Purpose;*
- ❑ *Facility to be used;*
- ❑ *Type of automated procedure;*
- ❑ *Types of data;*
- ❑ *Structures;*
- ❑ *Program constructs;*
- ❑ *Expressions and operators.*

Examples of the types of automated procedure are:

- ❑ *the creation of sub-directories and the removal of files with some common character in their name from one directory or sub-directory to another directory or sub-directory;*
- ❑ *the creation of a routine which initiates a particular type of document, creates specific elements within the document and enables the entry of variables such as name and address or invoice and payment details;*
- ❑ *the creation of a screen menu which enables the user to identify what software application they wish to access, such that entry of a character initiates the required software.*

One of the automated procedures must include the use of variables which are entered via a user prompt and field entry area on the screen.

Task 6.15 PC 3 & 4

Using a typical PC based system of your own, in your place of work or where you study, the stored program development tools, available programming languages and associated documentation, implement (create) automated procedures to meet the two specifications produced for Task 6.14.

6.3.5 Evaluation

Having produced a working representation of an automated procedure, it is useful to evaluate the working solution in order to deduce the following details associated with it's production:

- ❑ Costs;
- ❑ Benefits;
- ❑ Fitness for purpose;
- ❑ Possible improvements.

Costs

The production of any computer-based solution will consume both time and economic resources to complete the production:

❏ It may have been necessary to purchase development tools to undertake the production. Should such tools not be required on future projects, then the costs are directly attributable to the production of this single solution. It may have been better to use existing development tools which although they may not have been the most suited would not have necessitated additional acquisitions;

❏ The production was completed in a measurable time period. Was the time period acceptable? Could the production time have been shortened and if so at what cost?

Benefits

The evaluation of the operation of the automated procedure will provide the necessary information to deduce the benefits directly attributable to it's use. Such benefits include shorter processing times, easing of user activities, standardised procedures, more easily accessible information and more accurate information.

Question 6.53

Identify five possible benefits which may occur through the use of automated procedures.

Fitness for purpose

The evaluation of the operation of the automated procedure will identify whether it functions as required and possibly where it may be deficient. A negative evaluation may also question whether the procedure was suitable for automating.

Possible improvements

An evaluation of the *costs*, *benefits* and *fitness for purpose* associated with the production of the automated procedure will provide the necessary information to ascertain what (if any) improvements can be made to the automated procedure and the production of future procedures. Only having used the automated procedure is it possible to deduce the overall benefits gained by it's use and it's fitness for purpose. It may be that the automated procedure functions as specified and it's use provides measurable benefits. It may also be that:

❏ use of the automated procedure incurs additional administration tasks (both manual and additional automated procedure usage);

❏ use of the automated procedure causes unacceptable time delays;

❏ users may find it difficult to use;

❏ it may not actually represent a solution to the original requirement.

The possible improvements could indicate:

❏ changes to the functionality of the automated procedure requiring amendments to be made to the working representation;

❏ activities to simplify the use of the automated procedure without amending it.

Question 6.54

What four aspects associated with automated procedures should be evaluated?

Finally, the evaluation may alternatively indicate necessary amendments to the system used to run the automated procedure, such as additional memory, disk storage and memory management.

Task 6.16   PC 5

Using the automated procedures created in Task 6.15, evaluate both procedures and produce notes describing the findings of your evaluation.

Answers to questions in Unit 6

Answer 6.1 Development of systems software requires the developer to possess the necessary technical understanding of the computer because the software being developed has to control and manage the computer correctly and efficiently.

Answer 6.2 Applications software generally represents any software which doesn't provide for the overall control of the computer, as depicted by systems software packages, permitting the end-user to process information in some manner and produce a desired result with a minimum technical understanding of the computer.

Answer 6.3 A software package or program which provides the means to develop further programs may be regarded as both systems software and applications software because although being an element of systems software, it is used by an end-user, namely, a programmer in a similar manner to any typical applications software.

Answer 6.4 The main purpose of an operating system is to control the operation of the computer and the flow of information around the computer in order to execute further applications.

Answer 6.5 The 'User Friendliness' aspect of a program represents the flexibility and ease with which the user interacts with the running application both through the actions associated with input and format with which the output is presented.

Answer 6.6 A programming language permits the program developer to lay down a solution in a more human readable form. Each programming language is more suited to developing solutions to particular problems than others. Thus, the correct language should be used to efficiently develop a suitable solution.

Answer 6.7 A programming language provides the means to explicitly state the instructions and order in which such instructions are to be executed to derive a desired outcome. The information submitted to a program generator defines the user's requirements and is not concerned with how the requirement is achieved.

Answer 6.8 The application developer is able to concentrate on the function of the application rather than develop endless interface handling routines of their own.

Answer 6.9 The developer has the need to use standardised user interface software easily permitting development to be concentrated on the functionality of the package being developed. The end-user has the need to interact with packages with a minimum of technical awareness of the system being used.

Answer 6.10 The major purpose of development software is concerned with aiding the production of further software packages.

Answer 6.11 Information handled by a program is referred to as data.

Answer 6.12 Textual documents were processed by text editors, word processors and desk top publishing packages.

Answer 6.13 The Microsoft Office packages providing the processing of the identified information forms are:
- Textual documents – Word (Word Processor);
- Numbers – Excel (Spreadsheet Manager);
- Graphical information – PowerPoint (Drawing Package);
- Structured Data – Access (Database Manager).

Answer 6.14 Solid modelling techniques permit designers to model three dimensional objects and scenes under differing conditions.

Answer 6.15 One such example is a domestic automatic washing machine which may include micro-processor based control software to manage functions such as water levels during wash cycles and water temperatures during wash cycles.

Answer 6.16 The expert system package represents both the knowledge base of the equivalent human expert and a set of decision making procedures used by the equivalent human expert. An expert system is only as good as the knowledge base and decision making rules it is provided with. Should there be a flaw in this information, then the overall system is flawed.

Answer 6.17 There can only ever be one outcome, why compute it? Any variations would require the production of an alternative slightly different solution.

Answer 6.18 Data elements may take various forms:
- A whole number;
- A floating-point number;
- A single character;
- A string representing a collection of characters;

❏ A composite structure, also known as a *Data Structure.*

Answer 6.19   The best suited data element forms would be:
- ❏ Person's salary – whole number;
- ❏ Car Registration Number – string;
- ❏ Stock Quantity – whole number;
- ❏ Average value – floating-point value;
- ❏ Post code – string.

Answer 6.20   4th. generation languages permit the user to define a required task without having to detail how to do it whilst a solution written in a 3rd. generation language must describe precisely how a required task is to be accomplished.

Answer 6.21   The 3rd. generation language representation is textual and more readable to a human whilst the machine language representation is the form other languages are usually translated into by means of *Compilation* or *Assembly*. At this level, the form is numeric, the processing of which is accomplished through the interpretation of the numbers contained there-in by the machine's micro-processor.

Answer 6.22   The two forms of translation are Compilation and Assembly.

Compilation provides the means to translate high-level languages such as 3rd. generation languages into a form more easily understood by the micro-processor.

Assembly provides the means to translate lower-level assembler languages into a form more easily understood by the micro-processor.

Answer 6.23   The names associated with the three basic control structures are:
- ❏ Sequence;
- ❏ Selection;
- ❏ Iteration (also known as repetition).

Answer 6.24   The purpose of each of the three basic control structure is:
- ❏ Sequences – a set of program statements;
- ❏ Selections – permit the natural order of processing program statements to be adjusted, permitting alternative processing;
- ❏ Iterations – permit the repetition of a set of program statements.

Answer 6.25   The manner in which the user makes a selection falls into one or more of the following categories:
- ❏ function key;
- ❏ character key;
- ❏ multiple key combinations;
- ❏ menus;
- ❏ object or icon selection.

Answer 6.26   The menu list may be:
- ❏ displayed as a drop-down menu which appears hanging down as the expansion of an option previously visible upon the screen;
- ❏ displayed as a list at a specific point upon the screen alongside an associated entity, possibly a sub-menu following previous menu option selection;
- ❏ displayed centrally upon the screen.

Answer 6.27   Short-hand keys were introduced to provide the user with a quick and immediate means of selecting an available option.

Answer 6.28   Traditionally, programs were developed using the following program development tools:
- ❏ Text editors;
- ❏ Translators (Compilers and/or Assemblers);
- ❏ Linkers.

Answer 6.29   Present-day development packages use Independent Development Environments (IDEs) embodying the necessary development tools to produce a working solution. Working programs can be easily developed by experienced developers. However, the ease with which changes can be made supports the hacking of code in a vain attempt to make a flawed program work.

Answer 6.30   Each language has a formal definition comprising two aspects:

Syntax – a set of grammatical rules defining how keywords, symbols, expressions and statements may be structured and combined.

Semantics – a set of rules that define the meaning of the language's constituent parts, that is what actually occurs when such elements are executed.

Answer 6.31   Pseudo code is a Program Development Language (PDL) tool representing a syntax free language form permitting the developer to specify the structure of a program solution without unnecessary concern to the rigour of the syntax of the eventual program language

Answer 6.32   Usually a macro represents a series of user entered key-strokes or actions which can be initiated by entering a key or selecting a window button which the user has previously defined as representing the macro.

Answer 6.33   It is not logically correct to attempt to display the eventual total and average without first deducing them. In turn, these values cannot be deduced without first obtaining the two values.

Answer 6.34 Multiple-choice processing would require the multiple nesting of IF-THEN-ELSE constructs to process the statement sequence associated with the selection. The CASE construct provides a simpler means of defining the required structure.

Answer 6.35 The iteration constructs would be:
- ❏ the number of iterations is known? – FOR;
- ❏ the number of iterations is variable? – WHILE or REPEAT-UNTIL.

Answer 6.36 Such additional forms provide for larger and smaller range values and are again generally used to control the amount of memory required to store data items.

Answer 6.37 Briefly describe the type of information associated with:
- ❏ Integer numbers – whole numbers;
- ❏ Real numbers – floating-point numbers;
- ❏ Characters – single letters;
- ❏ Strings – a collection of individual characters;
- ❏ Booleans – a TRUE / FALSE indicator.

Answer 6.38 A data type represents a description of a form of data such as an integer, real or string where-as a data item is an actual instance of a piece of data (variable). A data item can be manipulated in some manner.

Answer 6.39 VAT would be represented by a real or floating-point value.

Answer 6.40 An array comprises many occurrences of the same data type.

Answer 6.41 An array comprises many occurrences of the same data type but a record comprises a group of related data elements each denoting a field within the record.

Answer 6.42 A primary key represents a field associated with unique values whilst the entries associated with a secondary key may include duplicate entries.

Answer 6.43 3 and 15.

Answer 6.44 TRUE, FALSE and TRUE.

Answer 6.45 TRUE, TRUE and TRUE.

Answer 6.46 It is beneficial to use automated procedures to reduce input error, speed up processing and standardise procedures.

Answer 6.47 Automated procedures speed up processing because the text depicting each command to be undertaken is immediately available following the completion of the preceding command.

Answer 6.48 Generally, a user needs to perform activities such as backing-up information. Such tasks need not always be undertaken by a person familiar with the technicalities associated with file naming, directory and sub-directory conventions.

Answer 6.49 Macros provide the user with the ability to define their own short-hand instructions. Usually a macro represents a series of possible user entered key-strokes or actions which can be initiated by entering a key or selecting a window button which the user has previously defined as representing the macro.

Answer 6.50 An example such as one of the following word processing macros which:
- ❏ delete a user specified number of text lines. The user must be prompted for the number of lines to delete;
- ❏ include the text of a user specified file. The user must be prompted for the name of the file.

Answer 6.51 Unlike macros processed within a specific application, batch files represent command scripts which are submitted to the operating system for processing.

Answer 6.52 The three types of automated procedure are:
- ❏ macro – best suited to simplifying user interaction within a particular application;
- ❏ batch file – best suited to simplifying user interaction with the operating system;
- ❏ program – best suited to providing automated procedures not suitable for implementation as macros or batch files.

Answer 6.53 The five benefits identified are shorter processing times, easing of user activities, standardised procedures, more easily accessible information and more accurate information.

Answer 6.54 The four aspects associated with automated procedures which should be evaluated are:
- ❏ Costs;
- ❏ Benefits;
- ❏ Fitness for purpose;
- ❏ Possible improvements.

Unit 6 Sample Test Paper

1. What is an operating system?

   A A piece of systems software
   B A piece of applications software
   C A utility
   D A program development tool

2. What is an Independent Development Environment?

   A A stand-alone computer system dedicated to developing software
   B A programming language
   C An application dedicated to the development of software
   D A Development Environment produced by an individual company

3. What forms of software represent Program Development Tools?

   A Compilers, assemblers and file management routines
   B Operating systems, compilers and electronic mail
   C Text editors, compilers, assemblers and linkers
   D Word processors, compilers, linkers and electronic mail

4. Graphical information is processed by what form of application package?

   A Database manager
   B Drawing package
   C Word Processor
   D Spreadsheet manager

5. A Database manager package generally processes which of the following:

   A Numerical and statistical information
   B Raw text and layout details
   C Raw data, structure details and queries
   D Raw data, Raw text and structure details

6. Assuming a Spreadsheet contains the values 10 in A1, 15 in B1, 20 in C1 and 25 in D1 whilst E1 contains the formula =SUM(B1,D1)*2, what will be displayed in E1?

   A 60
   B 80
   C 140
   D 120

7. Medical diagnosis is a subject area suited to which of the following software packages?

   A Expert systems
   B Modelling
   C Controlling
   D Word processing

8. A record data type is associated with which of the following data forms?

   A composite structure
   B An array
   C A string of characters
   D A whole number

9. Which data form is most suited to representing a telephone number?

   A A whole number
   B An array of whole numbers
   C A record
   D A string

10. Which of the following language lists contain only 3rd generation languages?

    A SQL, LISP
    B Pascal, FORTRAN, TURBO Assembler and COBOL
    C Pascal, ADA, FORTRAN and COBOL
    D SQL and Pascal

11. The basic programming control structures are?

    A Sequentials, Selections and Iterations
    B Sequences, Selections and Iterations
    C Sequences, Selectors and Iterations
    D Sequences, Selectors and Repeaters

12. A successful compilation or assembly produces which modules for input to a linker?

    A Source modules
    B Executable modules
    C Object modules
    D Micro-code modules

13. Which iteration construct should be used when the number of iterations is known?

    A FOR
    B WHILE
    C REPEAT-UNTIL
    D IF-THEN-ELSE

14. What term best describes an array?

    A A collection of characters
    B Many occurrences of the same data type
    C A collection of associated but different data types
    D A record consisting of different data fields all of the same data type

15. What is produced by a Linker?

    A An Object Module
    B A Source Module
    C A Link Module
    D An Executable Load Module

16. How is a window based icon represented?

    A As a graphical image
    B As a drop-down menu
    C As an application window
    D As a list of control-key combinations

17. What does the arithmetic expression 2+3*11-4 evaluate to?

    A 51
    B 35
    C 23
    D 31

18. If the identifier X contains the numeric value 10, what expression will evaluate *TRUE* and define X as being in the range 0 to 100 inclusive?

    A (0 <= X) OR (X <= 100)
    B (0 <= X) AND (X <= 100)
    C (0 < X) AND (X < 100)
    D (X<= 100) OR (X>= 0)

19. How is a macro processed?

    A By an application
    B By the operating system's command interpreter
    C By the processor
    D By another means

20. What does a batch file represent?

    A A collection of user files
    B A collection of macros
    C A command script
    D A collection of programs

by **Mike Watkins**

Database Development

Introduction

Data Analysis or Data Modelling is a requirements analysis technique that is used to describe the data and information needs of an organisation and the data model produced provides a solid foundation on which to develop the organisations application systems. Data modelling, together with process modelling, are the basic techniques of current structured systems analysis and design methodologies (see Unit 5) that are used to construct application systems to meet the requirements of its users.

Data Analysis is also an essential technique to be carried out prior to building any application system using a relational database management system. Prior to designing and implementing a relational database application a conceptual data model of the application should be constructed and this used to design a logical database that can be then implemented using a relational database software package.

Data analysis consists of applying one or both of the two complementary activities, Entity Relationship Modelling (ERM) and Normalisation. If both techniques are applied to the same system then the models produced will provide a checking facility regarding the correctness of the model. The two techniques analyse an application from different starting points, ERM is a top-down activity that moves from the general to the specific, while Normalisation is a bottom-up activity.

In the first element of this unit you will learn how to develop a data model using both data analysis techniques and how the data model is used to design a relational database system to meet the application requirements. Implementation of the design is dependent on the database software package to be used and is outlined in the last two elements, for more detailed guidance you will need to refer to a specialist text on the particular database package available to you.

Create Relational Database Structures for a Given Specification

Introduction

In this element we will develop your skills to construct data models of application systems using the techniques of Entity Relationship Modelling and Normalisation. On completion of the element you should be able:

- ❏ to list and define the key-terms of entity-relationship (E-R) modelling;
- ❏ to draw an E-R diagram to represent simple application systems;
- ❏ to list and define the key-terms of normalisation;
- ❏ to perform normalisation on a set of un-normalised data through to third normal form;
- ❏ use the data model to produce a logical relational database design as set of relational tables.

■ Data and Information Resources

Data and information are important resources of any organisation whether it be private or public, a road haulage company, a building society, a tool hire firm, a school or the inland revenue. For an organisation to operate it is essential that its data is as accurate and complete as possible to provide a basis that enables effective real-time, short term and long term decisions to be made. Creation and maintenance of data also costs money so it is worthwhile to make the effort to get things right.

The information required by an organisation will change as it responds to its internal operations and external environment. Information is raw data that has been processed eg(*totalled, averaged, sorted, analysed, evaluated*) in such a way that it means something to the organisation. Very often the same raw facts are manipulated in different ways by different information systems of the same organisation.

■ Stable Data and Dynamic Processes

Within any organisation the types and structure of data used does not change very much over time, *data is said to be stable*. However, the application processes that obtain information from the data are often subject to rapid change and new processes are constantly being developed, *processes are said to be dynamic*.

Figure 7.1 Process skyscrapers built on a stable data foundation

7.1.1 Data Model

In order to use a database system to develop and implement process applications a data model of the application area should be constructed by carrying out a *requirements analysis*. The analyst will investigate the data and information as they actually exist within a real world application by collecting documents and interviewing users about their use of the data and their requirements for the application.

From the analysis, a data model is constructed that will provide a *conceptual* model of the real-world application from which a database can be *logically* designed and then *physically* built using a database software package.

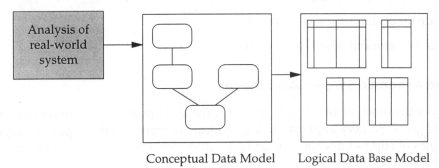

Conceptual Data Model   Logical Data Base Model

Figure 7.2 Application System Models

■ Conceptual Model

The conceptual data model is a diagram that shows related groups of data items and the associations that exist between them. The data model provides a useful tool for communications between the application *developer* and the application *users* during the analysis phase of a project. The model provides a representation of the application data in a way that is independent of any software that will be used to implement the application.

■ Data Analysis

The activity of discovering the structure and use of data within an application is called *data analysis*, the diagrammatic model that is produced is called an *Entity-Relationship Model (ERM)*

363

and shows the individual data groups of the application, its *Entities* and the associations that exist between them, its *Relationships*.

Question 7.1

The Entity Relationship diagram is:

A) A logical model

B) A physical model

C) A conceptual model

D) An organisational model

■ Top-Down Activity

Data analysis is a top-down activity that takes a broad brush approach to discover the structure of data within an information system application based on the organisations view and rules of the application. It is started at the top by looking first for entities, then identifying associations that exist between them and finally becoming more specific by adding attributes. The analyst will gain an understanding of the application and gather the necessary information by interviewing application users, collecting data and getting answers to such questions as:

What does the system DO? or What is the system required to do?

What items and objects does it handle?

What events are significant?

What decisions are taken and why?

What are the organisation's business rules?

What is the norm and what is the exception?

■ The Ashgrove Surgery Data Model

In Unit 5 the outcome of one component of the systems analysis activity was an ER diagram of the Ashgrove Surgery application. The diagram is reproduced in figure 7.3 together with some examples of support documentation to illustrate what you are required to produce having carried out a data modelling activity.

Entity Definitions:

Client A person who is registered with the surgery as a patient and allocated to one of the doctors lists.

Employee A person employed by the surgery to provide a medical service to clients, this includes Doctors, Nurses and ancillary staff.

Appointment An event at a particular time and place where a client receives a medical service from an employee. A patient sees the doctor about some medical condition.

Prescription A document issued to a client and signed by a doctor to allow the client to obtain a treatment medicine(s) for their medical condition. It may be issued as a result of an appointment or may be a repeat prescription.

Relationship Definitions:

An appointment *must be conducted* by an employee, an employee *may conduct* many appointments. Not all employees are allowed to conduct appointments.

A prescription *must be signed* by an employee. An employee *may sign* many prescriptions. Not all employees are allowed to sign prescriptions.

A client *may receive* many prescriptions. A prescription *must be for* one client.

A prescription *may be caused* by one appointment. One appointment *may cause* many prescriptions.

A prescription *must consist of* one or more lines. A prescription line *must be on* one prescription. A prescription line *must be for* one treatment medicine. A treatment medicine *may appear on* many prescription lines.

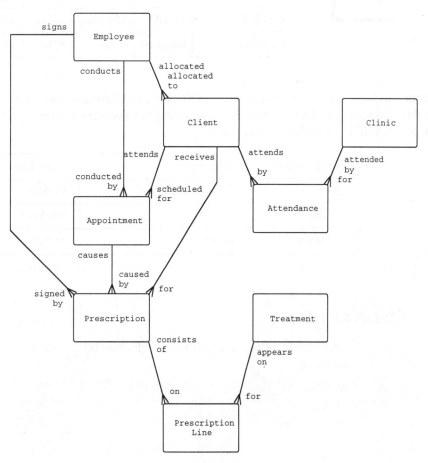

Figure 7.3 Ashgrove surgery ER model

■ **Entity-Relationship Model**

The ERM is the deliverable of the data analysis activity. It is a diagrammatic representation or model of the application system that uses a very simple symbol set and shows:

❑ *Entity Types*   items of interest to the application about which data is kept;

❑ *Attributes*   characteristics of individual entities relevant to the application;

❑ *Relationships*   associations that exist between entities within the application.

The ERM diagram does not contain any computing technical terms or jargon and after a little explanation of the symbols used is easily understood by the application users. It provides a good communication tool between the developer and the client users.

Entity Type: CAR

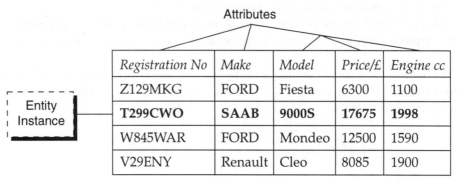

Registration No	Make	Model	Price/£	Engine cc
Z129MKG	FORD	Fiesta	6300	1100
T299CWO	**SAAB**	**9000S**	**17675**	**1998**
W845WAR	FORD	Mondeo	12500	1590
V29ENY	Renault	Cleo	8085	1900

Figure 7.4 Instances of the Entity 'CAR'

This data can have an association with an entity type GARAGEs who are franchised to service particular makes of car. The relationship that exists between the entity type CAR and the entity type GARAGE is 'franchised to service'.

Garage Name	Address	Franchise
Jones	Treforest Ind Est	FORD
Cardiff Saab	Cardiff	SAAB
Williams	Gloucester	Renault

Figure 7.5 Instances of the Entity 'GARAGE'

Question 7.2

Data characteristics of an entity type are called?

A) Fields

B) Columns

C) Attributes

D) Properties

Question 7.3

An individual occurrence of a particular entity type is called?

A) An entity instance

B) An entity appearance

C) An entity class

D) An entity record

Question 7.4

An association between entity types is called?

A) A relation

B) A relationship

C) A link

D) A franchise

The ERM should provide an accurate representation of the data requirements of an application which can act as a *framework* on which to develop a computerised system. The emphasis of the data analysis activity is on Entity Types and the Relationships that exist within the application, NOT on the processing of entities.

Entities

■ Entity Type

This is a thing or object of significance within the application area about which data and/or information is held in a *record* or needs to be known:

Application Area	Entity Types (or Class)
Hospital	– Patient, Ward, Doctor, Drug
College	– Lecturer, Student, Course, Module
Vehicle Hire	– Car, Model, Client, Hire
CD Library	– CD, Member, Loan, Reservation, Fine

■ Discovering Entity Types

Entity types are often *nouns* in sentences from an application description or scenario obtained from the analyst's investigation of the application area within the organisation. They usually represent real things that have an identity within the application.

Entities for a CD-library application are shown in *italic* in the outline system description that follows.

> 'The CD Library stocks *CDs* which may be borrowed by *members* on loan. Members may also make a *reservation* for any CD *Title* currently not available and the *loan* may be liable to *fines* if the *borrower* is late returning a CD.'

Question 7.5

Identify the entities in the following college description.

'Students on an IT course study different units that cover a specific topic area. Each unit is delivered by a least one member of staff who is also responsible for setting and marking unit assessments.'

■ Entity Instance

An entity instance is a single particular occurrence of an entity type. There will normally be many instances of an entity type within an application. Each instance of an entity type must be *distinctly identifiable* from all other instances of that entity type.

Entity Type   *Instances or Occurrences*
CD TITLE   Bruce Springstein Greatest Hits
                         Simply the Best
                         Bedtime Stories
MEMBER   Mike Rocking
                         Kate Dancer
                         Chris Serious

■ Entity Symbol

An entity type is represented in the ER diagram using soft box that is labelled with the entity name:

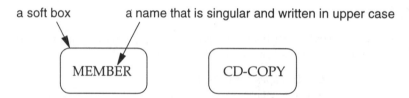

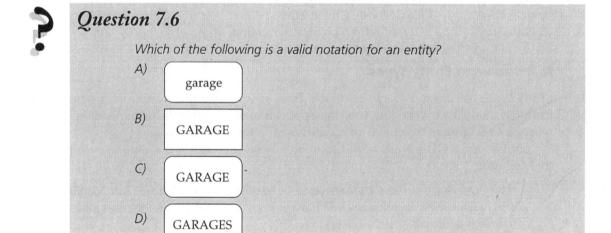

■ Entity Definition

Each entity identified and given a name should have a brief description that defines precisely the entity within the context of the application.

> 'A CD-TITLE is a reference to a music CD, at least one copy of which has been acquired by the library for loan to its members'.

This definition includes those music CDs stocked by the library. It excludes those music CDs that the library hasn't acquired and all Computer CDs or Multimedia CDs.

Question 7.7

What other information does the definition provide?

A) The library stocks every music CD produced

B) There may be more than one copy of some CDs

C) There is only one copy of each CD

D) There is more than one copy of all CDs

In a student college application an entity might be described as:

> *Lecturer:* 'An academic member of staff who has a teaching responsibility for one or more courses and who may also be undertaking research and/or consultancy activities.'

this definition excludes administrative or technical members of staff.

Attributes

Attributes are *fields* and represent the named properties or characteristics of a particular entity type that are relevant to the application area. The values of an entity's attributes distinguish one instance of a particular entity type from another instance of the same type.

A Lecturer entity might have the attributes:

LECTURER (Staff No, Name, Title, Address, Home Tel No, Gender, Date of Birth, Salary, Email Address, Room No, Tel No, Grade)

A Golf club member might have the attributes:

GC-MEMBER (Member No, Name, Tel No, Membership Type, Fee Amount Paid, Handicap, Last Revision Date)

In the CD library system some attributes of different entity types would be:

Entity Type	Attributes	————————Entity Instances————	
MEMBER	Membership No	0123	0345
	Member Name	Mike Rocking	Kate Dancer
	Address	21 Zeppelin St	73 The Crescent
	Tel No	5566778	6573821
	Gender	Male	Female
CD-TITLE	Reference No	RKS005	CLC101
	Title	Greatest Hits	100 Best Tunes Vol 1
	Artist	Bruce Springstein	Various
	Year	1995	1990

The MEMBER Mike Rocking has other characteristics such as that he drives a Ford Maverick, banks with MoneyTakers, has a dog Jack, but these attributes are not of any relevance to the CD library application.

Question 7.8

Which one of the following do you think is a relevant additional attribute for the MEMBER entity type

A) Membership Class, such as Adult, Junior, OAP

B) Car Registration No

C) Income per annum

D) Make of CD player

An attribute will perform one or more of the following functions for an entity type. It will:

☐ *Identify* the entity, to distinguish one entity type instance from another instance;

☐ *Describe* the entity, to provide a meaningful representation of an entity instance;

☐ *Classify* the entity instance as belonging to some particular group;

☐ *Quantify* the entity instance to indicate its size in terms of amounts or dimensions;

☐ Express the entity *state*, to indicate an instance's current status where this is subject to change over time.

Question 7.9

For the functions of Identify, Describe, Classify and Quantify choose one attribute of the LECTURER entity that performs that function.

■ Attribute Domain

Each attribute has associated with it a range or set of values it may take called the attribute *domain*. The domain will also show any structure that an attribute value may take.

The domain of the attribute *date of birth* might be:

A valid date after 1900, in the format dd – mmm – yyyy

Thus '12-Jul-1947' is a valid date, whereas '12/07/47' is not valid for this domain definition.

The GC-MEMBER attribute *MembershipType* might have as a domain a set of specific values such as ('MA', 'MJ', MV', 'M5', FA', 'FJ', 'FV', 'HW', 'FF'), that represent codes for the type of membership taken out by the member.

The domain definition for a particular attribute will specify some of the following characteristics:

☐ the type of data the attribute value is – *a number, money, text, date*;

☐ the maximum size or length of a value, *Cash Card PIN – 4 digits* ;

☐ a format that the attribute value would take, *a cash card withdrawal date dd/mm/yyyy*;

☐ a range of values that the attribute value should lie in, *cash card withdrawal amount – between 0 and 50*;

☐ allowable set of values and whether it may be null, *gender – 'M' or 'F'*;

☐ the attribute's meaning or description, – *pounds sterling amount of withdrawal*.

The domain definition can be part of a data dictionary and is used to provide guidance for specifying attribute properties when defining the data during database implementation using a Data Base Management System.

Attribute	
Name:	Card PIN
Meaning:	Secret PIN for card usage
Data Type:	Character
Format:	nnnn (4 digits)
Values:	Null not allowed

Attribute	
Name:	Transaction Time
Meaning:	Date and time card used
Data Type:	Date/Time
Format:	Date - dd/mm/yyyy
	Time - hh:mm
Range:	Date - must be valid and after the last transaction date
	Time - hh 0 - 23
	mm 0 - 59
Values:	Null not allowed

Attribute	
Name:	Card Holder
Meaning:	Name of account holder
Data Type:	Character 30
Format:	Left justified
Values:	Null allowed

Attribute	
Name:	Amount
Meaning:	Amount of cash withdrawn
Data Type:	Money
Format:	nn.nn
Range:	0.00 - 50.00
Values:	Null allowed

Example Domain Definitions

Relationships

■ Associations

Within an application entity types do not exist in isolation but have associations with other entity types. A relationship is an association of significance to the application that exists between entity types. A relationship is a two-way association between the participating entity types:

❏ A client hires a car — the *hires* relationship associates a client with the hire car and the car with the hirer.

❏ A lecturer teaches a module — the *teaches* relationship associates a lecturer with the module(s) he/she teaches and a module with the lecturer(s) that teach it.

❏ A member borrows a CD — the *borrows* relationship associates a member with the CDs he/she currently has on loan and the CD with the member who currently has it on loan.

■ Discovering Relationships

Relationships are often *verbs* that link entity types in sentences from an application description or scenario obtained from the analysts investigation of the application area within the organisation.

'The CD Library stocks CD Titles copies of which may be *borrowed* by members on loan. Members may also *make* a reservation for any CD currently not available and the loan may be *liable* to fines if the borrower is late returning a CD.'

They can also be discovered by constructing example lists of possible associated entity type instances and linking a member of one list with one or more members of the other list:

Figure 7.6 Relationship occurrences between two entities

Figure 7.6 shows that a MEMBER may borrow one or more CD-TITLEs and a CD-TITLE may be borrowed by several MEMBERS.

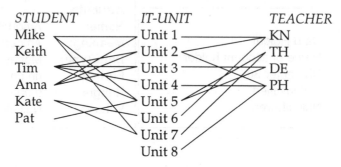

Figure 7.7 Relationship between three entities

Figure 7.7 shows that a STUDENT may study several IT-UNITs, some STUDENTS study no IT-UNIT. A TEACHER delivers one or more IT-UNITs, an IT-UNIT is delivered by one or more TEACHERs.

■ Relationship Symbol

A relationship is represented by a *line* that links two associated entity types. The line also shows:

- ❒ the degree of the relationship;
- ❒ the membership rules for the relationship;
- ❒ components for a link phrase to help define the relationship.

■ Relationship Definition

Each relationship identified and represented in the model should be defined within the application. The definition should clearly indicate which entities are associated by the relationship and state for each entity its membership of the relationship.

'Each listed CD-TITLE must have one or more CD-COPYs, a CD-COPY must be of a listed CD-TITLE.'

This definition excludes having a listed CD-TITLE for which there may be no actual CD-COPY available for loan. It also excludes having a copy of a CD for loan that is not listed as an available title.

■ Relationship Degree

The Degree of a relationship states the number of instances of one entity type that are associated with one instance of the other entity type. There are three values of significance – *zero, one, many* (more than one). If the relationship actually exists then zero is only a possibility when membership of the relationship by the entity type is *optional*.

In figure 7.7, STUDENT 'Mike' is associated with three instances of IT-UNIT, IT-UNIT 'Unit 8' is not associated with any instance of STUDENT and IT-UNIT 'Unit 2' is associated with two instances of TEACHER.

There are three categories of relationship degree and all three include zero as a possibility:

■ One to One   1 : 1

An instance of one entity type is associated with just one instance of another entity type.

The library CD purchase rule is that it will aquire just one CD-COPY of each CD-TITLE.

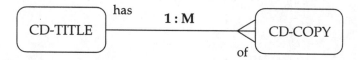

'A CD-TITLE *has one* CD-COPY, a CD-COPY is *of one* CD-TITLE'

■ One to Many 1 : M

An instance of *one* entity type is associated with *many (one or more)* instances of another entity type. The many end of the relationship line is represented by a trident like shape called a 'crows foot':

one   many

The library CD purshase rule is that it will acquire at least one (many) CD-COPY of each CD-TITLE.

'A CD_TITLE *has many* CD-COPYs, a CD-COPY is *of one* CD-TITLE'

The entity type CD-TITLE is called the *owner* or parent while the entity type CD-COPY is called the *member* or child of the relationship.

■ Many to Many   M : N

One instance of entity type 'A' is associated with many instances of entity type 'B' and one instance of entity type 'B' is associated with many instances of entity type 'A'. Both ends of the relationship line have 'crows feet'.

A library reservation rule is that MEMBERS can reserve several CD-TITLEs. This means that popular CD-TITLEs can be reserved by many members.

'One CD-TITLE may be reserved *by many* MEMBERS, one MEMBER may be the reserver *of many* CD-TITLEs'

Question 7.10

For each of the following relationship definitions choose the correct degree classification.

i) Each salesperson is allocated a company car, a company car is assigned to one salesperson:

	S'Person		Car
A)	1	:	N
B)	N	:	1
C)	1	:	1
D)	M	:	N

ii) Each department has at least one employee, an employee works in one department:

	Dept		Employee
A)	1	:	N
B)	1	:	1
C)	M	:	N
D)	N	:	1

iii) Each project involves one or more employees, an employee may work on more than one project:

	Project		Employee
A)	1	:	N
B)	M	:	N
C)	N	:	1
D)	1	:	1

iv) Each project has a leader, an employee may lead more than one project:

	Project		Employee
A)	1	:	N
B)	N	:	1
C)	1	:	1
D)	M	:	N

■ Membership

In any associations we can ask whether the entity types participation in the relationship always exists or may exist. Can we find at least one instance of an entity type that exists but does not participate in a particular relationship with another entity type.

In figure 7.7 STUDENT 'Keith' is not associated with any instance of IT-UNIT and IT-UNIT 'Unit 8' is not associated with any instance of STUDENT.

Is there a CD-TITLE for which there is no actual CD-COPY or is there CD-COPY that is not a valid CD-TITLE.

> Due to loss or damage there **may** be a CD-TITLE for which there is no CD-COPY available. Any CD-COPY available **must** be of a CD-TITLE.

The membership of the relationship between CD-TITLE and CD-COPY is different for each entity type. The CD-TITLE has *non-obligatory* or *optional* membership of the relationship, while the CD-COPY has *obligatory* or *mandatory* membership. This means that an instance of CD-TITLE can exist without an instance of an associated CD-COPY but an instance of CD-COPY can only exist if its associated instance of CD-TITLE exists.

CD-TITLE

CD No	Title	Artist	Label
32375	The Very Best Of	EAGLES	WARNER
27333	**History**	**AMERICA**	**WARNER**
58472	Your 100 Best Tunes Vol 1	Various	DECCA

CD-COPY

CD/Copy No	Date Acquired	Price/£
32375/1	01/04/1994	11.99
32375/2	23/06/1995	11.99
58472/1	15/05/1990	9.99
32381/1	**06/12/1993**	**10.75**

Figure 7.8 Instances of 'CD-TITLE' and 'CD-COPY'

In figure 7.8 CD-TITLE '27333' has no current copies, this is OK. However, CD-COPY '32381/1' has no matching CD-TITLE, this is an example of data inconsistency and this should not occur.

■ Relationship Symbols

The lines that represent relationships also show the *membership rules* for a particular relationship. The form of the line used indicates:

- ❑ the degree of the relationship (1 : 1 or 1 : M or M : N);
- ❑ the membership rules of the relationship and whether an associated entity type is optional or not.

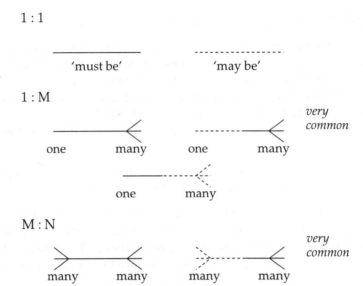

1 : 1

'must be'   'may be'

1 : M

one   many   one   many   *very common*

one   many

M : N

many   many   many   many   *very common*

many   many

Where a line is dotted that end of the relationship is read as 'may be', a solid line reads as ' must be'.

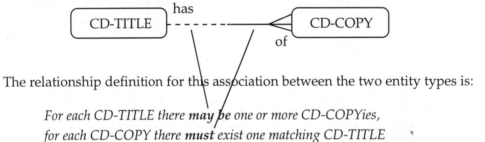

has

CD-TITLE ------< CD-COPY

of

The relationship definition for this association between the two entity types is:

*For each CD-TITLE there **may be** one or more CD-COPYies,*
*for each CD-COPY there **must** exist one matching CD-TITLE*

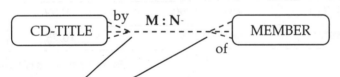

by   M : N

CD-TITLE >----< MEMBER

of

*'A CD-TITLE **may be** reserved by many MEMBERS,*
*one MEMBER **may** reserve many CD-TITLEs'*

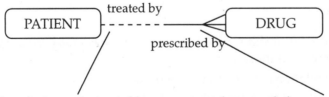

treated by

PATIENT ------< DRUG

prescribed by

*Each patient **may** be treated by one or more drugs, each drug **must** be*
prescribed to a patient

Question 7.11

Which of the following is the correct representation of the following relationship definition:

A customer may place one or more contracts, a contract must be made for one customer.

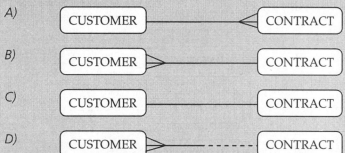

A)

B)

C)

D)

Question 7.12

Which is the correct relationship definition of the diagram shown:

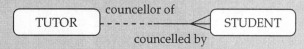

A) *A tutor must be the counsellor many students, a student must be counselled by one tutor.*

B) *A tutor may be the counsellor of one student, a student must be counselled by many tutors.*

C) *A tutor may be the counsellor of many students, a student must be counselled by one tutor.*

D) *A tutor may be counsellor of one student, a student must be counselled by one tutor.*

Question 7.13

Which is the correct relationship definition of the diagram shown:

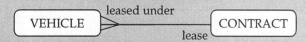

A) *A contract must lease one or more vehicles, a vehicle must be leased under one contract.*

B) *A contract may lease one or more vehicles, a vehicle must be leased under one contract.*

C) *A contract may lease one vehicle, a vehicle may leased under one contract.*

D) *A contract must lease one vehicle.*

Question 7.14

Which is the correct representation of the relationship definition given:

A hospital patient may occupy a ward, a ward may be occupied by one or more patients.

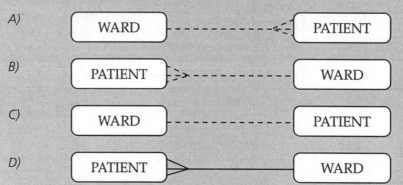

A)

WARD - - - - - - - - - - -< PATIENT

B)

PATIENT >- - - - - - - - - - - WARD

C)

WARD - - - - - - - - - - - PATIENT

D)

PATIENT >———————— WARD

Question 7.15

Which of the relationship definitions is NOT valid for ER diagram shown?

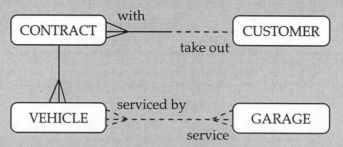

A) A garage may service many vehicles, a vehicle may be serviced by many garages.

B) A contract must be for one or more vehicles, a vehicle must be leased under one contract.

C) A customer may drive one vehicle, a vehicle must be driven by one customer.

D) A customer may take out one or more contracts, a contract must be with one customer.

Question 7.16

Which of the following relationship definitions is NOT valid for the ER diagram shown?

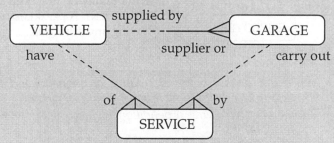

A) *A vehicle must be supplied by one garage, a garage may be the supplier of many vehicles.*

B) *A vehicle may have one or more services, a service must be of one vehicle.*

C) *A vehicle must be serviced by the garage that supplied it, a garage supplying a vehicle must service it.*

D) *A garage may carry out many services, a service must be by a garage.*

■ Relationship Definitions and Membership Rules

The membership rules of an entity type within a relationship has a significant effect on the meaning of the relationship and can constrain how an application will operate.

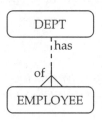

A DEPARTMENT may have one or more employees, an EMPLOYEE must belong to a DEPARTMENT.

This means that EMPLOYEE instance cannot exist without having first been allocated to a DEPARTMENT. A DEPARTMENT can exist without having any EMPLOYEES.

A DEPARTMENT must have one or more employees, an EMPLOYEE must belong to a DEPARTMENT.

This means that EMPLOYEE instance cannot exist without having first been allocated to a DEPARTMENT. A DEPARTMENT cannot exist without having any EMPLOYEE.

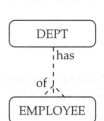

A DEPARTMENT may have one or more employees, an EMPLOYEE may belong to a department.

This means that EMPLOYEE instance can exist without having first been allocated to a DEPARTMENT. A DEPARTMENT can exist without having any EMPLOYEES.

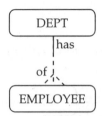

A DEPARTMENT must have one or more employees, an EMPLOYEE may not belong to a department.

This means that EMPLOYEE instance can exist without having first been allocated to a DEPARTMENT. A DEPARTMENT cannot exist without having any EMPLOYEE.

In the Tasks 7.1 to 7.3, read each scenario and list the entities and relationships. Construct an ER model using the correct symbols to represent relationship degree and membership. Write a definition for each entity and build link phrases to define each relationship.

Task 7.1   PC 1

Students on a GNVQ award study several units. Each unit is delivered by at least one lecturer, a lecturer may be involved in the delivery of several units. Assessment of a unit requires students to complete several assignments.

Task 7.2   PC 1

A college department prints technical reports authored by its lecturers. Not all lecturers are authors. Each technical report is classified as belonging to one particular topic area. Some topic areas have yet to have any reports printed.

Task 7.3   PC 1

In a zoo each species of animal consumes one type of food, which may also be eaten by more than one species. Zoo keepers usually supervise at least one animal.

Keys

Each entity type discovered during the modelling process will have a set of attributes that provide a picture of the entity as a whole, it must also be possible to distinguish one instance of an entity type from another. The entity key has a unique value for each entity instance, this means that the field chosen has a value that is never duplicated or the same as that of another instance of the same entity type.

■ Simple or Elementary Key

This type of key is on made up of a *single* attribute. For a STUDENT entity type the attribute *Enrolment No* may be used as it is unique to each entity instance, attributes *Name or Date of Birth* would not be unique. In a PRODUCT entity the attribute *Item No* would be unique, an INVOICE would have a unique *Invoice No* as an attribute.

■ Compound or Composite Key

This type of key is one made up from two or more attributes joined together. A CHEQUE entity would use *Bank Sort Code/Bank Account Number/Cheque Number* to ensure uniqueness to distinquish one instance of CHEQUE from another. In a golf club competition a CARD entity would use *Competition date/Member No* to distinguish each instance of competition card.

■ Primary Key

The *primary key* of an entity type is a simple or compound key that makes it possible to distinguish one instance of that entity type from another instance of the same type.

The primary key:

❐ *uniquely identifies each instance of an entity type;*

❐ *must have a value, can never be null;*

❐ *should not be longer than needed to ensure uniqueness.*

By knowing the primary key value of an entity type a particular instance can be identified and it's other attribute values made known.

Student Enrolment Number, Flight Number, National Insurance Number, Insurance Policy Number

are all examples of attributes that uniquely identify the entity type they belong to.

Banking Application:
Entity Types:

Bank Branch	*Bank Account*
Bank Sort Code	**Bank Sort Code**
Bank Name	**Account Number**
Bank Address	Account Name
Bank Telephone No	Account Address
	Account Type
	Current Balance

The attribute *Bank Sort Code* uniquely identifies a particular branch of a bank, whereas to uniquely identify an account at a particular branch requires both the *Bank Sort Code* **and** the *Account Number*.

Knowing the value of the attribute Account Name will not guarantee uniquely identifying an instance of Bank Account, there may be several accounts with the same Account Name within the same bank or at different banks.

Question 7.17

Which of the following would uniquely identify a cheque drawn on an account?

A) Bank Sort Code/Account Number/Cheque Date

B) Account Number/Cheque Number

C) Bank Sort Code/Account Number/Cheque Number

D) Bank Sort Code/Account Number/Date/Cheque Number

Question 7.18

A VEHICLE entity type has the following attributes:
Manufacturer Name, Model Name, Registration Number, MOT Month, Engine Size, Body Colour, Trim Colour, Year Made
Which of the following would be suitable Primary Key Attribute?

A) Manufacturer Name/Model Name

B) Registration Number

C) Year Made/Model Name/Body Colour

D) Model Name/Year Made/Body Colour

Question 7.19

A Patient entity type has the following attributes:
Patient No, Name, Home Address, Ward, Bed No, NI Number, Date of Birth, Gender, GP Name, Admit Date
Which of the following would NOT be suitable as a primary key attribute?

A) Patient No

B) Ward/Bed No/Admit Date

C) Name

D) NI Number

Question 7.20

How many instances of an entity type must a value of a primary key identify?

A) Exactly one

B) None

C) One or more

D) Zero or more

■ Foreign Key

A primary key of one entity might well be an attribute of another entity. A Foreign Key is an attribute of one entity that has a value that is the primary key value of another entity.

In the *Bank Account* entity type above the attribute *Bank Sort Code* will have a value that uniquely identifies a particular instance – primary key – of the *Bank Branch* entity type.

Company Sales Order Application
Entity Types:

Sales Order	*Customer*
Order Number	**Customer Account No**
Order Date	Customer Name
Customer Account No	Customer Address
Order Total Amount	Balance Outstanding
	Credit Limit

Product

Product Code
Product Name
Product Price
Supplier Account No
Quantity in Stock

Supplier

Supplier Account No
Supplier Name
Supplier Address
Telephone No

The value of a foreign key attribute may be null (not have any value). However when the attribute is not null then it's value then it must be a valid one – there must be an instance of the other entity type having that value as its primary key.

Sales orders may be taken from customers who do not have a sales account with the company and pay by cash. In this case the attribute *Customer Account No* of the entity type *Sales Order* would have a null value. Should the attribute *Customer Account No* of *Sales Order* have a value then it must match one instance of the *Customer* entity type.

Question 7.21

A hospital system has two entity types, PATIENT and WARD. A PATIENT entity type has the following attributes:

Patient No, *Name, Home Address, Ward Id, Bed No, NI Number, Date of Birth, Gender, GP Name, Admit Date*

Which of the following may be a foreign key?

A) Ward Id

B) Patient No

C) Bed No

D) Date of Birth

Usually the foreign key attribute refers to an instance of a second different entity type, but it is possible for it to refer to another instance of the same entity type. An EMPLOYEE entity type has the following attributes:

Staff No, Name, *Department Id*, Grade, *Manager*, Salary

The attributes *Department Id* and *Manager* are both foreign keys.
The value of the *Department Id* attribute must be a primary key value of a *DEPARTMENT* entity type.
The value of the *Manager* attribute is the *Staff No* of an instance of the same *EMPLOYEE* entity type.

Instances of entity type EMPLOYEE:

Instances of entity type EMPLOYEE:

Staff No	Name	Dept Id	Grade	Manager	Salary
80125	Davies	IS	SL	82014	24000
81006	Jones	SE	FL	81807	30000
81203	Morris	SE	SL	81006	25000
81807	Harris	SE	HOD		35000
82014	Williams	IS	FL	81807	39000

Instances of entity type DEPARTMENT:

Dept Id	Department Name
CS	Computer Systems
IS	Information Systems
SE	Software Engineering

Figure 7.9 Foreign Key links

■ Recursive Relationship

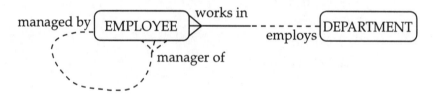

In this model the *manages* relationship is between one instance of the EMPLOYEE entity and another instance of EMPLOYEE.

One employee may be the manager of one or more other employees, some employees may not have a manager.

■ Multiple Relationships

In many applications two entities may exist that have more than one relationship with each other. Consider the entities *PERSON* and *PLACE* (a city, town or village), one relationship is *'birth-place of'*, a second is *'lives in'*:

'Each person must be born in one place, each place may be the birth-place of many persons.'
'Each person must live (or have lived) in many places, a place is the home of many persons.'

■ Resolution of Many to Many Relationships

If the ERM contains any M:N relationships these should be resolved into two 1:N relationships by creating a new intersection or link entity. This intersection entity will have at least two attributes, the *primary keys of both original entities*, there are often other attributes that characterise this *new* entity.

In a sales order application an order is for one or more products and a product may be required in many orders, this is modelled as:

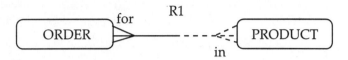

This M:N relationship R1 is resolved by adding a perhaps obvious intersection entity *'ORDER-LINE'* that is linked to both *'ORDER'* and *'PRODUCT'*.

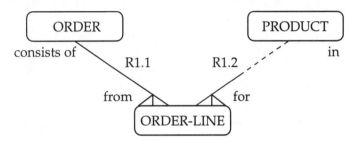

Note: The ends of the relationship on both ORDER and PRODUCT are now of **degree 1**, while the ends of both relationships on ORDER-LINE are of **degree N**.

There are now two relationships replacing the original one:

R1.1: *Each order must consist of one or more order lines, each order line must be from one order.*

R1.2: *Each order line must be for one product, each product may be requested in many order lines.*

The ORDER-LINE entity would have as a minimum the following attributes:

ORDER-LINE(***Order No, Product Code***, *Quantity Ordered*)

Order No provides a foreign key link to the *ORDER* entity and **Product Code** is a foreign key link to the *PRODUCT* entity. The third attribute is the Quantity Ordered for a particular product in a particular order.

During employment with an organisation an employee can have many jobs, a job in the organisation can be given to many employees.

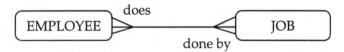

This M:N relationship is resolved by using an APPOINTMENT intersection entity:

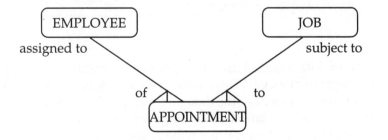

Note: The ends of the relationship on both ORDER and PRODUCT are now of **degree 1**, while the ends of both relationships on ORDER-LINE are of **degree N**.

An attribute of APPOINTMENT would be the date a particular employee is assigned to a particular job, another could be the salary given:

APPOINTMENT(***Emp Id, Job Id***, *Date Appointed, Salary*)

Question 7.22

Which is the correct resolution of the M:N relationship shown:

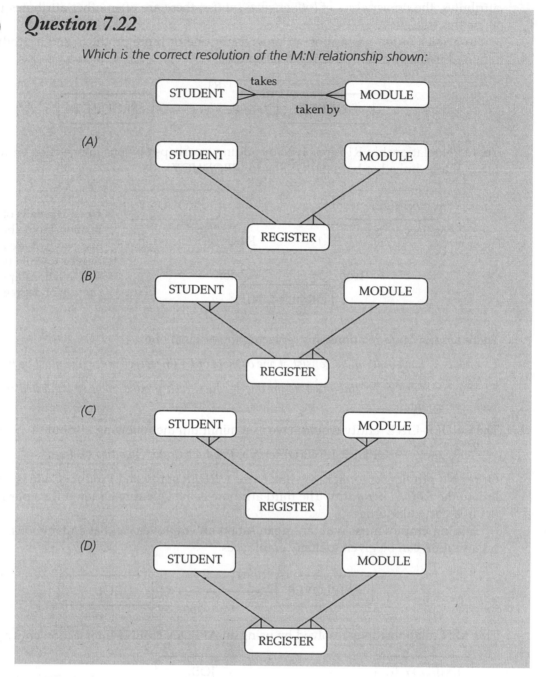

Data Dictionary

For most applications the volume of data collected during requirements analysis will be quite large and difficult for a single analyst to manage. When more than one analyst is working on the application the need to co-ordinate and manage the data and information collected is even greater. Analysts within a team will need to share their findings and make reference to each others data specifications and definitions. As the application develops, database designers and programmers may require access to this information. This extra data about the system and its data is collected and defined in a system *data dictionary*.

A data dictionary is a system *data catalogue* or *data warehouse* that lists and defines all elements of an application system. A simple manual data dictionary may just provide an alphabetic listing of data items and how they combine to make up records and will include a simple syntax to represent alternatives and repeated items. Computerised dictionaries will provide additional features for managing the application data and process structures.

The dictionary will record data collected in the requirements analysis activities of process (DFD) and data (ER) modelling:

- data attributes and any other basic data *elements*, including aliases for the same item, range specifications and validation rules;

- data types (*text, number, currency, date*) that are used to define the format or domain of data elements;

- entity names and definitions or other data *structures* that are combinations of data elements, together with any comment regarding the usage within a particular entity examples and volumetric data;

- relationship descriptions, including the entities associated, the link phrase and examples;

- data *flow* and data *store* descriptions;

- process descriptions that describe the input, output and logic processing of an application process.

By constructing a data dictionary an analyst should have the *name* and *description* of each data element and provide answers to such questions about a data item as:

- its size or length;

- its format or structure;

- its meaning and what its used for;

- other names (*aliases*) that may be used to reference it in the system;

- where it is used within the system.

The data element 'ROAD':	First line of an address
	House number and Name of Road
	Up to 30 text characters
The data structure 'ADDRESS':	Three lines plus post code
	ROAD
	TOWN
	COUNTY
	POST CODE
The data structure 'ORDER':	This is a confirmed request for stocked items received from an account customer.

Order No
    Order Taken Date
    Taken By Initials
    Order Required by Date
    Customer Authorisation No
    Account No of Customer
    Name of Customer
    Address of Customer
One or more of:
    Item Code
    Item Description
    Item Quantity

As the application is developed additional data can be added to the data dictionary such as information about the computer programs that process the application data. The dictionary can maintain cross-reference information associated individual items of data with the programs that process them. If an item should change its definition eg *a text field of two characters being increased in length to four characters,* the data dictionary will be able to indicate the effect of this change on pieces of software.

■ Templates

Document templates can be prepared for each component required within a dictionary and are filled in by the analyst. Using standard documents ensures completeness of data and consistency of presentation.

Figure 7.10 shows two such templates for entities and relationships, other templates can be used for defining attributes, domains or data types, any rules or constraints, process descriptions etc.

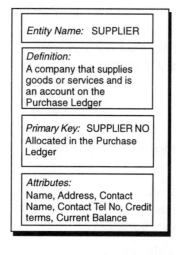
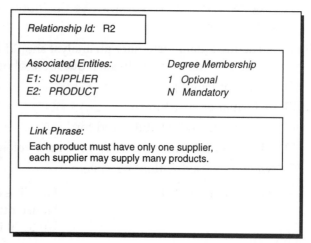

Figure 7.10 Entity and Relationship templates

■ Meta-data

The data dictionary can be implemented as a manual set of documents or as a computerised database, the content of a data dictionary is known as *meta-data* – data about data, its the database designers database. Relational database systems store data about the database in tables in the same way that it stores application data.

■ CASE Tool Support

CASE tools used to computerise diagram drawing for ERMs and DFDs will often have a data dictionary component that provides screen versions of document templates to enable each element of the system to be described. As diagrams are constructed using the tool all their components will automatically be entered into the data dictionary, after building the diagram further details about such things as attributes and their data types may be added by the analyst. The data stored by the CASE dictionary tool will be cross-referenced and analysts can examine and check out its contents for completeness and consistency. A variety of reports are usually provided to assist the analyst and provide hard-copy system documentation.

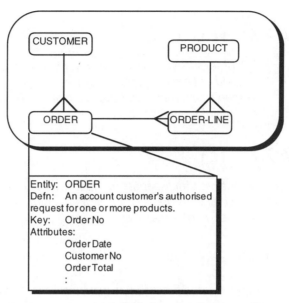

Figure 7.11 A CASE drawn ER diagram with Entity definition window

■ Schema Definition

A data base schema is a definition of the database that describes its logical components. For a relational database these will include definitions of its tables (entities), each column (attribute) and its data type (domain) together with any indexes (keys). Some CASE tools will use the contents of the data dictionary that refers to an ER model for an application to automatically generate a relational database *schema* using data definition commands of SQL.

 In Tasks 7.4 to 7.10 identify the entities, relationships, degree and membership of each relationship in each scenario and draw an E-R diagram. Suggest a primary key attribute and at least one other attribute for each entity.

Task 7.4   PC 1   *C3.3*

A parent has one or more children. A child can only attend one school but a a school but a school has many pupils. A parent may be a parent governor of one school and a school has many governors.

Task 7.5   PC 1   *C3.3*

A credit card company needs to know who holds each credit card. Normally they are interested in the card holder for whom the account is held. There may be several cards issued for one account each held by an authorised person. There may be different types of card having different interest rates and repayment terms.

Task 7.6   PC 1   C3.3

CVL divides its vehicles available for hire to customers into model types. Over a period of time a customer may hire many vehicles and a vehicle may be hired by many customers. Vehicles are maintained by different garages. A garage may maintain many vehicles.

Task 7.7   PC 1

Patients visit their dentist for treatment. A treatment may involve just one visit or several visits. Each visit is at an appointed time and the patient is billed on completion of a treatment.

Task 7.8   PC 1

An architect's practice has many projects. Each project is divided into one or more phases. Architects submit monthly timesheets made up of activity lines that show hours worked on phases of particular projects. Some architects are project managers.

Task 7.9   PC 1

A company's area sales office employs salespersons who are representatives for one or more customers. Customers place orders for one or more products that the company sells. In each area office on salesperson is the office manager.

Task 7.10   PC 1

A school has many students and offers many GCSE subjects. A GCSE subject may be taken by many students, and a student must take one or more GCSE subjects. In each subject taken the student receives a grade.

7.1.2 Normalisation

Introduction

Element 7.1.1 has described data modelling that results in producing *normalised* data groups of attributes each identified by a primary key. In this section a second technique of *Normalisation* is described that has very strong associations with the relational database model proposed by EF Codd. Normalisation is a bottom-up data modelling process that, like ER modelling, provides a framework for development of application systems that is independent of physical data storage and access requirements. The objective of normalisation is to produce a set of *normalised relations* that can be used to implement a relational database. It is a process that is complementary to ER modelling and provides a means of checking the completeness and consistency of the ER model. Before using a relational database package either normalise the application data or build an ER model or preferably do both!

■ Dr E. F Codd

The principles of normalisation were defined by Dr E F Codd of IBM in a research paper first published in 1970 and highlighted the need to separate the user view of data from its physical implementation. This, and other papers that followed, defined a new *Relational data base* model that allowed the user to view a database as a collection of *relations* made up of *tuples* and *attributes*, coupled to a formal Relational theory that had a Mathematical basis. Normalisation or Relational Data Analysis is generally associated with the *relational database* model but is really independent of the type of data base or file system to be used.

■ Tables, Columns and Rows

In Codd's relational model the data is stored in two-dimensional relations(*tables*) that consist of tuples(*rows*) and attribute(*columns*) – bracketed words are the more common terms of today's relational databases.

Relational Theory	Relational Database	Data Model	File Processing
Relation	Table	Entity	File
Tuple	Row	Occurrence	Record
Attribute	Column	Attribute	Field

Figure 7.12 Summary of terminology

The requirements of relation or table are:
- ❐ a *table* has a unique name to identify the data group stored;
- ❐ a *column* has a name to identify a particular attribute of the data group. A column name is unique to the table it belongs to, but the same name may be used to identify a column in another table. The values held in the same column of each row must all belong to the columns *domain* or data type;
- ❐ a *row* represents a single instance of the data group and must be uniquely identifiable;
- ❐ all values in the table are single-valued, each cell can only hold a single value, muli-valued or repeating groups are not allowed;
- ❐ different tables that have columns that take their values from the same domain may be *joined* via those columns.

Normalisation is a process, a series of steps that converts one table's (relation) representation of data that may have certain problems, into two or more tables that do not have those problems.

Question 7.23

Normalisation is also known as?

A) Eliminate Data Redundancy

B) Relational Data Analysis

C) Relational Formalisation

D) Normal Formalisation

■ Why Normalise?

Data held in an un-normalised format will usually contain a certain amount of data redundancy and suffer from undesirable side effects when being processed.

❒ *Redundancy* occurs when multiple copies of the same data are stored in the data base. This storage of the same data in different places results in a waste of storage space and more importantly the need to make multiple updates if the duplicated data changes.

❒ *Update side effects* are a direct result of holding multiple copies of the same data. If all copies of duplicated data are not changed during an update then the data becomes inconsistent. The update process will need to know about every copy of a piece of data and must ensure that ALL copies are changed. It can be very difficult to achieve this in many systems and may never be guaranteed.

❒ *Insert side effects* can occur when new data cannot be added to the system until some other event has taken place that causes the creation of some other associated data.

❒ *Delete side effects* can occur when the deletion of one piece of data results in the loss of some other associated data.

A company offers training courses to its employees and its branch offices keeps records of employees requests for enrolment on courses during the year. An employee can only enrol on one course at a time and each course has a standard fee and duration. Below is a table showing some instances of the stored training records of a branch office for the year.

Table Name: *Staff Training Courses*

Staff No	Emp Name	Room No	Tel No	Course Id	Course Title	Days	Grade	Paid	Fee in £s
66575	Cox	J130A	2267	C500	Concurrency	1	M	Y	125
69130	Watkins	J114	2648	C200	ER Modelling	3	M	Y	300
70200	Eyres	J114	2648	C300	ADT	2	D	N	225
86250	Mortimer	J224	2215	C200	ER Modelling	3		N	300
86425	Dunne	J224	2215	C400	OO Design	5		N	450
88500	Davies	J218	2436	C300	ADT	2	M	Y	225
92020	Stubbs	J224	2215	C200	ER Modelling	3	P	Y	300
93124	Norris	J123	2471	C300	ADT	2		Y	225

Figure 7.13 Staff Training Course Table

The format of the data in figure 7.13 exhibits the following side effects:

❒ Redundancy – All the data about courses C200 and C300 is repeated several times.

❒ Update side effect – the fee for course C300 has been increased from £300 to £330, this modification will require three updates to be made to each of the occurrences of course C300.

Question 7.24

How many changes are required to the above data if Dunne reports that the room telephone number is not 2215 but 2251?

A) One

B) Two

C) Three

D) None

❐ Insert side effect – a new training course C600, UNIX is offered. The data attributes about this course cannot be added until at least one employee enrols on it.

❐ Delete side effect – suppose that 86425, Dunne decides to withdraw from course C400. Because that employee is the only one enrolled, deletion of that employee will also lose all data about the course.

■ Normal Forms

The normalisation process is a step by step technique that transforms un-normalised data groupings through a series or *normal forms* into simplified normalised data groups from which the original data can be reconstructed.

The process starts by obtaining a representation of the un-normalised data from application source documents such as forms and reports. Always use documents with actual data values entered on them, never carry out normalisation from blank documents that just have headings on them. The actual data will aid understanding of the structure of a document and give meaning to fields on it.

The un-normalised data is first represented as a list of attributes which are then transposed through a series of normal forms.

Each stage of the process transforms data from one Normal Form to the next Normal Form.

Un-Normalised Form	UNF or	0NF	*High*
First Normal Form	FNF	1NF	
			Data Redundancy
Second Normal Form	SNF	2NF	
Third Normal Form	TNF	3NF	*Low*

■ Objectives of Normalisation

The process of normalisation aims to produce a set of well-formed data structures that meet the following objectives:

❐ they provide non-loss decomposition of data or information. This means that having performed normalisation it is possible to regenerate the original un-normalised data;

❐ they contain a minimum amount of data redundancy;

❐ they are NOT susceptible to data maintenance side effects that result in data becoming inconsistent or even lost.

Question 7.25

Which of the following is NOT a valid reason for normalising data?

A) Reduce data redundancy

B) Cut out maintenance side effects

C) Make processing of data more efficient

D) Simplify the structure of data

■ Un-normalised Form UNF or 0NF

The first stage of normalisation is to make a list of the un-normalised data items (attributes) associated with a document. Forms, reports and existing computer screens are usually structured in this way and they are a good source to provide a starting point for the normalisation process. Figure 7.14 shows a UNF list prepared from a *Purchase Order* by listing the documents field names and looking out for items that are repeated in a group.

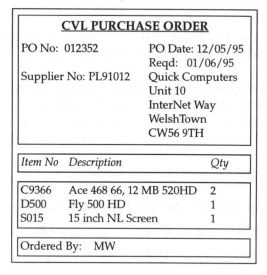

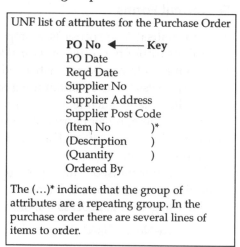

Figure 7.14 Step 1 – Document to UNF Attribute list

Knowledge about the attributes, the application process within the enterprise and any rules that may apply is required. For attributes, it is necessary to know their possible values, any format they may have, their meaning and how they may be associated with other attributes on the document.

Always use documents with real data on them, do NOT use blanks having no data filled in. Completed documents will assist understanding and may often provide additional information not explicitly represented on the form. A user may often write additional data where there is no column or box heading for it, in other words there exists other important attributes that the document doesn't cater for.

■ Choose a Key

Having obtained a list of un-normalised data attributes, either choose a *simple key* of one attribute or a *compound key* that is a combination of attributes to uniquely identify **one** instance of this particular data group. Try not to invent a non-existent attribute to do this, use compound keys to achieve the unique identification. In figure 7.14 *PO No* has been chosen to uniquely identify each Purchase Order data group.

■ Functional Dependence

This is an association between two attributes within the attribute list, where one attribute is dependent on another in some way for its meaning. An attribute 'Y' is said to be functionally dependent on attribute 'X' when if given a value of 'X' the value of 'Y' will also be known. Attribute 'X' is said to be the determinant of attribute 'Y'.

> *Staff No is the determinant of Employee Name.*
> *Course Id is the determinant of Course Title, Course Duration and Course Fee.*
> *Po No is the determinant of PO date, Reqd date and Customer.*

Staff No is NOT the determinant of Course Id or Course Name.
Course Id is NOT the determinant of Staff No or Employee Name.
PO No is NOT the determinant of Customer Name.

■ Determinancy Diagram

The training register kept by a company has revealed the following attribute list:

Staff No, Name, Room No, Internal Tel No, **Course Id**, Title, Duration, Fee, Grade, Paid Indicator

A compound key of the attributes *Staff No* and *Course Id* uniquely identify each instance of an entry in the register. The functional dependency of the other attributes are shown below:

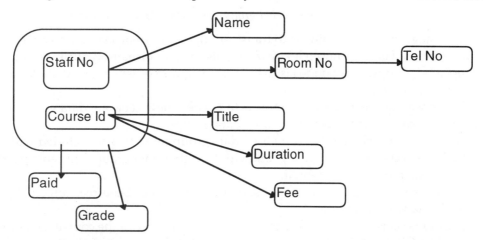

Figure 7.15 Functional Dependency Diagram

Figure 7.15 shows that *Grade* is dependent on *Staff No plus Course Id* **not** just the *Staff No* of an employee.

Questions 7.26 to 7.28 refer to figure 7.15

Question 7.26

Duration is dependent on which of the following?
A) Staff No
B) Staff No/Course Id
C) Course Id
D) Title

Question 7.27

Which of the following is the determinant of Tel No?
A) Staff No
B) Room No
C) Staff No/Course Id
D) Name

Question 7.28

Which of the following is the determinant of Paid ?
A) Staff No
B) Course Id
C) Staff No/Course Id
D) Grade

■ First Normal Form   1NF or FNF

'Remove repeated groups to a separate data structure'

The first stage of normalisation is to transform the un-normalised data to a First Normal Form representation. Having chosen a key for the list of un-normalised attributes they are scanned for repeated groups. A good idea is to bracket the group of repeating attributes and mark them with an '*' as in figure 7.14.

The repeating attributes are removed to create a new separate data group leaving behind the non-repeating attributes in their own data group.

The key of the original un-normalised data group must also be included with the repeating attributes, it becomes a foreign key link with the other data group. This ensures that the original UNF data group can be rebuilt.

Consider the training course data shown earlier. It has been rearranged slightly to group the staff data within courses.

The *Course Id* is chosen as a key to identify each instance of the course data group. For some courses like C200 there is now a repeated group of staff data – *Staff No, Emp Name, Room No, Tel No, Grade, Paid*.

Course Id	Course Title	Days	Fee in £s	Staff No	Emp Name	Room No	Tel No	Grade	Paid
C200	ER Modelling	3	300	69130	Watkins	J114	2648	M	Y
				86250	Mortimer	J224	2215		N
				92020	Stubbs	J224	2215	P	Y
C300	ADT	2	225	70200	Eyres	J114	2648	D	N
				88500	Davies	J218	2436	M	Y
				93124	Norris	J123	2471		Y
C400	OO Design	5	450	86425	Dunne	J224	2215		N
C500	Concurrency	1	125	66575	Cox	J130A	2267	M	Y

Figure 7.16 Training Course Data rearranged to show repeating group

Break out the repeated group of attributes taking with them the key of the original complete un-normalised data group:

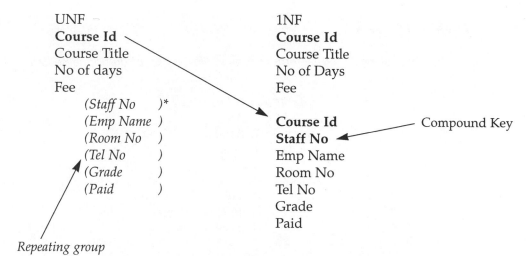

UNF
Course Id
Course Title
No of days
Fee
    (Staff No   )*
    (Emp Name)
    (Room No   )
    (Tel No   )
    (Grade   )
    (Paid   )

Repeating group

1NF
Course Id
Course Title
No of Days
Fee

Course Id
Staff No   ←   Compound Key
Emp Name
Room No
Tel No
Grade
Paid

The original data is now in First Normal Form, the single un-normalised data group has been transformed into two data groups *Course* and *Course-Staff*. The key of the Course-Staff data group is a compound one made up of Course Id and Staff No. The attribute *Course Id* of the Course-Staff data group is also a foreign key and establishes a link between the two data groups so that the original data group can be rebuilt from these two data sources.

Data group: **Course**   *Key:* **Course Id**

Course Id	Course Title	Days	Fee
C200	ER Modelling	3	300
C300	ADT	2	225
C400	OO Design	5	450
C500	Concurrency	1	125

Data group: **Course -Staff**   *Key:* **Course Id/Staff No**

Course Id	Staff No	Emp Name	Room No	Tel No	Grade	Paid
C200	69130	Watkins	J114	2648	M	Y
C200	86250	Mortimer	J224	2215		N
C200	92020	Stubbs	J224	2215	P	Y
C300	70200	Eyres	J114	2648	D	N
C300	88500	Davies	J218	2436	M	Y
C300	93124	Norris	J123	2471		Y
C400	86425	Dunne	J224	2215		N
C500	66575	Cox	J130A	2267	M	Y

Figure 7.17 Training Course data in 1NF Tables

With the data in the form of figure 7.17 several drawbacks have already been overcome:

❑ the course data is stored only once so that data duplication is reduced;

❑ a new course can now exist without having any staff take it.

Task 7.11 PC 2

Produce first normal form from the following set of un-normalised attributes.

UNF
Project code
Project Type
Project Title
Delivery date
    (Staff No   )*
    (Staff Name   )
    (Salary   )
    (Date Joined Project)
    (Time Allocation   )

Task 7.12 PC 2

UNF
Ward Name
Ward Type
Ward Tel No
No of beds
    (Bed No   )*
    (Patient Admit Id   )
    (Patient Name   )
    (Patient Tel No   )
    (Admit Date   )

■ First to Second Normal Form   2NF or SNF

'Break out part key dependencies'

This transformation is only concerned with those data groups that have a compound key, an identifier that is made up from more than one field. The dependency of each attribute in that data group is examined to check if it is dependent on the whole key or just a part of the key.

The *Course-Staff* data group has a compound key of *Course Id/Staff No*, the dependency of each remaining attribute of this data group is checked. Some may have the whole key as a determinant but others have only part of the key as a determinant, *the attributes that have a part key determinancy are broken out with their determinant.*

Course Id/Staff No is the determinant of *Grade* and *Paid*, so these are full-key dependent and are left alone.

Staff No is the determinant of *Name, Room No, Tel No*, so these attributes are part-key dependent and must be broken out with *Staff No*.

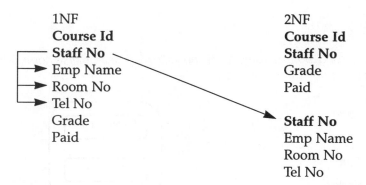

The *Course* data group has a simple key so is unaffected by the transformation to second normal form:

Course Id
Course Title
No of days
Fee

Course Id
Course Title
No of Days
Fee

In Second Normal Form there are now three data groups, *Course*, *Course-Staff* and *Staff*. The Staff No attribute of Course-Staff is a foreign key and establishes a link to the Staff data group.

Course Id	Course Title	Days	Fee in £s
C200	ER Modelling	3	300
C300	ADT	2	225
C400	OO Design	5	450
C500	Concurrency	1	125

Course Id	Staff No	Grade	Paid
C200	69130	M	Y
C200	86250		N
C200	92020	P	Y
C300	70200	D	N
C300	88500	M	Y
C300	93124		Y
C400	86425		N
C500	66575	M	Y

Data group: **Staff**
Key: **Staff No**

Staff No	Emp Name	Room No	Tel No
69130	Watkins	J114	2648
86250	Mortimer	J224	2215
92020	Stubbs	J224	2215
70200	Eyres	J114	2648
88500	Davies	J218	2436
93124	Norris	J123	2471
86425	Dunne	J224	2215
66575	Cox	J130A	2267

Figure 7.18 Training Course data in 2NF tables

With the data in the form of figure 7.18 another drawback has been overcome:

❏ A new member of staff can now exist without having to do a course

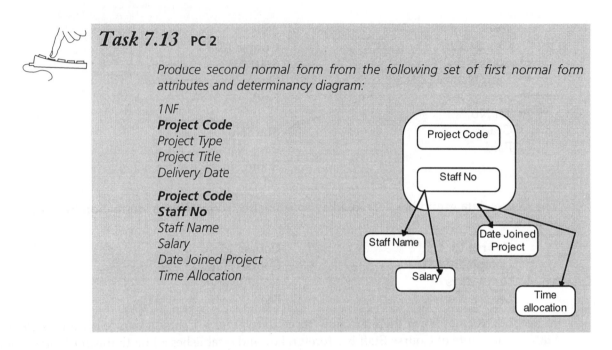

Task 7.13 PC 2

Produce second normal form from the following set of first normal form attributes and determinancy diagram:

1NF
Project Code
Project Type
Project Title
Delivery Date

Project Code
Staff No
Staff Name
Salary
Date Joined Project
Time Allocation

■ Second to Third Normal Form   3NF or TNF

'Break out non-key dependencies.'

This transformation applies to all data groups. In each data group a non-key attribute is examined to check if it is dependent on some other non-key attribute.

In the Course data group all attributes are dependent on the key Course Id.

In the Course-Staff data group both attributes are dependent on the whole key.

However in the Staff data group the attribute Tel No is dependent on another non-key attribute Room No and is not dependent on the key Staff No, it is Room No that is the determinant of Tel No. The determinant attribute and its dependent attribute(s) are broken out to form a new data group.

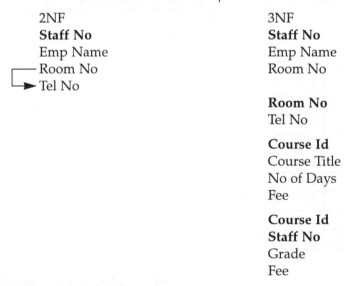

2NF
Staff No
Emp Name
Room No
Tel No

3NF
Staff No
Emp Name
Room No

Room No
Tel No

Course Id
Course Title
No of Days
Fee

Course Id
Staff No
Grade
Fee

The *Room No* attribute of the *Staff* data group is now a foreign key linking to the *Room* data group.

In Third Normal Form there are now four data groups each having its own key and linked together by their foreign key attributes.

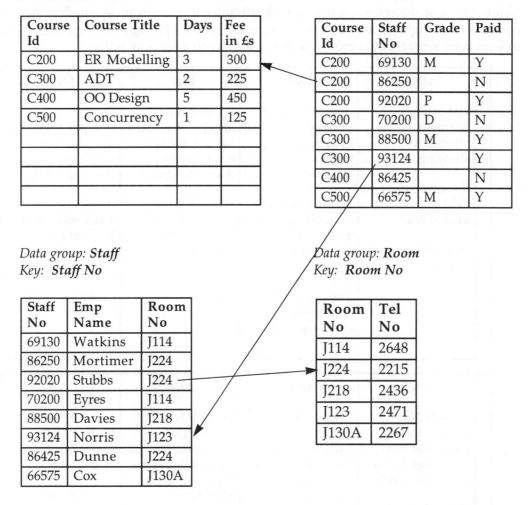

Course Id	Course Title	Days	Fee in £s
C200	ER Modelling	3	300
C300	ADT	2	225
C400	OO Design	5	450
C500	Concurrency	1	125

Course Id	Staff No	Grade	Paid
C200	69130	M	Y
C200	86250		N
C200	92020	P	Y
C300	70200	D	N
C300	88500	M	Y
C300	93124		Y
C400	86425		N
C500	66575	M	Y

Data group: **Staff**
Key: **Staff No**

Data group: **Room**
Key: **Room No**

Staff No	Emp Name	Room No
69130	Watkins	J114
86250	Mortimer	J224
92020	Stubbs	J224
70200	Eyres	J114
88500	Davies	J218
93124	Norris	J123
86425	Dunne	J224
66575	Cox	J130A

Room No	Tel No
J114	2648
J224	2215
J218	2436
J123	2471
J130A	2267

Figure 7.19 Training Course data in 3NF Tables

This final transformation shown in figure 7.19 has removed the data duplication caused by repeating the Tel No attribute with the Room. It also allows a Room to exist without having any staff occupy it.

The four data groups of Third Normal Form are said to be fully normalised and can also be used to construct an ER model where each data group is an entity and the foreign key links are relationships.

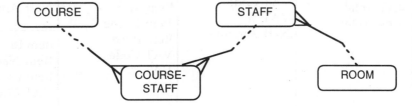

■ A Document Template for Normalisation

Divide a sheet of paper into four columns one for each normal form. Label them as shown in figure 7.20. List the set of un-normalised attributes in the left most column, then fill in the columns to the right as normalisation progresses. Identify Primary keys, repeating groups and foreign keys, separate data groups within a stage with a horizontal line.

UNF	1NF	2NF	3NF
List of un-normalised attributes showing: the chosen key field in bold or underlined; repeating groups in (...) *	Attributes split into separate data groups having broken out repeated groups. Identify keys of each group and any foreign key links using @ Key of repeated group will be a compound one of at least two fields	Further data groups created by having broken out part-key dependencies. Identify keys of each group and any foreign key links @	Further data groups created by breaking out non-key dependencies. All groups have a key and foreign key links @ clearly shown.

UNF	1NF	2NF	3NF
Invoice No Invoice Date Customer No Customer Name Customer Addr (Item Id)* (Item Name) (Item Price) (Quantity) (VAT Code) (VAT %) (Nett Amount) Nett Total VAT Total Gross Total	**Invoice No** Invoice Date Customer No Customer Name Customer Addr Nett Total VAT Total Gross Total **Invoice No @** **Item Id** Item Name Item Price Quantity VAT Code VAT % Nett Amount	**Invoice No** Invoice Date Customer No Customer Name Customer Addr Nett Total VAT Total Gross Total **Invoice No @** **Item Id @** Quantity Nett Amount **Item Id** Item Name Item Price VAT Code VAT %	**Invoice No** Invoice Date Customer No @ Nett Total VAT Total Gross Total **Customer No** Customer Name Customer Addr **Invoice No @** **Item Id @** Quantity Nett Amount **Item Id** Item Name Item Price VAT Code @ **VAT Code** VAT %

Figure 7.20 A template for Normalisation

Task 7.14 PC 2

Produce third normal form from the set of second normal form attributes and determinancy diagram:

2NF
Order No
Customer Acc No
Customer Name
Customer Address
Order Date
Order Total

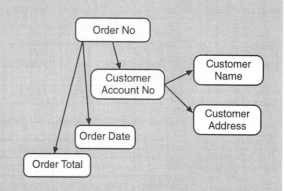

Task 7.15 PC 2

Normalise though 1NF, 2NF to 3NF the following un-normalised data group and data dependency shown about Research/Technical Reports produced by staff of a college. A single report is identified by a unique report number, is in a particular field of interest and may have several authors:

UNF
Report No
Report Title
Report Type
Date Submitted
Field Code
Field Title
    Author Staff No
    Author Name
    Author E-mail
    Department Id
    Department Name
    Room No
    Tel No

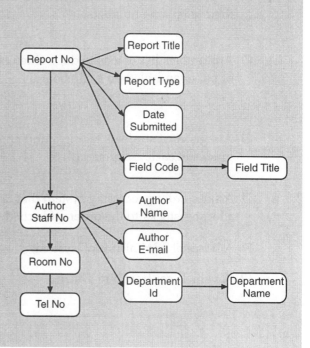

Task 7.16 PC 2

The table below shows data instances of projects worked on by employees of a small software house. Produce a list of attributes in UNF showing clearly the primary key for the data group and those attributes that repeat in an instance and carry out the first step of normalisation to 1NF.

Identify the functional dependencies implicit in the table and complete the normalisation to 3NF.

Emp Staff No	Staff Name	Dept Id	Dept Name	Project Id	Project Title	Project Manager Id	Man Name	Emp Start Date	Emp Charge Rate (£s)
8503	Lennon	15	Analysis	94010	PP Archs	8402	Smith	01/04/1994	300
				93021	M Printers	8402	Smith	14/09/1993	275
				93004	B Garages	9001	Roberts	07/02/1993	275
8910	Starr	21	Design	94010	PP Archs	8402	Smith	08/08/1994	225
				94015	AS Jewels	9001	Roberts	14/12/1994	250
9002	Jones	15	Analysis	94010	PP Archs	8402	Smith	22/01/1995	350
9005	Evans	18	Testing	93004	B Garages	9001	Roberts	02/01/1995	200

7.1.3 Relational database Structures

Data Base Management Systems

■ What is a Data Base?

A data base is a collection of data that is organised to provide a user with easy access to information. Examples of data bases in every day use are:

❐ A person's filofax having lists of contacts and their telephone numbers;

❐ A plumbers list of jobs to do, written on pieces of paper and filed on a clip board;

❐ A register of students taking a unit and their grades in each assignment;

❐ A sales order processing system that takes customer orders, allocates stocks to the order and schedules its delivery;

❐ A hospital administration system;

❐ A vehicle contract hire system.

A database system is a self-describing organised collection of integrated data records. This means that within a database management system (DBMS) are stored:

❏ *the source data of user applications, stored in the form of tables and fields;*

❏ *data associations that represent relationships that exist amongst the stored data and integrates that data;*

❏ *meta-data or stored data dictionary that defines the data stored and the structure of that data.*

■ DBMS Objectives

The objectives of a DBMS are to:

❏ *provide facilities for data definition, data storage and data manipulation;*

❏ *ensure the accuracy and consistency of stored data;*

❏ *ensure data integrity by protecting it from damage by authorised users;*

❏ *ensure data security by protecting it from unauthorised users;*

❏ *make application development easier, more cost effective and produce more flexible systems.*

■ Types of Databases

DBMSs are applicable in many different ways throughout an organisation. There are three categories:

❏ Personal or Individual Databases

These are used by an individual within the organisation to keep track of entities that are of importance to him or her. These databases have the following characteristics:

Single-user, Micro-computer based, End-user developed, Piece-meal development, Little if any central control, Duplication of data and activities, Single application per data base, Relatively small data volumes, Simple views of data, Single record group access and Basic security data access requirements.

❏ Workgroup or Department Database

These store and process data that are important to an integrated group or department within an organisation. This workgroup is usually responsible for carrying out the day to day activities of some organisational function. The database is used to integrate their activities and keep track of entities important to the workgroup. These databases have the following characteristics:

Multi-user, Skilled user population, Clerical lower management users, Mini or Micro computer based, Networked or Star LAN configuration, Specialist development, Integrated organisational function application, Medium to large data volumes, Integrated views of data, Multi-record group access, Shared data access, sophisticated security integrity requirements, database administration requirements.

❏ Organisational Database

These store and process data that are important throughout the organisation, from the senior executive management, through middle management down to clerical or shop-floor operations level. They integrate the activities of many departments, they are multi-functional and keep track of entities of importance to all aspects of the organisation. Within this type of system the activities of one user workgroup can have an affect on the activities of another. These databases have the following characteristics:

Multi-user, Naive or casual or skilled users, Clerical to top-management users, Mini-mainframe based, Star or distributed LAN/WAN configuration, Specialist developed, Multi application,

405

Large to very large data volumes, Multiple views of data, Shared data access, Major security and integrity requirements, Major database administration requirements.

■ Database Users

Except for single-user databases a DBMS will need to be able to support a variety of users from the very naive to the more sophisticated database expert. The user requirements will stretch from simple very limited data access to full data base administration and development activities. Access to the database may be local or remote, be on-line or batch, support client server. The users can be classified into groups that are dependent on their degree of database expertise and/or their requirements for interaction with the database:

❑ *Naive end-users*, these may not be and need not be aware of the presence of the DBMS. The user will require guidance through each step of database access, perform a very limited set of operations, have access to a precise portion of the database.

An example of such a user group are users of the 'hole in the wall' banking machines. Their use is menu structured, they provide a simple and small set of allowable operations and provide access to individual accounts only. They also have a simple and reasonably effective security system to prevent unauthorised access.

❑ *On-line end-users*, these are more specialised users who communicate with the database either directly via an on-line workstation driven by the DBMS itself, or via a user interface driven by an application program. These users are aware of the database and will have a certain degree of expertise in the limited interaction that they are permitted. The more expert of this user group may actually be able to carry out ad-hoc data access using a data manipulation language such as SQL.

❑ *Application Developers*, this group includes database designers and application programmers who are responsible for developing and maintaining the application software and user interfaces. The application software may be developed either in a 3GL host language that has extensions to provide database access, several 3GLs now support embedded SQL or using a 4GL application development environment that partners a particular DBMS (Oracle SQL*Forms) or can be integrated to a DBMS (Focus).

❑ *Database Administrator (DBA)*, this is an individual or group who administer the database by exerting centralised control over the whole database and its use. The DBA has highly specialised knowledge of the DBMS, its applications and their use of the database. It takes responsibility for granting access rights and other aspects of database security, backup and recovery. The DBA is the sole authority for database changes, modifications and maintenance of meta-data.

Task 7.17 PC 1, 2 & 3   *C3.2*

In your school or college or any organisation to which you have access, find out if a database system is used. Write a short report of no more than 500 words about what the system is used for, who are its users, what software and hardware is used and how it was developed.

■ DBMS Components

A DBMS is a large and complex software system. It often requires extensive disk space for both it's own software components and it's data that will tend to grow in volume over time. Where on-line backup is required then the data storage requirements will more than double. There are several main components:

- ❑ *The DBMS Engine*, this is a core component of the DBMS and it's primary function is to convert logical input-output requests from the other software applications to physical input-output requests that are passed on to the resident operating system. It is also responsible for memory and input-output buffer management.

- ❑ *Database Tools*, these are pieces of software that are used for defining, modifying and generally administering the database. These support the database data definition language and data manipulation language facilities; the user access rights; meta-data definition, maintenance, querying and reporting; database monitoring and tuning; backup and recovery facilities.

- ❑ *Processing Interface/Query Processor*, that provides access facilities to stored data that is utilised by end-users directly or through application software. It will contain libraries of routines for use with 3GL host languages, host language pre-compilers. The query processor may share some responsibility with the DBMS engine for optimising user access queries.

- ❑ *Application Development tools*, for the development of end-user applications. These include screen/form, report and menu painters, code generators. This software component may be integrated as part of the complete DBMS package or may be a third party add-on that can interface to several different DBMSs. These tools will require access to the database meta-data.

■ Advantages of Databases

Creating applications using a database management system offers several advantages for both the applications developer and the applications users:

- ❑ Centralised management and control over an organisations data. Data is a valuable resource of any organisation and like any other asset should be managed;
- ❑ Provides a degree of data independence from application software easing software maintenance problems;
- ❑ Can reduce data redundancy and provide better data consistency;
- ❑ Provides data sharing, greater data availability and application integration;
- ❑ Improved data integrity and security;
- ❑ Can resolve conflict and enhance adherence to standards;
- ❑ Can improve application development productivity.

■ Disadvantages of Databases

As with many other things what we gain in having the above advantages we pay for with some drawbacks that are associated with using a DBMS:

- ❑ DBMS software can be costly. Single user Micro databases are reasonably cheap, their networked brothers are more expensive and there may be several hidden costs. Multi-user DBMSs are very expensive products;
- ❑ DBMS software is greedy and can eat up system resources;
- ❑ Backup and recovery procedures may be quite complex and will impose a significant overhead on both facilities and operation;
- ❑ Specialised staff required for both application development and database administration;

- Data and usage interference by one application on another and organisational conflict;
- Performance issues, can be slow, may optimised across whole user group not just one application.

Question 7.29

Why do users of database applications often complain about their performance, that they take longer to do certain processes than conventional file applications?

Relational Database Systems

A relational database is one type of database system that stores its data in tables of columns and rows. Before using such a system the database must be logically designed and this design defined using the facilities of a relational database product. How the logical design is physically implemented will depend on the database software product and is of little concern to the majority of the database users be they application developers or users.

Logical Relational Database Design

The *ER data model* coupled with the process of *normalisation* provides a *conceptual* view of the data and its relationships necessary to meet the requirements of an application system. A Relational Database holds data in *tables* and *logical design* requires representing the data model in table form.

■ Relational Table

A relational *table* is the implementation of an entity type, it is composed of:
- *columns* that represent entity *attributes*;
- *rows* that represent entity *instances*;
- has a unique *name* within the database application;
- each column within a table should have a unique name but column names need not be distinct amongst a set of tables. Column names common to several tables should be qualified with the table name and use a dot (.) operator to ensure uniqueness – *table-name.column-name*;
- A *primary key* for a table will enable each row to be uniquely identified. The primary key may be a *simple* one of one column or a *compound* one composed of several columns.

Each entity of the conceptual model is represented by a table and its attributes by columns. Relationships are either inferred from common attributes that link associated entity tables through the use of *foreign keys* or will require their own table that will include foreign key links to associated entity tables.

■ Database Schema

A *schema* is the logical definition of a database is described using a Data Definition Language or DDL of a particular database management system. The schema is stored in the computer and used by the database software during the building and running of applications.

■ Subschema views

Subschemas can be derived from the schema to provide a definition of a portion of the database needed by an individual piece of application software. The subschema allows the application to *view* only the parts of the database it is allowed to access.

■ Objectives of Logical Database Design

When specifying a database the designer should bear in mind the following objectives:

❒ to minimise the number of tables subject to the rule that data is in at least First Normal Form;

❒ each row of a table must have a unique identifier, its primary key and there must not be any rows in a table having a primary key with a null value.

ER Models to Relational Tables.

For a simple model involving two entities with one relationship between them, in addition to the number of entities the number of tables required depends on:

❒ the degree of the relationship – 1:1 or 1:N or N:M;

❒ the membership of the each entity within the relationship – mandatory or optional.

■ 1:1   Relationships

Consider two entities EMPLOYEE and CAR having the following attributes:

EMPLOYEE   (***staff-id***, *name, department, birth-date, salary*)
CAR   (***reg-no***, *model, mileage, tax-month*)

❒ Both entities have mandatory membership

'Every employee has a company car, every company car is used by an employee'

EITHER

One table EMPCAR is created to hold the attributes of both entities the employee and the car. The primary key could be either the employee's staff-id or the car's reg-no attributes.

EMPCAR   (***staff_id***, *name, reg-no, department, birth-date, salary, model, mileage, tax-month*)

Always ask the question 'is this really one single entity?', if there is any doubt **DO NOT** merge into one table.

OR

Two tables are used one for each entity, the relationship is established by posting the primary key attribute of one entity as an additional foreign key attribute of the other.

EMPLOYEE1 (***staff-id***, *name, department, birth-date, salary*)
CAR1   (***reg-no***, *model, mileage, tax-month, staff-id*)

409

or
EMPLOYEE2 (***staff-id***, *name, department, birth-date, salary, <u>reg-no</u>*)
CAR2　　　　(***reg-no***, *model, mileage, tax-month*)

❏ One entity membership is mandatory, other entity has optional membership.

'Every company car must be used by an employee, but not all employees have use of a company car.'

The CAR entity has mandatory membership of the relationship, the EMPLOYEE entity has non-mandatory membership.

Use two tables, one for each entity type. Post the primary key attribute of the entity having optional membership (EMPLOYEE.staff-id) as a foreign key attribute of the entity having mandatory membership. The foreign key attribute must never be null.

EMPLOYEE3 (***staff-id***, *name, department, birth-date, salary*)
CAR3　　　　(***reg-no***, *model, mileage, tax-month, <u>staff-id</u>*)

The attribute *staff-id* of table CAR3 must never be null.

❏ Both entity types have optional membership.

'A Company car may be used by an employee, an employee may have use of a company car. There may be company cars not assigned to any employee.'

Use three tables, one for each entity and one to represent the relationship when a company car is assigned to an employee.

EMPLOYEE4 (***staff-id***, *name, department, birth-date, salary*)
CAR4　　　　(***reg-no***, *model, mileage, tax-month*)
CAR-EMP　　(***reg-no***, *staff-id*)　　or　　EMP-CAR(***staff-id***, *reg-no*)

This is a preferred solution particularly if there is some other attribute(s) associated with the assignment of a car to an employee such as *date-assigned* and *usage-mileage*. It will also accommodate the possibility of a change in the degree of the relationship should a car be re-assigned to another employee.

CAR-EMP　　(***reg-no***, *staff-id, date-assigned, usage-mileage*)

OR

Use two tables as above and allow a null value for the foreign key attribute. If there was additional associated data attributes, these would also need to be stored as extra attributes in one of the tables and null values allowed for these as well:

EMPLOYEE5 (***staff-id***, *name, department, birth-date, salary, <u>reg-no</u>, date-assigned, usage-mileage*)
CAR5　　　　(***reg-no***, *model, mileage, tax-month*)

The EMPLOYEE5 table is not in Third Normal Form, however for logical design of relational data bases data need only be in First Normal Form.

Question 7.30

Normalise EMPLOYEE5 to Third Normal Form.

❐ **1:M Relationships**

Consider the two entities WARD and PATIENT having the attributes shown:

> WARD   (***ward-id***, *name, type, no-of-beds*)
> PATIENT   (***patient-id***, *name, address, birth-date, admit-date*)

❐ *One* entity membership is optional, *Many* entity has mandatory membership

'*A ward may contain many patients, a patient must be assigned to one ward.*'

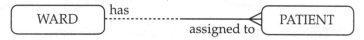

Two tables are required, one for each entity with the primary key attribute of the *One* entity posted as an additional foreign key attribute of the *Many* entity.

> WARD1   (***ward-id***, *name, type, no-of-beds*)
> PATIENT1   (***patient-id***, *name, address, birth-date, admit-date, <u>ward-id</u>*)

❐ *One* entity membership is optional, *Many* entity has optional membership

'*A ward may contain many patients, however a patient may be assigned to a ward. Some patients are not assigned to any ward.*'

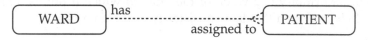

EITHER

Use two tables but allow the foreign key attribute *ward-id* to have null values, this also requires *admit-date* to be allowed a null value

OR

A preferred design is to use a third table to represent the relationship. The primary key attributes of both entities are posted as foreign key attributes of the new table. The primary key of this table will be a compound one of the the two posted attributes and null values would not be allowed. Other attributes may be associated with the relationship and would make up other columns in the table.

> WARD2   (***ward-id***, *name, type, no-of-beds*)
> PATIENT2   (***patient-id***, *name, address, birth-date, admit-date*)
> ADMIT   (***<u>ward-id, patient-id</u>***, *admit-date*)

Question 7.31

In ADMIT why are ward-id and patient-id in bold and underlined?

■ N:M Relationships

Regardless of membership rules three tables are required, one for each entity and one for the relationship. The primary key of the relationship table will be a compound one made up of from the primary key attributes of each entity table. Additional attributes of the relationship would be columns within its table.

Normally the ER model will have resolved any M:N relationships and replaced them with an intersection entity and two 1:N relationships which would be represented in the logical design using the rules given earlier.

'A patient may be given several drugs as a treatment for their illness, a drug may be issued to several patients.'

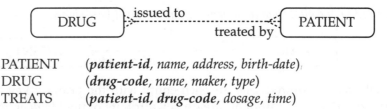

PATIENT	(***patient-id***, *name, address, birth-date*),
DRUG	(***drug-code***, *name, maker, type*)
TREATS	(***patient-id, drug-code***, *dosage, time*)

❐ Entity Integrity Rule

A primary key must have a unique value for each row of a table. A primary key must never have a null value.

❐ Referential Integrity Rule

A foreign key attribute of a table must either have a null value or have a value that matches a primary key value of the table to which it points. Enforcement of these two rules help maintain the data consistency of the data base.

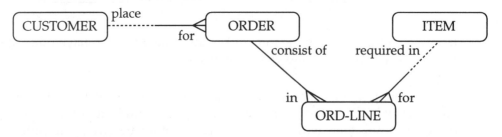

The table implementation of a customer order data model is shown below. The table primary keys are in bold and foreign keys are underlined. The lines connecting the tables show how they are linked together to implement the model.

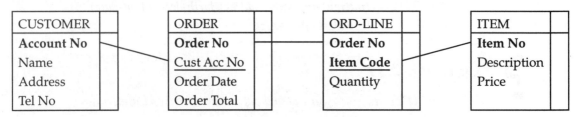

Figure 7.21 A table representation showing foreign key referential integrity links

Task 7.18 PC 3

Produce a skeleton table structure for the following ER model and entity attribute lists:

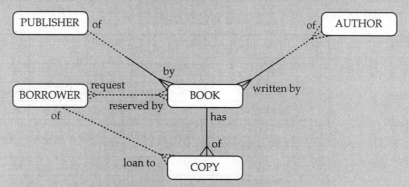

PUBLISHER	(**pub-code**, name, address, tel-no)
AUTHOR	(**author-id**, name, birth-date, nationality)
BOOK	(**ISBNo**, title, edition, pub-date, class, price)
BORROWER	(**member-no**, name, address, tel-no, birth-date, status)
COPY	(**access-no**, aquired-date, price)

A book copy on loan to a borrower must be returned on or before the loan due date else a fine is levied on the loan. When a borrower reserves a book the date and time the reservation is made is recorded.

Task 7.19 PC 3

Design logical database table structures for any of the data models you have produced earlier in this unit.

■ Indexes

Many operations on a relational database will require the retrieval from a table of a row or collection of rows that satisfy some selction criteria, other operations will require the retrieval of data from more than one table based on some common characteristic. Where large tables are used the retrieval times may become excessive and provide a poor response time.

Creating table indexes and using them to retrieve rows can greatly speed things up and get response times down. Which fields to index in a table is an important aspect of physical database design and will depend on the type of retrieval activities to be performed. In most cases selected fields will be used for permanent indexes to speed up the high volume processing activities. Some databases allow indexes to be created, used to improve a particular processing activity and then dropped.

However, indexes take up space, they are effectively small tables of two columns, the *key value* and the *row number* where that value is stored. Where a table has multiple indexes created for it, insert of a new row or update of row fields may result in excessive activity to update each index. There are databases in existance where the space required for indexing is as big or exceeds that required for storing actual data.

■ Primary Key Indexes

Each database table must have a primary key that uniquely identifies each row. It is customary for all but the smallest of tables to create an index on the primary key. Use of the index will speed up selection of rows from one table if the primary key is specified and vastly improve multi-table retrieval through use of foreign keys.

Row No	Reg Number	Make	Model	Body Type	Price in £s	Eng Type
1	M111AAA	FORD	Mondeo 1.6LX	H	12000	P
2	M222BBB	FORD	Mondeo 1.8GL	S	13500	P
3	M333CCC	FORD	Escort 1.7TD	E	11500	D
4	L444ZZZ	ROVER	620i	S	13400	P
5	L555XXX	ROVER	620i	S	13400	P
6	L666YYY	VW	GOLF 1.6CL	H	10500	P
7	M444DDD	VW	Passat 1.8TD	E	12500	D
8	M555EEE	BMW	318i Touring	E	16500	P
9	L111GGG	RENAULT	19TD	H	11500	D
10	M666FFF	RENAULT	Clio Oasis 1.9D	H	8500	D

Figure 7.21 Data Table Structure, Reg Number as Primary Key

Reg No	Rec No
L111GGG	9
L444ZZZ	4
L555XXX	5
L666YYY	6
M111AAA	1
M222BBB	2
M333CCC	3
M444DDD	7
M555EEE	8
M666FFF	10

Each key item in the index will be unique (there will not be any duplicate key values), there will be one entry for each row of the table and the index is usually held in sequential key order, while the data in the actual table may be in the order in which the rows were inserted.

Figure 7.22 Primary Key index table

■ Secondary or Alternative Keys

Indexes can also be built on other columns to enable rapid retrieval on non-key fields. The index structure will be similar to that of the primary index, but duplicate values will usually exist as more than one row will have a field that matches the secondary key value. In figure 7.21 a secondary index could be built on the *Body Type* and/or the *Engine Type*. There would be an entry for each value of the *Body Type* field and one or more record numbers of the rows having that value.

Task 7.20 PC 3

Construct the secondary indexes on Body Type and Eng Type for the data of figure 7.21

Create Data Input Forms for a Database

Introduction

This element deals with implementing a relational database using a desk top micro database product. There are many micro based database products available today and most of them claim to be relational and many provide the user with powerful windows based facilities for the development of database applications. All database applications will involve the use of tables, forms, queries and reports. In this element and Element 7.3 the creation and use of these items is described.

The first step is to define the database table structures, their columns and data types. Having defined the database tables, forms can be built to allow input of data to populate the table, queries developed to interrogate the stored data and reports built that use the table and query structures. The detail of doing most of these activities is very dependent on the database software product being used and is beyond the scope of these last two elements and reference should be made to a specific texts for a particular relational database product.

It also introduces SQL (*Structured Query Language*) a language specifically developed for processing data held in databases. Today SQL is accepted as a standard for database processing and is supported by many relational database products such as ORACLE, Informix, Microsoft Access, Borland Paradox and Dbase.

On completion of this element you should be able:

❑ to understand how a relational database is defined and processed using SQL;

❑ to use a relational database package to create database tables using a variety of field data types;

❑ to create table indexes and understand how they are used during database processing;

❑ to use a relational database package to create and use data entry forms to populate tables;

❑ to specify validation checks on selected fields with suitable error messages;

❑ to understand what meta-data is and how it is used to support a data dictionary.

Relational Database Implementation

Having completed the logical design that specifies the relational model's tables the next step is to implement the design using a relational database system. There are many different relational DBMS available on micros, minis and mainframe systems. Popular micro based products are Access, Paradox, Approach and the Xbase clones, while Oracle, Ingres and Informix are available on minis running Unix, IBM's relational product is DB2 and there are many more.

With all these products the first step of implementing a database is to define that database using some *Data Definition Language or DDL*. Using the DDL the tables, columns, their datatypes, keys and indexes are defined.

Having defined the database its tables can be populated and the stored data accessed, processed and manipulated using a *Data Manipulation Language or DML*.

Each product has its own DDL and DML syntax and many also include a particular relational language called the *Structured Query Language or SQL*. In fact SQL has been accepted as a standard by ANSI since 1986 and many non-SQL systems now support it.

■ SQL

A relational database system is one that users see as a collection of tables in which data relationships are established using common values called foreign keys. SQL provides a standard for the definition and manipulation of data in a relational database:

❐ to specify a portable syntax for data definition and data manipulation commands;

❐ to enable the definition of data structures and processing operations for designing, maintaining, and accessing a relational database;

❐ to provide facilities to ensure the integrity and security of the database.

Relational DBMS support of SQL is usually provided using a simple SQL on-line interpreter that allows users to enter a single SQL command that is immediately executed on the database. Microsoft Access and Visual Basic, Borland Paradox and other desktop database software products have very strong SQL facilities.

SQL DDL commands create and modify the database schema description while its DML commands operate on the stored data.

■ Data Definition Language Commands

DDL commands are used to create the tables, table indexes and user views. This involves defining:

❐ the *base* tables of the database, their keys, attributes or columns and the data-types of each attribute;

❐ table indexes to speed-up access to data stored in the tables. An index can be specified on elementary or compound columns of the table. A primary index will not allow duplicate values, whereas a secondary index may permit duplicates;

❐ views, these are a virtual or imaginary table, constructed from columns of one or more related base tables. The view provides a 'window' into the database and the data it presents is derived from the base table data. They are useful for query and report processing and can also provide data security by providing restricted access to stored data via a user specific view.

Tables, indexes and views can be created, modified and dropped from a database. Dropping of tables containing data must be approached with caution, as this will result in data loss. Indexes and views may be dropped with no data loss implications.

❐ *Creating Tables*

```
CREATE TABLE        car (
                    PRIMARY KEY (reg_no),
                    reg_no          CHAR(7)          NOT NULL ,
                    make            CHAR(20) ,
                    mileage         INTEGER,
                    tax_month       CHAR(3),
                    price           MONEY,
                    purch_date      DATE,
                    eng_size        INTEGER,
                    body_type       CHAR,
                    eng_type        CHAR              ) ;
```

```
CREATE TABLE          emp (
                      PRIMARY KEY (staff_id),
                      staff_id          INTEGER          NOT NULL ,
                      name              CHAR(15) ,
                      dept_id           CHAR(2) ,
                      d_o_b             DATE ,
                      salary            MONEY                  ) ;

CREATE TABLE          usage (
                      PRIMARY KEY (reg_no, staff_id),
                      FOREIGN KEY (reg_no) REFERENCES car
                      ON DELETE RESTRICT,
                      FOREIGN KEY (staff_id) REFERENCES emp
                      ON DELETE CASCADE,
                      reg_no            CHAR(7)          NOT NULL ,
                      staff_id          INTEGER          NOT NULL ,
                      assign_date       DATE ,
                      use_miles         INTEGER                ) ;
```

The NOT NULL clause on the primary key fields enforce *entity integrity*. The *foreign* key clauses in *usage* enforces *referential integrity* to prevent usage of cars that do not exist or by employees who do not exist. The *delete* clause specifies the action to be taken by the database if the parent row of *car* or *emp* is deleted. RESTRICT prevents the deletion of a *car* row if there are *usage* rows that reference it. If an *emp* row is deleted CASCADE allows the deletion of *usage* rows that reference it.

Task 7.21   PC 2 & 3

Using a database package available to you, find out what data types it provides to define column domains.

❏ *Creating Indexes*

Indexes improve database access to individual rows of a table and should be built for columns that are frequently used in search criteria. An Index can be created prior to carrying out some database activity and dropped afterwards.

```
CREATE UNIQUE INDEX          cidx          ON car (reg_no) ;

CREATE UNIQUE INDEX          eidx          ON emp (staff_id) ;

CREATE UNIQUE INDEX          uidx          ON usage (reg_no, staff_id) ;

CREATE INDEX                 didx          ON emp(dept) ;
```

❏ *Creating Views*

A view provides a defined 'window' into the database, it may just show selected columns of one table or may combine columns from several tables. Views provide a security feature to prevent users having access to sensitive data and a convenience feature to make the database easier to use.

```
CREATE VIEW     c_ford     AS
                SELECT     *                    {* means all the columns }
                FROM       car
                WHERE      make = 'FORD' ;
```

Question 7.32

What would a user 'see' when accessing the database via 'c_ford'?

```
CREATE VIEW     car_user     AS
                SELECT       usage.reg_no, assign_date, use_miles, name, make
                FROM         usage, emp, car
                WHERE        usage.reg_no = car.reg_no
                AND          usage.staff_id = emp.staff_id ;
```

car_user will provide the user with a view of data amalgamated from three tables.

❑ *Changing Tables*

The columns of a table can be altered in size or additional columns inserted into a table. Changing a table can be problematic if it contains data, so approach this activity with caution.

```
ALTER TABLE     emp
      ADD       (sex          CHAR) ;
ALTER TABLE     emp
      MODIFY    (dept         CHAR(4) ) ;
```

❑ *Privacy and Security*

The GRANT command is used to protect the database from unauthorised users by enabling users to be classified with varying degrees of privileges and access rights to data.

```
GRANT  CONNECT  TO mike  IDENTIFIED BY cymru ;          {data base access only }
GRANT RESOURCE  TO chris IDENTIFIED BY wales ;          {database modification}

GRANT SELECT ON car TO mike;                            {restricted to one table}
GRANT SELECT INDEX ON emp TO chris ;            {restricts database modification}
```

Task 7.22 PC 2 & 3

Investigate the privacy and security features of your own database package?

■ Desktop RDMS

Microsoft Access is one of several relational database systems available on micro-computers. The package is part of the Microsoft Office suite and can integrate with other software packages. Access is a desktop relational database management system with a built-in applications generator for Windows GUI. It provides extensive facilities for database definition and database application development using forms, reports and queries. Other desktop products such as Paradox, Approach, Dbase for Windows provide similar facilities.

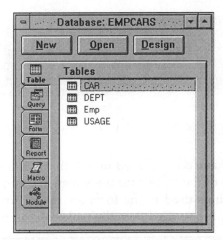

Access, like its competitors provides good support for tables, forms, queries and reports, with easy to use designers that provide a step by step guide to laying out each item.

New - enters design mode to create new items;

Open - runs an existing item;

Design- modifies an existing item.

The data used by forms and reports can come from single tables, queries or multiple tables. Forms built on one table can have sub-forms based on a second table.

Figure 7.23 Access Design and Use Window

■ Create/Define a Table using Access

The design table window is used to name and provide properties of each table column or in Access terminology field. The fields are listed in the top pane and extra properties about a field are shown in the bottom pane. Switching between panes is achieved using the mouse or the function key <F6>. Help facilities about data types and other properties are available using the function key <F1>.

Reg_No is a seven character text field, it is the primary key of the table and is indexed with no duplicate values allowed.

Other properties allow definition of field format, field caption to be used in auto generation of forms and reports, validation rules and error messages.

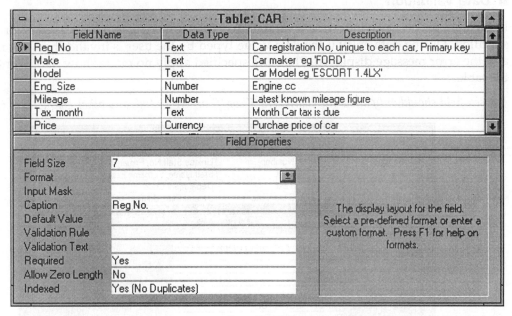

Figure 7.24 Access Table definition window with Field Property window

419

Task 7.23 PC 2 & 3   *N3.1*

Using your own database package create a table using the design specification for a small database application you are developing.

■ Populate a Table

Once created a table can be populated and have data entered into it, through use of a default form. The form design projects the structure of the table onto the screen and provides an easy to use data entry facility. The column headings used in the form are taken from the *Caption* property of each field, if no *Caption* property is specified then the table column name is used.

Reg No.	Manufacturer	Model	Eng cc	Mileage	Tax Mth	Purchase Price	D
L123SDW	FORD	MONDEO 2.0	1990	22150	SEP	$11,750.00	
L345AAA	VW	GOLF	1600	25000	JAN	$11,000.00	
L346AAA	VW	GOLF	1600	23000	JAN	$11,000.00	
L450AAA	ROVER	600i	1600	22000	JAN	$12,000.00	
L451AAA	ROVER	600i	1600	27000	JAN	$12,000.00	
L553HWO	ROVER	600i	1600	19750	DEC	$12,450.00	
L678BBB	FORD	ESCORT 1.4Est	1400	20000	APR	$11,000.00	
L679BBB	FORD	ESCORT 1.4Est	1400	19000	APR	$11,000.00	
M007BON	PEUGEOT	306XL	1400	7000	DEC	$10,560.00	
M299CWO	SAAB	900i	1998	1325	APR	$16,750.00	
M29ENY	RENAULT	CLIO 1.9D	1880	5600	AUG	$8,175.00	
			0	0		$0.00	

Record: 1   of 11

Figure 7.25 Default form for CAR table with data values

■ Data Validation

In the field properties window data validation checks can be set and associated error messages specified. During data entry if the data value typed by the user is invalid then this is trapped and the error message displayed. The rules specified apply no matter how data is entered into the table.

The sex field should only allow the characters 'F' or 'f' or 'M' or 'm', any other character is invalid.

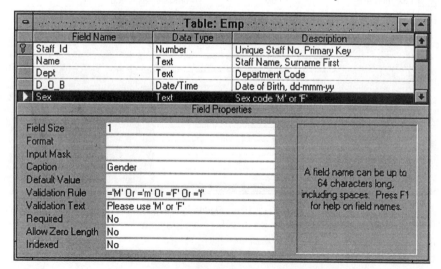

Figure 7.26 Field Property window showing data validation rule for 'Sex' column

420

In figure 7.27 the user has entered a 'D' in the *Gender* column which has been trapped by the validation rule and the validation text error message displayed.

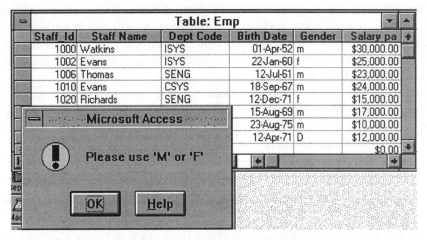

Figure 7.27 Error window display caused by validation check on 'Gender' column

Task 7.24 PC 2 & 3   N3.2

Using your own database package add data validation checks to the table defined in Task 7.23 and then populate the table with date using a default table form.

Task 7.25 PC 2 & 3   N3.1

Using your own database package define all other tables of the application.

■ The User Interface

The user interface describes the way the application will look to its users via its forms and reports. Design of the user interface is subject in its own right and is usually referred to as Human Computer Interaction (HCI). However, here are some simple guidelines to be used when designing the user interface:

- ❐ provide a logical view of data that is familiar to the user;
- ❐ be consistent, make all screens have the same look and feel;
- ❐ give control to the user to enable them to choose what to do, provide feedback to the user about what the system is doing and be forgiving;
- ❐ where possible offer selection to the user rather than make them remember.

■ Data Entry Forms

All information system applications have a requirement to collect and display data using customised screen forms. The table based data entry screen shown earlier was build by default and mirrored the table and is not really suitable for data entry in an application. A form can be customised and made to look like manual forms from which data is entered. A sales order entry form would look very much like the actual paper based sales order, a holiday booking form would closely resemble a booking document. In addition to data entry forms may also be used for enquiries.

Forms are built or designed using the form design window feature of a product such as Access and allow use of foreground and background colour to highlight data, definition of field templates and formats, use of multi-choice controls where the user selects one, setting of default values, data validation checks, calculated fields, single and multi-record forms, sub-forms and many other features.

A feature of the window will be a toolbar that is used to add field and other features to the form, the Access toolbar is shown on the left of figure 7.28. In addition to the toolbar the actual form area will have grid lines to aid placement, vertical and horizontal rulers for sizing and vertical and horizontal scroll bars.

Each form designed must be based on a database table or query previously defined, a query may involve the joining of more than one table. There are three basic areas to a form:

☐ an optional *header* section that contains static heading text, graphic images and form button controls;

☐ a *detail* section that is the main body of the form that labels, displays and allows entry of data to table or query fields using the toolbar control objects;

☐ an optional *footer* section similar to the header.

When setting up window features such as list boxes, combo boxes and options groups in a form, Access provides Wizards to guide you through setting up each box. Each feature of a form has associated with it a set of properties that are assigned values during the form design process. Most of the property elements are set by default as design takes place but some will need to be specifically set. Properties can be viewed, set and amended through a property window usually activated by double-clicking the form object.

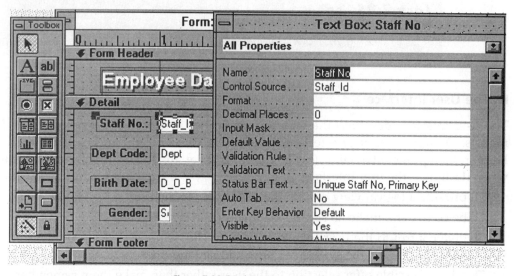

Figure 7.28 Employee Form design window showing toolbar and property window

A form can be built from an empty design window or more easily by using the form Wizard auto-generation feature that guides the user through the initial steps. Having obtained an initial design additional features can be added using the toolbar.

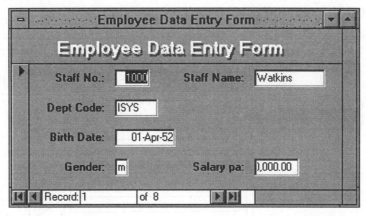

Figure 7.29 A customised Employee form

The form of figure 7.29 is based on the single table Emp and allows creation and modification of employee data.

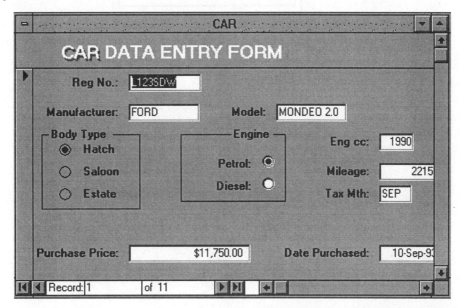

Figure 7.30 Form with Radio button field options

Facilities for form design are provided by the toolbar of the product and most include such features as *radio buttons* shown in figure 7.30. Each option is associated with a specific field value such as '1', '2' and '3' for 'Hatch', 'Saloon' and 'Estate' respectively. Other controls include support for graphics and many other GUI features of colour, form texture and field or text relief.

Task 7.26 PC 2 & 3

> *Using your own database package design and built data entry screens for each table.*

■ **Tables, forms and windows**

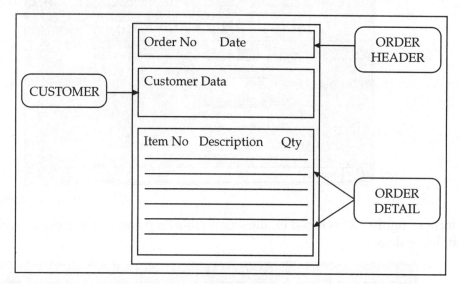

Figures 7.31 How forms are related to tables and queries or views.

Create Database Reports

Introduction

This element follows on from the Element 7.2 and deals with querying and reporting from a database using a desk top micro database product. Most of the products provide facilities for building queries on top of the base tables of the database and are able to extract data from joining several tables. The base tables or the queries can be used as a basis on which to develop reports.

It also shows how SQL can be used to query the database using its Data Manipulation Language features of its SELECT command.

On completion of this element you should be able:

❐ to design and implement reports that access database tables;

❐ to build and use database queries and construct reports based on those queries;

❐ to understand how a relational database is processed using SQL.

■ SQL

Element 7.2 gave SQL DDL commands to define and create a database, in this element DML commands are described that access and operate on the stored data.

■ Data Manipulation Language Commands

The DML commands of SQL are used to interrogate the database by enabling retrieval of data by selecting from one or more tables. Using SQL the database user is able to specify what data is required, from where and in what format. The basic SQL DML command that does all this is the *SELECT* statement. The SELECT statement has three distinct components:

SELECT   that lists the columns from tables or views;

FROM   that identifies the tables or views from which the columns are chosen;

WHERE   that includes the conditions for row selection within a single table or view, and the conditions for joining two tables or views.

❐ *Single Table Access*
Show all attributes of emp
SELECT *   FROM   emp ;

Show particular attributes of car.
SELECT reg_no, make, price FROM   car ;

Which cars must be taxed in June?
SELECT reg_no, make   FROM   car   WHERE   tax_month = 'JUN' ;

Find the lowest, highest and average prices of cars.
SELECT MIN(price), AVG(price), MAX(price) FROM car ;

How many cars are Volkswagen?
SELECT COUNT(*)   FROM car WHERE make = 'VW' ;

Find the lowest, highest and average prices for each make of car.
SELECT make, COUNT(*), MIN(price), AVG(price), MAX(price)   FROM car
GROUP BY make
ORDER BY make ;

❏ *Multi Table Access*
Get employee names and the car each one uses.
SELECT emp.staff_id, name, dept_id, reg_no, assign_date, use_miles FROM emp, usage
     WHERE emp.staff_id = usage.staff_id ;

Find staff numbers of employees using ROVER cars.
SELECT staff_id, car.reg_no, make, assign_date FROM usage, car
     WHERE usage.reg_no = car.reg_no
     AND   make = 'ROVER' ;

Department alphabetic list of employee names and the cars they use.
SELECT name, dept_id, car.reg_no, make, assign_date, use_miles FROM emp, car, usage
     WHERE   usage.staff_id = emp.staff_id
     AND   usage.reg_no = car.reg_no
     ORDER BY dept_id, name ;

List the cars used by female employees.
SELECT make, car.reg_no, assign_date FROM emp, car, usage
     WHERE   sex = 'F'
     AND   emp.staff_id = usage.staff_id
     AND   usage.reg_no = car.reg_no ;

What car does WATKINS drive?
SELECT car.reg_no, make FROM car, usage, emp
     WHERE   name = 'WATKINS'
     AND   emp.staff_id = usage.staff_id
     AND   usage.reg_no = car.reg_no ;

Question 7.33

Write SQL to show all the data in the car table.

Question 7.34

Write SQL to find the value of the lowest, highest and average salary

Question 7.35

Write SQL to show which cars are driven by females in reg no sequence.

■ Query Builder

Support for simple queries and Query By Example facilities exist in most desk top products. Simple queries are like views and display specified columns from one table or two or more tables joined via a foreign key. QBE extends this facility by allowing the user to specify selection criteria for picking rows from database tables. A QBE activity will place selection criteria on specific columns of the query and only the rows that satisfy the criteria are displayed.

The screen in figure 7.32 shows the *Usage* table joined via its foreign key field *Staff_Id* of the *Emp* table. Individual fields that make up the view or query are then selected from both tables using a drop-down list box.

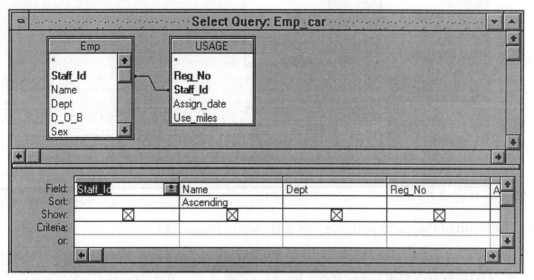

Figure 7.32 Building a query from two related tables Emp and Usage joined by the Staff_Id column

■ Query Data Display

Execution of the above query will yield data from both tables joined by the foreign key Staff_Id. The data has been sequenced by staff name.

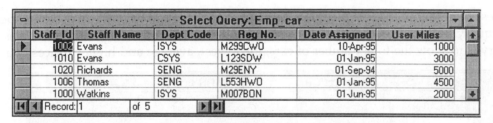

Figure 7.33 Default query display of selected Emp and Usage table columns

■ Query By Example

QBE allows the user to find and retrieve pieces of data from the database. QBE uses a query form that has *selection criteria* set in fields. These are then used to retrieve data that have values that satisfy the criteria. The query design is altered to add selection criteria to individual fields.

To retrieve only those car users belong to the 'ISYS' department.

427

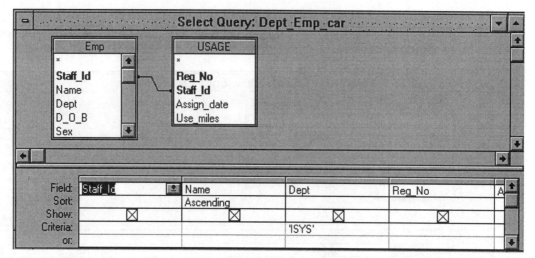

Figure 7.34 A QBE selection to show 'ISYS' department's staff vehicles

The result of the query in figure 7.34 is shown in figure 7.35.

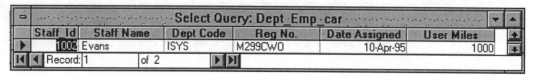

Figure 7.35 Query result of staff vehicles for department 'ISYS'

■ SQL Aggregate Functions

Access offers support for SQL and its aggregate functions can be used on columns specified in the query builder. Figure 7.36 shows the drop down list of available SQL functions and the query is to show the total number of cars, the lowest, average and highest prices of a car.

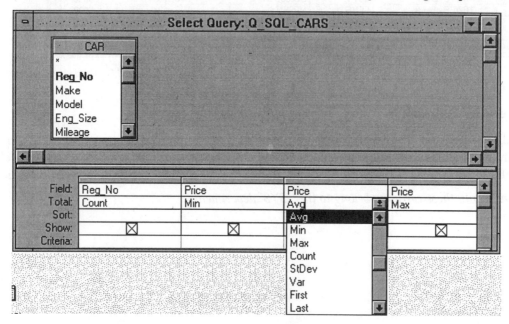

Figure 7.36 Specifying an SQL aggregate function 'Avg' in a query

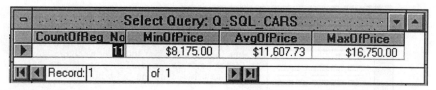

Figure 7.37 Result of running SQL 'Avg' aggregate query

■ Database Reporting

A Report based on the contents of a database is usually the final product of most database applications. Reports may be simple lists of a tables contents or may be based on a query that joins several tables. Sometimes a printed version of a form may serve as a report, such as an order form in sales order processing application. However, more often than not a report will provide another view of the data stored in the database.

Unlike a form or query a report is not a screen-based item but is meant to be printed on continuous or sheet-fed stationary in portrait or landscape format and may use up several pages. This means that a screen view of a report will not always be legible and for it to be legible only a portion may be visible. Reports are output-only items and their data values of the underlying tables cannot be modified.

Reports are designed using the report design window which in Access provides similar grid, ruler and toolbar facilities to the form design window. Again Access provides a help Wizard to generate initial reports based on selected tables or queries. The report Wizard has a number of standard report formats the most useful of which is the Groups/totals report that list details of records in specified order within groups, with group summary data. An initial report developed using the Wizard can be easily customised to meet user requirements.

Like a form a report can be divided into several sections:

❑ a *header and footer* that appear once at the beginning and end of the report respectively. The report header can provide a report title and date, the footer can show grand totals;

❑ a *page header and footer* that appear at the top and bottom of each page in the report. the page header will have report field page headings and while the footer may hold page totals and page number details;

❑ a *page body* that may contain groups of data that may be nested and each having a header and footer. When a new group starts headings are printed, during processing of the group lines are printed, values are accumulated and total and summary data such as averages are printed when the group ends. Suppressing of repeated values within the group;

❑ within the group will be text and data field values that provide the lowest detail of the report;

❑ lines, boxes, text fonts and styles can be used to make the report more readable.

Reports and the items that they are composed of, all have properties characteristics that are initially set by default during report generation but can be modified by the designer.

■ Report Generation

This process starts by selecting a report type, table or query to be used as a basis for the report and then proceeds to field selection for inclusion in the report.

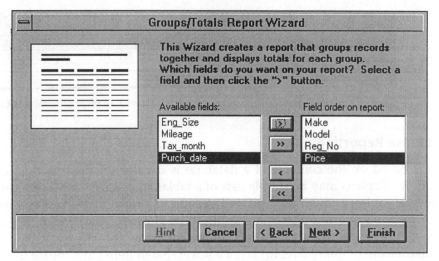

Figure 7.38 Field selection from CAR table into a report

■ Report Groups

The report type to be produced will be a group/total report and the field(s) to group data by must be specified. For data to be grouped it must be capable of being arranged into some sequence that brings the group together.

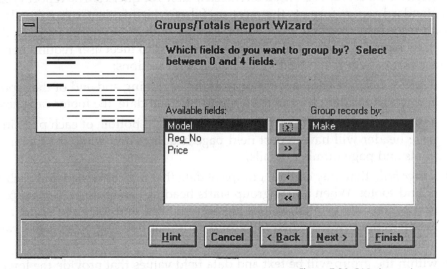

Figure 7.39 CAR data to be grouped by 'Make'

■ Report Sorting

The sequence of the groups and the data within the group can be specified.

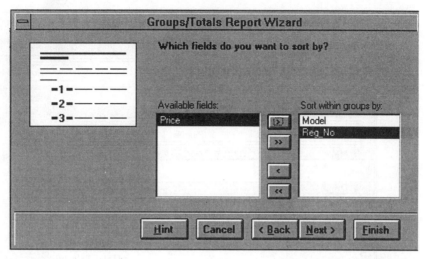

Figure 7.40 Data to be sorted within a group by Model/Reg No

■ Report Output

The report produced provides totals and other group summary data at the end of each group.

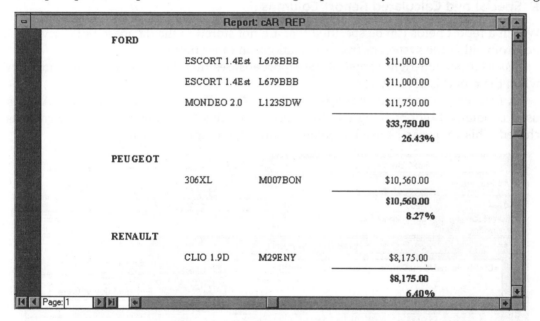

Figure 7.41 Group/totals report output

■ Report Design

The report design window is shown in figure 7.42 Items in bold are report headings while those in lightly boxed fields are database table column items. Summary function accumulators are towards the bottom of the window.

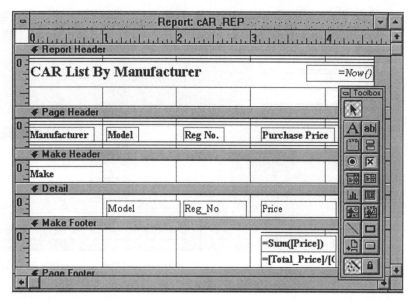

Figure 7.42 Report design window

■ Special and Calculated Report Columns

Within a report fields can be specified that are not stored in the database but derive their values from either the system or from calculations on other fields.

Now() in the top-right corner of the report ensures that the current system date is printed when the report is actually run.

A field value can be calculated from other values. The number of months a CAR has been used is obtained by obtaining the difference in months from now to when the car was purchased. This value can be used to obtain the average monthly mileage.

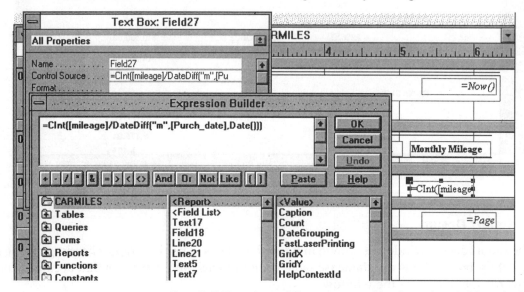

Figure 7.43 Expression to derive average monthly mileage, items in [..] are database fields

Task 7.27 PC 2 & 3

N3.3

Using your own database, produce a number of reports for your application. At least one report should involve grouped data and use calculated values.

Students taking modules on a HND scheme belong to different awards. The final subject mark given to student in a module is based on course work and exam performance, the mark is also graded.

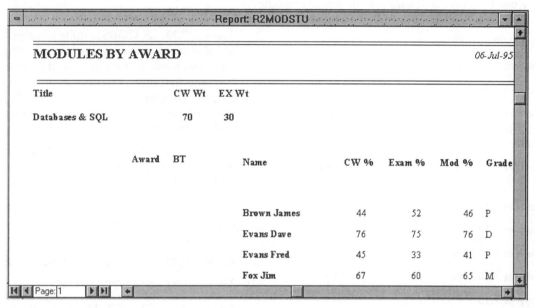

Figure 7.44 Module student report with calculated fields

The value of the Mod% column is calculated from other report data:

$$Mod\% = ((CW\_Mark * CW\_Wt) + (Exam\_Mark * EX\_Wt))/100$$

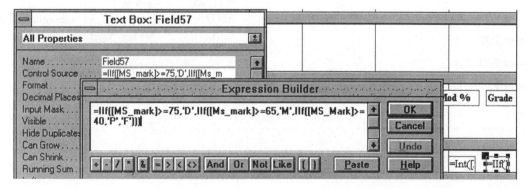

Figure 7.45 Expression for determining module grade

The Grade awarded is determined by testing the module mark column, 75 or more gets a 'D', 65 to 74 gets 'M', 40 to 64 gets 'P' and below 40 gets 'F'.

These calculations are set in the expression builder of each fields properties.

433

Answers to questions in Unit 7

Answer 7.1   C

Answer 7.2   C

Answer 7.3   A

Answer 7.4   B

Answer 7.5   Students, units, staff, unit assessment. Only one IT course so ignore it, topic area is attribute of unit

Answer 7.6   C

Answer 7.7   B

Answer 7.8   A

Answer 7.9   Identify - Staff No or Email Address; Describe – Name or address; Classify – Gender or Grade; Quantify – Salary.

Answer 7.10   (i)   C   (ii)   A   (iii)   B
               (iv)   B

Answer 7.11   D

Answer 7.12   C

Answer 7.13   A

Answer 7.14   B

Answer 7.15   C

Answer 7.16   C

Answer 7.17   C

Answer 7.18   B

Answer 7.19   C

Answer 7.20   A

Answer 7.21   A

Answer 7.22   D

Answer 7.23   B

Answer 7.24   C

Answer 7.25   C

Answer 7.26   C

Answer 7.27   B

Answer 7.28   C

Answer 7.29   A DMBS is quite a complicated piece of software of many layers through which requests for data filter. It handles all database activities, checking that integrity rules are not being violated, piecing together data from several sources to respond to requests. All this activity places a performance overhead on the system.

Answer 7.30   EMPLOYEE6(**staff-id**, name, department, birth date, salary)
CAR-EMP6(**staff-id, reg-no**, date assigned, usage-milage)

Answer 7.31   They form a composite primary key for ADMIT

Answer 7.32   Only rows of 'FORD' cars.

Answer 7.33   SELECT * FROM car;

Answer 7.34   SELECT MIN(salary), AVG(salary), MAX(salary) FROM emp;

Answer 7.35   SELECT make, car.reg_no, assifgn_date FROM emp, car, usage
WHERE   sex = 'F'
AND   emp.staff_id = usage.staff_id
AND   usage.reg_no = car.reg_no
ORDER BY   car.reg_no;

Unit 7 Sample Test Paper

1. A systems investigation will identify the data that comprise the system. Which of these is used to model that data?

   A data flow diagram
   B decision table
   C entity relationship diagram
   D program variables

2. What will be included in a systems analysis investigation report?

   A a user guide
   B program specifications
   C file and record designs
   D a data model

3. Which of these would you NOT expect to find in a data dictionary?

   A entity definitions
   B data types
   C decision tables
   D relationship definitions

4. Which of the following would improve data consistency within an application?

   A a data dictionary
   B normalised structures
   C large disk capacity
   D specifying primary keys

5. Which is achieved by normalising data?

   A data redundancy is minimised
   B data is organised to a standard format
   C data is more portable
   D data access is quicker

Questions 6 – 8 relate to the following scenario.

A hockey club has about 20 players who take part in a number of matches throughout the season.

6. Which is the degree of the relationship 'plays in' between PLAYER and MATCH?

   A 1:1
   B 1:N
   C M:N
   D N:1

7. In each match one player will be captain. Which is the degree of relationship 'captains' between PLAYER and MATCH?

   A 1:1
   B 1:N
   C M:N
   D N:1

8. Which is the correct membership for the 'captains' relationship?

   A PLAYER is optional, MATCH is mandatory
   B PLAYER is optional, MATCH is optional
   C PLAYER is mandatory, MATCH is mandatory
   D PLAYER is mandatory, MATCH is optional

Questions 9 – 11 share answer options A to D based on the following scenario.

Students take and are assessed in a module delivered by a member of staff.

A
Module Code
Module Title
CW weighting
EX weighting
Staff No
Staff Name
(Student No   )*
(Student Name   )
(CW mark   )
(EX mark   )

B
Module Code
Module Title
CW weighting
EX weighting
Staff No

StaffNo
Student No
Staff Name
Student Name
CW mark
EX mark

C
Module Code
Module Title
CW weighting
EX weighting
Staff No
Staff Name

Module Code
Student No
Student Name
CW mark
EX mark

D
Module Code
Module Title
CW weighting
EX weighting
Staff No

Staff No
Staff Name

Module Code
Student No
CW mark
EX mark

Student No
Student Name

9. Which tables are in 1NF?
10. Which tables are un-normalised?
11. Which tables are in 3NF?

12. An initial E-R diagram is shown, however it has been found that cars are being reallocated to employees, this means that several employees are associated with one car.

Which change is required to correct the E-R diagram?

A rename the EMPLOYEE entity as EMPLOYEES

B introduce a new entity ALLOCATE

C introduce a second relationship

D change the degree of the relationship

13. An initial E-R diagram is shown, however it has been found that for some book titles the library has no book copies at all.

Which change is required to correct the E-R diagram?

A change the many end of the relationship to one

B change the one end of the relationship to optional

C change both ends of the relationship to optional

D do nothing

Questions 14 – 15 relate to the following scenario.

A new entity *hires* has to be developed in the E-R diagram shown, it also has attributes of *date* and *days-out*.

14. Which set of tables matches the new situation?

A customer(**account no**, name, date)
   hire(**reg no, account no**)
   vehicle(**reg no**, model, day rate, days out)

B customer(**account no**, name)
   hire(**reg no, account no**)
   vehicle(**reg no**, model, day rate, date, days out)

C customer(**account no**, name)
   hire(**date,** days out)
   vehicle(**reg no**, model, day rate)

D customer(**account no**, name, date)
   hire(**reg no, account no,** date, days out)
   vehicle(**reg no**, model, day rate)

15. Which is the correct new E-R diagram?

A

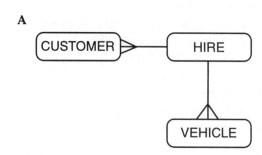

B

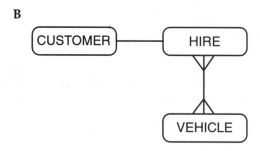

C

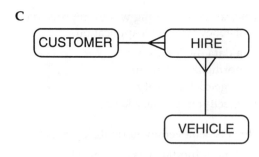

D

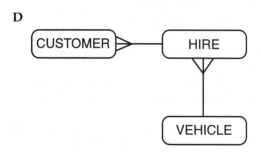

Questions 16 – 20 relate to following scenario.

You are creating a data dictionary for part of a sales ledger system. Data about invoices sent to customers include Invoice No, Invoice Date, Customer Account No, Customer Contact Name, Invoice Amount and whether it is paid or not.

The following data types are available:

- A   numeric
- B   text
- C   date
- E   logical

Which of the data types would you use for?

16. Invoice Amount
17. Paid indicator
18. Customer contact name

19. Which is a candidate to be a foreign key?

- A   Invoice Date
- B   Invoice No
- C   Customer contact name
- D   Customer Account No

20. Which is a candidate to be a secondary key?

- A   Invoice No
- B   the month of Invoice date
- C   Invoice amount
- D   the paid indicator

21. Meeting rooms in an IT department are available for booking by staff and students. Booking(room no, bookee id, date, time, duration, purpose). Which would be a primary key for Booking?

- A   room no
- B   room no/date/time
- C   room no/date/duration
- D   room no/bookee id

Questions 22 – 24 refer to the E-R diagram and attribute tables shown, for an architects practice.

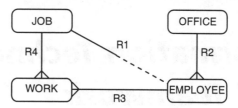

JOB(job no, title, location, client)
OFFICE(Code, address, tel no)
EMPLOYEE(Staff id, Name, Tel no, grade)
WORK(job no, staff id, hours)

22. Which is the correct definition of the *manages* relationship R1?

- A   All employees manage jobs and all jobs are managed
- B   Some employees manage many jobs, a jobs has one manager
- C   Each employee may manage one jobs, each jobs must have a manager
- D   Some jobs are not managed and all employees manage a jobs

23. Which is the correct amendment to the attribute tables to implement R1?

- A   JOB(job no, title, location, client, staff id)
- B   EMPLOYEE(staff id, name, tel no, grade, job no)
- C   OFFICE(Code, address, tel no, staff id, job no)
- D   No change

24. Which is the correct amendment to the attribute tables to establish the *works from* relationship R2?

- A   OFFICE(Code, address, tel no, Staff Id)
- B   EMPLOYEE(Staff Id, Name, Tel No, grade, Office Code)
- C   OFFEMP(Office Code, Staff Id)
- D   No change

by **Mike Watkins**

Information Technology Projects and Teamwork

Introduction

IT has an important role in most organisations today, and there are many success stories of how application of IT has benefited an organisation. However, many organisations have their own IT horror story where an IT project has gone wrong and was far from being successful. These projects have generally been poorly managed and have been characterised by missed deadlines, escalating costs and poor quality of final deliverables.

The IT activities of information systems application development and computer programming in particular are often considered to be individual activities that involve creativity and imagination. However, in practice, IT development activities are usually a mix of individual and team working.

The development and implementation of an IT system whether it involves the conversion of some manual system to a computer based system or the re-development or improvement of an existing computer system is a *project*. It will have a recognised beginning and end, and will normally consist of a series of stages that reflect the development methodology being used.

With small projects the end date may be just a few months after the start date and will involve just one or two people. Many IT projects will take more than a year to complete and are likely to involve a large number of people who have the necessary IT and other skills needed to complete the project successfully.

The IT project process commences when a client asks a developer to tender for producing an IT system. The client will provide an outline *statement of requirements* from which the developer is expected to produce a *proposal document* that contains an outline *system specification* together with a *costing statement*, which can be very risky for the developer if based simply on the outline requirements provided.

To help reduce the risk in the time available, the developer will gather as much relevant information as possible about the IT project and use this to prepare the proposal document. This will outline how the developer aims to meet the clients requirements and how much will be charged for doing it!

The IT project is undertaken by a *project team* who will possess the necessary skills and drive to get the job done. The team and the work of the project will be managed by a project leader who will need to possess the people skills of *leadership*, *diplomacy* and *control* in addition to any technical expertise.

Project management is about directing the resources of people, time and money to complete the project in an orderly manner on time, within budget and to an acceptable quality. This will involve activities of project *planning*, *organising*, *scheduling*, *monitoring* and *control*. A feature of many IT projects is that it is often difficult to judge how near completion a project is. IT projects often exhibit the characteristic of being 95% complete for more than 50% of the project duration.

The people factor of projects makes project management a complex and difficult task. A good project manager is usually a good people manager, a person will not be a good project manager unless they are a good people manager. Being a project manager is a very responsible position and can be well rewarded financially. However when things go wrong the project manager gets the blame and when things go right the project manager usually gets little praise.

The aim of this unit is to provide an awareness of how projects are undertaken, how project management is used to plan, organise, schedule, monitor and control project activities and to enable you to be an effective member of a project team.

Element 8.1 deals with the characteristics of IT projects and describes how projects are undertaken and managed. Elements 8.2 and 8.3 are really about your own personal activities when undertaking an IT project as part of a team.

Element 8.1

Explore Information Technology Team Projects

Introduction

This element looks at projects and IT projects in particular, how they are planned, resourced, organised, scheduled and monitored, which are basically the activities that comprise project management. Project management is not something unique to IT, every project needs managing whether it is an IT project like a student administration system or a civil engineering project like the Channel Tunnel or a mountaineering project to climb Everest. Neither is project management something new, it was needed to construct the Pyramids. Today there are methods to help the project manager, what makes project management difficult is people and a project is usually a very social event.

On completion of this element you should:

❑ have an understanding of why projects need to be planned;

❑ have knowledge of how projects are organised and scheduled;

❑ have an awareness of how projects are monitored and controlled;

❑ have an ability to apply project management methods to projects of limited scope and duration.

■ **What is a Project?**

A project is something that you don't normally do and very often hasn't been done before and is usually viewed as a significant activity within its own environment. A project will have one or more of the following features:

❏ a *goal*, this is some principal outcome that the project seeks to achieve. Prior to doing the project its goal did not exist or had not yet been achieved. On completion of the project the goal will exist or have been achieved, something will have changed or things are not the same as before the project started;

❏ some *objectives*, these are more specific outcomes or deliverables that the project aims to achieve and against which the success of the project can be measured;

❏ a *leader* who manages and monitors the project, and who has ultimate responsibility for its success or failure. The person who gets the blame when things goes wrong and who doesn't get praised when things work out all right;

❏ a *team*, a group of people that come together at the start of the project with the aim of getting it done. The team members will have responsibility for various jobs that make up the project and are managed by the project leader;

❏ a *deadline*, a date by which the project should be successfully completed and milestones that when reached are a measure of progress in moving towards the project goals and objectives;

❏ a *budget*, an amount of money made available to finance the project and which should not be exceeded;

❏ *complexity* that comes from the project goal or product being itself complex and the methods needed to achieve the goal are also complex. Complexity can be reduced by dividing the project up into stages or phases that can be broken down into tasks which helps simplify things. Problems also seem less complex if you have previous experience of solving them or similar ones.

Here are some examples of projects that you may have been involved in or know of:

❏ A holiday, perhaps with your family or a group of friends;

❏ Selecting and buying a new bicycle;

❏ A school or college trip to visit an IT exhibition;

❏ Learning to drive and passing a driving test;

❏ Redecoration of a room in a house;

❏ Changing a classroom to become a computer laboratory;

❏ Installing an e-mail system;

❏ Making a group presentation as part of an Advanced IT award;

❏ Construction of the second Severn crossing.

Task 8.1 PC 1 & 2

Describe a project that you have been involved in or know of. What was it's goal? Identify the project leader. Did it involve a team, a deadline, a budget? Try an list some stages or tasks that needed to be performed during carrying out the project.

Task 8.2 PC 2

Obtain a copy of a national or local newspaper, turn to the jobs section. Scan the jobs on offer and list any that involve joining a project team or that mentions the word project.

Question 8.1

What does the statement '95% complete for 50% of the time' signify about IT projects?

■ Software Project Crisis

Application software and systems development projects or any IT project have a history that goes back only to the 1940s. This contrasts with civil engineering projects that has a history stretching back thousands of years to the early Roman, Greek and Egyptian civilisations.

The history of IT systems development has many examples of systems that have been completed on time and within cost, to the satisfaction of both user and developer. However, this rosy picture has tended to be the exception rather than the rule. Most IT employees can provide examples of systems that have overrun their costs by more than 100% of the planned budget, overrun their timescales by similar percentage amounts.

Whether delivered to time and budget or not, many systems have not met the users needs by being unreliable, not user friendly, difficult to change and not generally able to do the job intended. This has often been due to project planning concentrating on the 'programming' phases while ignoring or not spending enough time in specifying what needs to be achieved and agreeing this with the user.

Task 8.3 PC 1 & 4

Investigate and describe an IT project that has failed completely or doesn't meet the needs of its users or was over time or over budget?

■ Characteristics of IT development

Trying to keep IT development within time and cost predictions has obviously been a problem to the IT industry. The following factors of IT development contribute to the problem:

❑ *objectives*, the project objectives are unclear and not understood or agreed by everyone at the start of the project. The developers have their view, the actual client users of the system have their expectations and the client management may have yet another view;

❑ *communication*, IT system development involve people and there is a great deal of interpersonal communication both spoken and written. This poses several problems that are due to misunderstanding when using natural language, users being vague about their needs and developers use of computer jargon. The problem of communication exists between people within the IT application developers organisation, within the IT application client organisation and between the client management, client user and the developer themselves.

❐ *complexity*, IT application systems usually involve a degree of complexity measured in terms of the very size of the system and the complex nature of the task being undertaken. A one fold increase in complexity of a system will increase the difficulty of creating that system by much more than that. This problem may be made worst by having poor management and an undisciplined approach to systems development.

❐ *project management*, planning at the start of the project may be vague, and poor during the project monitoring and control of work done. There is a failure to spot problems early, by identifying deviations from schedule, budget or objectives. Failure to control changes to earlier agreed specifications and poor evaluation of the final project deliverable;

❐ *newness*, IT systems development is a relatively new activity and to date has failed to develop good practices that are common in other engineering disciplines. Some success has been achieved in improving the software coding activity through structured programming techniques, the software development activity through use of software engineering principles and the systems development activity through use of structured methodologies and project management.

■ IT Development Methodologies

As a result of analysing the causes of IT failures structured methodologies were specified. These sought to provide a framework for the development of IT or software projects. Their aim is to reduce the errors introducing during the life of a project, to deliver something *that works, is to cost, to time and meets the needs of its users*.

Many popular methodologies are based on the *software project life cycle*, this divides the software project into a prescribed set of phases or stages that consist of a set tasks usually carried out one after another.

Question 8.2

Name some software project development methodologies that you are aware of?

A set of typical stages for a project life cycle would be:

❐ *Feasibility Study*, that initially gathers further relevant information in order to flesh out the clients original statement of requirements and provides a more detailed project proposal and costing. It may arise that this activity reveals that the project is infeasible and should not start at all;

❐ *Requirements Analysis*, to gather more detailed information and obtain a thorough understanding of the nature of the application and the requirements of its users;

❐ *Systems Design*, devising a computerised solution to meet the requirements identified and specifying how it will work;

❐ *Implementation*, development of the computer software to implement the design;

❐ *Testing*, running of the software to check if it meets its design and requirements goals;

❐ *Installation*, shipping the developed code to the user site and training of the users in its use;

❐ *Maintenance*, revising and correcting the existing code to overcome errors or revised requirements.

Question 8.3

What is the difference between the feasibility and the requirements analysis stages?

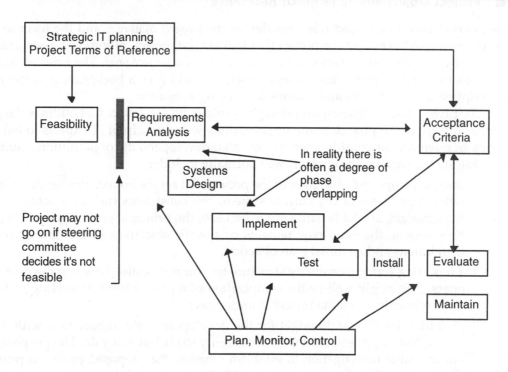

Figure 8.1 Typical phases of an IT project life cycle

Question 8.4

In figure 8.1 some arrows between Acceptance criteria and phases are double headed. Can you deduce why this is?

Having the project divided into a set of phases can help project management and the project leader is able to exert better project control. The leader can monitor each phase and should be able to receive an early warning if things go wrong so that recovery can be initiated. The leader should also seek to ensure that the techniques and methods applied during each phase are sound and well implemented which should reduce bad practices, spot errors early and in the end produce a better quality product.

The *prototyping* development methodology that seems more suited to the smaller type of IT project has a less formal structure and will require the project leader to specify phases or events to assist the monitoring and control activities. However, with prototyping the involvement of the user is a major component and this can provide the developers with early feedback if things are not going to plan. Prototyping may also make the user feel that things are more complete than they really are and has the affect of raising their expectations of an early finish date. If prototyping is used the developer must take care not to include additional features requested by the user that were outside the original specification. If the changes are essential, a new set of requirements, specifications, costings and timeline should be established. If the original objectives for the project are woolly and vague then prototyping can help firm things up or may open up a can of worms. Projects developed using the prototyping methodology still require project management.

■ Project Objectives or Terms of Reference

At the very start of a project it is essential for the project manager and the team to have very clear terms of reference for the project that will get the project rolling. The users initial request for a project to be undertaken will be in the form of a *project brief*. The brief identifies a new need that cannot be met using current systems. It will give a background to the problem, a description of the problem and reasons for seeking a solution.

The project brief will be expanded slightly into *terms of reference* that outlines the goal, *objectives* and *scope* of the project. Many organisations seek the help of IT experts to help draw up terms of reference for consideration by potential developers, the organisation's auditors often provide such a service. The contents will normally include:

- ❐ the goal, scope and objectives of the project that set the boundaries for the project. These will list problems of any current system, any constraints such as a definite completion date, budget, available hardware to be used, the principal goal or general objective of a new system, the main requirements or specific objectives of the new system, recommendations and an initial plan of action;

- ❐ a reporting and responsibility structure for communication between the user and developers. This might well be the composition of a project *board* or *working party* who will meet regularly when the project is underway;

- ❐ an initial deadline and budget for the developers to say report back with a feasibility report. Not all projects start with a feasibility study but many do. The purpose is to carry out an initial investigation to establish whether the proposed project is possible to be developed within the constraints specified or to establish better cost and time estimates for consideration by the user.

On receipt of the feasibility report, the scope and objectives can be firmed up and a project strategy specified that will enable the systems objectives to be met and aim to balance the project cost, time and quality features.

Question 8.5

What additional information should be specified at the start of a project?

■ CVL & CBS

This is a small case study that will be used to present some of the activities of carrying out a project. CVL is a client that wishes to undertake an IT project and has decided to employ CBS as the developers of the system.

- ❐ **Background**

    CVL is a vehicle leasing company that provides vehicles to its customers on three year lease agreements. CVL can supply any make, model of vehicle that it obtains from local franchised garages. Vehicle leases can be with or without maintenance and customers are invoiced on a monthly basis. CVL finances the purchase of leased vehicles through hire purchase arrangements that it has with some local finance houses.

CVL currently has a lease fleet of some 300 vehicles spread over about 100 customers. The board of CVL believe that its customer service is second to none, its charges are very competitive and that the lease market is set for expansion. They have set a target of increasing their fleet to some 1500 vehicles over the next three years and their customer base to more than 300. They would like to meet this expansion in business through their current staffing or even with one or two less staff.

Computer systems are used by the accounts section but the actual lease sales operation is manually operated.

❏ Problems

Several problems have been identified with their current manual system:

(i)   as the fleet as grown, monthly invoice preparation has become very time consuming and errors regularly occur with a number of customers not being invoiced correctly;

(ii) initial contact with CVL occurs when a customer requests a quotation for leasing a particular type of vehicle. Quotation preparation is quite an involved calculation and can only be carried out by certain sales personnel. Quotations are also often misplaced and need recalculating;

(iii) the vehicle maintenance ledger is very out of date and does not reflect the current history of the vehicle. Knowledge of more detailed running costs of particular make and model of vehicle would, the directors believe, give CVL a competitive advantage;

(iv) there is regular disagreements between the CVL accounts section and CVL sales regarding each months business activities. Accounts also receive the complaints from customers who have been incorrectly invoiced and are very concerned that these mistakes cause delays in settlement of the invoice;

(v)   enquiries by customers or accounts involve extensive manual cross referencing and can tie up staff for a considerable time.

The planned expansion would only increase the above problems and the directors feel that the system needs computerising. CVL has an IT project!

❏ Requirements

The *system goal* is allow the planned fleet increase to be achieved with the same or reduced staffing while improving customer service and system operations.

Specific objectives are:

(i)   to provide a computerised quotation facility for use by sales staff. The system should be able to hold standard quotes that may be tailored to the needs of individual customers by the salesperson. The facility should enable quote details to be carried forward into the lease details should the customer accept the quote;

(ii) to set up and manage the leases and their associated vehicles throughout the period of the lease and produce monthly customer invoices;

(iii) to keep detailed records of each maintenance event that a vehicle undertakes and to raise any invoices that recharge the customer for work not covered by the lease agreement;

(iv) to produce monthly reports showing new sales, sales by customer, terminated leases, detailed or summarised maintenance costs by vehicle or make, model;

(v)   to provide enquiry facilities by customer, by lease, by vehicle;

(vi) to integrate with the account system and avoid duplicate data entry. To provide audit trail reports for reconciliation by the accounts section;

(vii) to ensure the security and integrity of CVL leasing and accounting data. Prevent unauthorised access to system and sections of system, where possible prevent authorised user violation of data integrity and provide data backup and restore facilities.

☐ **Constraints**

- *Timescale*, the system to be operational for the expected rush of new business after August 1st.

- *Hardware*, new hardware to be purchased that provides multi-user access to CVL personnel and allow integration with the accounts system.

- *Software*, multi-user operating system, relational database with integrated bespoke software developed to meet main requirements of CVL and to provide an interface to the accounts system.

- *Costs*, an initial budget of three thousand pounds is available to finance a feasibility study and produce a functional specification and detailed costing to meet CVL requirements by December 1st.

The above CVL project terms of reference were prepared with the assistance of CVL's auditors who employ IT specialists to assist their clients. CBS's involvement with CVL was recommended by CVL's auditors.

In many projects an outline requirements specification is prepared by the auditor's staff and distributed to a number of companies who then bid for the contract. Usually the specification will have more details than that given above but is often insufficient for accurate estimating to be done.

8.1.1 Purpose of Planning

Planning is one process of project management concerned with identifying project tasks, estimating the effort needed to complete each project task and the scheduling of those tasks. This involves finding answers to the following questions and documenting them using project planning methods:

☐ *what needs to get done?* Identify what tasks have to be completed;

☐ *how long will it take to complete each task?* Estimate task duration, when can a task start and when should it be completed by;

☐ *which tasks happen before other tasks?* Determine task relationships and the order of carrying them out;

☐ *who or what will carry out each task or be responsible for it?* Identify resources to be used in order to complete each task.

■ What is Project Management

For any IT project to be completed successfully it must be planned and managed in a proper manner, which is why the life-cycle methodology is so popular. Most of us do manage or have managed projects during our lives. Project management may not be difficult particularly if the project is not too big. The aim of project management is to:

produce a product or achieve some goal on time, within budget and for a product, that is working correctly.

Project management has three main functional aspects that are linked together, project *planning and scheduling*, project *organisation* and project *monitoring and control*. These combine to manage and direct project resources in order to meet established objectives.

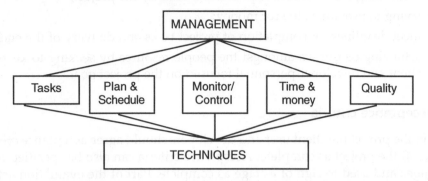

Figure 8.2 Project management elements underpinned by techniques

The project *objectives* will normally include the budgetary elements of time and cost and the quality element on completion of the project. The project *resources* will normally include the principal components *people, time* and *money* supported by accommodation, materials and equipment. Resources are normally subject to some restrictions or control called *constraints*.

A Computer Lab project will have the goal of converting a classroom to a computer laboratory with a prescribed number of workstations for students. It will have some cost constraint of an allocated budget, an amount to spend on labour and materials. It will have a time constraint of needing to be ready for the start of the new academic year. There will be quality constraints of health and safety, student workspace, workstation performance and software availability.

Project management itself takes time and will consume project resources it terms of team members time. It is an often underestimated activity within the overall project budget. It is mainly concerned with managing people!

Question 8.6

Estimating the cost of an IT project is an example of which?

A *Planning*

B *Monitoring*

C *Organising*

D *Scheduling*

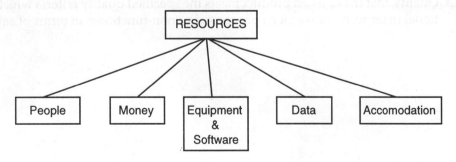

Figure 8.3 Project resource elements

The project management planning phase will provide a basis for the following integrated set of activities:

- ❏ controlling the resources required and used by the project;
- ❏ trying to provide value for money;
- ❏ meet deadlines for completion of project tasks and delivery of the end product;
- ❏ achieving consensus amongst the people resource by seeking to keep the eyes of both client and developer personnel focused on the project goal.

■ Acceptance criteria

Early in the project the client user and developers should agree acceptance criteria that are used to sign off the project as complete. Acceptance criteria can also be specified at the start of project stages and used to sign of a stage as complete. Part of the evaluation activity for the project or a stage will use the acceptance criteria and check against the actual project or stage outcomes.

In their simplest form acceptance criteria could be test data with expected results. The test data are input to the software and results produced compared to the prepared expected results. For systems such as those of accounting, this process may involve several months of 'testing' and may be achieved by parallel running.

Other acceptance criteria are:

- ❏ target dates hit, within and at end of stages and final delivery;
- ❏ system functions implemented and 'correct';
- ❏ usability of the system, ease and consistency of use;
- ❏ hardware performance, system response times, utilisation and volumetric data;
- ❏ security, reliability and maintenance;
- ❏ within budget and time.

■ Time, Cost, Quality Triangle

Acceptance criteria need to be realistic and achievable and project management need to be aware that high quality, early delivery and low cost may not go together. These three components are factors of several criteria:

- ❏ Time, that the project meets its goals and objectives by the agreed deadline, its delivered on time;
- ❏ Cost, that the project is delivered within the specified budget, which may be an amount of real money or some paper cost of person-days per week of the project;
- ❏ Quality, that the finished product meets the specified quality criteria which may be functional in terms of transactions per second or non-functional in terms of say easier to use.

If time and cost are fixed and a project is running over on both aspects then quality must suffer. If quality is to be maintained then there must be an increase in time and/or cost.

As with most things quality costs money, although in IT projects throwing money at a project will not guarantee the quality of the final project;

To do things in a shorter time normally requires more effort which means more mandays which in turn increases costs.

Figure 8.4 Quality, cost and time triangle

Question 8.7

Acceptance criteria are NOT used to?

A evaluate time

B evaluate cost

C evaluate progress

D evaluate quality

■ Constraints

The project planning activity needs an awareness of several different types of constraint that might apply and may determine the order of tasks:

❑ development constraints, IT development usually have to done in a particular sequence, design follows analysis;

❑ client constraints, imposed by the client and normally specified in the terms of reference or unearthed by the feasibility study;

❑ external constraints, imposed by events not directly under the control of the project developers, such as delivery of hardware;

❑ resource constraints, imposed by the availability of resources such as developer personnel with specific data communication skills or access to computer time.

Question 8.8

The customer's accounts manager has a months leave and the accounting system acceptance testing cannot take place until her return. What type of constraint is this?

A development

B resource

C customer

D external

■ Risks

Project planning also needs to assess the risk factor of the project or certain tasks. There are a number of risk categories that are common to many IT projects:

- ❐ the level of interfacing with other applications;
- ❐ client experience of IT, regarding their unfamiliarity with IT development characteristics, its jargon and methods;
- ❐ the newness or novelty of the application;
- ❐ experience of the development team in terms of skill levels and of experience with like or similar tasks;
- ❐ overall size of the project, risk increases with size;
- ❐ hardware and software systems factors, of using 'state of the art' technology that has not yet been proven.

Question 8.9

Development staff turnover on a project is an example of what risk?

A   customer

B   developer

C   newness

D   hardware

The chances of success are improved if the budget and time constraints are realistic and there is low risk, the project has a structure that can be broken down and compartmentalised, the developer has previous experience and it is not to large a size. The client and the developer should aim to reach a **consensus** very early in the project regarding what is realistically achievable within the various constraints that apply to the project and the risks that exist.

The CBS & CVL system will involve the following constraints and risks:

Skill problems might be:

- ❐ the hardware installation will require wiring of CVL premises, which may be carried out by external contractors;
- ❐ CVL site preparation may involve small building works projects;
- ❐ data take on may require the use of contracted data entry staff.

Risk areas might be:

- ❐ late delivery of hardware ready for data take on. A fallback position would be to rent similar hardware to carry out this task;
- ❐ late delivery of software will always cause problems. Fallback, schedule a phased delivery and installation of software;
- ❐ accounts interfacing problems. Fallback, produce hard copy for hand keying.

Task 8.4   PC 1

For a project that you know of, or a case study in your library, list some project objectives in terms of its main goal and any constraints that were applied to it.

8.1.2 Project organisation activities

This is concerned with how the people resource of the project will be organised and managed throughout the project. Normally within an IT project having determined the work to be done it is divided and allocated to positions or individuals. These may be organised into groups or teams based on the type or function of the work to be done. Each group will have specific roles and responsibilities and may operate at various levels within the project that are similar to the strategic, tactical and operation managerial levels of any organisation. Initially this organising structure will be very small but for large IT projects it grows as the project develops and will shrink as the project nears completion.

■ Project Players

An IT project will involve people from different organisations or different sections of the same organisation. There are two principal groups, the *project client or customer* who wish it to be built and the *project developers or supplier* who have responsibility for building it.

```
┌─────────────────────┐        ┌─────────────────────┐
│   Project Client    │        │  Project Developer  │
│     (Customer)      │        │     (Supplier)      │
│        CVL          │        │        CBS          │
└─────────────────────┘        └─────────────────────┘
```

Figure 8.5 The project players

These two groups can be further subdivided as follows:

- ❏ the project developers will consist of firstly the project team who actually do the development day in and day out and secondly senior management who have an overseeing role and have little direct involvement in the daily activities of the project;
- ❏ the project client will consist of firstly client management who have requisitioned the project and secondly client users who will use the finished product in their daily work activities.

For the CVL project the initial feasibility study will involve two personnel from CBS, Mark a computer systems specialist and Jeff an business analyst and account specialist.

At CVL the project is monitored by David a director, day to day communication with CBS is via Mike the chief sales manager and Jane the accounts manager. CBS will have access to leasing and accounts staff during their investigation.

Role Definition and Assignment

When a project gets the go ahead, client and developer people will usually be organised into project management groups at different levels and have different types of roles and responsibilities. Figure 8.6 shows a set of typical groups organised around the project manager who will have membership of many of the groups. For large IT projects there is likely to be a hierarchical structure similar to that of many organisations, this will also require several tiers of management such as stage managers reporting to an overall project manager.

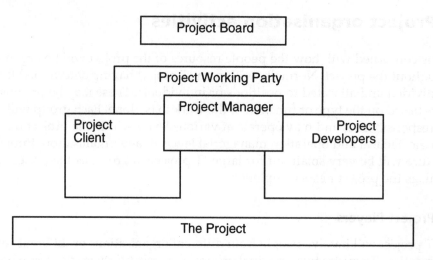

Figure 8.6 The interacting groups of a project

■ Project Board

At the top level, members of these groups will constitute a *project board* or *steering committees* who will usually hold formal meetings infrequently, say every three months, but may hold one off meetings to address any major project developments or problems. Members of the project board from both sides may contact each other informally to try and clear any issues that may have been brought to their attention. It's responsibilities include:

❒ at the start the project board will have approved the project and pledged resources to it;

❒ provide project guidance and direction to maintain its viability;

❒ monitor the use of time and money resources, the adherence to standards and quality;

❒ approve all project plans and sign off completed work;

❒ agree and delegate action plans to resolve any issues passed up to it;

❒ report back to senior management.

The CVL Project Board will be composed of CVL and CBS personnel.

Dave a CVL director, Mary the IT specialist from CVL auditors, John CBS director and Mark CBS project leader.

■ Project Working Party

The project itself will be under the control of the project leader and there will be more regular progress or trouble-shooting formal meetings, say monthly or as required, of a *project working party* chaired by the project leader and having representatives from the client and developer. Again there may be informal contact between both sides to address any issues that spring up. It's responsibilities include:

❒ before the start of any project phase prepare a plan and allocate work;

❒ monitor the actual work to meet cost, time and quality constraints;

❒ evaluate completed work with respect to standards and acceptance criteria;

❒ provide guidance and direction to development teams;

❒ monitor and control project progress, deal with exceptions and initiate any corrective action;

❒ take action on plans passed down to it by the project board;

❏ agree and action any plans to resolve issues highlighted by the client or developers;

❏ report back to project board.

The CVL project working party will be Mark CBS project leader, Jeff CBS business analyst, Mike CVL sales manager and Jane CVL accounts manager.

■ Project Development Team

This organising element of a project is closely associated with the planning activity, having formulated a project plan the project manager must organise the project by creating a project team or teams and deciding:

❏ what kinds of staff are required to carry out the project;

❏ what duties need to be performed;

❏ what responsibilities are associated with each position;

❏ the lines of communication within the team and with any external entities.

This activity will bring together people with the required skills to form a development team under a team leader who may also double as the project manager. The team leader will be an experienced person who will be responsible for such day to day activities as, allocation and reallocation of work, evaluation of completed work, approving designs and testing strategies and release of completed products. The team will hold formal team meetings to review work completed, address problems, share experience and knowledge and to plan future work.

The CBS development team will be Mark project manager and analyst/programmer, Maggie a senior software developer, Jeff the business analyst and accounts specialist, Rich a software developer/hardware technician and Pam of customer support. All have the CVL project as their main activity but they are also allocated to other activities.

Question 8.10

What other activities at CBS might be allocated to Mark or Maggie?

Task 8.5   PC 4

Find out how your school, college or any organisation you have access to, goes about undertaking an IT project. Identify the client, the developer(s), the manager and the steering committee. You may not be able to clearly label all four!

■ Project Teams

By using a project team the people associated with the project are organised within the boundaries of the project and gives them a strong sense of identity with the project. Additionally a project team will enable quicker decision making and reduce communication paths amongst the people.

However, some people work better as individuals and may not be good 'team players', on the other hand some people produce their best when belonging to a team. Project teams also create barriers and team members can become very inward looking and not share their expertise or experience gained with other project teams.

What is a Team?

A team is selected and built, this applies equally to sports teams and IT project teams, they are not simply a random collection of individuals. The team will have an identity and its existence will be known to others. Teams associated with success will have people wishing to join them, while those associated with failure will have members wishing to leave.

Teamwork is responsible for much of the work carried out in organisations whether it be a hospital maternity ward, a car engine plant production line or a computer migration job. Teams can be permanent or temporary. Permanent teams exist to carry out their activities and responsibilities each and every working day. Temporary teams are formed to carry out a new additional activity for a specified period of time and when that is completed the team is disbanded or severely reduced in size. For a team to be effective it requires team building.

Question 8.11

Are the teams that exists in a hospital maternity ward permanent or temporary?

Team Building

This is an activity that may not occur naturally and may require an organisation to undertake team building development to foster a team ethos. This is particularly important for permanent teams or temporary teams that have a project duration in excess of say one year. Team building involves such things as:

- size and composition of the team. Team sports such as rugby, hockey, football and cricket have a specific size but the composition of its members can be determined by the next match to be played. IT teams will require certain skills in particular positions like a sports team, but the size will depend on the project;

- selection of people to fill team positions. The aim is not to put 'square pegs in round holes', nor try to allocate people to jobs for which they are totally unsuited. Staff development will enable less experienced staff to try something new and make a success of it;

- allocation of responsibility within the team. Collective acceptance of the team structure and the responsibilities associated with each position for decisions taken within the team and of the outcomes from the team;

- team leader, who will exhibit leadership by focusing the team on the job to be done, diplomacy in resolving internal and external people problems and management to monitor and control the project work and the project team;

- working with other team members that requires the inter-personal skills of co-operation, sharing of ideas, acceptance of suggestions and modification of own ideas, providing support to others and not undermining the work of others.

The team will take a collective responsibility for its work, it will tackle and solve problems as a group. It should be aware of its strengths, weaknesses, opportunities and threats, together with the feelings of its members.

■ Team structure

An IT project of any reasonable size will require a team to be assembled to undertake the various tasks that make up the project. The roles that compose a team will depend on the job to be undertaken and may be different for the various phases of the project. Team size will depend on the size and duration of the project, large projects will be composed of several separate teams each having responsibility for a particular component. For any team, keeping it as small (eight or less) as possible has its advantages:

- ❑ communication problems are reduced, it will be easier for all the team to meet in one place at one time;
- ❑ members will work closely, helping each other, sharing understanding, knowledge and experiences;
- ❑ work produced is more likely to be seen as a product of the team who have a collective responsibility for it.

An effective ideal team will need people to fulfil the following roles:

- ❑ a leader to manage and co-ordinate the team, keeping it focused on its goal and objectives;
- ❑ an ideas person, who is creative, innovative and good at solving problems;
- ❑ workers, who carry out the main working tasks of the team;
- ❑ a critic, who questions methods or activities, highlights problems, monitors progress;
- ❑ a team builder, who keeps the team together, makes it work and maintains harmony.

One person may play more than one role and some teams may not have all of the roles filled. How well a team operates will be affected by its make up and the characters of team members is important. It may be not always possible to build a team of temperamentally compatible people, who all get on well and like each other, the work must be done. The team leader has a responsibility to make the team work.

During a small IT project a typical team will require a number (about four from the developer side) but not all of the following people and one person may fill more than one role:

- ❑ a team leader who manages the team and may double as an analyst or developer;
- ❑ a systems analyst or analyst developer, responsible for requirements analysis and system design;
- ❑ a software developer, responsible for implementing designs using a 3 or 4GL development environment;
- ❑ a hardware and systems specialist, responsible for hardware installation, configuration and trouble shooting;
- ❑ a client trainer and user support, training in use of systems and daily hand holding;
- ❑ administrative support; clerical and secretarial duties in support of team;
- ❑ client user representative, to provide a user perspective, evaluation and feedback;
- ❑ marketing expert, if the product is to be sold more widely.

For example a Computer Based Learning project team may be composed of:

- ❑ a team manager, responsible for planning, progress and may also have design and technical skills;
- ❑ graphic designers, responsible for art work and special effects;
- ❑ media specialists, responsible for shooting or editing media sound or vision takes;
- ❑ CBL software authors, responsible for development of material using an authoring package;

❏ academic content providers, responsible for scripting material;

❏ evaluators, to evaluate and comment on the finished product.

For small projects the developer team members will often be working on more than one project. This will be particularly true of senior staff who will divide their time as required. Teams may also shrink or grow as the project develops with specialised staff being called in as required and they will often flit from project to project. The client representation may also change as the project evolves and will end with the client eventually evaluating the project. However for larger projects team members tend to be dedicated to a specific project but may still have to undertake odd one-off tasks.

■ Confidential Data

At whatever level of involvement in a project, if the developers are external to the client then all members of the development team must respect the confidential nature of the client's data and procedures that they have access to during the projects life. Copies of client data or paperwork should all be securely filed and not be accessible to any other client or non-member of the project team.

In the CVL system its customer list or the way it composes a quotation for a customer would be quite useful data for a competitor or the customers themselves. CBS staff involved in the project will need to respect the confidentiality of any data or information that they have access to and ensure that any CVL documents are secure at all times.

Question 8.12

Which group gives formal approval to the requirements analysis system specification?

A project board

B project manager

C development manager

D project working party

Task 8.6   PC 2

For a project you know of list the team members, their titles and responsibilities. Classify members as one of the 'ideal' team roles.

8.1.3   Project scheduling

Project planning and replanning are important activities of project management, all but the smallest of projects will be broken down into stages or phases. People have compared doing a project to making a journey where the project goal is the journey destination and the project plan is the route map to make that destination. For any journey there may be several different routes to get to the destination and there may be many alternative forms of transport to use. In coming up with an itinerary (journey plan), the resources available and any constraints must be taken into account.

Question 8.13

List some resources and constraints that may apply to a journey.

A plan for the whole project will show the major stages of the project indicating their main activities with start and end dates. Each stage can itself be planned in the same way and refined into a set of more detailed task plans usually involving people as shown in figure 8.7.

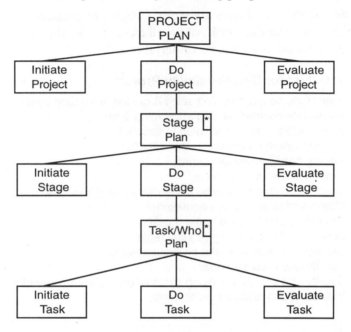

*Figure 8.7 Project plan refined into stages, refined into tasks
(the * indicates zero or more)*

In figure 8.7 the initiate activity at the start of each level sets objectives or terms of reference for the activity and agrees acceptance criteria against which the activity will be evaluated on completion. The evaluation activity at the end of each level checks the work done against the acceptance criteria thus providing a built in degree of quality control.

Task Analysis

When performing task analysis, proceed in a top-down manner by first listing a set of general top level project stages or phases. Each one of these can be broken down and refined into more specific tasks which may be refined further into sub-tasks or jobs. The refinement should stop when each job can be completed by an individual in about week or less. Each task should be described and where possible a method should be specified for use in carrying out the task. Define the end of task goal or objective and any quality criteria that can be used to measure success.

By doing this the project manager should be able to estimate task, stage and project duration times that will also allow a review progress on a weekly basis and will be responsible for signing off the task as completed.

For each task check these against:

❏ *Resources*, hardware, software, services, time and budget;

❒ *Skills*, required to achieve each task successfully, some may require training or use of external contractors;

❒ *Responsibilities*, showing who is responsible for what;

❒ *Risks*, identify risk areas that can affect project progress, allow some slack of extra time and be aware of a fallback position.

For small projects these activities may not be to difficult to organise, however for larger projects project management is a very important activity which can determine the success or failure of the project.

In carrying out the CVL feasibility study CBS might prepare a task list as shown in figure 8.8. CBS might have a standard task list for all feasibility studies that they undertake, although for some projects not all tasks will be undertaken.

Task List for CVL Feasibility Project

Investigate contract leasing sales & customer support systems;
Investigate contract leasing accounting systems;
Investigate integration of sales to accounts;
Specify outline requirements specification;
Specify hardware requirements;
Obtain hardware quotations;
Specify software requirements, packages and bespoke;
Obtain software package quotations;
Estimate bespoke development costs;
Specify and cost training requirements;
Specify and cost data take on requirements;
Specify any building works;
Specify and cost any ongoing costs when system is operational;
Prepare report and present findings.

Figure 8.8 Task List for CVL Feasibility

Question 8.14

For a summer holiday project list the tasks that need to be performed, indicate by when each task should be completed and list any constraints that could apply.

Task 8.7   PC 3

For the Computer Lab project list the stages or tasks that need to be carried out to complete the project.

■ Effort

Effort is estimated in terms of the resources that are required to complete a task and the time and cost that this requires. Depending on the duration of the task effort is expressed in one of the following units:

❒ *person-hours*, used for very small tasks;

❒ *person-days*, equivalent to about six person-hours, used for small size tasks;

❒ *person-weeks*, equivalent to five person-days, used for small to medium size tasks;

❏ *person-months*, equivalent to about four person-weeks, used for medium large size tasks;

❏ *person-years*, equivalent to about twelve person-months, used for large size tasks;

If the duration of a task is estimated as fifteen person-days then it is expected that one person will take fifteen days to complete the task, or perhaps two people will take eight days or maybe three people six days. Beware, not all tasks are divisible amongst many people and when more people are allocated to a task more time is taken up with them communicating with each other and time is also required for management of the team.

Question 8.15

Why, for a task estimated as 24 person-days is it unlikely to be completed on time by four people in six days?

The amount of time needed to complete a task assumes that a person is working on the task full time. Allocating one person part-time to a task will lengthen the time taken to complete the task, but the task effort remains the same. A person working full-time is one person unit, a person working part-time for 2 days a week is 0.4 person units.

Question 8.16

Why is a part-time person that works 2 days a week equal to 0.4 person units?

The task *effort* or *duration* is the *total amount of work time* needed to do a task like 20 person days or 4 person weeks.

Question 8.17

A task has been estimated to take 10 days, the person allocated to it can only work on it for 40% of their time, how long will it take to complete the task?

Question 8.18

CVL Feasibility Study

CBS estimated this to be 15 person days of effort or duration and decided that their two people Mark and Jeff should complete in 7.5 days, Mark to handle the sales contract systems, hardware and bespoke software specifications, Jeff to handle the accounts systems and preparation of hardware and software quotations. However both Mark and Jeff had other commitments and could only commit 2 days a week. Thus CBS estimated it would take 4 weeks (20 days) to do the job. They felt safe with this estimate as the deadline December 1st was more than a month away. Are they?

In carrying out their work on the feasibility Mark or Jeff might delegate some activities to other people in CBS. Having specified the hardware requirements Jeff could pass the obtaining of quotations from hardware suppliers to Pam who has experience of doing this.

Having estimated effort in terms of person days for each task, costs can be calculated by multiplying by the charge rate per day for the skill necessary to do the task.

For the feasibility study CBS are prepared to receive a fixed fee of £3,000 in the hope that the actual project will be quite profitable for them.

■ Estimation Dilemma

Before an IT project gets off the ground, clients or bosses often want to know how much is it going to cost and when will it be completed? At the very beginning of a project giving an accurate answer to both of these questions is very difficult. Another similar situation is that a fixed budget has been set for carrying out the project.

Estimating how long an IT task should take is not easy and is largely due to two factors:

❑ experience, to date IT does not have a long enough history of experience for estimating as found in non IT areas such as engineering or building;

❑ the conceptual nature of many IT tasks, a new IT project is often a concept, it isn't real or concrete and therefore there isn't a really detailed view of how large a task it really is.

In order to provide a reasonable estimate of time and cost a certain amount of analysis of the problem, an understanding of the project issues and at least some preliminary design is necessary. For any task experience of similar activities can help, one formula that can be used is to provide three estimates for each task, at *best* estimate or *shortest*, at *worst* estimate or *longest* and on *average* estimate. These are combined to provide the estimated task duration or costs:

$$\text{Task estimate} = \frac{\text{longest} + (4 \times \text{average}) + \text{shortest}}{6}$$

Question 8.19

A task has been estimated as 70 days worst case, 26 days best case and 36 days average, what is the task estimated duration?

However many bids are made for IT contracts based on little if any real in depth understanding of the project and its requirements. These IT projects have been doomed from the start due to not enough time or insufficient budget being allocated to do a good job. The project leader should aim to be realistic about setting deadlines and not make promises that he or she knows cannot be met. Also project management takes time and costs money.

■ Estimation tolerance and fallback

To help the estimation activity the estimator needs access to historical data about similar projects so that the experience gained on earlier projects can be taken into account when estimating for a new project. The experienced planner will try and build into the plan a degree of tolerance or *margin for error* on each task to allow for any slippage. For run of the mill activities then the tolerance can be quite a small percentage of the estimated effort, for more risky or constrained activity the tolerance should be a higher percentage or even an alternative or *fallback* activity planned, for when things really go wrong. Increasing time allowed for activities will also increase costs and could make the project infeasible, so building in big tolerances may result in the project never getting started or allocated to the developer.

■ Task sequence

The order in which tasks are carried out is important. Some tasks must take place and be completed before others can start, the second task is *dependent* on the first. Some tasks may be able to be carried out at the same time as each other.

Before the task of installing IT equipment can be started, the task of ordering and delivery of the equipment must have been completed and before that task can start the task of selecting and receiving supplier quotations must have taken place. It may be possible to commence installation before all equipment has been received so part of these two tasks could take place at the same time.

Two application programs are to be developed. Both programming tasks can be broken down into three phases, design, coding and testing. The tasks have been allocated to one developer, a programmer analyst. There are several ways in which the developer can carry out the development:

❐ Complete all phases of program one before starting the first phase of program two:

❐ Work on the phases of both programs simultaneously, this will increase the elapsed time taken to develop each program.

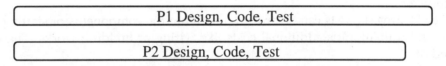

❐ Complete the design phase of program one as a single task, then commence the coding phase of program one while simultaneously commencing the design phase of program two:

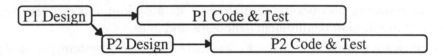

Task No	Task Name	Duration	Predecessor
10	Agree Terms of Reference	2 days	none
20	Requirements Analysis	15 days	10
30	Agree Acceptance criteria	4 days	10
40	Produce full requirements specification	5 days	20, 30
45	Agree test data	5 days	30
50	Design System	10 days	40
60	Develop System	50 days	50
70	Produce system stationary (forms, reports)	10 days	40
80	Write support documentation	10 days	60,70
90	Test System	10 days	45, 80
100	Install system	5 days	90

Figure 8.9 Task list with duration and predecessors

Question 8.20

Why is information about project tasks needed?

Task 8.8   PC 3

For a project construct a task list, estimate the duration of each one and show the sequence in which they should be carried out.

■ Project Costs

Having estimated how long each task should take and obtained quotations for any equipment or additional services a project costing can be prepared. The project costing will show a breakdown of the main components and the overall total cost known as the 'bottom line'. If the project is to be undertaken by external suppliers the costing is their quotation for doing the job. However, projects undertaken by an organisation's own IT staff should always be costed, a 'paper cost'. The costing will form the conclusion of a feasibility study if one has been undertaken.

For IT projects costs can be broken down into the components of staffing, hardware, software and training plus additional costs like wiring or building works. These costs are composed of:

❏ staffing, charges for the project team of developers, trainers and their administrative support;

❏ hardware, contributing to these costs will be: number of workstations including main computer or server; processor, size of main memory and hard disk capacity of each workstation; networking requirements, data backup and recovery requirements; data communication requirements, modems and lines;

❏ software, contributing to these costs will be: operating system; licensed number of users; packages; bespoke development; data communications software;

❏ training, costs of special 'courses' for using supplied software;

❏ sub-contractors, costs for carrying out all types of building works including wiring;

❏ data entry, costs to set up system by taking on basic data, this may require the use of external agency staff to shorten the time this would take;

❏ computer time, costs may be incurred buying time on a computer in order to get some tasks completed;

❏ other, these costs can include travel and subsistence and consumables.

Where software and hardware is 'off the shelf', costing is obtained from specifying requirements to the supplier who will quote for their supply. Where a project has a bespoke software requirement these costs can seem very high in comparison to other cost components, this is because bespoke software development is a highly labour intensive activity with high daily rates that are often dependent on the seniority of staff used. The project leader would command a much higher charge rate than a trainee software developer. However, some developers may have a universal standard charge rate for their clients but would still cost the project internally using a varying cost rate based on salaries and other overheads.

Assuming all units of money are in pounds sterling, CBS has the following charge rates based on overheads and staff wages:

Senior analysts/developers like Mark and Jeff	300 per day
Programmers and hardware technicians	200 per day
Training	250 per day

They charge customers on average 250 per day dependent on the who they are and the job to be done. They also apply an adjustable profit margin to the final accumulated cost based on a senior directors 'feel' for the job.

$$Bespoke\ cost = No\ of\ days\ effort \times rate\ per\ day$$

In the CVL project Mark's feasibility study activities have revealed that the system can be broken down into a number of components that require bespoke development. One of the components is the Quotation sub-system to allow a customer quotation to be prepared.

Mark has charged £4,500 for this. He arrived at this figure as follows:

Quotation System Tasks	Person	Time	Rate	Cost
Design System	Mark	3 days	300	900
Code & Test system	Maggie	10 days	200	2,000
	Rich	5 days	150	750
	Totals	18 days		3,650
Profit margin			@ 20%	730
				4,380

Mark rounds this figure up to £4,500, he feels that there is some slack in his costing and he may be able to reduce costs if he needs to.

Question 8.21

Which is NOT recommended when making a cost estimate of task?

A check the estimate with data about previously completed similar work

B check the estimate with those of similar tasks in the same system

C check the estimate with the clients estimate for the work

D check the estimate with those for tasks of much different complexity

For the CVL project Mark and Jeff have prepared a system proposal that provides details of costs for the system:

```
Contract Leasing proposal for CVL
Prepared by:      Mark and Jeff of CBS
Detailed Costing;
```

Hardware

Central Server: 1 12 Mbyte, 1 Gbyte Tape streamer	IBM PC compatible 486/66	3500.00
Workstations: 6 8 Mbyte, 200 Mbyte	IBM PC compatible 486/33	4800.00
Network & Comms:	Network cards, cable for main site	2500.00
	Comms link and modems to remote accounts office	750.00
		11550.00

Software

Operating System – 8 user license WinNetOS	1200.00
Database – 8 user license WinRelDB	1600.00
	2800.00

Bespoke development for contract leasing:

Customer/Contracts sub system	4500.00
Contracts Quotation System	4500.00
Vehicle & vehicle maintenance sub system	9000.00
Sales Invoicing	4500.00
Accounts interface	3000.00
	25500.00

Accounts Packages all 8 user licenses:

Sales Ledger	900.00
Purchase Ledger	900.00
Nominal Ledger	1200.00
	3000.00
Total Systems Cost	**£42850.00**

Maintenance

Hardware on-site 8 hour callout	1200.00 per year
Bespoke software	2500.00 per year
Packaged software	300.00 per year
Total Maintenance	**£4000.00**

Figure 8.10 CVL cost proposal

■ Project Milestones

These are often significant events during the progress of a project that indicate the achievement of some intermediate goal. Reaching of a milestone is a measure of project progress and *major* or *external* and *minor* or *internal* milestones can be set at the outset of the project and indicated in the project schedule.

Milestones, major or minor, are part of the project monitoring process and review the work that has been achieved. Any difficulties or problems that arise should be resolved or a way specified for their resolution.

Major milestone points are used by the client or project board to monitor progress and are significant project events usually associated with some planned deliverable such as the feasibility study or system proposal or system installation.

Minor milestones are used by the development team to mark significant planned development events such as the design of the accounts interface, integration of accounts system. They exist between major milestones.

Informal personal milestones may be used by individuals in the development team to set target dates and judge progress.

At major milestones points a complete project walkthrough may be held and the status of the project against the plan thoroughly reviewed. The outcome from this process might indicate that the project is beginning to seriously divert from the plan. This is the signal for a project reappraisal to take stock of the situation, re-assess it, re-group and re-plan by the re-scheduling of activities, the re-allocation of some tasks and the possbile request for additional resources. It is important to face up to facts as things are and not as they were planned.

Small slippage at personal or minor milestones may not at first seem significant but, *a month or year's delay occurs a day at a time!*

On projects that are running late, it is very tempting to assign more personnel to tasks that are overdue. Rather than have the effect of getting things done on time this strategy often results in making things run even later.

Question 8.22

Which of the following is a poor example of a milestone?
A the completion of requirements analysis
B the completion of 75% of system implementation
C the completion of systems testing
D the completion of installation of data communications hardware

Task 8.9   PC 3 & 4

List major, minor and personal milestones for a project you are involved in or have investigated in the library.

When faced with a number of personal tasks to do, you will need to prioritise your activities against any planned milestones that need to be hit. If you do have a choice, don't put off a task that you believe will cause you problems, do this first, otherwise you might just keep putting it off. Problems not dealt with today will still be there tomorrow.

■ Availability of Resources

Project scheduling is about allocating resources such as people with particular skills to tasks *when* they are required. For each task the resources required should be identified and their availability established. Restricted access to a resource or a delay in a resource becoming available can affect the elapsed time for a task regardless of how long the estimated time says the task should take.

To prepare a building for installation of a multi-user computer system will involve such tasks as:

❏ delivery of work desks and chairs from an office supplier;

❏ wiring of rooms using an electrician or wiring sub-contractor to provide electrical and network connections for the computer and each work-station;

❑ altering the building structure using a building sub-contractor;

❑ fitting of floor coverings using a specialised sub-contractor.

For this overall task to be completed successfully the availability of the various subcontractors must be established and a commitment from them to meet some planned schedule obtained.

In application software development a task that is often underestimated is the testing of completed software modules. The task will require a significant amount of access to hardware on which to run the software under test. It has been estimated that to test a piece of software will require 10 person-days or 60 person-hours. Of this total time a third, 20 hours is required in computer access time.

Question 8.22

What is happening in the other 40 hours?

However, the computer needed for the testing task is only available for 1 hour in each working day. This means that testing will require 20 days, which is double the total time estimated for the task. If the original time estimate is to be met then access to the machine must be provided outside the normal working day in the evenings or early mornings or at weekends.

■ Gantt Chart

A Gantt chart is a graphical technique used to present project tasks against a time axis and shows the *planned* timing or *scheduling* of tasks(stages or activities). The time axis is written along the top margin and the name of each activity is written down the left margin. A rectangle or line is drawn level with the name of an activity with its start and end points indicating under the time axis when it is scheduled to start and finish. The order of tasks is shown, with tasks that may take place at the same time or those that must take place in sequence clearly visible. Milestones are also marked with a precise date for hitting them.

Within the chart, different box shading or colours can be used to represent tasks. A chart can be produced for different levels of the project. A top level Gantt chart would show the main stages of the project and might include client and developer tasks. A stage level Gantt chart would show the principal tasks of each stage. A Gantt chart can also be produced for a person resource showing the start and end dates of tasks they are responsible within the project.

The figures below were produced using Microsoft Project, a Windows tool for project planning and scheduling.

For the CVL project CBS have to install and set up the accounts systems and also develop integrating software for interfacing the sales contract data to the accounts. Mark the project manager, has identified the following tasks and durations for this sub-project. He has also allocated the CBS staff resources to the tasks. He has produced a critical path for the project and is aware of the critical activities. Figures 8.10 to 8.12 show Marks planning.

	Task Name	Duration
1	Accounts Training	3w
2	Interface Design	2w
3	Develop Interface	8w
4	Develop Reports	4w
5	Install & set up accounts	1w
6	Accounts Data Take on	8w
7	Integrate	1w
8		0d

Figure 8.11 Accounts system task list

The first thing Mark did was set a start date of April 1st 1996 for the project and to draw up a task list for the Accounts system sub-project, which is shown in figure 8.11. Tasks 2, 3, and 4 are bespoke software development for running the interface between the sales contract system and accounts package. Tasks 1, 5 and 6 are accounts system task. Task 7 is the testing of integration of the systems.

Next Mark prepared a list of CBS staff resources that were part of the CVL project team and available to work on the accounts sub-project. The list is shown in figure 8.12.

CVLACC.MPP

	Resource Name	Initials	Group	Max. Units	Std. Rate	O
1	Mark	M	A/P	1	$25,000.00/y	
2	Maggie	M	A/P	1	$30.00/h	
3	Pam	P	AC/T	1	$30.00/h	
4	Jeff	J	AC/T	1	$35,000.00/y	
5	Rich	R		1	$25.00/h	

Ready | NUM

Figure 8.12 Accounts CBS resources list

Marks next task was to set up a Gantt chart that showed the duration of each task. He then sequenced tasks by linking tasks together. Task 1 and task 5 had to be complete before task 6 could start, task 2 had to be complete before either tasks 3 or 4 could start.

Having built the Gantt chart Mark then allocated staff resources to each task. Half of both Jeff's and Pam's time would be spent on task 1. Half of Jeff's time would be spent on task 5. Mark's and some of Maggie's time would be spent on task 2. the chart is shown in figure 8.13, the connecting lines show tasks that are linked. The diamond is a milestone for the end of the project on 21st of June which is well before the 1st August deadline for the whole project.

	Task Name	Duration	April 24 31 7 14 21 28	May 5 12 19 26	June 2 9 16 23 30	July 7 14 21
1	Accounts Training	3w	Jeff[0.5],Pam[0.5]			
2	Interface Design	2w	Mark,Maggie[0.25]			
3	Develop Interface	8w			Maggie	
4	Develop Reports	4w		Rich		
5	Install & set up accounts	1w	Jeff[0.5]			
6	Accounts Data Take on	8w			Pam	
7	Integrate	1w			Mark	
8		0d			6/21	

Figure 8.13 Accounts Gantt chart

Question 8.24

In figure 8.13, list two tasks that are done in sequence and two that are done in parallel?

Question 8.25

What other milestones could Mark have set for the project?

Task 8.10 PC 3 & 4

Prepare a Gantt chart for a project you are involved with.

Critical Path Method (CPM)

There will be many paths or routes through a Gantt chart from the start of the earliest task to the end of project. The start time of an task is going to be determined by the latest finish time of any task that precedes it. In order to establish what actions should be taken when any problems occur, the project manager needs to be aware of:

❑ the critical tasks of the project schedule, those tasks that if delayed or allowed to overrun will most likely impact on the project's finish date by making it late;

❑ any tasks that have some slack, that if delayed will not impact on the project finish date;

❑ the effect of actual task progress on the project finish date and the effect of rescheduling or re-estimating any activity.

CPM is an important technique for project managers and the method is outlined here as an indepth analysis is beyond the scope of this text.

■ Dependent Tasks and Network Diagrams

Task B is dependent on task A if it cannot start until task A has finished. Software implementation is dependent on software design. A diagram can be drawn that show how tasks are related or dependent on one another. In figure 8.14 tasks are represented by lines that are labelled with the task name and show it's duration. Each task line is started and ended by an event represented by circles. The complete network represents the events as a time sequence from left to right.

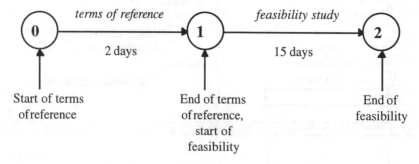

Figure 8.14 Network events and tasks

468

In addition to numbering the events the circle will also show two time details:

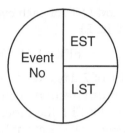

Figure 8.15 Event symbol

❏ *earliest start time* or EST, is the earliest time each event can occur at. These are calculated in a *forward* process working from event 0 that has an EST of zero, through the sequence of dependent tasks and terminates on the final end of project event. After event 0 the subsequent ESTs are calculated by adding the line duration connecting from one event to the next. In figure 8.14 event 1's EST will be 2 (0 + 2), event 2's EST will be 17 (2 + 15). Where more than one task line links to an event then it's EST is the latest or largest EST value calculated for each link. In figure 8.16 task 9's EST is the largest of [20(15 + 5), 18(10 + 8), 24(12 + 12)], which is 24. So task 9 cannot start until day 24 because prior to that not all tasks it is dependent on will have finished.

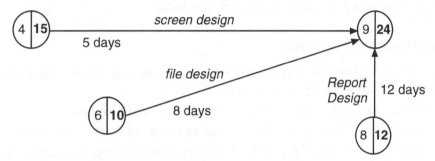

Figure 8.16 Earliest start times for task 9 dependent on tasks 4, 6 and 8.

❏ *latest start time* or LST, is the latest allowable time an event can occur at. These are calculated using a *backward* process from the final event through to the starting event. The LST for the final event is set the same as it's EST, for prior events their LST is calculated by subtracting the duration of the task line linking the two events. Where more than one line links back to an event its LST is the smallest or earliest LST value calculated for each link. In figure 8.17 event 20's LST will be 50 (60 – 10), event 19's will be 47 (50 – 3). For event 18 the LST is the smallest of [37(47 -10), 30(50 – 20)], which is 30. This process continues back to event 0 which should always end up with an LST of zero, if this isn't the case an arithmetic mistake has been made.

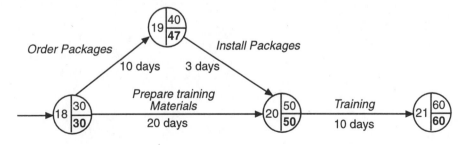

Figure 8.17 Calculation of latest start time for task 18

469

■ Float time or slack in the schedule

Having calculated both the EST and LST for each event the network can be analysed by calculating the *float time* of each event, its EFT:

$$EFT = LST - EST$$

Event 19 in figure 8.17 has an EFT of 7 days, while events 18 and 20 have EFT of zero.

The EFT is a measure of how much freedom there is for scheduling the task that is complete when the event ends. The larger the EFT the more freedom there is in scheduling that task without delaying the project. However if the event EFT is small or zero then this will limit flexibility of scheduling and a delay for the tasks that those events end will result in the project being late. Events that have an EFT of zero are said to be on the critical path for the project. A delay of any task on the critical path will lead to the project being late.

Question 8.25

In figure 8.17 which tasks are on the critical path?

By knowing which tasks have some float or slack available the project manager may be able reallocate resources from them to more critical tasks.

■ Shortening the Schedule

The schedule may need to be shortened because it costs to much or it does not meet the project deadline. A schedule can be shortened by:

- ❒ overlapping more tasks which may require more resources;
- ❒ increase the working time by scheduling weekend work or overtime;
- ❒ reduce the scope of the project objectives, thus reducing the number of tasks;
- ❒ allocate more resources to critical tasks to speed up their completion.

Question 8.26

Which of the above methods may reduce costs?

Task 8.11 PC 4

Construct an activity network diagram using the tasks, durations and dependencies shown below. Which tasks are on the critical path?

Task	Duration	Dependencies
T1	3w	
T2	2w	
T3	0.5w	
T4	11w	T2, T3
T5	11w	T2, T3
T6	15w	T2, T3
T7	1w	T2, T3
T8	11w	T7
T9	6w	T7
T10	6w	T7
T11	5w	T8, T9, T10
T12	5w	T4, T5, T6, T11
T13	4w	T2
T14	5w	T12
T15	4w	T12
T16	4w	T13, T14, T16

Managing slippage

Very often some tasks take longer than planned and may cause the project to slip or miss a milestone. This can be due to several reasons, underestimated, unavailability of a resource or more complicated than expected. It is important to be aware of things not progressing as planned as early as possible. The later in the project things like this are detected the less time there is available to do something about it. There will be a need to assess what has actually been done and what needs to be done and then estimate the effort required to do it. Slippage can be handled by:

❏ using up any available slack if the task is not critical;

❏ assessing the impact of the delay on the project if there is no slack;

❏ allocate additional resources to the task, this will only work if the new resources have familiarity with the task to be completed, if they don't then further time is required to bring them up to full speed;

❏ initially deliver the project minus the task or with reduced functionality for the task;

❏ negotiate an extension with the client user, if this is the only option then request as big an extension as the client will permit. There is nothing worst than asking for repeated extensions.

Having built his Gantt chart Mark can then construct a CPM or PERT network to find out which tasks are on the critical path for this project. The critical path is shown in figure 8.18 and shows that the tasks 1,6 and 7 are critical and must be completed on time. Slippage on any one of these tasks would delay the finish date. However Mark knows that there is some slack in his estimates so things should go all right, he is a little worried about task 7.

Question 8.27

Why do you think Mark is worried about task 7, Integrate?

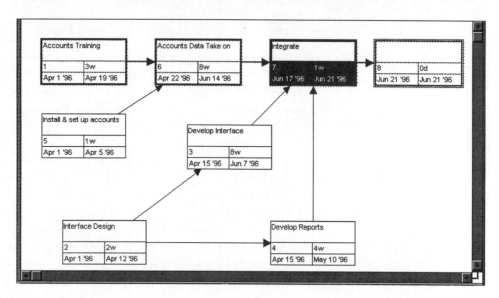

Figure 8.18 Accounts critical path

A node of the PERT network shows the earliest start times and latest finish times for each task as shown in figure 8.19. Task 7 is preceded by tasks 3, 4 and 6, all of which must be complete before 7 can start. Task 7's earliest start time must be after the latest finish time of these three tasks, which is June 14th for task 6.

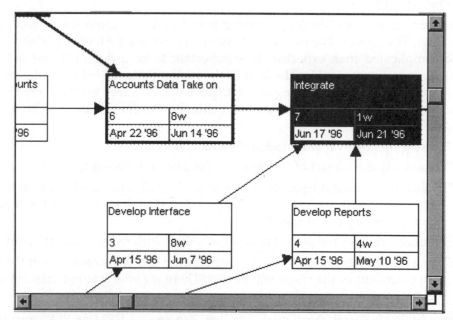

Figure 8.19 PERT detail showing node fields

In addition to the diagrams Mark also makes out task sheets that show clearly task start and finish dates with resources allocated to each one.

	Task Name	Duration	Start	Finish	Predecessors	Resource Name
1	Accounts Training	3w	Apr 1 '96	Apr 19 '96		Jeff[0.5],Pam[0.5]
2	Interface Design	2w	Apr 1 '96	Apr 12 '96		Mark,Maggie[0.25]
3	Develop Interface	8w	Apr 15 '96	Jun 7 '96	2	Maggie
4	Develop Reports	4w	Apr 15 '96	May 10 '96	2	Rich
5	Install & set up accounts	1w	Apr 1 '96	Apr 5 '96		Jeff[0.5]
6	Accounts Data Take on	8w	Apr 22 '96	Jun 14 '96	5,1	Pam
7	Integrate	1w	Jun 17 '96	Jun 21 '96	6,3,4	Mark
8		0d	Jun 21 '96	Jun 21 '96	7	

Figure 8.20 Accounts task sheet

The accounts system Gantt chart of figure 8.13 shows there is plenty of slack for task 4 and some for tasks 3 and 5, however there is little slack on any other tasks. Task 6 of CBS accounts has a long duration time and could be shortened by making available more resources. The accounts systems involve three ledgers, sales, purchase and nominal. The take on to these systems could be scheduled in parallel with additional resources being bought in. Figures 8.21 and 8.22 shows the effect of doing this with agency staff being used for sales and purchase ledger. The finish time for the project has come forward to June 14th.

	Resource Name	Initials	Group	Max. Units	Std. Rate	Ovt. Rate	Cost/Use	Accrue At	B
1	Mark	M	A/P	1	$25,000.00/y	$0.00/h	$0.00	Prorated	S
2	Maggie	M	A/P	1	$30.00/h	$0.00/h	$0.00	Prorated	S
3	Pam	P	AC/T	1	$30.00/h	$0.00/h	$0.00	Prorated	S
4	Jeff	J	AC/T	1	$35,000.00/y	$0.00/h	$0.00	Prorated	S
5	Rich	R		1	$25.00/h	$0.00/h	$0.00	Prorated	S
6	Agency	A		2	$150.00/d	$0.00/h	$0.00	Prorated	S

Figure 8.21 Two agency persons added to the resource list

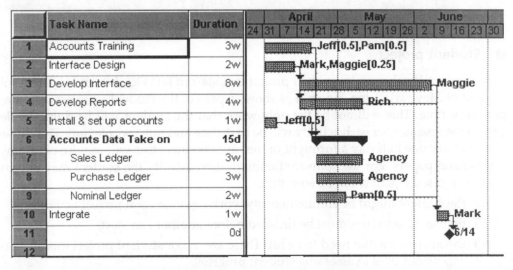

Figure 8.22 New Gantt chart with accounts data take on split into three parallel tasks

Question 8.28

Which task is now critical to determining how early the project finishes? What could be done to shorten its duration?

473

■ Project Progress

As the project is underway the progress or completion percentage can be shown against each active task.

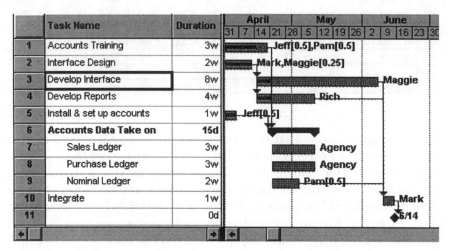

Figure 8.23 Progress of accounts system as at April 21st

From figure 8.23 Mark can see that bespoke development tasks 2, 3 and 4 are on schedule but task 1 is slightly behind. Task 1 should have been completed by April 21st, but is only 75% complete as shown by the dark line within the task box.

Question 8.29

Should Mark be concerned about this?

■ Student project

A student undertakes an individual project that start in late October and must be submitted at the end of May early June. Figure 8.24 shows a plan of the student's project activities over that period of time. This will not be the only work that the student will be doing while studying and so the resource for each activity will be part-time and not a whole unit. The student decides to spend say one half day a fortnight on research because this will require obtaining copies of articles and papers. For the software familiarisation activity the student may allocate one day a week. From the plan it can be seen that:

❏ the student might be simultaneously working on several project activities;

❏ that some activities must be finished before another can start;

❏ the milestones that need to be hit. These are major student project monitor points that a supervisor uses in assessing student progress.

Figure 8.24 also shows the progress of the student project at the beginning of December. It seems the student would need to concentrate on the Requirements Specification activity to hit the presentation milestone.

	Task Name	Duration	Qtr 4, 1995 Oct Nov Dec	Qtr 1, 1996 Jan Feb Mar	Qtr 2, 1996 Apr May Jun
1	Project research	80d			
2	Requirements Specification	45d			
3	Project Initial Presentation	5d			
4		0d	12/8		
5	Software Familiarisation	40d			
6	Design Prototype HCI	40d			
7		0d		2/4	
8	Prototype Production	90d			4/26
9		0d			
10	Evaluate Prototype	15d			
11	**Project Documentation**	**125d**			
12	Initial documentation	30d			
13	Research documentation	30d			
14	Prototype Documentation	50d			
15	Evaluation Documentation	5d			
16		0d			5/24
17	Project Final Presentation	5d			

Figure 8.24 Student project Gantt chart showing actual progress

In the student project Figure 8.25 of a PERT network shows the activities on the critical path to be, *Prototype production, Project documentation and Project Final Presentation* It will come as no surprise to many project students that getting the documentation done is a critical activity.

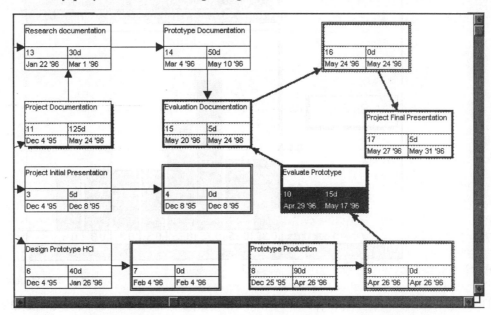

Figure 8.25 PERT diagram of student project

■ Resource Loading

The loading of a resource measures how busy the resource is during a period of time. A person working on one task could be working just to their capacity, however someone allocated to several tasks can easily get into a situation where they are having to work over capacity.

Mark can look at the loading of staff on the accounts system, he has some concerns about the work loads of Jeff and Pam. Figures 8.21 show their work loading for the period of the accounts project.

475

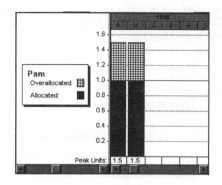 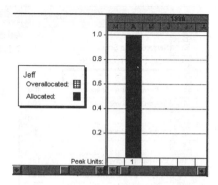

Figure 8.26 Pam and Jeff loading

Question 8.30

What does Pam's graph show? What can Mark do?

Similarly the loading of the student resource can be viewed through the projects life-cycle as shown in figure 8.27.

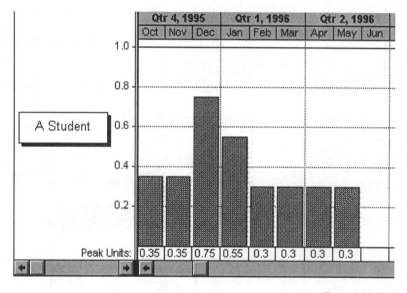

Figure 8.27 Student resource loading

The student resource loading shows that on the time estimates used and the allocated effort from the student slightly exceeds the 20% planned for most of the time. The peaks around Christmas and the new year could well be handled as a result of vacation time. Also the loading around Easter is not high and this would be a good time to pick up any slippage if things fall behind schedule.

8.1.4 Methods of controlling projects

Project control has three components:

❏ *monitoring*, where actual time, cost and quality are compared against planned;

❏ *detection*, of deviations where actuals move outside planned tolerances;

❏ *correction*, actions triggered by detection of things not going according to plan.

It is applied throughout the life of the project, at the end of one stage, the beginning of another and at any milestone. However, during a stage or prior to a milestone being reached control should detect any deviations from plan. Project control also has responsibility for managing change to the project.

Project Monitoring

Project monitoring is about collecting data from a variety of relevant sources connected with the project. The data provides information that is used to control the project by making and acting on decisions. Time and cost data for project developer staff can be accumulated from weekly or monthly time sheets. Project status reports can be produced at each level of the project as outcomes from formal project review meetings. The frequency of meetings will depend on the level of the participants within the project. High level meetings, involving very senior staff of the project board, might meet every three months or in the middle of and at the completion of important phases. Lower level meetings, involving development staff, might occur weekly each Monday morning to review progress, to deal with any technical issues and spread new information.

■ Time Recording

Staff time sheets completed weekly or monthly can be used to gather time and hence cost data for the project. The entries on a person's timesheet will detail all the work they have done during the period covered and might well contain data relevant to more than one project and non-project data. The record should identify the project tasks worked on and the time spent doing it.

CBS Weekly Time Sheet

Name: Maggie   Week Ending: 07/07/95
Staff Id: 005

Project/ Task Id	Task Description	Mon	Tue	Wed	Thu	Fri	Sat/ Sun	Total
C001/093	Interface Code	4	4	3	3			14
C001/094	Interface Test	2	2	2	1			7
P005/015	Data Model			2	3			5
P005/015	User Meeting					2		2
C001/090	WP meeting	1						1
	Help Desk		1		1	1		3
	leave					4		4
	Totals	7	7	7	7	7		35

Figure 8.28 Weekly timesheet of staff task time

These times can be accumulated against the different project/tasks and costed using the appropriate charge rate for the member of staff.

■ Time, Cost Reporting

Cumulative or monthly cost reports can be produced from this data that provide detail or summary views of costs by project, by project/task and by project/task/staff. Many companies would use a relational database to set up project task time and cost plans, to record the timesheet data against the project tasks and use the data sorting and grouping facilities to produce the a variety of reports.

CBS Project Monthly Cost Breakdown

Project: C010   CVL Contract Leasing   Period: 01/01/96 – 31/03/96

Task	Month	Days	Cost/£	Task Total	Project Total
010	Jan	2	300		
				300	
020	Jan	10	1800		
	Feb	5	900		
				2700	
030	Feb	2	400		
				400	
040	Feb	5	1000		
				1000	
050	Feb	2	400		
	Mar	8	1500		
				1900	
060	Feb	5	1000		
	Mar	15	3000		
				4000	
					11300

Project: C020   CVL Accounts Interface

Figure 8.29 Monthly summary report of actual task costs

■ Project progress

The project manager must be able to see the status of the project at any time and be able to make a formative judgement as to whether it is ahead or behind schedule, is it within budget or running over budget.

The Gantt chart can be updated with information that show actual progress against what was planned. As well as monitoring actual progress the project manager will constantly need to re-appraise this progress by estimating what remains to be completed and how long will be required to do this. Graphs and other presentation methods can be used to show actual performance against planned performance and to predict task or project completion at current rates of progress.

A project task has been estimated as requiring 20 person-days. If 12 person-days have been logged against the task then we might estimate the task is 60% complete. However, we might re-appraise the progress to date and conclude that there is in fact a further 18 person-days of effort required to complete the task successfully. How complete is the task now?

The re-appraisal has estimated that the task actually required 30 person-days and 12 have been completed, so the task is in fact only 40% complete.

$$\% \text{ complete } = \frac{\text{person-days spent to date}}{\text{person-days spent to date} + \text{person-days remaining}} \times 100$$

$$= \frac{12}{12+18} \times 100 = 40\%$$

■ Common Problems

All but the smallest of projects will run into trouble with tasks not starting on time or taking longer than planned. The project manager should be aware of the following problems that occur quite frequently:

❐ fluctuations of staffing levels due to staff leaving, holidays and illness;

❐ underestimating support resources needed to perform certain tasks – typing support, client user availability, accommodation;

❐ assumption that external activities will be completed on time.

Experienced project managers will be aware that such problems often can't be prevented and should include some slack in the plan to cover such eventualities.

■ Project Management Methods

In the mid eighties attention began to focus not just on software or systems development methodologies but on the management of software projects. The structured methodologies tended to be concerned with methods and techniques to be applied within each stage and provided tick lists for monitoring progress. Project management needs to address the issue of managing what goes on in a phase and needs not only to manage time and but also quality. There have always been tools for project management but their use lacked a framework to provide a discipline for effective operation. PRINCE (**PR**ojects **IN** Controlled Environments) is one such method that is widely used in the UK and its name describes its purpose very well.

■ Team Meetings

Team meetings are necessary to carry out a number of project management tasks. Technical and development staff often view meetings as a necessary evil and can't wait for them to be over. This feeling is often brought about by these people having to sit through meetings that were allowed to deviate from what was planned and dealing with things that were of little or no interest to them.

At every level in the project hierarchy, a formal meeting should be planned for a set time and place, have a specific purpose, with an agenda and any support documentation produced and circulated to all participants in advance.

The first meeting that kicks the project or a stage off, or final meeting that signs off a project or stage are usually a little different from the more regular project meetings. The meetings embedded in the project, whatever their level, will take the form of reviewing a past period and planning the next period. Project personnel will report what was planned, review what was actually done and present a plan of what to do next. Any exceptions will be highlighted and their justification and impact discussed.

■ Meeting organisation

All meetings should have a chairperson and a minute secretary or at least someone to make some notes of any major issues or outcomes from the meeting. The chairperson should keep the meeting on track and not allow it to stray outside its remit. Outcomes from the meeting should be action lists with the names of associated staff and any deadline for completion. As soon as possible after a meeting agreed minutes should be filed and copies circulated to all participants. See Unit 2 for further details.

Meeting Memo		
Purpose: To Plan Data take On	Date: 12 Mar	
	Time: 09.30	
Place: CBS Office, Cardiff	Length:2hr	
To Attend:		
CBS: Mark, Jeff, Maggie		
CVL: Mike, Jane		
Agenda		
A. CONTRACTS		
1. DT-on Preparation		
2. DT-on Software		
3. DT-on Schedule		
B. ACCOUNTS		
4. Accounts Package Training		
5. Accounts Set up		
Items Required		
DT-on screen forms		

Meeting Action				
Purpose: To Plan Data take On		Date: 12 Mar		
		Time: 09.30		
Place: CBS Office, Cardiff				
Present:				
CBS: Jeff, Mark				
CVL: Mike, Jane				
No.	Minute		Action On	By Date
1	Screen form amendments		Maggie	09/04
2	Software Testing underway		Mark	28/04
3	Arrange Agency DT-on staff		Jeff	24/04
4	Contract Dt-on		Jeff Mark	08/05
5	Accounts Training		Jeff Pam	01/04
6	Chart of accounts		Jeff Jane	24/04

Figure 8.30 Meeting agenda and action List

For the CVL project meetings are held between CBS and CVL users, figure 8.30 shows an agenda and resulting action plan from one such meeting.

Duties of chairperson:

❒ know why the meeting is taking place and what it is seeking to achieve;

❒ starts, runs and ends the meeting;

❒ introduces items from the agenda, asks individuals to present items of agenda and invites participation and discussion;

❒ keeps control of meeting and monitors time and business;

❒ checks minutes at a later date.

Duties of participants:

❒ be prepared, read supplied documentation before hand;

❒ when asked, report to the meeting, at other times make a contribution where appropriate;

❒ take their own notes;

❒ carry out actions placed on them;

❒ agree minutes of previous meeting.

A useful practice to adopt for documenting any meeting is, to hold the meeting in the morning and use the afternoon to write up the meeting minutes and action plan. This is particularly good when investigating a system and holding meetings with users. The documented notes should then be available for circulation early the next day.

■ Reviews

A review process within a project is a quality assurance mechanism that will involve a group of people examining work that has been completed or is still underway. The review can be applied to designs, implemented software, documentation and to project progress. The objective is to review the work and identify any problems, inconsistencies or defects that may be present. It may also assist in resolving a problem. The important thing about a review is that it is the work being reviewed and not the person or persons carrying it out. Personality clashes should be left outside the review room.

The reviewer(s) must be knowledgeable about the work under review, should be able to make an effective contribution to the process, analyse the work presented and offer constructive comment about it.

A review may take many forms, a good method is for the originator(s) of the work to *walk-through* it with the reviewer(s). The structured walk-through is a formal meeting with a chairperson and takes the form of the originator(s) presenting copies of their work to the reviewers and then performing a verbal walk-through the work describing why things have been done in a particular way.

An alternative form is for the reviewer(s) to look at the work privately, prior to the review meeting and then use the meeting to discuss their observations under the control of a chairperson. The review process can occur without meetings where the originator of the work passes it to a peer for observations. This is less formal and works best when both parties have a degree of respect for each other's abilities.

Types of reviews:

❑ management reviews, high level reviews largely concerned with progress against plans and schedules. They are often held at project milestones or checkpoints;

❑ technical reviews, middle level quality reviews, concerned with carrying out a technical analysis of the system or system component against it's specification;

❑ development reviews, low level review, concerned with development activities of design, implementation and testing. The intention is to check the use of standards, detect errors or potential problems.

The comments made during the review and the outcome should be documented. If no or only minor problems are unearthed, then the work can be signed off with the condition that required changes are made. A reviewer should follow this up. Where major changes are needed then the changes should be actioned, planned and a further review scheduled.

■ Project Documentation

For the project management to be effective it must know what's going on and inform people. This will require that the project management process be visible and means documentation in either paper or electronic format. There are a number of types of project documentation:

❑ project brief and terms of reference so all the team should be aware of the project's goal and objectives;

❑ project plans, task estimates and schedules, produced to predict, monitor and control the project;

❑ project standards, used in development for design and implementation. They also include document and procedure standards to be used during the project;

- working documents, these systems documentation from the requirements document, through systems design and specification, software specification and design to test strategies and end-user documentation;
- minutes, memos and reviews to record the communications between project participants.

■ Change Control

There are many reasons why a project change might arise. Whatever the cause all changes should be formally documented and managed. Changes result from some issue being identified that needs to be dealt with. Typical causes of issues being raised are:

- system specification error;
- failure of the system to meet a functional or usability requirement;
- specification changes due to new ideas that may result in improving an aspect of the system;
- specification changes due to an additional function not originally included;
- specification changes due to external factors that impact on the project, government legislation, organisation IT policy changes;
- resource issues such as budget and staff shortages.

Any change should be formally requested to the project manager who may then present it to the project board. The change request is a record for a proposed modification to the project with details of its justification and any impact it may have. The outcome resulting from the request should be formally documented. Very often, for projects that are poorly documented and managed, disputes arise between the client and developer. Many are a result of little dialogue between the client and developer, producing a system that fails to meet the client's expectations in that system functions are omitted or changed, other functions included, usability and performance problems.

■ Evaluation

On completion of the project or a project stage, the completed work and the activities of doing the work should be evaluated. The acceptance criteria set up at the start of the project or stage provide a checklist. The evaluation activity cover the following:

- that all planned products are complete and there are no outstanding issues;
- review and summarise actual against planned performance in terms of time, money and quality;
- assessment of the effectiveness of the work methods and any methodologies used within the project and to manage the project;
- acceptability of performance and functionality criteria with reasons for any deviation;
- recommendations for future enhancements or modifications in light of experience.

From the developers point of view evaluation can be summarised as:

- Did we deliver a product to user requirements? If not, why not? Were any deviations justified. Is the user happy?
- Did we produce the product within the time plan?
- If not, why did it occur, was the extra time justified, what lessons are learnt?
- Did we produce it within cost estimates?
- If not, did we loose money? If so can any new work recoup some losses?

From the clients point of view evaluation can be summarised as:

❏ Did we get the product expected?

❏ If not, what's missing, does it do the job, is it usable?

❏ Was it on time?

❏ If not, what caused the delay? Was it justified?

❏ Was it to cost?

❏ If not, what extra was involved? Was it justified?

❏ What extra work needs to be done, how long will that take and what will it cost?

Task 8.12 PC 1 & 2

For a particular week fill out a timesheet showing the time you spent on each school or college activity.

Contribute to an Information Technology Project

Introduction

This element is about being an IT team member, having a role in an IT project team and making a contribution to its activities. To do this you must undertake an IT project with your fellow students that will require you to undertake some group work activities. While working on one project it should be possible for you to undertake different roles from stage to stage or task to task and thus widen your experience. It is to be hoped that you are able to partake in more than one project and thus apply any experienced gained or lessons learnt on one project to the next one.

The actual tasks to be performed will depend on the IT project being undertaken, whatever they are you will need to apply the project management activities and methods described in Element 8.1 together with the specific IT knowledge and skills covered in the Units 1 to 7.

8.2.1 Objectives

■ Choosing a project

An IT project will require you to undertake a group activity in which you are expected to produce a system and its support documentation. In doing so you will have to demonstrate that you and the group have understood the problem, are able to solve the problem and can deliver that solution.

When carrying out an IT project in a school or college environment there is one problem that needs to be addressed, *who is the client*? An ideal situation would be to have a real client with a real problem to be solved. Local small businesses, sports clubs, other organisations and your school or college might be a source of such projects. Your tutors may also have a list of suitable projects that they have built up over the years.

If you come up with your own new project, then you will initially have to play the 'client' in specifying the project's terms of reference and then hand this role over to your tutor for the remainder of the problem. An excellent activity in this situation is for one group plus tutor to take the role of the 'client' and another group to take the role of the 'developer'. The 'client' specifies the project terms of reference and the 'developer' undertakes the project. The tutor's role is one of support for the 'client' to ensure that the project stays within bounds.

Characteristics of this type of project is that:

❏ it has a fixed time span. It starts at a particular time in the academic year and must be completed by a specified time;

❏ it is unlikely to be the only activity that you are involved in while at school or college. This means that you have so much time per week say one day to allocate to the project;

❏ the project must not be trivial or over ambitious that it can't be finished in the time available. Your tutors should be able to help you get a project of about the right 'weight'.

General guidelines for characteristics of a suitable IT project are:

❏ choose something that interests you or your group, a first meeting of the group could be a 'brain storming' session to come up with a project, be imaginative. Don't be afraid to take on something that may require a little 'research' in order for you to tackle it properly;

❏ has a goal supported by clearly identified objectives that are specific to the system requirements;

❏ is of a size that allows it to be divided into identifiable stages;

❏ requires investigation and analysis of user needs;

❏ requires solutions to be found that are compatible with the scope and constraints;

❏ requires implementation of solutions either by specifying manual procedures or activities or by using computer software.

Some examples of IT projects are:

❏ vehicle or item hire system;

❏ small sales catalogue of specialised goods like sports equipment or jewellery;

❏ video shop membership and rental;

❏ newsagent's business;

❏ sports club administration;

❏ analysis of sports centre data to provide management information;

❏ a banking demonstration system for use by primary schools;

❏ project time recording system.

■ Terms of reference

At the start of the project your team will need to draw up terms of reference for the project that you wish to undertake. This will require you to hold at least two meetings.

The first meeting will be a preliminary one where you will introduce yourself to each other, you might like to describe your personal and IT strengths and weaknesses, what IT activities you like doing and don't like doing. Outcomes from the meeting is to select a chair person and secretary for the next meeting, these roles can be rotated around the group as the project develops. An action on all participants to think about a suitable project and be prepared to present it at the next meeting.

The second meeting is more formal and has a purpose of choosing a project and forming it's terms of reference. It will have:

❏ a chairperson, who has the aim of getting a positive outcome from the meeting. The meeting must finish with everyone being in agreement about the chosen project;

❏ a secretary, who will make notes about the discussions and build up outline terms of reference.

Before finishing the meeting the next one should be scheduled, where the terms of reference can be discussed in greater detail. The chairperson and secretary should get together to write up the terms of reference and circulate copies (e-mail is useful for this) to each group member for them to read by the next meeting.

The outcome from these activities should be a short report that has the following format:

❏ Group name;

❏ Project Title;

❏ Project background and reasons for it;

❏ Outline requirements and objectives of the solution;

❏ Scope and Constraints;

❏ Acceptance criteria;

❏ Timescale.

8.2.2 Roles and responsibilities

During the project roles and responsibilities should be allocated formally to group members. Some of the roles will be administrative and others technical, a good idea is to rotate the roles amongst the project team bearing in mind individual strengths and weaknesses. The project will not meet its aims if say one person is secretary all the time and does no technical work. Obviously someone who is weak technically or administratively will need help and guidance from within the team. If a person likes accounts then that person might be best suited to managing the time/cost budget, but this should not be the only role taken on.

One role that must be fulfilled is that of team leader who will drive the project on, the team leader need not chair all meetings, also the team leader should not do all the work. It is essential that the team take collective responsibility for it's work. The range of roles include:

❏ accountancy

❏ administration;

❏ development;

❏ design;

❏ production.

8.2.3 Performance

Working in a team will allow you to develop your group working and personal skills that are transferable to any situation. As a team member you will be aiming for job satisfaction to enable you to work effectively and efficiently. These are improved if the team provides:

❏ skill variety, carrying out of a number of different tasks that are challenging and promotes interest;

❏ task identity, tasks are useful, meaningful, understandable and doable;

❏ freedom, members are able to take responsibility for how tasks are done but knowing it will be subject to review;

❏ feedback, the team is supportive, members collaborate and are not competitive.

The performance or effectiveness as a member of a team can be judged by:

❏ level of enthusiasm about being in the team and reliability as a team member;

❏ ability to communicate with fellow members, awareness of the teams activities, keeping the team informed of their activities, attendance at meetings;

❏ willingness to undertake tasks allocated and their adaptability;

❏ co-operation and participation in discussions and decision making;

❏ willingness to put forward own ideas, acceptance that these might be criticised and not taken up;

❏ ability to listen to others, accept their ideas and be willing to modify own ideas;

❏ support of the group and other group members and don't undermine the work of the group;

❏ willingness to see praise given to the group for work they have done, to accept responsibility for the groups activities and it's outcomes.

The criteria for judging work performance are dependent on the tasks that are undertaken, the following form a useful checklist:

❏ meetings: degree of preparation, body language, attentive, puts forward views;

❏ written work: is well presented with few or no errors, relevant, is clear and concise, about the right length and correct layout and produced on time;

❏ technical: knowledge and understanding of methods and techniques, ability to apply to problems, productivity and monitoring of progress;

❏ effort: judgement of work to do, quality of work produced, quantity of work produced. Ability to hit deadlines with a quality product that satisfies most or all acceptance criteria;

❏ time management: ability to judge progress, level of resources used to do job, such as own time, machine time and other resources.

Task 8.13 PC 2

Form a project team. Hold initial meetings to choose a project and develop initial terms of reference.

Prepare and make a short presentation of 10–15 minutes that outlines your project's goals and objectives.

Keep minutes of all meetings held.

Evaluate an Information Technology Team Project

Introduction

This element is about undertaking an evaluation of an IT project on it's completion. Evaluation against acceptance criteria is built into project management, it is difficult if the acceptance criteria are not precise and the client and developer may then dispute that the project meets requirements. In a wider sense evaluation includes evaluating not just the completed system but also the operation of the project.

Project evaluation

The quality of the completed project can be measured against it's objectives, detailed requirements and its ability to satisfy agreed acceptance criteria. It would be unusual for a project to be perfect and hit everything on completion. However providing that it serves its main function it should be possible to sign it off and release it.

Evaluation meetings can be held with the client where issues are raised and discussed. Many IT products are subject to pre-release evaluation to selected users who have agreed to partake in the evaluation exercise. Their experiences of using the product can be obtained through:

- ❐ developers observing their use of it and noting problems as they arise;
- ❐ sending out specially prepared questionnaires for completion by the user;
- ❐ using special error or usage log forms to record missing functions, inconsistencies and errors;
- ❐ user and developer meetings to discuss observed problems.

For project management, evaluation is concerned with checking what actually occurred against what was planned. The information collected throughout the project coupled to team experiences are useful data for carrying out any future projects. The evaluation of the project will take the form of a critical analysis of the project, obtaining feedback from both the development team and the client. The critical analysis should be based on comments obtained from all parties. The comments obtained should:

- ❐ be formative and constructive if the aim is to improve matters:
- ❐ clearly and concisely identify any problems or issues of significance;
- ❐ be objective and based on the original agreed terms of reference, not on some private expectation;
- ❐ reflect the situation accurately and not be based on rumour or incorrect application.

The report produced from the critical review can be constructed around the following sections which summarise what was produced and how it was produced:

- ❐ the final product: quality of the final product, based on the end of project evaluation;

❐ development strategy: use the accumulated costs and time figures to check if things went to time and were within cost. Were development methods used best suited to the tasks? It should be possible to identify critical tasks that really caused problems. What was the productivity level of the team? Would any alternative methods have been better?

❐ resource strategy: use resource usage records to identify where there were any resource problems. What skills were in short supply, was access to the computer for development a problem, was administrative support for preparing documentation lacking?

❐ management strategy: was the team structure right? Were issues and problems dealt with effectively and efficiently? Did the team communicate effectively with each other and with the client? Were they a team? Is there evidence that proper meeting and other records were kept and filed? Was the leadership effective? How well did the decision making process work?

As a result of the critical review the developers can undertake an appraisal of both their staff and working methods with aim of improving performance in areas that caused problems. This may require that team members undertake appraisal of their performance on the project where they are made aware of how their contribution was judged. From this it should be possible to identify areas for improvement and specify ways of achieving that improvement.

Task 8.14 PC 3

On completion of a project prepare an individual report that evaluates the project and your contribution to it. The report should include:

❐ *how well the project met its goal and objectives;*

❐ *what activities the team did best, did worst;*

❐ *what activities you did/liked best, did/liked worst;*

❐ *what difficulties were experienced and the reason for them;*

❐ *how well were deadlines adhered to;*

❐ *how you have benefited by partaking in the project.*

Answers to questions in Unit 8

Answer 8.1 For many IT projects developers are forever (for 50% of the project lifetime) saying that its nearly finished (95% complete), but the project never seems to get completed.

Answer 8.2 Your answer may include prototyping, SSADM, Rapid application development (RAD).

Answer 8.3 Feasibility is a less detailed study that provides an overview of system requirements and establishes time and costs. Information gained in a feasibility study provides a basis for requirements analysis which, if the project goes ahead naturally follows on.

Answer 8.4 As the project progresses through later stages more detailed information about the system becomes available which might result in the acceptance criteria being modified with the agreement of client and developer.

Answer 8.5 Acceptance criteria.

Answer 8.6 A

Answer 8.7 C

Answer 8.8 C

Answer 8.9 B

Answer 8.10 Software development for other CBS projects or maintenance of installed systems.

Answer 8.11 Permanent. Individuals or groups may undertake specific roles, but they act as a permanent team.

Answer 8.12 A

Answer 8.13 Amount of money for transport, time available to make journey.

Answer 8.14 Tasks: Collect brochures, choose holiday, check availability of chosen holiday, book holiday, pay for holiday.
Constraints: when you can go, how much you have to spend, access to airport, personal circumstances like young children or disabilities.

Answer 8.15 the task may not be easily divisible four ways. Time will also be taken up by the four people having to communicate.

Answer 8.16 2 days out of 5 day week is 0.4 or 40%

Answer 8.17 25 days

Answer 8.18 Jeff and Mark each put in 0.4 person units = 0.8 in total. The elapsed time estimate for this work is 20 days so effort = 0.8 x 20 = 16 days which is within the one month deadline. However, its a tight situation.

Answer 8.19 40 days

Answer 8.20 The project manager will break the project into tasks in order to estimate time, costs and resources required. Completion of tasks will help monitoring of progress.

Answer 8.21 C

Answer 8.22 B

Answer 8.22 Desk checking of test results and revising test plans

Answer 8.23 Sequence tasks 1 and 5, parallel tasks 3 and 4

Answer 8.24 End of accounts set up, end of accounts training.

Answer 8.25 Tasks 18, 20 and 21

Answer 8.26 Reduce the scope

Answer 8.27 It is a high risk task, involving integration with another application.

Answer 8.28 Task 3, could get Rich to help Maggie.

Answer 8.29 Not having training complete may delay the accounts take on, which could cause problems with the agency. However, there is plenty of slack in the take-on activity.

Answer 8.30 Pam has more work to do than she has time, Jeff is under utilised on this activity so if he has time Mark could reallocate some of Pam's work to Jeff, otherwise Pam might have to work extra hours which will increase costs.

Unit 8 Sample Test Paper

1 Which of the following is NOT a project?

   A arranging a trip to an IT exhibition
   B setting up a help desk for new students
   C selecting an e-mail system
   D going shopping each Saturday

2 An early stage in a IT system project would be:

   A start implementing the system
   B collect relevant information about the system
   C start designing the system
   D organise staff training

3 An IT project is planned in order to:

   A monitor and control use of resources
   B produce the best possible system
   C meet customer requirements
   D identify the aims of the project

4 Which of the following is NOT an appropriate planning activity for an IT project?

   A setting deadlines
   B identifying individual tasks
   C creating test data
   D setting targets and goals

5 Which of the following is TRUE about an IT project plan?

   A it is used by the client to judge the developer's ability
   B the client is involved in its production
   C it will contain software design details
   D it will contain hardware specifications

6 A role of the IT project board is to:

   A pledge resources to the project
   B plan the project
   C allocate staff duties
   D carry out development

7 Acceptance criteria for an IT project are established:

   A near completion of the project
   B just before project testing
   C early in the project
   D when design is complete

8 Dividing an IT project into stages or phases will:

   A keep the user informed
   B eliminate all errors
   C aid planning
   D reduce staffing requirements

9 Which of the following is NOT part of an IT project terms of reference?

   A project goal and objectives
   B project scope and boundaries
   C project development method
   D project problems

Questions 10 – 11 refer to the following statement.

'A new IT project must be implemented under the WOS operating system.'

10 Where would you expect to find such a statement?

   A in the requirements specification
   B in the terms of reference
   C in the acceptance criteria
   D in the end-user documentation

11 The statement can be classified as a:

   A risk
   B requirement
   C problem
   D constraint

12 Who will be responsible for analysis of an IT system?

   A the client
   B the developer
   C the project board
   D the client's auditors

13 Which is NOT the role of a project manager?

   A monitoring project progress
   B increasing the project budget
   C reporting to the project board
   D partaking in quality reviews

14 Who would investigate the sales potential of a new IT product?

    A project manager
    B developer's accountant
    C marketing analyst
    D IT specialist

15 Who would be responsible for implementing an IT system design?

    A a software developer
    B a systems analyst
    C an end-user
    D an administrator

16 An IT project team has recruited a new computer graduate. What role would be most suitable?

    A project librarian
    B systems analyst
    C hardware technician
    D project manager

17 In scheduling, which is NOT required about a project task?

    A what resources it needs
    B when will it take place
    C which task it follows
    D how it will be tested

18 A milestone used on a project is:

    A a significant event
    B a measure of distance through the project
    C an error marker
    D a reminder indicator

19 A useful aid to estimating the duration for a task is:

    A knowing when it is needed
    B the users knowledge of it
    C data about doing something similar on another project
    D having a project management tool available

20 A diagram that shows a schedule of project tasks is:

    A a flowchart
    B a dataflow diagram
    C a gantt chart
    D a module chart

21 Which is NOT shown in a CPM network?

    A task duration time
    B task float time
    C task identification
    D task resource

22 Tasks on a critical path have a float time:

    A greater than zero
    B equal to zero
    C less than zero
    D equal to the task duration

23 To shorten project time the project manager should first of all:

    A inspect all tasks looking for time savings
    B ask for additional resources
    C inspect critical tasks looking for time savings
    D inspect non-critical tasks looking for time savings

24 The project working party meets weekly. Actions and decisions taken are recorded in:

    A memos to management
    B minutes
    C reports
    D letters to client

25 The project manager must record how the project is proceeding to meetings of the project board. What would the manager produce for the board?

    A the original plan and schedule
    B a presentation showing actual progress against planned progress
    C copies of client's correspondence
    D a list of completed tasks

26 The evaluation of an IT project will take place:

    A immediately after testing
    B immediately after installation
    C immediately after design
    D within three months of installation

27 At a review meeting with the client a number of points of detail are raised that you dealt with satisfactorily. What else should you do?

A list the items raised and answers given

B forget all about them

C raise the matter with more senior management

D list the items raised and answers given and raise them with the project working party

28 How would you judge a team member's effort?

A by ability to meet deadlines

B by quality of work

C by quality of work and ability to meet deadlines

D by their time management

29 How would you judge if a team member is a good software developer?

A the HCI implementation

B their knowledge of software technicalities

C the volume of work produced

D the time taken to correct errors or make changes

30 How would you monitor your own contribution to a project?

A by checking progress against personal milestones

B by being helpful to other team members

C by being helpful to the team leader

D by noting down comments from other team members

Index